Hillel Guide To
JEWISH LIFE
ON CAMPUS

REMOVED FROM THE COLLECTION
OF PRINCE WILLIAM PUBLIC
LIBRARY SYSTEM

S0-BYJ-091

THE PRINCETON REVIEW

Hillel Guide To JEWISH LIFE ON CAMPUS

Fourteenth Edition

Edited by Ruth Fredman Cernea, Ph.D. and Jeff Rubin

REMOVED FROM THE COLLECTION
OF PRINCE WILLIAM PUBLIC
LIBRARY SYSTEM

Random House, Inc.
New York

www.randomhouse.com/princetonreview

Princeton Review Publishing, L.L.C.
2315 Broadway
New York, NY 10024
E-mail: comments@review.com

Copyright © 1999 The Princeton Review

All rights reserved under International and Pan-American Copyright Conventions. Published in the United States by Random House, Inc., New York, and simultaneously in Canada by Random House of Canada Limited, Toronto.

ISBN 0-375-75470-9

ISSN 1090-4859

Designed by Dinica Quesada

Photo research by Ruth Fredman Cernea, Ph.D.

Production Coordinator: Greta Englert

Manufactured in the United States of America on partially recycled paper.

9 8 7 6 5 4 3 2 1

Fourteenth Edition

ACKNOWLEDGMENTS

It is our pleasure to acknowledge the many devoted, talented people who contributed to this book. Thanks, first, to the campus Hillel professionals and advisors who took time from their demanding jobs to respond to our queries. Jennifer Dublin performed stellar work in gathering and collating data. Gillian Granoff, Cori SaNogueira, and Lisa Sowers were assiduous in collecting information. David Kruger, Hindy Chinn, Melissa Miller, and Elizabeth Munsey provide the ongoing digital backbone of this work. Thanks to Nurite Notarius-Rosin and our colleagues in Hillel's International Center who are a constant source of support, and to Hillel International Director and President Richard M. Joel for bringing about the "provoking infrastructure" that makes renaissance possible.

—Ruth Fredman Cernea, Ph.D., and Jeff Rubin, editors

Contents

HILLEL

CONGRATULATIONS!

As a prospective college student, a world of possibilities is opening before you. Hillel: The Foundation for Jewish Campus Life would like to help you get the most out of your college experience and achieve your dreams.

Hillel's 500 Foundations, Affiliates, and Regional centers will connect you to new friends, new experiences and new means of Jewish expression. Hillel can offer you everything from sports to community service, social activities to Jewish studies, professional mentoring to religious services—all contributing to your college experience and to a renaissance of Jewish life. As the largest Jewish campus organization in the world, Hillel has the tools, resources and professionals to help you define your future according to your own interests and needs.

But first you must select the college that is right for you. This book, the Hillel Guide to Jewish Life on Campus, *is a great first step. This guide provides profiles of more than 500 colleges and universities, descriptions of the rich variety of Jewish activity alive on campus today. More than that; the guide offers you a network of Hillel professionals and advisors around the world who can provide first-hand insight into campus life. Contact them by phone or e-mail.*

When it comes to choosing a college, one size doesn't fit all. The same is true for choosing your Jewish experience on campus. I urge you to choose a college that fits you academically, socially, professionally, and Jewishly. Hillel is here to help. See what it can offer you.

RICHARD M. JOEL
PRESIDENT AND INTERNATIONAL DIRECTOR
HILLEL: THE FOUNDATION FOR JEWISH CAMPUS LIFE

The Foundation for Jewish Campus Life
B'nai B'rith Hillel Foundations
1640 Rhode Island Avenue, N.W.
Washington, DC 20036
(202) 857-6560 • (202) 857-6693 Fax
www.hillel.org • E-mail: info@hillel.org

PART ONE | *What Is Hillel?*

Introduction

HILLEL: CREATING A JEWISH RENAISSANCE ON CAMPUS

Hillel, the Foundation for Jewish Campus Life, is dedicated to bringing meaningful and celebratory Jewish experience to all Jewish members of the university world. As the organized Jewish community's designated agent on campus, Hillel encourages and assists students, faculty, campus professionals, and community leaders in creating rich social, intellectual, activist, and spiritual experiences for the Jewish student community according to locally defined needs and interests. Guiding principles of all endeavors are a commitment to quality and to Jewish pride and peoplehood, and a belief in a valued heritage and positive Jewish future.

Hillel's seventy-year sponsorship by B'nai B'rith has been fortunate and productive, growing from a small chapter at the University of Illinois to a presence on hundreds of campuses throughout the world. During this time, Jewish students—once tentative residents of many campuses—have become increasingly comfortable and welcomed at America's colleges. Now, with approximately 85 percent of all young Jewish Americans going to college, the entire Jewish community is joining with Hillel in a new and unprecedented partnership to effectively meet the challenges and opportunities presented by this complex Jewish campus population.

Where Jewish students once struggled for acceptance at many colleges, now they are often bewildered by the range of intellectual, professional, and social possibilities open to them. Jewish students have another very precious possibility available, one that can help define all the others while adding meaning and value to their lives: the opportunity to grow Jewishly. Hillel's vision and mandate are to help students create exciting and varied Jewish experiences, so that no matter which professional path they choose, their lives will be continually enriched.

Hillel's structure reflects its expanded and acknowledged role within the Jewish community:

The Foundation for Jewish Campus Life serves as Hillel's operating agency, taking responsibility for quality assurance, program accountability, and fiscal integrity for the network of campus Hillels and for Jewish campus life in general. The Foundation's Board of Directors includes students as well as other leaders from all areas of Jewish communal life.

Hillel's International Board of Governors is chaired by Edgar M. Bronfman and co-chaired by Charles Schusterman and Michael Steinhardt. This group of respected community leaders and philanthropists provides counsel, guidance, and support for the Foundation for Jewish Campus Life.

B'nai B'rith Hillel Commission continues to provide encouragement and support to Hillel.

Hillel's International Center in Washington, D.C., provides leadership, administrative supervision, national accreditation, professional training, and development support for Hillel Foundations, Regional Centers, and other Hillels throughout the world. The International Center also coordinates national student programs and initiatives, encourages participation by national lay leadership, and coordinates community relations.

Hillel Regional Centers provide guidance and supervision to Hillels in major metropolitan areas and adjacent communities. These centers also coordinate regional programs and services for students, and provide information about campus life to the local metropolitan area.

Campus-Based Hillels encourage students to develop activities according to their own needs and interests. Campus Hillels act as advocates for Jewish interests within the university setting, facilitate the campus programs of cooperating Jewish agencies and institutions, and are centers of information about off-campus Jewish educational and other experiences. Hillel Foundations are professionally staffed and supervised by Hillel; other local Hillels, especially those on campuses with smaller Jewish populations, are usually staffed by volunteers, such as faculty advisors or local professionals.

Local Advisory Boards provide direction and guidance to campus-based Foundations and Regional Centers. These Boards include community members, students, and faculty.

THE STEINHARDT JEWISH CAMPUS SERVICE CORPS

The Jewish Campus Service Corps creates activities for Jewish college students throughout the campus, wherever Jewish students live and study. The Jewish Campus Service Corps (JCSC) is a new cadre of recent college graduates who encourage and assist Jewish students in creating vital and engaging Jewish communities on America's college campuses. The JCSC helps organize events and activities, taking into account students' interests, time schedules, and preferred locations, such as the Greek houses, the dorms, satellite campuses, the dining halls, the sports fields. The JCSC owes its inception to a challenge grant by Michael Steinhardt of New York—a challenge that has been met by other philanthropists in many communities. Additional challenge grants have been provided by Jan Mitchell of New York, Hadassah, and Steven Spielberg's Righteous Persons Foundation.

The one-year JCSC Fellowship is highly competitive. Applicants must demonstrate strong involvement in campus life as undergraduates, such as membership in a sorority or fraternity, student government, campus newspaper, social action programs, resident advisor program, or similar activities. They may come from any Jewish background and need not have been previously active in Jewish campus life; they must, however, demonstrate a basic understanding of Judaism, an enthusiasm for Jewish values and continuity, creativity, and an ability to work well with others. The JCSC Fellows receive training by national Hillel in cooperation with the local Foundations and supervision by a local Hillel professional. Outstanding Fellows are offered the opportunity to serve a second year, and are designated Senior Fellows. Fellows who wish to pursue a career in Hillel may apply to become Steinhardt Scholars, a program that provides graduate school scholarship and professional mentorships to JCSC alumni.

HILLEL'S STEINHARDT JEWISH CAMPUS SERVICE CORPS
List of Participating Campuses/Hillels with Fellows

*New Campus; #Senior Fellow

1. American University Hillel

2. Amherst Hillel House—University of Massachusetts—Cheryl Gordon

3. Arizona State Hillel Foundation—Jessica Fainsztein

4. Bryn Mawr/Haverford—Haverford College Hillel—Jessica Cooper#

5. Carnegie Mellon University—Alison Ross

6. Center for Jewish Life at Duke University—Nanci Steinberg

7. *Chicago City Wide—Heather Landesman

8. *Cincinnati Hillel Foundation—University of Cincinnati—Ryan Schultz

9. Cleveland Hillel Foundation—Gary Shyken#

10. Cornell University Hillel Foundation—Joanna Paley

11. CUNY Queens—Hillel at Queens College—Meredith Farrell

12. CUNY Queens—Hillel at Queens College—Rosy Kimchi#

13. Florida State University Hillel Foundation—Andy Carrol#

14. Hebrew University Beit Hillel—Laurie Hahn

15. *Hillel Foundation of Metropolitan Detroit

16. Hillel of Greater Baltimore—Johns Hopkins University—Shelly Richelson

17. Hillel of Greater Baltimore—Towson State University

18. Hillel of Greater Baltimore—University of Maryland Baltimore County—Shira Korman

19. Hillel Foundation of Greater Houston—Ilana Gauss

20. Hillel at the George Washington University

21. Hillel of New Orleans—Scott Pranis

22. Hillel of Orange County—Irvine-Renee Gindi

23. Hillel of Palm Beach/Broward County—Shoshana Kapnik

24. *Hillel of San Diego—Community Colleges—Rachel Gold

25. Hillel of San Diego—San Diego State University—Myron Breitstein University of Connecticut

26. Hillel of San Diego—University of San Diego Hillel Foundation—Chase Kohn#

27. Hillel at Stanford—Iris Rave

28. Hofstra University Hillel—Amy Krivosha

29. Indiana University—Rony Keller

30. Kent State University

31. MIT Hillel—Lisa Katz

32. Miami University Hillel Foundation—Ellary Spiezer

33. Michigan State University—Michelle Acosta

34. Milwaukee Hillel Foundation—Carmit Harari

35. Multi Campus Hillel of Greater Philadelphia—Rachel Salis

36. *Multi Campus Hillel of Greater Philadelphia—Drexel University—Maureen Levinkron

37. New York University—Rena Dascal#

38. Northwestern University Hillel—Jen Lacoff

39. *Oberlin Hillel Foundation—Kate Palley

40. Ohio State University Hillel—Rena Gelb

41. Ohio State University Hillel—Cydney Singer

42. Ohio University Hillel Foundation—Rochelle Young

43. Penn State Hillel Foundation—Jeremy Adelman

44. Princeton University—Eleanor Stein

45. Rochester Area Hillel Foundation—Lisa Sandler

46. St. Louis Hillel Center—Washington University—Jamie Harris-Gershon#

47. St. Louis Hillel Center—Washington—University—Nina Sackheim

48. *SUNY, Albany

49. SUNY, Stony Brook—Rachel Jurisz

50. Syracuse University Hillel—Tamara Kramer

51. Tel Aviv University

52. Tufts University—Yosh Schulman

53. University of Arizona Hillel Foundation—Bethany Weinstein

54. University of California—Berkeley Hillel Foundation—Eli Savage#

55. University of California—Los Angeles Hillel Foundation—Cari Rezman

56. University of California—Santa Barbara Hillel Foundation—Kelly Rotman

57. University of Chicago—Shayna Klopott

58. University of Connecticut Hillel—Nicole Uritz

59. University of Florida Hillel—Eliot Sokalsky

60. University of Georgia

61. University of Hartford Hillel—Stephanie Melofsky#

62. University of Illinois—Urbana-Champaign—Erin Boxt

63. University of Iowa—David Leventhal

64. University of Kansas

65. University of Maryland College Park—Katy Goldwater

66. University of Maryland College Park—Stacy Blumenthal

67. University of Miami Hillel—Sara Marion

68. University of Miami Hillel—Florida International University—Andrea Karpel

69. University of Michigan—Megan Nesbit

70. University of Minnesota Hillel—Gordon Eick

71. University of Missouri, Columbia Hillel Foundation—Gabe Bodzin

72. University of Pennsylvania Hillel—Emily Cook#

73. University of Pittsburgh Hillel—Mike Levinstein#

74. University of Rhode Island Hillel—Sharon Grainer#

75. University of South Florida Hillel—Alysha Goldstein

76. University of Texas—Austin Hillel—Aaron Lippman

77. University of Virginia—Laura Hinkes

78. University of Washington Hillel—Stefanie Hader#

79. University of Wisconsin Hillel Foundation—Julie Seltzer

80. Vancouver Hillel Foundation—Sam Kadish#

81. Yale University Hillel

Hillel Centers

THE FOUNDATION FOR JEWISH CAMPUS LIFE
B'NAI B'RITH HILLEL FOUNDATIONS

Hillel International Center

1640 Rhode Island Avenue, NW
Washington, D.C. 20036
(202) 857-6560
Fax: (202) 857-6693
E-mail: info@hillel.org
Web: www.hillel.org

Edgar M. Bonfman, Chairman
Charles Schusterman and Michael Steinhardt,
   Co-Chairmen, Hillel International Board of Governors
Chuck Newman, Chairman, Board of Directors
Robert Spintzer, Chairman, B'nai B'rith Hillel Commission
Richard M. Joel, President, The Foundation for Jewish Campus
   Life; International Director, Hillel

Baltimore

Hillel of Greater Baltimore
1515 Reistertown Road
Baltimore, MD 21208
(410) 653-2263
Fax: (410) 653-7809
E-mail: abukake@uno.com

David Raphael, Executive Director

Campuses served: Goucher College, John Hopkins University, Loyola College, Peabody Institute of Music, Towson State University, University of Maryland—Baltimore, University of Maryland—Baltimore County.

Boston

Hillel Council of Greater Boston
233 Bay State Road
Boston, MA 02215
(617) 353-7210
Fax: (617) 353-7214
E-mail: smendales@wn.net; psheinman@wn.net
Samuel Mendales, Executive Director
Patti Sheinman, Assistant Director

Campuses served: Babson College, Bentley College, Berklee College of Music, Boston College, Boston University, Brandeis University, Curry College, Emerson College, Fitchburg State College, Framingham State College, Harvard University, Lesley College, Massachusetts Bay Community College, Massachusetts Institute of Technology, New England Conservatory of Music, Northeastern University, Simmons College, Suffolk University, Tufts University, University of Massachusetts—Boston, Wheelock College.

Chicago/Illinois

The Hillels of Illinois
One South Franklin Street/Ben-Gurion Way
Chicago, IL 60606
(312) 664-5667
Fax: (312) 855-2479
E-mail: psaiger@juf.org

Rabbi Paul Saiger, Executive Director

Campuses served: Chicago Kent School of Law, DePaul University, Illinois State University, John Marshall Law School, Loyola University, Northeastern Illinois University, Northern Illinois University, Northwestern University, Oakton Community College, Southern Illinois University, University of Chicago, University of Illinois—Chicago, University of Illinois—Urbana-Champaign.

Los Angeles

Los Angeles Hillel Council
900 Hilgard Avenue
Los Angeles, CA 90024
(310) 208-6639
Fax: (310) 824-7194
E-mail: losahillel@aol.com

Eitan Ginsburg, Acting Executive Director

Campuses served: California Institute of Technology, California Polytechnic University—Pomona, California State University—Northridge, Claremont Colleges (Claremont McKenna, Harvey Mudd, Pitzer, Pomona, and Scripps Colleges), Los Angeles Pierce College/Woodland Hills, Los Angeles Valley College, Occidental College, Santa Monica College, Southwestern University Law School, University of California—Los Angeles, University of California—Santa Barbara, University of Judaism, University of Southern California, Whittier College School of Law.

Miami/Florida

Florida Hillel Council Regional Center
1100 Stanford Drive
Coral Gables, FL 33146
(305) 661-8549
Fax: (305) 661-8540
E-mail: FHC@flahillel.org

Rabbi Mark S. Kram, Executive Director
Linda Levin, Associate Director
Nancy Berlin, Associate Director

Campuses served: Barry University, Broward Community College, Florida Atlantic University, Florida International University, Florida State University, Hillsborough Community College, Jacksonville University, Lynn University, Miami-Dade Community College, New College, Nova Southeastern University, Palm Beach Community College, Rollins College, Santa Fe Community College, Stetson University, Tallahassee Community College, University of Central Florida, University of Florida, University of Miami, University of North Florida, University of South Florida, University of Tampa.

Montreal

B'nai B'rith Hillel Foundation of Montreal, Inc.
3460 Stanley Street
Montreal, Quebec H3A 1R8
Canada
(514) 845-9171
Fax: (514) 842-6405
E-mail: info@hillel.montreal.gc.ca

Joseph Muyal, Director, French Services
Jodi Goroff, Jewish Campus Service Corps Fellow

Campuses served: CEGEP St. Laurent, Concordia University, Dawson CEGEP, Marianopolis CEGEP, McGill University, Universite du Montreal, Vanier College.

New York City

Hillel of New York
381 Park Avenue South, Suite 613
New York, NY 10016
(212) 696-1590
Fax: (212) 696-0964
E-mail: hillel.of.ny@jon.cjfny.org

Robert Lizhtman, Executive Director

Campuses served by full-time professional staff: Baruch College, Brooklyn College, Columbia University, C.W. Post, Hofstra University, Hunter College, Nassau Community College, Pace University—Pleasantville, Queens College, Queensborough Community College, Saint John's University, Sarah Lawrence, State University of New York—Purchase, SUNY—Stony Brook.

Affiliated campuses: Adelphi University, City College, Cooper Union College, Fashion Institute of Technology, John Jay College, Long Island University—Brooklyn, Marymount College, New York Institute of Technology, Pace University—Downtown, Parson School of Design/New School, Polytechnic University, Pratt Institute.

Philadelphia

Hillel of Greater Philadelphia
202 South 36th Street
Philadelphia, PA 19104
(215) 898-8265
Fax: (215) 898-8259
E-mail: hillelgp@pobox.upenn.edu

Rabbi Howard Alpert, Executive Director
Rabbi Bonnie Goldberg, Associate Director

Campuses served: Beaver College, Bryn Mawr College, Bucks County Community College, Community College of Philadelphia, Delaware County Community College, Delaware Valley College, Drexel University, Harcum Junior College, Haverford College, La Salle University, Penn State University—Ogontz, Philadelphia College of Textiles & Science, Swarthmore College, Temple University, University of Pennsylvania, Ursinus College, West Chester University.

Toronto

Toronto Jewish Campus Services
3101 Bathurst Street, Suite 401
North York, Ontario M6A 2A6
Canada
(416) 785-1465
Fax: (416) 785-8271
E-mail: zkaye@yorku.ca
Web: www.Jewishcampusservices.com

Zac Kaye-Toronto, Executive Director
Pearl Gropper Berman, Assistant Executive Director

Campuses served: Carleton University, McMaster University, Queens University, University of Ottawa, University of Toronto, University of Waterloo, University of Western Ontario, University of Windsor, York University.

Washington, DC

Hillel of Greater Washington
6101 Montrose Road, Suite 201
Rockville, MD 20852
(301) 468-3422
Fax: (301) 468-3641
E-mail: ssjea@aol.com
Web: www.tamos.net/~hillel

Dr. Shulamith R. Elster, Executive Director
Bonnie G. Scheinker, Assistant Director
Alexis Kilstein, Jewish Campus Service Corps Fellow

Campuses served: American University, Catholic University, Gallaudet University, George Mason University, George Washington University, Georgetown University, Howard University, Montgomery College, Mount Vernon College, Northern Virginia Community College, Prince George's Community College, University of Maryland.

HILLEL FOUNDATIONS ON CAMPUSES

Hillel Foundations serve as the infrastructure for Jewish life on campus. Each Foundation is professionally staffed, has a lay board, and is supervised by the Hillel International Center or a Regional Center. Hillel's Accreditation Program ensures that each Hillel Foundation meets the highest standards of quality service to the campus community. The accreditation process includes self-studies, site visits, and the development of strategic plans. During the next few years, each Hillel will have participated in this process. Hillels that have already been granted accreditation are marked with an asterisk.

UNITED STATES

Arizona
Arizona State University*
University of Arizona*

California
California State University of Northridge*
Hillel at Claremont Colleges
  Claremont Colleges
  Claremont Graduate School
  Claremont McKenna College
  Harvey Mudd College
  Pitzer College
  Pomona College
  Scripps College
Hillel at Pierce & Valley Colleges
  Los Angeles Pierce College—Woodland Hills
  Los Angeles Valley College—Van Nuys
Hillel Foundation of Orange County
  California State University—Fullerton
  University of California—Irvine
Hillel of San Diego
  San Diego State University
  University of California—San Diego
San Francisco Hillel
  San Francisco State University
  University of California—San Francisco
  University of San Francisco
Stanford University
University of California—Berkeley*
University of California—Los Angeles
University of California—Santa Barbara
University of California—Santa Cruz
University of Southern California*

Colorado
Hillel Council of Colorado
  Colorado State University
  University of Colorado
  University of Denver

Connecticut
University of Connecticut*
University of Hartford
Yale University

Delaware
University of Delaware

District of Columbia
American University
George Washington University

Florida
Broward/Palm Beach Hillel Foundation
  Broward Community College
  Florida Atlantic University
  Palm Beach Community College
Florida State University
Greater Miami Hillel
  Florida International University
  Miami-Dade Community College
  University of Miami
University of Florida
University of South Florida

Georgia
University of Georgia

Illinois
Northwestern University*
University of Chicago*
University of Illinois—Chicago*
University of Illinois—Urbana-Champaign*

Indiana
Indiana University*
Purdue Unviersity

Iowa
University of Iowa

Kansas

University of Kansas

Kentucky

University of Louisville

Louisiana

New Orleans Hillel Center—Tulane University

Maryland

Hillel of Greater Baltimore
  Goucher College
  John Hopkins University
  Towson State University
  University of Maryland—Baltimore County
University of Maryland—College Park

Massachusetts

Boston University*
Brandeis University
Harvard University and Radcliffe College*
Massachusetts Institute of Technology*
Northeastern University
Tufts University*
University of Massachusetts—Amherst*
Wellesley College

Michigan

Michigan State University
Hillel of Metro Detroit*
  Oakland Community College
  Wayne State University
University of Michigan*

Minnesota

University of Minnesota

Missouri

University of Missouri—Columbia
Washington University*

Nevada

University of Nevada—Las Vegas

New Hampshire

Dartmouth College

New Jersey

Princeton University*
Rutgers University

New York

Cornell University*
CUNY—Baruch
CUNY—Brooklyn College*
CUNY—Hunter College
CUNY—Queens College
Hillel of Westchester
Hofstra University
Ithaca College
New York University
Sarah Lawrence College
SUNY—Albany
SUNY—Buffalo
SUNY—Purchase
SUNY—Stony Brook*
Syracuse University
University of Rochester*

North Carolina
Duke University
University of North Carolina—Chapel Hill*

Ohio
Case Western Reserve University
Kent State University
Miami University
Oberlin College
Ohio State University*
Ohio University
University of Cincinnati

Oklahoma
University of Oklahoma

Oregon
University of Oregon

Pennsylvania
Hillel of Pittsburgh*
  Carnegie-Mellon University
  University of Pittsburgh
Multi-Campus Center*
  Temple University
  Drexel University
Pennsylvania State University
Swarthmore College
Tri-College Hillel
  Bryn Mawr College
  Haverford College
University of Pennsylvania*

Rhode Island
Brown—RISD Hillel*
  Brown University
  Rhode Island School of Design
University of Rhode Island

Texas
Hillel Foundation of Greater Houston
  Rice University
  University of Houston
Texas A&M University
University of Texas

Virginia
George Mason University
University of Virginia

Washington
University of Washington*

Wisconsin
University of Wisconsin*
University of Wisconsin—Milwaukee

OUTSIDE THE UNITED STATES

Australia
Monash University
University of Melbourne
University of New South Wales
University of Sydney

Austria
Jewish Community of Vienna

Beloroussia
Minsk Hillel

Canada
British Columbia
University of British Columbia

Ontario
Jewish Campus Services of Toronto
  University of Toronto
  York University

Quebec
McGill University*

Great Britain
London Hillel Foundation

Israel
Haifa University
Hebrew University*
Technion-Israel Institute of Technology
Tel Aviv University

Moldavia
Kishinev Hillel

Russia
Moscow Hillel
St. Petersburg Hillel Center

Ukraine
Kharkov Hillel
Kiev Hillel

Hillel in Cyberspace

WWW.HILLEL.ORG

Web technology is changing faster than you can say Y2K, and Hillel is keeping pace. Hillel's newly redesigned Web page promises to integrate the latest technologies to make information more accessible and lively. Hillel's Web site, www.Hillel.org, offers:

- *An online, updated version of this book, including a complete list of Hillel Foundations, Affiliates, Regional Centers, and partner agencies.*

- *Links to Hillel Web sites around the world.*

- *Links to university Web sites worldwide.*

- *Complete information on scholarships available to Jewish students.*

- *Links to important Jewish Web sites, including sources of Jewish learning.*

- *Explanations of Jewish holidays and customs.*

- *Audio and video excerpts from Hillel conferences.*

- *Instant access to a wealth of Hillel programming information.*

- *Information and online registration for Hillel conferences.*

- *Information and online registration for Israel 2000, a free trip to Israel through Hillel from Birthright Israel.*

- *The latest information on Hillel events and achievements.*

PART TWO | *Getting the Most Out of College*

Getting the Most Out of Your College Years

This book can help you choose the right college and get the most out of your college years. Hillel's international network of Foundations, affiliates, and partner agencies can help you academically, socially, professionally, and, of course, Jewishly. The guide below will help you to use the resources of this book most effectively. Visit the Hillel Web site for updates and additional information: www.Hillel.org.

CHOOSING A COLLEGE

- *Read the entries in this book to learn about the campuses you are interested in.*

- *Visit the Web page of Hillel Foundations at the schools to get additional information.*

- *Contact the campus Hillel professional by telephone or E-mail to get a firsthand account of the campuses.*

- *Visit the Hillel Foundation or campus contact person during your campus tour to speak with professionals and students.*

- *Invite a Hillel professional—an expert on college life today—to speak to your school, synagogue, or community group about how to get into college and get the most out of your college years.*

FINDING SCHOLARSHIPS

- *Visit the college scholarship database of Hillel's Web page (www.Hillel.org) to find out about scholarship opportunities for Jewish students.*

ADJUSTING TO COLLEGE LIFE

- *Contact the campus Hillel professional by telephone or E-mail to find out how to adjust to those first weeks of school.*

- *Visit the Hillel Foundation when you arrive on campus. Hillel professionals or students may be able to arrange for an older student to serve as a mentor.*

- *Express, explore, and expand your Jewish identity through Hillel. Whether you have little Jewish education or a lot, Hillel has opportunities for you. Hillel Foundations offer social activities, sports groups, community service activities, religious services, informal Jewish studies, and much more.*

- *Strengthen your resume by taking an active role in Hillel. Professional schools and employers value demonstrated leadership skills.*

- *Apply for a program grant to create Jewish programming on your campus.*

Develop Leadership Skills

- *Become a Hillel leader and learn skills that will last a lifetime: group work, budgeting, public relations, fundraising, event planning, and more.*

- *Participate in the Schusterman Hillel International Leaders Assembly, the annual summer conference of more than 400 Hillel student leaders from around the world. Meet fellow Jewish students and learn how you can become a more effective leader on your campus. For more information, consult the Hillel Web page (www.Hillel.org).*

Do Community Service and Public Policy

- *Participate in the community service program of your campus Hillel Foundation and make a difference in the lives of others.*

- *Meet international political leaders, develop your public policy skills, and meet fellow Jewish activists at the Charlotte and Jack J. Spitzer B'nai B'rith Hillel Forum on Public Policy. Conducted with the Jewish Council on Public Affairs and the Conference on the Environment and Jewish Life, the conference has been addressed by such major world figures as Vice President Al Gore, former Israeli Prime Minister Shimon Peres, and Justice Antonin Scalia. The 2000 conference will be held in March in Baltimore. For more information, consult the Hillel Web page (www.Hillel.org).*

Distinguish Yourself

- *Earn a nomination for the Exemplar of Excellence Award from Hillel by demonstrating extraordinary leadership skills. Exemplar of Excellence Awards are given annually at the Schusterman Hillel International Leaders Assembly.*

- *Become a Jacob Burns Scholar and study the sources of Jewish ethics. Burns Scholars are named every year at the Charlotte and Jack J. Spitzer B'nai B'rith Hillel Forum on Public Policy.*

Learn More About Judaism

- *Set up a regular study session with your campus Hillel professional or participate in Hillel-sponsored Judaica classes.*

- *Find out about Jewish studies programs in the entries of this book.*

- *Participate in the Schusterman Hillel International Leaders Assembly or the Charlotte and Jack J. Spitzer B'nai B'rith Hillel Forum on Public Policy.*

- *Read the Resources section of this book to find other Jewish agencies that offer Jewish educational opportunities.*

- *Visit Israel. Read the Resources section of this book to find opportunities to visit Israel.*

- *Access the Hillel Web page (www.Hillel.org) for Jewish studies, to pose a question to a rabbi, or to find links to other sources of Jewish information.*

Find Professional Opportunities

- *Ask your Hillel Foundation staff if professional mentoring opportunities are available on your campus or in the region.*

- *Read the Resources section of this book to find other Jewish agencies that offer internship opportunities.*

Find Summer Jobs and Programs

- *Read the Resources section of this book to find Jewish agencies that offer summer jobs, educational programs, travel, and internships.*

Travel to Israel, Germany, and the Former Soviet Union

- *Participate in Hillel's Israel 2000, a free, ten-day trip to Israel made possible by a grant from Birthright Israel and the Jewish community. For more information, visit the Hillel Web page (www.Hillel.org).*

- *Read the Resources section of this book to find other Jewish agencies that offer trips to Israel or visit www.israelexperience.org for a complete list.*

- *Join Hillel's Bridge of Understanding trip to Germany. This annual summer program enables Jewish students to travel to Germany to meet fellow students and to study cutting-edge public policy issues. The program is co-sponsored by the German Ministry of Economics. Hillel's participation is made possible by a grant from Judy and Michael Steinhardt. For more information, visit the Hillel Web page (www.Hillel.org).*

- *Travel to the states of the former Soviet Union to help run Passover seders. A limited number of spots are available for students who wish to participate in the Rudin Family Passover Project, a program that provides seders for thousands of Jews throughout the former Soviet Union. For more information, visit the Hillel Web page (www.Hillel.org).*

AFTER GRADUATION

- *Use this book for graduate school as you would to find an undergraduate campus.*

- *Contact Hillel professionals and Regional Offices to find out about the campuses of your choice. Many Hillel Foundations and Regional Offices provide programs for graduate students.*

- *Join the Steinhardt Jewish Campus Service Corps. JCSC Fellows are hired by Hillel to work on campuses across North America to engage Jewish students who might not otherwise participate in Jewish life. For more information, visit the Hillel Web page (www.Hillel.org).*

- *Apply to become a Fellow in the Hillel International Center in Washington, DC, gain valuable professional experience as you touch the lives of thousands of college students. These Fellowships are: the David and Arline Bittker Fellow, serving as a liaison to Hillel student leaders; the Bronfman Fellow, working directly with the*

President and Executive Director; the Public Policy Fellow,
specializing in political action and community service;
and the Soref Fellow, assisting in promoting Jewish life
on campuses with fewer than 500 Jewish students.

A Guide to the Guide

Hillel Guide to Jewish Life on Campus is a comprehensive, all-purpose resource to help you make the right decisions concerning your college career. We provide you with the most up-to-the-minute information available so you can decide which institution will offer you the most enriching campus experience. Following is an explanation of the icons and key points covered in our Directory of Colleges and Universities.

 Courses and/or degrees in Jewish studies are offered.

 Programs for study or travel in Israel are offered.

 Kosher food is available.

 Jewish housing is available.

SCHOOL LISTINGS

Why are some schools listed, while others are not?

Hillel Guide to Jewish Life on Campus lists all colleges and universities where there is an identifiable Jewish presence and a source of information for prospective students. These sources include professional or volunteer staff, such as Hillel staff, faculty advisors, staff from local Jewish Federations and Community Centers, college chaplains, rabbis, and other members of the local community. Each of the campuses listed is part of the Hillel resource and information network, and each person named has agreed to answer questions about campus Jewish life.

If a school is not listed, it is unlikely that a Jewish student group is active on campus or that there is a specific spokesperson for Jewish interests on that campus. For information about such schools, call the nearest Hillel Regional Center or Hillel Foundation, or speak with the college chaplain.

If a school is listed, I can expect an active program for Jewish students on that campus, right?

Not necessarily. This guide includes some schools where a local community member has agreed to provide information for prospective students, although at present there is no activity for Jewish students on campus. Since the level of activity at some schools varies from year to year, especially where there are small Jewish enrollments, take nothing for granted. Call ahead. The most certain assurance of an active program is the existence of a Hillel Foundation or affiliated full-service agency.

ENROLLMENT FIGURES

How do you get the Jewish enrollment figures?

Jewish enrollment figures are "best guess" estimates suggested by personnel on each campus. They suggest the relative proportion of Jewish students to the general enrollment. A "guesstimate" may also be offered for the proportion of undergraduate to graduate students; since these populations rarely mix, prospective students should pay particular attention to the undergraduate numbers.

Counting Jews is difficult, especially on a large campus. Some colleges still circulate religious preference cards, but the response is always optional, and "Jewish" names are hardly definitive these days. Still, the figures will indicate whether there is a "critical mass" of Jewish students—a number large enough to permit a range of potential friendships and activities. This is a very important consideration in selecting a home for the next four years.

HILLEL AND OTHER JEWISH STUDENT ORGANIZATIONS

What is a "Hillel Foundation"?

A Hillel Foundation is a full-service community agency dedicated to fostering Jewish community and Jewish identity on campus. Hillel Foundations are guided by full-time professional staff whose sole job it is to facilitate Jewish community anywhere on campus—in the dorms, in the dining halls, on the quad, etc., and to serve as an advocate for Jewish interests on campus.

Each Hillel Foundation is supervised by the Hillel National or Regional Center and governed by a board of members of the local community and members of the campus community. Students are central to the governing processes of all Hillel Foundations. Campuses with large Jewish student populations have multiple staffs, including specialists in programming and outreach.

Each Hillel Foundation is indicated in the directory by the Hillel logo next to the listing.

Some campuses don't have a Hillel Foundation. What about these schools?

Jewish student groups exist on many other campuses. According to tradition or local option, some are called Hillel, some are Jewish Student Organizations, and some have other names. In a few places, the Jewish chaplain of the university is the full-time director of the program.

Most often the lack of a Hillel Foundation indicates a part-time program. Such programs may be staffed by a volunteer—a faculty advisor or the local rabbi—or by a professional who comes to campus a few days a week. In some locations, the

---

Many Questions, or How can I tell which schools have the best campus Jewish life for me?

Are there enough Jewish students to ensure many opportunities for friendships? Will I have a choice of friendship groups?

Where do Jewish students meet, aside from Hillel gatherings?

Are there "Jewish dorms"?

How "Jewish" are the "Jewish" fraternities and sororities?

Are Jews welcome in all fraternities and sororities?

Is the campus population familiar with Jews? Am I prepared to answer questions about Jews? What will I answer?

Will I feel comfortable identifying myself as a Jew on this campus?

What do I want as a Jew in college? What do I expect of the university?

Which interests or causes are important to me, as an American and a Jew?

Are there enough different possibilities for Jewish involvement, in case my interests change? What are they?

Are Jews on campus working for the homeless, the hungry, the disadvantaged, the environment? Are they involved in political action, women's groups, HIV/AIDS prevention?

Is there a Jewish arts festival, a theater group, a campus Jewish newspaper, creative religious services?

Do students have a strong voice in campus Jewish activities?

Where do Jewish activities take place on this campus?

Do many students commute, or go home for the weekends? If so, how does that affect the social life of the college?

If I plan to commute, how will I be involved with the campus Jewish community? When do they meet? Where?

What is the university policy regarding Jewish holidays? Are registration, Parents Weekend, graduation, or exams scheduled on Jewish holidays? In case of conflicts, can I take exams at another time? Will I have a problem going home for Passover or High Holidays?

How important is the religious affiliation of the college?

Does the university have a chapel? Are chapel services a regular part of student life? Will I feel comfortable attending these services? Will it be awkward to exclude myself from these services?

How does the college celebrate Christmas? What is expected of me? Will I feel comfortable not participating?

Is there a university chaplain? If so, do her/his responsibilities include campus Jewish life? Is there a Jewish chaplain?

What is the university policy concerning controversial speakers? Have speakers hostile to Jews been on campus recently? What was the reaction of the administration? the students? the faculty? the local community?

What is the campus climate concerning Israel? Are there anti-Israel activists on campus? If so, how will I handle this?

What do I know about Jewish music? Jewish art, literature, values, philosophy? Jewish history? Where can I find the answers on this campus?

full-time professional staff of the local Hillel Regional Center or nearby Hillel Foundation assumes responsibility for more limited programs on nearby campuses; in other areas, the campus is served by an outreach worker from the local Jewish community center or Federation.

Local community involvement and support varies greatly according to location, and affects the vitality and continuity of the campus program. All campuses listed are part of the national Hillel network of resources and information; Jewish students at every campus are encouraged to participate in national and regional events sponsored by Hillel and cooperating agencies with campus programs.

What difference does it make to me if there is a Hillel Foundation on campus, or simply a group guided by a volunteer?

The more resources—professional staff, numbers of Jewish students—the more likely it will be that the program will be diverse and active. Students at campuses without full-time professional guidance may have to assume an even greater responsibility for activities and social interaction. This can be a great opportunity for leadership; however, unless there are enough students equally interested in creating campus Jewish life, it can also be time-consuming and difficult.

Since it is hard to predict what you will enjoy as a college student—and what your interests and wishes will be when you are a junior or senior—think carefully before selecting a college that offers little Jewish community and companionship.

But I prefer a small campus, or one with a small Jewish population—one without a Hillel Foundation. Does this mean I have to forget about Jewish activity for four years?

Not at all. Just choose wisely. On such campuses, Jewish students may have a very satisfying Jewish life, with more small friendship circles, "chavurah"-style. Jewish students at small colleges, as well as colleges with small Jewish populations, get additional fellowship through regional activities, such as retreats or programs held with nearby campuses, or by participating in programs at universities with a Hillel Foundation.

Because the numbers of students are limited on these campuses, the level of activity is often dependent on the enthusiasm and commitment of a few students. This takes a bit more effort and more individual initiative: Think about whether this is your style—and check several campuses to see which ones offer the most potential Jewish options.

Jewish students at these schools can especially benefit from participation in national and regional activities, such as Schusterman Hillel International Leaders Assembly and the Spitzer public policy forum, or the national conferences, summer programs, and other opportunities sponsored by many agencies listed in this guide.

Another serious consideration before selecting a campus with a limited Jewish population is that the number of potential Jewish friends will also be limited. While, of course, your friendships will include individuals regardless of background, now is the time to think seriously about the importance of having friends who share your perspectives and experiences. Think also of how comfortable you are in settings where most people are unfamiliar with Jews.

Some campuses are very welcoming; others are less so. Advance planning can help you tell one from the other.

ADDRESSES/PHONE NUMBERS/E-MAIL/WEB SITES

I don't know if I'll even do anything with Hillel. Why is the address important to me?

Important? This is some of the most important information in this Hillel "consumer's guide"! It directs you to the people and places with the most specific information about your potential home for the next few years. Go and see! Call, write, E-mail, ask, research, check it out! Ask to meet other Jewish students. No one knows better than someone who has lived there for years.

Hillel in cyberspace: Many Hillels have home pages, others have Jewish student discussion lists, and all have students who talk to each other and can talk to you via the Internet. Carefully define your concerns and frame your questions very clearly—and then let E-mail take you to campus.

I'll be living on campus. What difference does the city or town make to me?

The local community can be a great resource for you: It may offer options for Jewish experience unavailable on campus—and it's especially important if you are selecting a school with a small Jewish enrollment or without a Hillel. Items you take for granted—

Are there Jewish faculty on campus? Who are they? Do they openly identify as Jews? Do they support Jewish interests? Do they speak out when necessary?

Is there a Judaic studies program? Which courses are offered, and how often? Who are the professors?

What are the opportunities for connecting with Israel on campus? Are there events on campus? Trips to Israel? Will the college give credit for study in Israel?

Does the university library have Jewish reference books?

Are Jewish students on this campus mostly Reform? Conservative? Orthodox? "Just Jews"? Does this make a difference to me?

Where will I go for High Holidays? Is it important to me to attend religious services just like the ones I know at home? What kind of services take place on campus? Do I want to try new forms of Jewish expression and experience?

Is the local Jewish community hospitable to Jewish students? Are students invited to their homes for holidays? To synagogues?

Is there a JCC nearby? Where will I find "Jewish" foods? Are there other Jewish places of interest in town? Do the local congregations match my religious preference? How will I get there?

Where can I attend a Passover seder if I can't get home? Where will I eat during Passover? Where will I get matzah? Will I be comfortable keeping Pesach (Yom Kippur, Hanukkah) if few other students are doing this?

Does the kosher food offered on campus or in the community meet my requirements? Who supervises the kashrut?

Is it in the Student Union or in a special building, or shall I contact a faculty advisor or the local Jewish Federation?

If there is no Jewish organization on campus, is there one nearby? Am I willing to travel to that campus for Jewish activities? Will I take part in regional programs? How will I get there? Do other students go?

Do I want to participate in national and international programs for Jewish college students? How will I learn about them?

Where will I find guidance on personal issues from a Jewish perspective?

I've already been to Hebrew School, or Sunday School, or Day School. Why should all of this matter now?

What is the campus climate concerning:

- *Alcohol*
- *HIV/AIDS*
- *Drugs*
- *Personal safety*
- *Anorexia, bulimia*
- *Sexual activity*
- *Date rape*

How will I handle these possibilities or temptations?

certain foods, matzah, other holiday needs, etc.—are not available in all locations.

Local Jewish communities are generally very hospitable to students far from home, but resources and interaction vary greatly. Large cities offer multiple activities and services for Jewish students—restaurants, familiar foods in the supermarket, many congregations, social events, and sports facilities. Small towns obviously have fewer resources, but the local Jewish population may be very involved in the Hillel program on campus. Check the geography.

ON CAMPUS

What will this paragraph tell me?

This is your key to the Jewish activity and comfort level of the campus. It will indicate if the university is supportive and encouraging of Jewish campus life: Although most universities welcome Jewish enrollment, some are better than others in fostering a just and caring campus climate.

A wide range of groups and events indicates a creative program with a strong degree of student involvement. The diversity of opportunities, not specific programs, is the important factor, since discrete activities may change from year to year according to student interest. A full and varied calendar indicates an open system, one that encourages you to join in when and how you like and—even better—implement your own ideas.

Highlights may include other general information about your potential campus home: Greek life, Jewish libraries or museums, speakers series, and similar data.

HOUSING

There are many places to live on campus. Which ones are listed in this guide?

The guide lists only Jewish residence houses, such as a bayit or a Hillel house, which are likely to have kosher kitchens. Most of these houses have limited space. If you are interested in such housing, inquire beforehand about room availability.

On some campuses, some dorms are known quite informally as the "Jewish dorms," where Jewish students congregate. If you are interested in Jewish companionship in your housing arrangements, but kosher dining is not a necessity, ask if there are dorms with a larger concentration of Jewish students, and request these dorms.

Jewish-oriented fraternities and sororities also have houses on many campuses. If this is an option, contact the fraternity or sorority directly. Addresses and phone numbers are listed in the "National Agencies and Institutions" section in the back of this guide.

I'm looking forward to becoming a Jewish Greek. I'll live in the house. This will be my Jewish campus life.

Some fraternities and sororities do maintain a predominantly Jewish membership—but this does not usually mean that Jewish interests or activities are well represented within the house, and it is very unlikely that the house will be kosher. And a "Jewish" house on one campus may not be very "Jewish" on the next; the situation varies widely according to the campus. See for yourself if the local chapter fits your Jewish needs and definition.

At some schools, Jewish Greeks are actively involved in campus Jewish life in partnership with Hillel. To know what to expect, visit the house, and discuss the policy and program with the national headquarters of the fraternity or sorority. Addresses and phone numbers are listed in the "Directory of Agencies."

KOSHER FOOD

I found a school with a kosher dining plan. I'm all set.

Almost. Before enrolling, make certain that the standards of kashrut satisfy your requirements. Who supervises kashrut on that campus? In some places, it is Young Israel; in others, the local rabbi acts as mashgiach. Also ask if kosher dining is included in the University meal plan, and if there is an extra charge.

I want to eat kosher, but not many schools have full kosher dining plans. What do I do?

If you cannot attend one of the few schools with full kosher dining facilities, there are several options:

> **Cook your own.** Find out if the local supermarkets carry kosher foods, and if you are permitted to live off campus and cook in your own kitchen. This entails a bit of work on your part and some isolation, since you will not be eating with your classmates. This is not usually desirable during the freshman year. Is eating on your own an option for you?

Eat vegetarian. Many dining halls now serve a full range of vegetarian foods. If being a vegetarian satisfies your kashrut requirements, discuss the menus with the dining hall staff.

Eat/live in a kosher residence house. A few Hillels have residence space with a kosher kitchen, and some campuses may have other kosher residence houses. In all cases, space is very limited. If this option is very important to you, be certain you can secure a place before making your final college selection.

Ask about frozen kosher meals. Some dining halls will provide frozen kosher meals on request. In practice, they get few requests. Again, discuss it with the dining hall staff. If the meals are available, is there an extra charge?

Live at home. A satisfying college experience does not depend on living away, and this option might be preferable to eating alone or with very few others in a house off campus.

RELIGIOUS SERVICES

Will I find religious services and rituals just like the ones I'm used to?

Yes, and no. On some campuses with large Jewish populations, there may be several student worship groups—Orthodox, Conservative (including egalitarian and, in a few places, non-egalitarian), Reform, etc. It is more likely that you will find an innovative service, often student-run, designed to accommodate the diverse campus population. On many campuses, students have created their own prayer books and haggadot for Passover, and you may also find new and unusual settings for traditional rituals, such as a seder in the desert, Jewish women's festivals, and special environmental seders Tu B'Shevat. The campus is an open opportunity to reexamine Jewish spirituality and Jewish ritual, and locate and create those forms that speak to you.

If, however, you prefer to go off campus to find more familiar religious settings, look for a campus close to a major Jewish metropolitan center. In such cities, you will have a wide selection of synagogues; in smaller communities, there may only be one or two. If you choose a college distant from a Jewish population center, check ahead to be certain that the local synagogue is comfortable religiously and convenient to campus: this is especially important if you keep the Sabbath.

JEWISH STUDIES

I don't know if I'll want to take Jewish studies courses, but just in case, what should I know?

College is an excellent time to ask questions and learn everything they never told you in Sunday School about being a Jew—and receive credit for your effort. You may be surprised at how many non-Jews are in your classes!

This guide indicates the university's degree programs in Jewish studies. A few schools have a full Department of Jewish Studies; many more have a Jewish Studies Program, an interdisciplinary program with courses in departments such as History, Anthropology, Sociology, Religion, Political Science, Philosophy, Languages, Literature, or the Middle East.

Also indicated in each listing is the approximate number of credit courses offered each term in some area of Jewish interest. Double-check the actual situation: the university catalog may list many courses that are offered over a two- or three-year period, but not available when you want to take them. Some schools have many course offerings, but do not offer a degree in Jewish Studies. Check before enrolling.

You may be able to cross-register for Jewish studies courses at a nearby campus or local institution. Is this option practical for you? What are the transportation requirements? Will you receive credit?

I really don't know much about things Jewish, and feel a bit out of place with people who know a lot. If I don't take courses for credit, how can I learn more?

Just ask your Hillel staff. They will be more than happy to arrange a special skills session, an informal class, a discussion group or event to fill in the gaps. You will find that you have plenty of company. This can also be your chance to experience that bar or bat mitzvah you missed. Or try the Internet. Many Hillel Web sites will lead you to answers, and the Internet offers many other such electronic avenues to learning, all in the privacy of your home. Some suggestions are in the Resources section of this guide.

STUDY IN ISRAEL

Suppose I want to study in Israel?

This guide lists university-sponsored or supported study opportunities in Israel, such as summer seminars or Junior Year Abroad programs. Some universities do not sponsor their own study opportunities in Israel, but will grant credit for such study through another university if arrangements are made beforehand. The Hillel Scholars program provides support for students studying for one year at the overseas programs of Hebrew University and Ben-Gurion University; information abut the Hillel Scholars program will be found in the Resources section of this guide.

I might want to visit Israel, but I'd rather work or travel.

Hillel is the clearinghouse for information about many other opportunities to experience Israel which are specially designed for college students. These programs are sponsored by a broad variety of agencies and institutions. Look under "Short-term and Summer Opportunities for Jewish University Students," in the Resources section.

STAFF

Why do some campuses have more staff than others?

Campuses with large Jewish student populations may have a large staff: a director who is a rabbi or an executive with advanced degrees in Jewish studies and communal service; an assistant director, with similar professional training; one or more program specialists; a member of Hillel's Jewish Campus Service Corps, who works with students throughout the campus; and several administrative staff. Other campuses, with similar Jewish student populations, have fewer staff, depending on local resources and support. The national Jewish community has recognized the disparity of resources for Jewish students according to the local situation, and is currently taking active steps—through its designated agent, Hillel—to ensure that similar campuses have similar and adequate levels of support and staffing.

Most campuses with smaller Jewish populations are served by part-time staff. Some schools are served as extensions of the nearby Regional Center or Hillel Foundation, or by professional staff coming to campus one or more days a week from local Federations or synagogues.

What difference does the number and background of staff make to the program?

The more trained people there are to devote full-time energy to Jewish students, the more likely it is that the program will be varied and vital. Part-time means just that: no matter how dedicated the professional or volunteer, he or she has less time to be with students. Faculty advisors—many of whom are quite caring and committed—must devote their primary energies to their academic responsibilities.

REGIONAL COOPERATION

Why should I care if the campus is part of a regional system?

Regional cooperation expands the opportunities for Jewish students—a fact of special importance to students at the smaller campuses. All Jewish students in the area, no matter what the status of the campus organization, are welcome to enjoy the programs, retreats and other resources of the nearby Foundation or Regional Center.

BUILDING

Why should I care if there is a new building on campus, a new center for Jewish campus life? I'm not certain I'll ever use it.

Think of a new building as a statement of the community's commitment to your Jewish future, not as an assemblage of bricks and mortar, no matter how beautiful. While Jewish campus life may be found anywhere and everywhere on campus, still, meeting space for any Jewish student who wants it, for any Jewish student group that needs it, should be available, pleasant, and efficient. These buildings testify to the belief of thoughtful and generous individuals, and of the Jewish community at large, that every Jewish college student is valuable to the future of Judaism.

In the past few years, new buildings—designed with student advice—have been built on several campuses, and others will rise in the next few years.

PART THREE | *Celebrating Jewish Life*

If I am not for myself,
who will be?

If I am only for myself,
what am I?

AND IF NOT NOW, WHEN?

—Hillel the Sage,
First Century B.C.E., Jerusalem

Celebrities Celebrate

We asked prominent Jewish figures to share how they celebrate their Jewish identity and to recommend how students can succeed in college and beyond.

Mayim Bialik

Starred in the movie Beaches *with Bette Midler and in the NBC television series* Blossom
Currently a senior majoring in neuroscience at UCLA

How do you celebrate your Jewish identity?

I celebrate my Jewish identity every way I can. I integrate my Jewishness into all of my interests: my *a capella* vocal group, the social causes I work for, my involvement in women's issues. Judaism gives a richness to every part of my life. I find that it makes my experience as a human being richer because it's rooted in history and ethnicity.

What advice would you give to college students to succeed?

Put behind the expectations others have for you, their ideas of what you should be doing. You have the opportunity to create a new life. Be open to new experiences. Be prepared and organized but take the time to let things happen to you. Good organization skills are a must.

Ann Landers

Syndicated columnist
Attended Morningside College

How do you celebrate your Jewish identity?

I am a longtime member of Temple KAM, a conservative synagogue. I am also a member of Temple Shalom, which is a Reform congregation. I never miss a Yom Kippur service, no matter where I am, anywhere in the world. I always say the blessings over the candles on Friday nights. My Jewish values were instilled in me very early in my life and they are my philosophical foundation for living. They have never changed. They are fidelity, honesty, decency, and a compelling desire to help others.

What advice would you give to college students to succeed?

Religion gives a sense of where to go in life, a sense of morality, decency, and integrity. It will keep you grounded. Stick with your values, regardless of the pressure you may encounter to do otherwise. If you know who you are and what you believe, your chances for succeeding are immeasurably improved.

Don't be afraid to fail. Any individuals who have been eminently successful in life will tell you that they failed many times before, at long last, they did succeed.

Sen. Charles E. Schumer (D-NY)

Harvard College '71, Harvard Law '74

How do you celebrate your Jewish identity?

I take great pride in my Jewish heritage, and at the core of that heritage—at the core of Judaism—is family. My family is extremely important to me. It is the focus of my life. One of my happiest moments as a father was celebrating my older daughter's bat mitzvah in Israel. I felt so proud of her, and proud to be Jewish. As a family, we celebrate the holidays together, and we make time throughout the year to worship as a family.

Jewish education is also a very important part of celebrating Judaism; it is important to understand what it means to be Jewish. My two daughters, Jessica and Allison, are enrolled in Hebrew school so that they can learn a love of Judaism and an appreciation of their Jewish heritage. I hope that they will pass this on to their families, like I have tried to pass it on to them. To me, being Jewish is very important; it gives me a spiritual core that helps to guide me in both my personal and professional lives.

What advice would you give to college students to succeed?

My advice to Jewish college students is don't be afraid to take some chances. At college, you have opportunities that you'll never have again. Thousands of your peers all in one place, living together, and learning together make for a thrilling and exciting environment. Afterward, you're going to wish that you took advantage of all of the experiences that college has to offer. Before you make the decisions that will affect the rest of your life—

graduate school and career choices, for example—you owe it to yourself to try as many things as possible. Obviously, there's no greater place to do that than in college. My experiences and those of my friends have proven to me that if you take a risk, and you fail, you can recover, but if you never take a risk, you never know what you might be missing. If you persevere and work hard, you can succeed at anything you put your mind to. Fear of failure should never deter you from following your convictions, and following your heart.

Mike Wallace

Co-Editor of CBS News'
    60 Minutes
University of Michigan '39

How do you celebrate your Jewish identity?

I am more an ethnic Jew than an observant Jew. But it is my Jewish heritage that instructs me to do unto others as I would have others do unto me.

What advice would you give to college students to succeed?

To a young person thinking about journalism as a potential way of making a living in the future, my advice is to forget about "communications" courses in college. Instead study history, economics, government, the arts. Learn at least one foreign language (French or Spanish probably). Study literature and do a lot of writing. And try to get yourself an internship during summer vacations with a newspaper, small or big, and/or a radio or television station. Then, if you decide you're serious about journalism, and you have the resources, a year in graduate school of journalism can be useful, but not absolutely necessary. And good luck. I cannot think of a more satisfying way to spend a working life.

Alan M. Dershowitz

Felix Frankfurter Professor of Law, Harvard Law School
Brooklyn College '59, Yale Law School '62

How do you celebrate your Jewish identity?

My favorite way to "do Jewish" is to study Jewish sources. I love reading the Torah, the Talmud, Maimonides, and especially the Responsa. Virtually no issue of contemporary importance was not debated in our tradition. I do not always agree with the canonical result, but the debate is always fascinating and the questions always probing. I use my familiarity with Jewish sources in my classroom teaching, in my courtroom advocacy, and in my writing.

Of course, I also love Jewish food. I guess my favorite moment would be reading a good Responsa while eating gefilte fish on a slice of challah.

The most important way in which I am Jewish is through my commitment to social justice. I take very seriously the biblical commands *"Tzedek, tzedek tirdof"* ("Justice, justice shall you pursue") and *"Lo tamod al dam reacha"* ("You shall not stand idly by the blood of your neighbor"). My commitment to international human rights arose out of my deep feelings for Jewish tradition. We were victims; now there are others, and we must never forget.

My least favorite way of "doing Jewish" is being told to accept a set of supernatural and irrational beliefs without question. I always question. When Maimonides declares that there are thirteen principles of faith and that doubting even one of them disqualifies a person from being considered a member of the Jewish community, I have the chutzpah to say Maimonides is wrong and that you can be a good Jew while questioning every single one of Maimonides' thirteen principles.

Celebrating Being Jewish on the College Campus

The renaissance in Jewish student life is being felt in America, Israel, Europe, and wherever Jewish students wander. They are exploring Judaism as they explore the world—creating, enjoying, experiencing, understanding, and learning what it means to be Jewish—individually and globally. Following are just a few of the ways Jewish students are celebrating their heritage—and fashioning it for themselves.

IF I AM NOT FOR MYSELF, WHO WILL BE?

Celebrating Being Jewish Through Fellowship

Retreats—Regional and national retreats offer companionship, Jewish understanding, and a marketplace of ideas for dynamic campus programs. Each August, hundreds of students from North America, Moscow, St. Petersburg, and Kiev gather at Hillel's Schusterman International Leaders Assembly. Others "retreat" to the February Western States Kallah in southern California, or to similar gatherings in New England, the Pacific Northwest, the Midwest, and other parts of the country.

At many colleges and universities, creative programs open doors for Jewish women's spirituality and participation.

Greeks—Greek Jewish Councils have been springing up on campuses throughout North America helping Jewish Greeks to experience their Judaism in their own setting. Nationally, Hillel has partnered with the Alpha Epsilon Pi fraternity and the Alpha Epsilon Phi sorority.

Hillel in the Former Soviet Union—Students in Moscow, St. Petersburg, and Kiev are learning what it means to be Jewish with guidance from Hillel at Hebrew University.

Celebrating Being Jewish Through the Arts

Theater—Jewish theater groups are alive and well at Washington University, George Washington University, Hebrew University, Brooklyn College, and the Universities of Michigan, Pennsylvania, and many more.

The Literary Arts—York University has *Dorot*; at Queens College it's *Kolot*; at Michigan, the Jewish student journal is *Prospect*. These are just a few of the student-initiated publications sponsored by Hillel.

Arts Festivals—Music, literature, photographic exhibits, and art are featured on most campuses throughout the country.

Orchestra—Immigrants from the former Soviet Union harmonize with other Israelis as part of Hebrew University's orchestra.

Choral Groups—Jewish *a cappella* groups can be found at Tufts, Columbia/JTS, Yale, Princeton, and Brandeis; Jewish choirs from West Point and the Air Force Academy tour the United States.

Purim Parody: The Latke-Hamantasch Symposium—Each year, professors debate the merits of these worthy foods—a new American Jewish tradition at the University of Chicago, George Washington University, and the University of Cincinnati.

Moshe and Miriam's Wedding—Jewish wedding ceremonies are more than hours of singing, dancing, and eating; they're an art form. Jewish students experience marriage in the Jewish tradition through mock weddings at Indiana, Columbia, Cal State Northridge, and many other campuses.

Jewish Music—From klezmer to concert to jazz, students enjoy Jewish music at cabarets and cafes.

Celebrating Being Jewish by Celebrating Jewish Diversity

Religious Experiences à la Carte—Reform? Conservative? Orthodox? Egalitarian/Conservative? Reconstructionist? Women's Minyan? All of the above? Keeping with the diversity that makes up the Jewish tradition, Hillel encourages this variety and is always looking for new ways to enrich the Jewish student experience. Kesher (Reform), Koach (Conservative Judaism), and Kedma (Orthodox) work as partners with Hillel to reach every Jewish student in his or her own way.

Many Histories—Sephardic, Ashkenazic, North African, or Israeli: We celebrate Jewish diversity through festivals, Sedarim, performance, and discussion.

Celebrating Being Jewish Through Spirituality

Creative Rituals—Ever have a Seder in the desert, in the dorm, or in the Greek house from a student-written Haggadah? Creative, customized Haggadoth reflect contemporary concerns: environmental Sedarim, feminist Sedarim, Sedarim that encourage Jewish Americans to relate their own exodus from the former Soviet Union to the Passover story.

Celebrating Being Jewish by Celebrating Israel

Israel Experiences—Israel is built into everything that Hillel does, whether it is our Foundations in Israel, supporting Israel politically, celebrating Israel Independence Day, or traveling to Israel. Through Hillel's Israel 2000 trip, Hillel is taking the lead in a historic plan to send thousands of Jewish college students to Israel, free of charge, courtesy of Birthright Israel. The brainchild of philanthropists Michael Steinhardt and Charles Bronfman, the program is intended to give all Jews aged fifteen to twenty-six their first trip to Israel to stimulate their involvement in the Jewish community. The Birthright Israel program augments Hillel's continuing relationship with the United Jewish Communities and other agencies to bring Jewish students to Israel.

Celebrating Being Jewish Through Study

Drop-In Study—Drop-in study and other classes are available at many Hillels, on the schedule or by request.

Belated Bar/Bat Mitzvah—It's never too late: If you missed out on this tradition when you were thirteen, many Hillels sponsor belated bar and bat mitzvah programs for young adults.

Professional Training—Hillel's Joseph Meyerhoff Center for Jewish Learning trains Hillel professionals to integrate Jewish studies and the exploration of Jewish texts throughout their student programs.

IF I AM ONLY FOR MYSELF, WHAT AM I?

Celebrating Being Jewish by Caring for Others

Feeding the Hungry—Hillel/MAZON sponsors special programs to collect money and food nationwide; students work in food banks and soup kitchens in Los Angeles, Boston, Washington, D.C., and other places.

Celebrating Being Jewish by Building Bridges to Understanding

Exchange Programs with Germany—Through Hillel's programs with Germany, students come to understand not only Jewish and world history, but their own identities as Jews today. Co-sponsored by the Korber Foundation.

Celebrating Being Jewish by Remembering

The Holocaust—Visits to the U.S. Holocaust Memorial Museum for students of all backgrounds are sponsored by Hillel. Campuswide Holocaust commemorations are a feature on most major campuses.

AND IF NOT NOW, WHEN?

Celebrating Being Jewish Through Social Activism

Community Service—Hillels around the country engage in community service in such areas as hunger, homelessness, environmental protection, and illiteracy.

Development—Students take the lead in raising money for their Jewish communities through annual Half Shekel campaigns for Jewish federations and through Hillelethons for their campus community.

Tzedek Hillel—Hillel has launched a new national program, Tzedek Hillel, in which Hillel Foundations make a special commitment to social action. Conducted in conjunction with the Nathan Cummings Foundation and MAZON: A Jewish Response to Hunger, the program aims to transform the lives of communities, Hillels, and Jewish students.

The Charlotte and Jack J. Spitzer B'nai B'rith Hillel Forum on Public Policy—Students address urban problems, hunger, Israel, church/state relations, women's issues, the environment, and other contemporary social and political issues at this annual conference, held in conjunction with the plenum of the Jewish Council for Public Affairs and the Coalition for the Environment and Jewish Life.

Celebrating Being Jewish by Becoming Leaders for Today and Tomorrow

Hillel's Charles and Lynn Schusterman International Leaders Assembly—This annual gathering develops leadership skills and Jewish knowledge while building a national network of cooperation and mutual inspiration.

Hillel's National Student Initiatives Grants—Have an exciting new idea for a campus program? Hillel is there to help make it happen, through the student-administered Student Initiatives Committee.

Fellowships in the Hillel International Center—These programs give professional experience to outstanding recent graduates. The Arline and David Bittker Fellow, the Jan Mitchell Fellow, the Public Policy Fellow, and the Bronfman Foundation place students' voices at the Center.

Journalism—Jewish student newspapers on many campuses welcome aspiring journalists.

AIPAC Leadership Development—Students get political training and education at the American Israel Public Affairs Committee's annual conference, as well as at other regional leadership development programs facilitated by Hillels on local campuses.

Jewish Law Students Associations—In the U.S. and in Canada, law students integrate professional and Jewish interests in conferences, meetings, and publications.

PART FOUR

Directory of Colleges and Universities

UNITED STATES

ALABAMA

AUBURN UNIVERSITY

Enrollment 22,000 (UG 19,000; GR 3,000)
Jewish 70 (UG 60; GR 10)

Hillel at Auburn University
316 Sanders Court
Auburn, AL 36830
(334) 821-9499
Fax: (334) 844-1084
E-mail: auhillel@auburn.mail.edu
Web: www.auburn.edu/aull

Margie Teeter, Advisor

Kosher Food
Vegetarian dining alternatives.

ON CAMPUS
Students and faculty celebrate holidays together, from Rosh Hashanah dinner to a community seder. Students are welcome to participate in discussion groups and adult education classes conducted by the local rabbi. The Jewish Student Organization Hillel meets at the Student Union once or twice a month for discussions, videos, and socializing. A Shabbat dinner for students is held at the advisor's house.

UNIVERSITY OF ALABAMA

Enrollment 15,600 (UG 13,100; GR 2,500)
Jewish 400 (UG 350; GR 50)

University of Alabama Hillel
c/o Department of Religious Studies
Box 870264
Tuscaloosa, AL 35487-0264
(205) 348-5271
Fax: (205) 348-9642
E-mail: lweinber@woodsquad.as.ua.edu

Dr. Leon J. Weinberger, Advisor

Jewish Studies
Aaron Aronov, Chair of Judaic Studies, offers Jewish Studies courses; rabbi emeritus and editor of University of Alabama's Judaic series offers courses on ancient Israel and the Middle East; Governor's Liaison to the Holocaust Commission offers Holocaust Studies program; Hillel Advisor offers courses on Jewish women's

lives and European Jewry; and Hebrew courses are offered by an Israeli teacher.

Kosher Food
Vegetarian dining alternatives.

ON CAMPUS
Hillel at the University of Alabama is housed in a spacious building with a chapel, an auditorium, and a library. It serves as the center of community for students, faculty, and those wishing to worship in a more traditional way. Lively and timely programming includes film festivals, open house and receptions for home football games, Tu B'Shevat Sederim, Purim, Hanukkah, and holiday celebrations. The Hillel Advisor may also be reached through the Judaic Studies program at 201 Manly Hall.

ALASKA

ALASKA PACIFIC UNIVERSITY

Enrollment 700
Jewish Few

Congregation Beth Sholom
7525 East Northern Lights Boulevard
Anchorage, AK 99504
(907) 338-1836
Fax: (907) 337-4013
E-mail: sholom@alaska.net
Web: www.alaska.net/~sholom

Rabbi Harry Rosenfeld, Advisor

ON CAMPUS
There are few Jewish students at Alaska Pacific University. Rabbi Rosenfeld teaches a general biblical studies class through the Religious Studies Department. He will be happy to discuss the situation at A.P.U. or at the University of Alaska with prospective students.

UNIVERSITY OF ALASKA

Enrollment 25,000
Jewish Few

Congregation Beth Sholom
7525 East Northern Lights Boulevard
Anchorage, AK 99504
(907) 786-1800
(907) 338-1836
Fax: (907) 337-4013

Rabbi Harry Rosenfeld, Advisor
See listing for Alaska Pacific University.

ARIZONA

ARIZONA STATE UNIVERSITY

Enrollment 42,000
  Jewish 2,200 (UG 1,700; GR 500)

Hillel Foundation at Arizona State University
1012 South Mill Avenue
Tempe, AZ 85281
(480) 967-7563
Fax: (480) 966-5402
E-mail: hillel@imap1.asu.edu
Web: www.public.asu.edu/~hillel

Rabbi Barton G. Lee, Director
Alison Riley, Program Director
Jessica Fainsztein, Jewish Campus Service Corps Fellow

 Jewish Studies
15 courses; Certificate in Jewish Studies.

 Study in Israel
ASU has connections with Hebrew University and Ben-Gurion University.

 Kosher Food
Hillel serves 1 lunch weekly; dormitory cooking facilities; kosher food is available locally.

ON CAMPUS

A special feature of the active Hillel program at Arizona are events that take advantage of the University's unique setting, such as a seder in the desert and a Grand Canyon campout on Sukkot. The various social, cultural, and religious activities include an annual Israeli Scholar-in-Residence and an active Israel program.

Highlights include the Teaching Scholar Program, the Rosh Chodesh Women's Group, the Freshman Leadership Opportunity Program, a mentor program, Chevra (serving young adults aged 21–23), geriatric internships, Kertzer research scholarships, and intramural sports teams.

Hillel's on-campus site includes a library, a lounge, and offices.

> *"We have a very strong Jewish population and our Hillel is very strong as well."*
>
> **Adam Moss, junior**

NORTHERN ARIZONA UNIVERSITY

Enrollment 16,000 (UG 12,000; GR 4,000)
  Jewish 300 (UG 270; GR 30)

Hillel at N.A.U.
PO Box 08005
Flagstaff, AZ 86011
(520) 523-3647
Fax: (520) 523-8056
E-mail: kjs@dana.ucc.nau.edu

Hedy Jacobson, Advisor

 Jewish Studies
1 Judaism class and 1 Holocaust class offered.

 Kosher Food
Kosher food is available in Phoenix, 2.5 away.

ON CAMPUS

Hillel at NAU was organized in 1970. Among the activites Hillel has sponsored are holiday celebrations, a Kristallnacht Remembrance Day booth in the Student Union, social events, Israeli dancing, ice skating, and hikes in Sedona and the Grand Canyon. The campus has a chapter of the fraternity AEPi.

The city of Flagstaff (50,000 people) has a synagogue with approximately 40–50 families. Students are invited to participate in all Jewish community activities. Some 10 Jewish faculty members teach at Northern Arizona University.

PHOENIX COLLEGE

Enrollment 7,000
  Jewish 70

Hillel
1012 South Mill Avenue
Tempe, AZ 85281
(602) 967-7563
E-mail: hillel@imapl.asu.edu

Rabbi Barton G. Lee, Director

Jewish students at Phoenix College and area community colleges are served by the Hillel Foundation at Arizona State University. See listing for Arizona State University.

UNIVERSITY OF ARIZONA

Enrollment 30,000 (UG 21,000; GR 9,000)
Jewish 3,500

University of Arizona Hillel Foundation
1245 E. 2nd Street
Tucson, AZ 85719
(520) 624-6561
Fax: (520) 624-7693
E-mail: mblumenb@u.arizona.edu
Web: www.w3.arizona.edu/~hillel/

Michelle Blumenberg, Director
Jonathan Freirch, Assistant Director
Belinda Lasky, Jewish Campus Service Corps Fellow

Jewish Studies

21 courses; B.A. (major/minor). The Judaic Studies Program offers an interdisciplinary curriculum, including courses in Modern and Biblical Hebrew, Archaeology and the Bible, Jewish Literature, Jewish Mysticism, and the Holocaust. In addition, the Program organizes speakers, programs, and conferences for the university and local communities. The University library has a strong collection of Rabbinics, the biblical era, and Jewish history. It also houses the Bloom Southwest Jewish Archives, the only regional archive devoted to the preservation of southwestern Jewish history. Judaic Studies, University of Arizona, 814 E. University Blvd., Tucson, AZ 85721-0432; (520) 206-9748; jus@u.arizona.edu.

Study in Israel

Haifa University and Ben-Gurion University have arrangements with the University of Arizona for study abroad. The UA Judaic Studies Program offers 1–2 scholarships per year for study abroad in Israel. Hillel also offers some scholarship funds for Israel. Hillel sends a group to Israel bi-annually with the UJA student winter mission. UA accepts credits from other Israeli universities and various other programs in Israel.

Kosher Food

Hillel: Monday through Friday 9:00 a.m.–2:30 p.m. at the Oy Vey Cafe, which offers vegetarian dining. Shabbat dinners are held bi-weekly at Hillel. The Cafe offers Passover lunches and dinners during the holiday weekdays. The University has vegetarian dining alternatives and dormitory cooking facilities. Kosher food is available in Tucson; there is a kosher butcher/food store and kosher bakery.

ON CAMPUS

The University of Arizona Hillel Foundation is committed to creating opportunities for all types of Jewish life to flourish on campus. Hillel at UA is centrally located on campus behind the Student Union. The Hillel Student Coordinating Committee/Va'ad oversees a wide range of social, cultural, political, social action, and religious activities. Student groups currently affiliated with Hillel include: Jewish Women's Group; UJA Challenge (community service and philanthropy); Hillel Hikers; Wildpac; Jewish Law and Medical Student Associations; GAP—Graduate and Young Professional Programs; FYSH—First Year Students of Hillel; and Kesher (for Reform students). Hillel coordinates three separate e-mail lists, one each for faculty/staff, undergrads, and grads.

The University of Arizona Hillel is well integrated into campus life and frequently co-sponsors events with University departments and a variety of student organizations. The annual Conference on the Holocaust usually receives funding from the student government. Hillel has also developed a Greek Jewish Council, which meets bi-weekly and provides programming for Jewish students involved in the fraternity and sorority system on campus. Approximately 13 percent of the undergrad students participate in Greek life. Hillel offers several leadership scholarships to assist students in attending Jewish conferences/study abroad in Israel.

"It is unbelievable how a Hillel can have soooooooo much diversity and fun at the same time. We do anything from skiing to rock climbing and regular Shabbat services to 25-hour Holocaust vigils. It seems that anyone can fit in here at U of A. If you just want to eat a bite at our cafe, use the computer lab, or just hang out, you've found the right place!"

Eric Grosman

ARKANSAS

UNIVERSITY OF ARKANSAS

Enrollment 16,000 (UG 12,000; GR 4,000)
Jewish 45 (UG 30; GR 15)

Hillel—Jewish Student Union
Sam Barg Hillel
Engineering Building, Rm. 324
University of Arkansas
Fayetteville, AR 72701
(501) 575-5590

Professor Dan Berleant, Advisor

ON CAMPUS

The local community is very supportive of Jewish student activities and services, which vary according to the interest of the students. Students attend High Holiday services at the local congregation.

CALIFORNIA INSTITUTE OF TECHNOLOGY

Enrollment 2,050
Jewish 100

c/o Hillel at Occidental College
1600 Campus Road
Box F-8
Los Angeles, CA 90024
(823) 259-2959
Fax: (323) 824-7194
E-mail: hillel@its.caltech.edu

Caty Konigsberg, Director

Kosher Food

Caltech has vegetarian dining alternatives, as well as dormitory cooking facilities. Caltech is a 40-minute drive from an observant community in Los Angeles.

ON CAMPUS

Caltech Hillel has monthly Sunday brunches and weekly Thursday noon programs of interest to students, including discussions and panels, speakers, and Israel-focused forums. An Israeli Folk Dance Group meets on campus weekly. International Day in May has featured Israeli dancing and food.

In addition to social programs, students are interested in applying scientific inquiry to non-science subjects, learning about Jewish holidays, traditions, and thought. There are opportunities to learn Talmud and Yiddish, and an annual Passover seder. Students are invited to the Jewish faculty's annual gathering.

Caltech is served by Hillel at Occidental College.

CALIFORNIA POLYTECHNIC STATE UNIVERSITY — POMONA

Enrollment 12,200 (UG 11,100; GR 1,100)
Jewish 400

Cal Poly Hillel
3801 West Temple Avenue
Building 26
Pomona, CA 91768
(909) 869-3608
(909) 607-2096

Jane Berman, Program Director

Jewish Studies

1 course on the Holocaust through the English Department.

Kosher Food

Vegetarian food available; matzah during Pesach.

Housing

Offered through Claremont Colleges Hillel.

ON CAMPUS

Hillel at Cal Poly Pomona is a small, yet flourishing, Jewish commuter community on campus. Students meet weekly and gather informally at the office each day. Jewish Culture Week, co-sponsored by Hillel and the University, is an annual spring showcase of music, dancing, Shabbat dinner, and Israel and Holocaust speakers put together with student input and planning. Hillel is also active in Cal Poly's Multicultural Task Force. AEPi, the Jewish fraternity on campus, is an active constituent of Hillel.

Cal Poly Pomona is associated with Hillel at Claremont Colleges, which offers a broad range of programs and services to students at affiliated schools.

CALIFORNIA POLYTECHNIC STATE UNIVERSITY — SAN LUIS OBISPO

Enrollment 17,000 (UG 16,000; GR 1,000)
Jewish 750

Hillel of SLO
Student Life and Activities
Box 88
San Luis Obispo, CA 93407
(805) 756-2476
(805) 756-2130
Fax: (805) 549-0852
E-mail: hillel@oboe.calpoly.edu;
jrabinov@oboe.calpoly.edu
Web: www.calpoly.edu/~sgoldenb/hillel

Professor Ken Barclay, Advisor
Professor Stu Goldenberg, Advisor

Jewish Studies

1 beginning Judaism course offered through the University.

Study in Israel

CSU Overseas Program in Israel.

ON CAMPUS

Hillel at Cal Poly is an intimate, well-organized, and highly student-led group, giving students great power to plan events and to lead an organization that represents Jewish life on campus.

In the past 4 years, Hillel has grown considerably, and students have represented SLO at national Hillel events, such as the Spitzer Forum for Public Policy and the Leaders Assembly. SLO's Web page won top honors in a national Hillel contest.

Each quarter, Hillel sponsors social events, including beach bonfires, hiking, camping, and Shabbat dinners. Students also have the opportunity to lead a Passover seder, Shabbat services, and the Holocaust Memorial Service. Above all, Hillel at SLO is dedicated to providing a comfortable place for Jewish students, whether the need is a family with which to share a holiday dinner, a tree planting experience on Tu B'Shevat, latkes on Hanukkah, or hamantashen on Purim.

"It may be a small Jewish presence, but the bonding among the Jewish students provides an experience like no other place. Students work together to provide a Jewish communal life. Unfortunately, the campus provides very little from a Jewish perspective. However, the University is open to listening to the Jewish students' suggestions."

Joel Mann, recent graduate

CALIFORNIA STATE UNIVERSITY—CHICO

Enrollment 15,000
Jewish 450

Chico State Hillel/JSU
643 Crister Avenue
Chico, CA 95926
(530) 343-7108
E-mail: ischiffman@csuchico.edu
Web: www.csuchico.edu/jsu/

Nitza Chiffman, Director
Dr. Samuel Edelman, Faculty Advisor

 Jewish Studies
4 courses; minor.

 Study in Israel
CSU overseas program in Israel.

 Kosher Food
Vegetarian dining alternatives.

ON CAMPUS
Hillel sponsors monthly Shabbat dinners at students' homes, as well as a women's group, which discusses literature and culturem and an annual student and faculty social hour that is held at the director's home. There is also an Israel Project, guest speakers, and a fall retreat.

"Jewish life at California State University—Chico is rich. Many Jewish professors are involved with Hillel, and we also have growing Modern Jewish and Israel Studies programs. The University Public Events Office very much supports Jewish culture and learning, and has brought to campus speakers such as Shimon Peres, who visited us in April."

Earl W. Jessee, senior

CALIFORNIA STATE UNIVERSITY—FRESNO

Enrollment 15,000
Jewish 70

c/o Temple Beth Jacob
406 W. Shields Avenue
Fresno, CA 93705
(559) 222-0664

Michael Lipson, Faculty Advisor
Regina Hansen, Coordinator

 Jewish Studies
2 courses; Hebrew.

ON CAMPUS
Jewish students meet for social activities, including potluck and Shabbat dinners. The two local synagogues and the Federation are supportive of Jewish campus activities.

CALIFORNIA STATE UNIVERSITY—FULLERTON

Enrollment 25,000
Jewish 1,500

 Hillel Foundation of Orange County
Bendat Hillel Center
250 E. Baker Street, Suite F
Costa Mesa, CA 92626
(714) 433-2478
Fax: (714) 433-2488
E-mail: ochillel12@aol.com
Web: www.faith.uci.edu/jewish/

Jeffrey T. Rips, Director
Todd Silverstein, Jewish Campus Service Corps Fellow

 Jewish Studies
4 courses; Jewish studies minor.

 Study in Israel
Semester at Tel Aviv University.

ON CAMPUS

The Orange County Jewish community is very supportive of Jewish student activities at the local colleges. Hillel has a good working relationship with the campus ministry, holds an annual Jewish arts festival, and participates in the West Coast Regional Kallah. Many programs are held jointly with Hillel at the University of California—Irvine. The Hillel Foundation of Orange County, based at these schools, serves as a resource for Jewish students at area community colleges.

The Orange County Regional Student Board ensures programming that includes California State University—Fullerton, University of California—Irvine, Chapman University, Fullerton College, Goldenwest College, Irvine Valley College, and Saddleback College.

CALIFORNIA STATE UNIVERSITY — LONG BEACH

Enrollment 28,000 (UG 15,500; GR 12,500)
Jewish 2,500

Hillel of Greater and W. Orange County
3801 E. Willow Street
Long Beach, CA 90815
(562) 426-7601
Fax: (562) 985-8579
E-mail: erika@lbhillel.org

Erika Silver, Director

 ### Jewish Studies
B.A. in Religious Studies; 5 courses.

 ### Kosher Food
Hillel provides occasional kosher meals, and kosher food is available locally. Hillel sponsors Shabbat dinners as well as Rosh Hashanah dinner, breakfast for Yom Kippur, a Purim feast, and Sukkah meals.

ON CAMPUS

Hillel has an office located in the University Interfaith Center. The University is supportive of Jewish activities.

Long Beach Hillel also serves Cypress College, Long Beach City College, Brooks Institute—Long Beach, and Cerritos College.

CALIFORNIA STATE UNIVERSITY — NORTHRIDGE

Enrollment 25,000 (UG 13,500; GR 11,500)
Jewish 3,500

 CSUN Hillel—Jewish Student Center
17729 Plummer Street
Northridge, CA 91325
(818) 886-5101
Fax: (818) 886-0152
E-mail: drmbloom@csun.edu
Web: www.csun.edu/~hfhil001

Rabbi Michael Bloom, Director
Lonee Frailich, Program Director

 ### Jewish Studies
18–20 courses offered annually. Minor only in Jewish Studies, which is integrated into a major in Religious Studies. CSUN's Jewish Studies Program provides strong advisement services for students interested in transfers, overseas study, graduate school, or preparation for entry to rabbinic, education, and communal service programs. Gender studies are an integral part of the curriculum. Professors work cooperatively with Hillel. Professor Jody Myers, Jewish Studies Program, CSUN, 18111 Nordhoff Blvd., Northridge, CA 91330-8354; (818) 677-3392, ext. 3007; jody.myers@csun.edu.

Study in Israel
Junior year abroad and other options.

ON CAMPUS

Northridge is a safe and comfortable suburban Los Angeles campus, located in the San Fernando Valley, with its large Jewish population. Eighty percent of the primarily commuter student population live within 30 minutes of the campus; 15 percent of the students live in dorms or apartments near campus. A wide variety of religious organizations are active at Northridge, and students with disabilities will find excellent support systems, including the National Center for the Deaf. Jewish students occupy leadership positions throughout the campus, in such organizations as the Associated Students, University Student Union, and the Daily Sundial. Jews are completely integrated into the University's important Greek system, which includes approximately 10 percent of Northridge's student population.

Hillel is the main Jewish center and organization at Northridge, offering an active, varied program based in a fine house. Students have created an active Israel Awareness Committee, and participate in area-wide retreats, a Mitzvah project, an annual Jewish awareness festival, dances, and social activities. This year, CSUN Hillel-Jewish Student Center successfully added a graduate social program, the Kosher Meat Market, with now has more than 200 members.

"Going straight into the heart of Jewish life on campus is very easy at CSUN. I attended Hillel events for the first time as a freshman last year, and I've been involved with Hillel since then. Leading Egalitarian services every Friday night has given me the confidence to know that I can accomplish anything. I also take Jewish studies classes and serve as a Secretary of AEPi fraternity. By getting involved with Jewish life, I've been able to improve my social life, conquer my fear of public speaking and connect with Judaism deeply."

Ryan Ross, sophomore

Hillel at Northridge is affiliated with the Los Angeles Hillel Council.

CALIFORNIA STATE UNIVERSITY — SACRAMENTO

Enrollment 21,900 (UG 13,300; GR 8,600)
Jewish 1,000

> Sacramento Hillel
> c/o Davis Hillel House
> 328 A Street
> Davis, CA 95616
> (530) 756-3708
> Fax: (530) 756-6076
> E-mail: hillel@mother.com
> Web: www.jewishsac.org/hillel/index.htm
>
> **Rabbi Kenny Kaufman**, Director
> **Bobbette Morvai**, Program Director
> **Cherryl Smith**, Student Advisor

 Jewish Studies
The Humanities & Religious Studies Department at CSUS offers an introduction to Judaism class and occasional seminars in Judaism.

Study in Israel
Sacramento Hillel, in conjunction with Davis Hillel, connects students for study at various universities in Israel such as the Hebrew University, Haifa University, and Tel Aviv University and for many summer Israel programs as well. Hillel also coordinates with the Northern California Hillel Council for an annual, highly subsidized, 3-week winter trip to Israel.

Kosher Food
Kosher food is available throughout Sacramento.

ON CAMPUS
The Sacramento Hillel is newly developing and is a service of the Sacramento Jewish Community Federation.

Sacramento Hillel holds monthly organizing meetings where students can meet and plan future programs. Sacramento Hillel offers regular bagel brunches, and participates in both the Western States Hillel Association Regional Kallah and the Hillel International Leaders Assembly. CSUS students are also invited to events at the nearby Davis Hillel.

CALIFORNIA STATE UNIVERSITY — SAN BERNARDINO

Enrollment 10,000 (UG 7,250; GR 2,750)

> Student Life Office/Hillel
> 5500 University Parkway
> Box 126
> CSU—San Bernardino
> San Bernardino, CA 92407
> (909) 880-5478
>
> **Larry Mink**, Advisor

 Jewish Studies
2 courses.

ON CAMPUS
Students participate in the Hillel Western Regional Kallah retreat. Hillel offers 2 small annual scholarships. The community provides home hospitality for the holidays.

CHAPMAN UNIVERSITY

Enrollment 3,000
Jewish 150

> Hillel Foundation of Orange County
> Bendat Hillel Center
> 250 E. Baker Street, Suite F
> Costa Mesa, CA 92626
> (714) 433-2478
> Fax: (714) 433-2488
> E-mail: ochillel12@aol.com
>
> **Jeffrey T. Rips**, Director

 Kosher Food
Annual Passover seder and Shabbat dinners.

ON CAMPUS
Chapman University students are invited to participate in all regional Hillel programs. Chapman has representatives on the Countywide Student Council.

Chapman University is served part-time by the Hillel Foundation of Orange County.

CITY COLLEGE OF SAN FRANCISCO

San Francisco Hillel Jewish Student Center
33 Banbury Street
San Francisco, CA 94132
(415) 333-4922
Fax: (415) 333-4926
E-mail: programs@sfhillel.org
Web: www.sfhillel.org

Seth Brysk, Executive Director
Jenna Balsavage, Program Director
Illya Mirtsyn, Emigre Program Director

City College of SF is served as an outreach program of San Francisco Hillel. See listing for San Francisco State University.

CLAREMONT COLLEGES

Hillel at the Claremont Colleges
McAlister Center
919 North Columbia Avenue
Claremont, CA 91711
(909) 621-8824
Fax: (909) 621-8304
E-mail: hillel@cgu.edu
Web: www.cuc.claremont.edu

Rabbi Leslie Bergson, Director
Noah A. Bleich, Program Director
Amy Perlo, Jewish Campus Service Corps Fellow

Jewish Studies
Various courses offered each year. Major in Jewish Studies is available through an interdisciplinary program.

Study in Israel
Junior year/semester abroad.

Kosher Food
Holiday, Rosh Hashanah, Yom Kippur break-the-fast, and all Passover meals. Otherwise, vegetarian dining alternatives.

ON CAMPUS

Hillel at Claremont Colleges serves Jewish students at the undergraduate and graduate schools that comprise the Claremont Colleges, including Claremont Graduate School, Pomona, Pitzer, Harvey Mudd, Scripps, and Claremont McKenna Colleges. Hillel is centrally located in the McAlister Center for Religious Activities. Hillel works cooperatively with many student organizations. Hillel's "70s" Sukkah, retreats, and Rosh Hashanah Dinner in the Garden are outstanding campus events. Hillel also brings in guest speakers and has special events throughout the year. Along with Hillel, Claremont Colleges have 2 Jewish student groups: Jewish Action Group (Pitzer) and Jewish Student Union (Pomona).

CLAREMONT GRADUATE SCHOOL

Enrollment 1,750
Jewish 75

Hillel at the Claremont Colleges
McAlister Center
919 North Columbia Avenue
Claremont, CA 91711
(909) 621-8824
Fax: (909) 621-8304
E-mail: hillel@cgu.edu
Web: www.cuc.claremont.edu

Rabbi Leslie Bergson, Director
Johnathan Bentwich, Program Director

ON CAMPUS

Special programs for Jewish graduate students are held periodically throughout the year.

See listing for Claremont Colleges.

CLAREMONT MCKENNA COLLEGE

Enrollment 1,082
Jewish 115

Hillel at the Claremont Colleges
McAlister Center
919 North Columbia Avenue
Claremont, CA 91711
(909) 621-8824
Fax: (909) 621-8304
E-mail: hillel@cgu.edu
Web: www.cuc.claremont.edu/interfth/page12.html

Rabbi Leslie Bergson, Director

See listing for Claremont Colleges.

CYPRESS COLLEGE

Enrollment 14,000
Jewish 100

Hillel Club
c/o Long Beach Hillel
3801 E. Willow Street
Long Beach, CA 90815
(714) 826-2220
Fax: (714) 527-8238
E-mail: din@lbhillel.org

Erica Hillinger, Director

Kosher Food
Locally available.

ON CAMPUS

Cypress College is a thriving community college with an active Hillel which is affiliated with Hillel at CSU—Long Beach. Students participate in social and educational activities on campus and in conjunction with CSU—Long Beach.

GOLDEN GATE UNIVERSITY

San Francisco Hillel Jewish Student Center
33 Banbury Street
San Francisco, CA 94132
(415) 333-4922
(415) 546-6968
Fax: (415) 333-4926
E-mail: sfhillel1@aol.com
Web: www.sfhillel.org

Seth Brysk, Executive Director
Jenna Balsavage, Program Director
Illya Mirtsyn, Emigre Program Director

ON CAMPUS

Shabbat dinners are held monthly on campus, as are occasional other programs. Golden Gate is served by the San Francisco Jewish Student Center.

See listing for San Francisco State Unversity.

HARVEY MUDD COLLEGE

Enrollment 702
Jewish 85

 Hillel at the Claremont Colleges
McAlister Center
919 North Columbia Avenue
Claremont, CA 91711
(909) 621-8824
Fax: (909) 621-8304
E-mail: leslieb@cuc.claremont.edu
Web: www.cuc.claremont.edu/interfth/page12.html

Rabbi Leslie Bergson, Director

See listing for Claremont Colleges.

HASTINGS COLLEGE OF LAW

Enrollment 1,400
Jewish 400

San Francisco Hillel Jewish Student Center
33 Banbury Street
San Francisco, CA 94132
(415) 333-4922
(415) 546-6988
Fax: (415) 333-4926
E-mail: sfhillel1@aol.com
Web: www.sfhillel.org

Seth Brysk, Executive Director
Jenna Balsavage, Program Director
Illya Mirtsyn, Emigre Program Director

Hastings is served by the Jewish Law Students Association and the graduate program of San Francisco Hillel. See listing for San Francisco State University.

HEBREW UNION COLLEGE— JEWISH INSTITUTE OF RELIGION

Enrollment 90
Jewish 90

3077 University Avenue
Los Angeles, CA 90007-3796
(213) 749-3424
(213) 747-6128
E-mail: lbarth@huc.edu
Web: www.huc.edu

Dr. Lewis Barth, Dean

See listing for HUC-JIR in Cincinnati, OH.

HUMBOLDT STATE UNIVERSITY

Enrollment 7,200
Jewish 200

Jewish Student Union
Humboldt State University
Department of Religious Studies
Arcata, CA 95521
(707) 826-5762
(707) 826-4126

Rabbi Lester Scharnberg, Advisor

 Jewish Studies
Major in religious studies.

ON CAMPUS

Activities vary according to the interest of the students.

LEE COLLEGE AT THE UNIVERSITY OF JUDAISM

Enrollment 180 (UG 90; GR 90)
   Jewish 180

Lee College Hillel
The University of Judaism
15600 Mulholland Drive
Los Angeles, CA 90077
(310) 476-9777
Fax: (310) 471-1278

TBA, Director

 Jewish Studies
40 courses; B.A., M.A.

 Study in Israel
Year abroad program.

 Kosher Food
All meals are kosher; vegetarian alternatives are available. Full kosher meal plan.

 Housing
Jewish residence: dormitory.

ON CAMPUS

Hillel at Lee College provides the structure for Jewish community life on campus for students in academic degree programs. Lee College students come from all walks of Jewish life and every type of community: Reform, Conservative, Orthodox, Reconstructionist, and secular. All participate in Shabbat, holiday, and cultural activities as they wish, exploring their Jewish identity in their own way.

Hillel provides a full Shabbat and holiday program in addition to activities that include an Israel Awareness Committee, a Judaism and the Environment recycling program, and educational projects that send students into the community to educate Jewish youth about issues such as AIDS, Zionism, and the environment.

University of Judaism's Los Angeles location places students in the midst of the second largest and most diverse Jewish community in the world. Local Jewish cultural activities include Israeli dancing, a Jewish museum, kosher Mexican food, and a Jewish film festival.

"As a whole, everything is comfortable."
   Jennifer Handy, junior

LOS ANGELES PIERCE COLLEGE—WOODLAND HILLS

Enrollment 13,200
   Jewish 1,500

 Hillel at Pierce & Valley Colleges
19720 Ventura Boulevard, Suite G
Woodland Hills, CA 91364
(818) 887-5901
Fax: (818) 887-7143
E-mail: hillelatpv@aol.com

Nomi Gordon, Director
Leya Witkowsky, Program Director
Rick Lupert, Judaic Program Coordinator

 Jewish Studies
1 course.

 Study in Israel
The College offers opportunities for study in Israel. For information on accepting credits from Israeli institutions, contact International Transcript Evaluation Committee at (310) 396-0720.

Kosher Food
Hillel faculty has a kosher kitchen. There is no kosher dining on campus, but there are many kosher restaurants in the West Valley.

ON CAMPUS

Pierce is a 2-year community, commuter college with an increasing Jewish student enrollment, located in a West San Fernando Valley suburban environment. Hillel programs are held jointly with Los Angeles Valley College, 10 miles away. The College is supportive of extracurricular organizations, including Hillel.

On-campus programs include weekly meetings, Jewish holiday celebrations, guest speakers, and the annual Jewish Awareness Month. The large Hillel House, located in Woodland Hills, has complete facilities for student activities including Cafe Hillel, a weekly coffeehouse with live music, parties, Israeli folk dancing, educational programs, and Shabbat programs. In addition, Hillel's diverse array of programs includes retreat weekends, a coed Jewish sports league, mitzvah/community service projects, Israel programs, and recycling and environmental projects. The Va'ad, Hillel's Student Board, provides a structure for student empowerment and leadership development.

LOS ANGELES VALLEY COLLEGE—VAN NUYS

Enrollment 16,500
Jewish 1,500

Hillel at Pierce & Valley Colleges
19720 Ventura Boulevard, Suite G
Woodland Hills, CA 91364
(818) 887-5901
Fax: (818) 887-7143
E-mail: hillelatpv@aol.com

Nomi Gordon, Director

 Jewish Studies
2 courses.

 Study in Israel
To receive credit for courses taken in Israeli universities, contact Internaitonal Transcript Evaluation at (310) 396-0720.

Kosher Food
The Hillel facility has a kosher kitchen. There are no provisions for kosher dining on campus, but many kosher restaurants are nearby in North Hollywood.

ON CAMPUS

LAVC is a community college located in a Jewish suburb in the San Fernando Valley. Hillel programs are held on campus and jointly with Pierce College in Woodland Hills, where the Hillel House is located. The college is supportive of extracurricular organizations, including Hillel.

On-campus programs include weekly meetings, Jewish holiday celebrations, guest speakers, and the annual Jewish Awareness Month. The large Hillel House, located in Woodland Hills, has complete facilities for student activities, including Cafe Hillel, a weekly coffeehouse with live music, parties, Israeli folk dancing, educational programs, and Shabbat programs. In addition, Hillel's diverse array of programs include retreat weekends, a coed Jewish sports league, mitzvah/community service projects, Israel programs, and recycling and environmental projects. The Va'ad, Hillel's Student Board, provides a structure for student empowerment and leadership development.

"Hillel has a very visible and positive presence at Valley College. Because it is a commuter campus, there is little sense of 'college life.' Therefore, Hillel's participation is very noticeable."

Robin Gilman, sophomore

LAVC Hillel also serves Los Angeles Pierce College.

LOYOLA MARYMOUNT UNIVERSITY

7900 Loyola Boulevard
Los Angeles, CA 90045

Rabbi Arthur Gross-Schaefer, Advisor
Naomi Zahavi, Advisor

 Jewish Studies
Introduction to the Old Testament, Religions of the World; Prophecy and Social Justice; Contemporary Judaism and Its Historical Background.

Kosher Food
Kosher food is available upon request in campus dining facilities.

ON CAMPUS

Loyola Marymount University is a Catholic university on the west side of Los Angeles. LMU Jewish community is associated with LMU Campus Ministry and the Los Angeles Hillel Council, and provides Jewish programming. All major Jewish holidays during the school year are observed. Rabbi Gross-Schaefer, who teaches in the School of Business Administration, provides spiritual leadership.

LOYOLA UNIVERSITY LAW SCHOOL—CALIFORNIA

Enrollment 4,000
Jewish 100

LMU Jewish Community
c/o Naomi Zahavi
900 Hilgard Avenue
Los Angeles, CA 90025-8200
(310) 338-7685
Fax: (310) 338-4366
E-mail: nzahavi@lmumail.lmu.edu
Web: www.lmu.edu/ministry/camp-min.htm

TBA, Director

Jewish Studies
1 course.

Loyola is served part-time as an outreach program of the Los Angeles Hillel Council.

MILLS COLLEGE

Enrollment 930 (UG 750; GR 180)
Jewish 50

Berkeley Hillel Extension
5000 MacArthur Boulevard
Oakland, CA 94613
(510) 845-7793
Fax: (510) 845-6446
E-mail: hillel@uclink2.berkeley.edu

Rabbi Rona Shapiro, Director

Mills College is served part-time by Hillel at Berkeley.

OCCIDENTAL COLLEGE

Enrollment 1,600
Jewish 160

Hillel at Occidental College
Herrick Interfaith Office
1600 Campus Road
Box F-8
Los Angeles, CA 90041
(323) 259-2959
(323) 208-6639
Fax: (310) 341-4959
E-mail: losahillel@aol.edu

Caty Konigsberg, Director

Jewish Studies
B.A. in Religious Studies, with Jewish Studies emphasis. Approximately 8 courses annually, including Introduction to Judaism, The State of Israel, Modern Jewish Thought, and Judaism After the Bible.

Study in Israel
Informal program for students who wish to study in Israel.

Kosher Food
Vegetarian dining alternatives and modest dormitory cooking facilities are located on campus. Kosher meats and bakery goods are available in North Hollywood, about 20 minutes away, and in Pico-Robertson, about 30 minutes away.

ON CAMPUS
Occidental's commitment to multiculturalism offers Jewish students a comfortable atmosphere. Hillel representatives are members of the Associated Students, Interfaith Student Council, and the Cultural Resource Center—building bridges with campus organizations. A large percentage of Jewish faculty on campus enjoy dinners, brunches, discussions, and holiday celebrations with students. Hillel meets weekly for lunch at the Herrick Interfaith Center. Students plan social events, such as movies, bagel brunches, or cultural events.

Faces in the Crowd is a voluntary program, consisting of students from many different organizations on campus. Students work during the spring and summer to produce a student-written program, which is performed for the entire freshman class during orientation week. The program increases understanding of differences (tradition, religion, race, sexual orientation, disabilities, gender) and creates goodwill and understanding. Occidental's Jewish students interact with students from many campuses at citywide events, dances, conferences, and Shabbats, as well as with the larger Los Angeles Jewish community.

Occidental Hillel also serves California Institute of Technology.

PITZER COLLEGE

Enrollment 880
Jewish 200

Hillel at the Claremont Colleges
McAlister Center
919 North Columbia Avenue
Claremont, CA 91711
(909) 621-8000 ext. 2096
(909) 621-8824
Fax: (909) 621-8304
E-mail: hillel@cgu.edu
Web: www.cuc.claremont.edu/interfth/page12.html

Rabbi Leslie Bergson, Director

See listing for Claremont Colleges.

POMONA COLLEGE

Enrollment 1,580
Jewish 140

Hillel at the Claremont Colleges
McAlister Center
919 North Columbia Avenue
Claremont, CA 91711
(909) 621-8000 ext. 2096
(909) 621-8824
Fax: (909) 621-8304
E-mail: hillel@cgu.edu
Web: www.cuc.claremont.edu/interfth/page12.html

Rabbi Leslie Bergson, Director

See listing for Claremont Colleges.

SAN DIEGO STATE UNIVERSITY

Enrollment 29,500
  Jewish 3,000 (UG 2,500; GR 500)

Hillel of San Diego/SDSU
5742 Montezuma Road
San Diego, CA 92115
(619) 583-6080
Fax: (619) 287-4506
E-mail: jtolley@aol.com
Web: www.rohan.sdsu.edu/dept/jsu/public_html

Jackie Tolley, Director
Joshua Epstein, Program Director
Myron Breitstein, Jewish Campus Service Corps Fellow

 Jewish Studies

20 and 25 courses annually; minor. The Lipinsky Institute for Judaic Studies, with 3 full-time and 3 interdisciplinary faculty members, sponsors numerous programs, including an annual Visiting Israeli Professorship, a weekly Judaic Studies Lecture Series, the Sieger Lectures on Diaspora Jewry (autumn), and the Glickman-Galinson Symposium on Modern Israel (spring). Lipinsky Institute for Judaic Studies, College of Arts and Letters, San Diego State University, San Diego, CA 92182; (619) 594-5338; lbaron@mail.sdsu.edu.

 Study in Israel
Junior year abroad.

Kosher Food
Vegetarian dining alternatives.

ON CAMPUS

Hillel/SDSU is the focus of an active Jewish community on the campus. The Jewish Student Union/SDSU organizes a variety of cultural, social, and Israeli events and works in conjunction with Hillel. Among the numerous activities are holiday celebrations, discussions, Shabbat services and dinners, lectures, and Yom Ha'atzmaut commemorations. Hillel/SDSU is located within 2 blocks of campus. Local synagogues and Jewish community agencies welcome student involvement and employment.

Students from San Diego's community colleges are welcomed and encouraged to get involved.

"Hillel has been a huge part of my college experience. It is so important for Jewish students to have Hillel, especially on a commuter campus like SDSU, to give them a focus for being Jewish."

Kara Pickman, fourth-year student

SAN FRANCISCO STATE UNIVERSITY

Enrollment 28,000
  Jewish 2,000 (UG 1,500; GR 500)

San Francisco Hillel Jewish Student Center
33 Banbury Street
San Francisco, CA 94132
(415) 333-4922
Fax: (415) 333-4926
E-mail: sfhillel1@aol.com
Web: www.sfhillel.org

Michal Heller, Director
Stacy Roberts-Ohr, Director of Student Activities
Heather Meiselman, Outreach Director/Jewish Campus Service Corps Fellow
Karen Watnick-Crane, Social Action Coordinator/Jewish Campus Service Corps Senior Fellow
Meirav Booch, Israel Coordinator
Seth Brysk, Executive Director
Jenna Balsavage, Program Director
Illya Mirtsyn, Program Director

 Jewish Studies
12 courses.

 Study in Israel
Hebrew University year abroad program.

ON CAMPUS

SFSU's Hillel House is 2 blocks from campus, and includes a library, TV lounge, snack food, and coffee. Hillel provides a full range of social, cultural, educational, and religious programming designed for the predominately commuter student population. Activities are held at various campus locations, the Hillel House, homes, and other venues throughout the city. Along with weekly vegetarian Shabbat dinners, Hillel sponsors activities for a wide variety of student interests including Ani V'Ata social action, Eco-Judaism Rosh Chodesh for women, Israel Action group, Russian Club, Graduate and Professional (GAP) graduate student group, Jewish Law Students Association (JLSA), and other groups.

San Francisco Hillel serves the metropolitan Jewish student population, including the following campuses: San Francisco State University, University of San Francisco, University of California—San Francisco, Hastings Law School, Golden Gate University, and the Community Colleges.

SAN JOSE STATE UNIVERSITY

Enrollment 28,000
Jewish 2,000

Hillel of Silicon Valley
14855 Oka Road, Suite 2
Los Gatos, CA 95030
(408) 358-3033 ext. 60
Fax: (408) 356-0733
E-mail: jamnjews@aol.com
Web: www.sjhillel.com

Lindsay Greensweig, Executive Hillel Director

Jewish Studies

11 courses at San Jose State; credit courses also at Santa Clara University.

ON CAMPUS

Hillel of Silicon Valley provides quality programs for more than 6,000 Jewish students attending the 8 local colleges, allowing them to explore the social, cultural, educational, and religious tapestries of Judaism. Hillel of Silicon Valley acts as the unifying organization for local campus organizations and activities, bringing together students from all college campuses for Shabbat dinners, holiday celebrations, social events, women's groups, social and political action, and other significant events. This is especially important in this commuter campus enviroment, where a sense of Jewish community is often difficult to achieve.

Hillel holds regular meetings and Shabbat dinners and sponsors holiday events throughout the year. Special activities such as retreats, guest speakers, and an annual trip to Israel are also part of the program.

Hillel of Silicon Valley is the local affiliate of Hillel: The Foundation for Jewish Campus Life. Its mission is to create an informed, celebratory Jewish community for Jewish college students, to deepen Jewish identity through social, cultural, and educational programs, to offer diverse opportunities for engagement tailored to students' needs, and to support Jewish interests on campus. Central to this mission is the development of Jews who will move from campus to community as positive, identified Jews with a stake in the Jewish future.

In addition to San Jose State University, Hillel of Silicon Valley serves San Jose City College, College of San Mateo, Santa Clara University, West Valley Community College, Evergreen Community College, DeAnza Community College, and Foothill Community College.

SANTA CLARA UNIVERSITY

Hillel of Silicon Valley
14855 Oka Road, Suite 2
Los Gatos, CA 95032
E-mail: jamnjews@aol.com

Lindsay Greensweig, Executive Hillel Director

See listing for San Jose State University.

SANTA MONICA COLLEGE

Enrollment 25,000
Jewish 1,500

Santa Monica Hillel Club
c/o Los Angeles Hillel Council
900 Hilgard Avenue
Los Angeles, CA 90024
(310) 453-6639
Fax: (310) 453-0752

Shelly Rothschild-Sherwin, Coordinator

Study in Israel

Summer study-abroad program.

ON CAMPUS

Santa Monica College is served part-time as an outreach program of the Los Angeles Hillel Council. Hillel at Santa Monica mirrors the rich diversity of Jewish students who attend SMC, and programs on campus range from social to religious. Speakers come to campus to address up-to-the-minute events, and social outings are arranged on weekends. In addition, all Santa Monica Hillel members are invited to participate in the larger events hosted by Los Angeles regional campuses (UCLA, USC, Northridge, etc.).

SCRIPPS COLLEGE

Enrollment 786
Jewish 100

Hillel at the Claremont Colleges
McAlister Center
919 North Columbia Avenue
Claremont, CA 91711
(909) 621-8000 ext. 2096
(909) 621-8824
Fax: (909) 621-8304
E-mail: hillel@cgu.edu
Web: www.cuc.claremont.edu/interfth/page12.html

Rabbi Leslie Bergson, Director

See listing for Claremont Colleges.

SONOMA STATE UNIVERSITY

Enrollment 7,500
   Jewish 700

Hillel—Jewish Student Organization
c/o San Francisco Hillel
33 Banbury Street
San Francisco, CA 94132
(707) 525-4720
(415) 333-4922
Fax: (415) 333-4926

Professor Richard Zimmer, Advisor

 Jewish Studies

Holocaust lecture series offered each spring for credit in various departments; optional credit available for off-campus courses.

 Study in Israel

Study abroad at Hebrew University.

Kosher Food

Vegetarian dining alternatives.

ON CAMPUS

Hillel meets weekly in the Student Union and plans monthly events for all college-age persons in Sonoma County, including students at Santa Rosa Junior College and the College of Marin. Sonoma's Holocaust film and lecture series is associated with the Alliance for Study of the Holocaust. Students may attend adult Jewish education classes at the local synagogue.

Sonoma State is served by the Northern California Hillel Council.

SOUTHWESTERN UNIVERSITY LAW SCHOOL

Enrollment 1,700

Jewish Law Students Association
Los Angeles Hillel Council
900 Hilgard Avenue
Los Angeles, CA 90024
(310) 208-6639
Fax: (310) 824-1794

Southwestern is served part-time as an outreach program of the Los Angeles Hillel Council.

STANFORD UNIVERSITY

Enrollment 13,600 (UG 6,600; GR 7,000)
   Jewish 2,000

 Hillel Foundation at Stanford
Old Union Clubhouse
Box Y
Stanford, CA 94309
(650) 723-1602
Fax: (650) 725-8530
E-mail: hillel@forsythe.stanford.edu
Web: www.stanford.edu/group/hillel

Rabbi Yoel Kahn, Director
Stephanie Shernicoff, Administrative Manager
Debra Feldstein, Executive Director
Hayley DeLugach, Program and Outreach Director
Nora Kushner, Director of Education and Programming
Iris Rave, Jewish Campus Service Corps Fellow

 Jewish Studies

25 courses; B.A., M.A., Ph.D., minor. Programs in departments of History, Religious Studies, and English. Special travel and research grant programs are available for study in Israel. Stanford's Program in Jewish Studies is an interdisciplinary program, covering all facets of the Jewish experience. Eight faculty members, including 2 endowed professorships, address the full expanse of Jewish history, literature, language, religion, and politics. More than 800 undergraduates and 16 full-time doctoral students take advantage of these course offerings each year. Undergraduate students may participate in the Jewish studies minor, in the honors program, or in an individually designed undergraduate major. The program offers 5 annual endowed lectures that bring distinguished scholars to campus, and a range of symposia, colloquia, and other special events.

Study in Israel

Credits accepted for study at Israeli universities.

Kosher Food

Daily and Passover through independent Kennedy Kosher Co-op; Hillel: Shabbat dinner twice each quarter, holidays including High Holidays when school is in session, occasional meals, and vegetarian dining alternatives.

ON CAMPUS

Hillel at Stanford is one of the most active campus organizations. Hillel is located in the center of campus, in the Old Union Clubhouse building. The facilities include a kitchen, an office, and an extensive library. Most of the programs are generated and run by the many student groups Hillel supports. These include social, religious, and Israel programs, along with lectures, discussions, and speakers. Hillel also co-sponsors programs with other Jewish organizations and different campus communities.

Hillel also coordinates a Jewish Culture week each year with different student groups, and a special committee putting together different types of programs to explore and celebrate Jewish culture. Hillel employs several student interns each year to work on a variety of projects including community service, publicity, Shabbat programming, and reaching out to other students throughout the campus. Hillel celebrates all holy days.

Jewish student groups include: Alpha Epsilon Pi fraternity, B'nai Biz (business school social group), Jewish Engineering Grads, Israeli Students Association, Jewish Book Club, Jewish Law Students Association, Jewish Medical Students Association, Jewish Students Association (undergraduate), Kadima (Jewish literary magazine), Kennedy Kosher Co-op, Orthodox Minyan, and Stanford Israel.

UNIVERSITY OF CALIFORNIA—BERKELEY

Enrollment 30,000
  Jewish 4,000 (UG 2,000; GR 2,000)

Berkeley Hillel Jewish Student Center
2736 Bancroft Way
Berkeley, CA 94704
(510) 845-7793
Fax: (510) 845-7753
E-mail: rabbi@uclink4.berkeley.edu
Web: www.jfed.org/Hillel.html

Rabbi Rona Shapiro, Executive Director
Joshua Miller, Program Director

 Jewish Studies
25 courses; graduate program in conjunction with Graduate Theological Union.

 Study in Israel
Education abroad programs through UC at Hebrew University, Jerusalem.

 Kosher Food
Hillel offers Shabbat meals and a full Passover meal plan, as well as other holiday and occasional meals. The University offers vegetarian dining alternatives and dormitory cooking facilities.

Students on the University meal plan are reimbursed for Passover meals taken at Hillel.

 Housing
Berkeley Bayit (10 students).

ON CAMPUS
The University of California—Berkeley is highly diverse and open-minded, offering a broad range of opportunities for students to explore their interests. These qualities are reflected directly in Jewish campus life, with an impressive selection of exciting people to meet, groups to join, and programs to attend. Students involved in Jewish campus life range from secular to Orthodox, cultural to religious, and from those who are very knowledgeable about Judaism to those who are just beginning to learn.

Berkeley Hillel is housed in the Reutlinger Center, directly across the street from the campus; facilities include kosher kitchens, a library, a lounge, a large social hall, and meeting rooms. Hillel's umbrella group Mitriah includes active Jewish student groups such as First Year Students at Hillel, AEPi fraternity, Tikkun (social action group), Taksim (social/cultural group), Intra-Mural Sports, Environmental and Outdoors Group, Jewish Law Students, Jewish Grads and Young Adults, Jewish Magazine, Women's Group, a Russian Jewish Group, Berkeley Bayit, United Jewish Appeal, Reform Kesher Group, Conservative Koach Group, Chevre Minyan (Orthodox Group), and Israel Action Committee. Regular student-led programming includes 3 spirited weekly Kabbalat Shabbat services and a Friday night dinner program that often lasts late into the night. Other activities include holiday celebrations, dance parties, lectures, camping trips, discussions, weekend retreats, movie nights, Jewish concerts, and regular classes in Israeli folk dancing, Jewish medical ethics, Jewish folk singing, swing dance, and a range of traditional text study. Berkeley Hillel also supports an outstanding array of special programs, including outstanding conferences on women's issues, multiculturalism, and graduate and professional concerns. Several of these conferences have won national Hillel awards. Hillel strives to offer something for everyone, and the enthusiastic staff is always ready to work with student leaders to crate new opportunities for Jewish involvement.

"Our Hillel exemplifies that purpose as it constantly brings Jews together as friends, as students, as individuals. It is a home by providing a place for students to feel comfortable, it is a family in that the bond we all share is great, it is a priceless educational opportunity in that it teaches students the value of leadership, of personal growth, of cooperation and of being good people."

Bev Slome, junior

"Hillel is a place that no matter what I can come here and it feels like home. I started just coming for the events. Slowly, I wanted to take part in planning and now I come here to do my studying and my everyday stuff. Hillel has opened up a lot of opportunities for me to get involved in the campus community. I have learned more about Judaism in the past year than I have learned in my whole life till now."

Rich Cain, sophomore

UNIVERSITY OF CALIFORNIA—DAVIS

Enrollment 23,500 (UG 17,600; GR 5,900)
Jewish 2,200

Davis Hillel
Hillel House
328 A Street
Davis, CA 95616
(916) 756-3708
Fax: (916) 756-6076
E-mail: hillels@aol.com
Web: www.jewishsac.org/hillel/index.htm

Rabbi Ken Kaufman, Executive Director
Meleasa G. Wishnick, Program Director
Collin Fala, Administrative Director

Jewish Studies

B.A., M.A., and Ph.D. options in Religious Studies. The Religious Studies Department offers classes in Hebrew, Hebrew scriptures, an Introduction to Judaism, and other occasional seminars on Judaism.

Study in Israel

The Davis Hillel connects students for study at various universities in Israel such as the Hebrew University, Haifa University, and Tel Aviv University, and for many summer Israel programs as well. Hillel also coordinates with the Northern California Hillel Council for an annual, highly subsidized, 3-week winter trip to Israel.

Kosher Food

Hillel offers Shabbat dinners once a month, a Passover seder, an annual Parents' Dinner, and other occasional meals. Kosher food, including meat, is available in nearby Sacramento.

Housing

The Bayit next to Hillel houses 5 students in a cooperative Jewish living environment. There is also another Jewish cooperative house on campus.

ON CAMPUS

Davis Hillel is committed to Jewish calendar programming and involving students in the conception and implementation of all events. Davis Hillel is located across the street from campus, in a comfortable house with a lounge, a library, a kosher kitchen, and offices.

Hillel offers a full range of social, cultural, educational, and religious programs, including classes, guest speakers, student-faculty discussions, community service programs, seder, Shabbat, and holiday celebrations. The annual Jewish Culture Week includes diverse events with artists, musicians, special services, lectures, and the annual Parents' Dinner.

Hillel encourages and supports various Jewish student groups such as the Jewish Student Union, Jewish Graduate and Professional Students, Jewish Law Students' Association, the Jewish fraternity Alpha Epsilon Pi, and Sigma AEPhi. These groups are welcome to use Hillel resources for their events. Hillel offers non-credit Hebrew and Torah classes as well as creative educational programs and lectures.

Hillel also coordinates programs with the local congregation, campus departments, local Jewish Community Federations, Northern California Hillel Council, the San Francisco-based Israel Project, and the Interfaith Campus Ministries. Hillel creates leadership opportunities for students, and provides leadership training through various conferences held throughout the year. Aid is available to students wishing to participate in many of the opportunities publicized by Hillel. Hillel also has a very active Advisory Board and is supported by the large number of Jewish faculty and staff on campus.

The Davis Hillel also serves students at the California State University—Sacramento.

UNIVERSITY OF CALIFORNIA—IRVINE

Enrollment 15,000
Jewish 1,000

Hillel Foundation of Orange County
Bendat Hillel Center
250 E. Baker Street, Suite F
Costa Mesa, CA 92626
(714) 433-2478
Fax: (714) 433-2488
E-mail: ochillel12@aol.com
Web: www.faith.uci.edu/jewish

Jeffrey T. Rips, Director
Todd Silverstein, Jewish Campus Service Corps Fellow

Jewish Studies

3 courses, with more planned; minor in Religious Studies. Endowed chair in Jewish History.

Study in Israel

Summer seminar and junior year education abroad program.

Kosher Food

Available at all Hillel events, including Shabbat dinners, Passover meals, and free weekly bagel brunches.

ON CAMPUS

The Jewish community of Orange County is very supportive of activities for Jewish students at area colleges. Hillel has a good working relationship with the campus ministry. Students enjoy on-campus programming as well as regional events, such as the annual West Coast Regional Kallah. Many students commute.

The Hillel Foundation of Orange County serves as a resource for all area schools, including California State University—Fullerton, Fullerton College, Chapman, Irvine Valley, Golden West, Orange Coast, Saddleback, and Rancho Santiago.

UNIVERSITY OF CALIFORNIA—LOS ANGELES

Enrollment 33,600 (UG 23,600; GR 10,000)
Jewish 4,200

Hillel Jewish Student Center
900 Hilgard Avenue
Los Angeles, CA 90024
(310) 208-3081
Fax: (310) 824-2247
E-mail: hillel@ucla.edu
Web: www.ben2.ucla.edu/~hillel

Rabbi Chaim Seidler-Feller, Director
Carol Bar-Or, Assistant Director
Andrea Nussbaum, Program Director
Cari Rezman, Jewish Campus Service Corps; Speilberg Fellow

Jewish Studies

36 courses; B.A., M.A., Ph.D. Chair in Holocaust Studies, Sephardic Studies, courses in women and Judaism, history, religion, language, philosophy, literature, folklore, sociology, and others. The Center for Jewish Studies: (310) 825-4355.

Study in Israel

Summer seminar and junior year abroad. Scholarships are available for study in Israel.

Kosher Food

Hillel offers weekly kosher Shabbat dinners, and lunches and dinners for Passover. Vegetarian dining alternatives. Dormitory cooking facilities. Kosher food is available locally.

Housing

The Westwood Bayit, a Jewish student cooperative within walking distance of campus, offers a kosher kitchen and a swimming pool. Alpha Epsilon Pi, the only Jewish fraternity at UCLA, is actively involved in Jewish campus life, and has a residential fraternity house.

ON CAMPUS

The full range of Jewish experience is available at UCLA, with Hillel as the center of activity and information.

A diverse group of students plans the program, which includes a campus newspaper, political and social action groups, cultural programs, programs in Business, Law and Medical Schools; grad student, alumni, and faculty groups; community internships, programs for Persian, Russian, and Israeli students; women's and environmental programs; an *a cappella* group; Holocaust Awareness Week; and a Jewish Arts Festival. The Center for Jewish Studies and Hillel sponsor major symposia and conferences. Jewish Greek life is very vibrant on campus. UCLA Hillel offers a special, highly selective program for Jewish students who are campus leaders, but who have not been actively involved in Jewish campus life.

A new facility located across from the center of campus and named the Yitzhak Rabin Hillel Center for Jewish Life is expected to open in fall 2000. It will include a computer center, a cafe, a basic Jewish reference library, and a kosher dining facility that will be administered by the University. This arrangement will allow UCLA to offer a kosher meal plan to students in the residence halls and to the entire campus community.

UNIVERSITY OF CALIFORNIA—RIVERSIDE

Enrollment 10,000
Jewish 750

Hillel/Jewish Student Union
Student Life and Leadership Center
Box 97
Riverside, CA 92521
(909) 787-5338
E-mail: hillel@mail.ucr.edu

Scott Silverman, President
Amber Fink, Vice President

Jewish Studies

4 courses specifically on Judaism; 1 comparison course.

Study in Israel

UC—Riverside offers ample Israeli study opportunities. Scholarships are available and credits are transferable.

Kosher Food

Hillel is in the process of establishing a Kosher House. Vegetarian dining is available.

ON CAMPUS

UCR Hillel's bi-monthly Shabbat programs are well attended. In addition to its regular programming, Hillel often sponsors special activities upon students' suggestions.

UNIVERSITY OF CALIFORNIA—SAN DIEGO

Enrollment 16,000
    Jewish 2,000 (UG 1,700; GR 300)

Hillel of San Diego/UCSD
Office of Religious Affairs 0081
502 University Center
La Jolla, CA 92093-0081
(858) 534-2521
Fax: (858) 534-5848
E-mail: Hillel@ucsd.edu Web: sdcc13.ucsd.edu/~ujs/
hillel.html

Rabbi Lisa Goldstein, Director
Michael Rabkin, Program Director
Chase Kohn, Vice President

Jewish Studies

15 courses. B.A., M.A. and Ph.D. in association with the Department of History. The Judaic Studies Program is interdisciplinary. Courses include Hebrew Bible, Archaeology of Israel, and Ancient Jewish History. An endowment in Judaic studies provides support for other programs, including endowed chairs, the Taubman Institute for Sephardic Studies, public lectures, library holdings, conferences, publications, archaeological excavations, and scholarships. Ms. Laurel Mannen, Judaic Studies Program, 0104, University of California—San Diego, 9500 Gilman Drive, La Jolla, CA 92093-0104; (619) 534-4551.

Study in Israel

Junior year abroad.

Kosher Food

Vegetarian dining alternatives. Residence hall cooking facilities in selected apartments. Shabbat dinners as scheduled.

ON CAMPUS

Hillel of San Diego at UCSD sponsors an ever-expanding agenda of programs, including social events, Israel-related programs, social action activities, and programs for Greek students. Hillel also holds cultural events, graduate student activities, and first-year programs.

Most recently, Hillel has started a Jewish Klezmer Festival and a March for Unity to celebrate Israel's birthday. Students have initiated innovative programs such as a student radio show, Shalom UCSD, and *Bubbe's Kitchen*, a Jewish cooking show.

Hillel of San Diego, located in the Office of Religious Affairs, is the focus of an active Jewish community on campus. In the absence of a permanent facility, students enjoy the opportunity to reach out by holding programs throughout the campus.

"UCSD offers a variety of programs to satisfy every Jew's needs. There are social, religious, Israeli, and social action programs offered (and all for free I might add!), just to name a few. There is a large presence on campus, but I wouldn't say the Jewish community is cliquish or exclusive in any way. Everyone whom I have met has been very open to new people and ideas. Rabbi Lisa Goldstein, who is the Hillel director for San Diego, and our own personal on-campus rabbi, is WONDERFUL! She makes Jewish life great. The JCSC fellow and program director are also integral to a successful Jewish community on campus. So far, there has been great success. Jewish life is taken seriously on campus, and many different Jewish people come together, from different backgrounds and levels of observance, to enjoy free Shabbat services and dinner every Friday night. Shabbat is one of the best things about UCSD. The Union of Jewish Students has done great things for the students and community around UCSD. I was fortunate enough to get the opportunity to go on the UJA Winter mission to Israel for 10 days. It was an amazing trip. Excellent subsidies are available at UCSD for any and all Jewish related conferences and sponsored trips. For me, financing is a must and the Hillel office on campus helps a lot."

Erin Slaten, sophomore

"It is hard for me to imagine how different things here would be for me if I had not gotten involved in Hillel. I come from a mixed house; my mom is Jewish, my dad is not. Growing up we had more of an absence of religion than any religion at all. However, I was very drawn to Judaism by the little I knew about it from Passover seders at my Grandma's or friends' bar mitzvas. I decided to learn more about Judaism when I arrived here.

"Hillel is a real presence in UCSD life. It seemed natural to get involved. I've attended classes with Rabbi Lisa, gone to many Shabbat dinners and over winter break I journeyed to Israel with UJA. All of these activities were made possible by Hillel. Now, I consider Judaism to be very central to who I am.

"Without a doubt, what makes Hillel here so fantastic are the people: Rabbi Lisa, Chase Kohn (the JCSC Fellow), and Michael Rabkin make Hillel friendly, fun and accessible. Often I just drop by the Office of Religious Affairs to sit down and talk.

> *"I am a member of Alpha Epsilon Pi at UCSD and we get incredible the support from Hillel. Rabbi Lisa, Chase, and Michael are always willing to help with RUSH efforts, philanthropy events and whatever else we might need. I think AEPi's relationship with Hillel is one of the reasons our chapter here is so successful."*
>
> **Ian Holloway, junior**

UNIVERSITY OF CALIFORNIA — SAN FRANCISCO

Jewish 500

> San Francisco Hillel
> 33 Banbury Street
> San Francisco, CA 94132
> (415) 333-4922
> (415) 546-6988
> Fax: (415) 333-4926
> E-mail: sfhillel1@aol.com
>
> **Seth Brysk**, Executive Director

UCSF is served by the graduate program of San Francisco Hillel. See listing for San Francisco State University.

UNIVERSITY OF CALIFORNIA — SANTA BARBARA

Enrollment 18,500 (UG 15,500; GR 3,000)
Jewish 2,000

> UCSB Hillel Foundation
> 777 Camino Pescadero
> Goleta, CA 93117
> (805) 968-1280
> Fax: (805) 968-3781
> E-mail: hillel@ucsb.hillel.org
> Web: www.west.net/~hillel/
>
> **Rabbi Stephen Cohen**, Executive Director
> **Melanie Sasson**, Assistant Director
> **Kelly Rotman**, Jewish Campus Service Corps Fellow

ON CAMPUS

While Santa Barbara in general and UCSB in particular have not been known in the past as major centers of Jewish life and culture, that is quickly changing. Santa Barbara is a haven of tremendous natural beauty, cultural richness, and rapidly increasing Jewish life, which is especially attractive to former residents of Los Angeles. The town has a large Reform synagogue, a vibrant Young Israel (modern Orthodox), and a small and very friendly Chabad. All of these groups extend a warm welcome to Jewish UCSB students. Every year Hillel co-hosts the Santa Barbara Jewish Festival with the local Jewish Federation, the largest annual Jewish event in town attracting more than 4,000 people from California's Central Coast.

Hillel at UCSB has grown into a dynamic network of communities. Between 70 and 100 students come every Friday night for services (style falling somewhere between Reform and Conservative) followed by a catered vegetarian dinner and a student-run program. The Isla Vista minyan meets weekly on Saturday mornings throughout the year at Hillel—an extremely spirited, intelligent gathering of mostly graduate students, faculty, and community people looking for an informal, authentic Jewish community.

UCSB has been reorganized as a Tzedek Hillel campus, one with a strong culture of social justice programming. Hillel also has an *a cappella* choir, Hilleluyah, as well as monthly Israel-related programs, social events, speakers, and similar activities and other cultural events. AEPi and AEPhi, national Jewish fraternity and sorority at UCSB, work closely with Hillel to create a strong Jewish presence on campus. Holocaust Remembrance Week, Jewish Cultural Week, Campus United Jewish Appeal, and Progressive Jewish Students Union are among the many events and organizations that also contribute to a vital Jewish campus life at UC—Santa Barbara.

Hillel looks forward to the completion of the Milton Roisman Jewish Student Center on campus by September 2000.

UNIVERSITY OF CALIFORNIA — SANTA CRUZ

Enrollment 10,000
Jewish 2,000

> Santa Cruz Hillel Foundation
> 222 Cardiff Place
> Santa Cruz, CA 95060
> (831) 426-3332
> Fax: (831) 426-1895
> E-mail: info@santacruzhillel.org
> Web: www.santacruzhillel.org
>
> **Lorin Troderman**, Executive Director
> **Jenn Yale**, Program Director
> **Esther Greenburg**, Program Director

Jewish Studies

4 courses. An individually designed major is possible via independent work with professors at UCSC and within the UC system. Recently endowed Chair in Holocaust Studies. Annual conference.

 Study in Israel

Hebrew University Year Abroad program.

Kosher Food

Hillel keeps a kosher kitchen and serves meals every other Shabbat. Campus and town offer a variety of vegetarian options. Students utilize the Hillel kitchen for an annual Passover meal co-op.

ON CAMPUS

Hillel at Santa Cruz is an informal environment for students to build a sense of Jewish community on campus, and is advised by a student advisory committee and a community board of directors.

Santa Cruz Hillel offers a range of cultural, social, educational, and religious programs for students at UCSC and Cabrillo College, and promotes Israel as a destination for study and travel. Jewish cultural arts programs are co-sponsored with the residence halls, individual colleges, and the Arts & Lectures Department. These include the annual Alternative Jewish Film Festival, Sukkot Autmn Harvest Music Festival, Festival and Reggae Shabbat, and Jewish Comedy Nite. Hillel hosts speakers on Jewish topics of interest including Jewish history, literature, politics, and Israeli culture, and offers quarterly classes in Hebrew, the weekly Torah portion, and Jewish spirituality. Student organizations include: Leviathan (a quarterly Jewish newspaper), Jewish Student Union (the campus secular forum for all Jewish students), Talmidei Shalom (exploring the mystical and traditional paths of Judaism), Jewish Students of Cabrillo (organizing activities for their campus community), Israel Action Committee (interested in Israel programming), and Eco-Ruach/Environmental Groups (focusing on rain forests, sustainable development, etc.)

"Jewish Comedy Nite was a bundle of laughs! It was good, clean Jewish fun—the best thing since sliced bread! I loved that Hebrew, The Chosen Beer co-sponsored it! The entire night was so much fun! I can't remember laughing so hard—ever!"

Ben Berger, sophomore

UNIVERSITY OF CALIFORNIA MEDICAL SCHOOL

Jewish 500

San Francisco Hillel
Jewish Student Center
33 Banbury Street
San Francisco, CA 94132
(415) 333-4922
Fax: (415) 333-4926
E-mail: sfhillell1@aol.com

Seth Bryst, Executive Director

ON CAMPUS

Holiday celebrations, lectures, and an annual Jewish Medical Ethics series are held.

See listing for San Francisco State University.

UNIVERSITY OF JUDAISM

 Jewish Studies

40 courses; B.A., M.A.Ed./B.Lit., M.H.L. with Rabbinic Ordination.

 Study in Israel

Year abroad program.

 Kosher Food

All meals on campus are kosher. Kosher kitchens are available in the dormitories. Vegetarian meals are available.

 Housing

Jewish residence: dormitory.

ON CAMPUS

Hillel at University of Judaism provides a structure and a place for Jewish community life on campus for students in academic degree programs. UJ students come from diverse backgrounds, experiences, and affiliations. At Hillel, students from all backgrounds participate in regular Shabbat, holiday celebrations, and cultural activities. Each student, through the support of Hillel, explores his or her Jewish identity in his or her own way.

Hillel at UJ provides regular Shabbat and holiday services, meals, and celebrations. The Israel Awareness Committee is active in planning regular events including Israel Independence Day activities. Students also participate regularly in community programs and projects that focus on issues such as AIDS, Zionism, and the environment.

The UJ is located in a beautiful section of Los Angeles, the second largest and most diverse Jewish community in the world. Local Jewish cultural activities include the Skirball Center, the Simon Wiesenthal Holocaust Museum, Israeli music, dining and dancing, a multitude of kosher restaurants (including kosher Mexican food), and Jewish film festivals.

UNIVERSITY OF REDLANDS

Enrollment 1,800 (UG 1,400; GR 400)
Jewish 50

Hillel
PO Box 3080
Redlands, CA 92373-0999
(909) 307-7785 ext. 2602
(909) 793-2121

Professor Mara Winick, Advisor

 Jewish Studies
3 courses.

 Study in Israel
Available for month of January (interim) for academic credit.

 Kosher Food
Students can pre-order vegetarian dining alternatives or use dorm kitchen facilities.

 Housing
Kosher house; 5 students.

ON CAMPUS

Students have monthly Shabbat dinners and an annual Passover seder and participate in the Hillel Western Regional Retreat. An annual campus Holocaust observance is sponsored by Hillel, the University, and the city. Hillel offers 2 small annual scholarships.

UNIVERSITY OF SAN FRANCISCO

Enrollment 5,744 (UG 3,855; GR 1,889)
Jewish 425

San Francisco Hillel
33 Banbury Street
San Francisco, CA 94132
(415) 546-4922
(415) 546-6988
Fax: (415) 333-4926
E-mail: sfhillel2@aol.com
Web: www.sfsu.edu/~hillel

Seth Brysk, Executive Director
Michal Heller, Director
Heather Meiselman, Outreach Director
Jenna Balsavage, Program Director
Illya Mirtsyn, Emigre Program Director

 Jewish Studies
Several courses each semester including Hebrew and Jewish History.

University of San Francisco is served by the San Francisco Jewish Student Center. See listing for San Francisco State University.

UNIVERSITY OF SOUTHERN CALIFORNIA

Enrollment 28,000 (UG 15,000; GR 13,000)
Jewish 2,400 (UG 1,200; GR 1,200)

 USC Hillel Jewish Center
3300 South Hoover Boulevard
Los Angeles, CA 90007-3356
(213) 747-9135
Fax: (213) 747-2671
E-mail: mjdavids@usc.edu
Web: www.usc.edu/dept/hillel

Matt Davidson, Program Director
Charles Briskin, Rabbinic Intern

 Jewish Studies
Hebrew Union College's Los Angeles campus serves as the Jewish Studies Department, offering a Jewish Studies minor and popular classes in Hebrew, Holocaust, and Jewish history; M.A. and Ph.D. joint programs between HUC School of Jewish Communal Service and USC Social Work.

Study in Israel
Year or semester abroad at Hebrew University or Tel Aviv University.

Kosher Food
Hillel offers weekly kosher dinners every Shabbat when school is in session on holidays; first night seder, lunches and dinners for Passover and Sukkot. Frozen kosher meals are available at campus locations in addition to vegetarian alternatives.

Housing
Shalom Housing, a Jewish residential unit on campus, enables students to keep kosher while still being part of the campus community. Bayit, an off-campus house with a kosher kitchen, is also shared by Jewish students.

ON CAMPUS

The USC campus is multicultural without being tense, with most students and groups seeing themselves as part of the "Trojan family." A significant percentage of USC faculty and many deans are Jewish.

The Hillel Jewish Center is a beautiful modern building located just across the street from the USC campus. It contains a large lounge with piano, entertainment center, TV, library, and Ping-Pong table; student offices with computer and modem; a sukkah patio; and a kosher kitchen under Orthodox supervision. Traditionally Jewish Greek houses on campus are AEPi and ZBT.

Hillel is the hub of Jewish life, offering a comprehensive program of activities to meet the needs of USC's mostly residential Jewish student population. Weekly Shabbat celebrations feature student or rabbi-led services and a gourmet kosher dinner. Other programs include the Jewish Filmmakers Forum; Kol Schirimm (Jewish *a cappella* group); monthly Havdalah happenings with Saturday night on the town; the Kesher Mentor Program, which connects students with Jewish faculty and staff; informal classes in Hebrew and Torah; and rotating exhibits in the Hillel Art Gallery. Students participate in the regional kallah over President's Weekend and in numerous citywide events, including dances and Shabbat/holiday celebrations.

USC Hillel has been awarded Hillel's national Elie Wiesel Award for outstanding programming in Jewish Arts and Culture and the William Haber Award for Programs of Quality for the Jewish Campus Community for its creation of the group AMJID Arabs, Muslims and Jews in Dialogue. AMJID engenders knowledge, respect, and mutual loyalty among student participants from these diverse religious and ethnic cultures. Hillel has also created JAATF (Jews and African Americans within the Trojan Family), which has become an important model for intergroup cooperation.

The Dean of Religious Life at USC is Rabbi Susan Laemmle. Rabbi Laemmle is always available to meet with students, coordinate interreligious programming, and advocate for the needs of Jewish and non-Jewish students on campus.

> *"The friendly staff and wide variety of programs offered extend the Trojan family beyond the classroom."*
>
> **Beth Strum, graduate student**

> *"Hillel has enabled me to explore my own Jewish identity more than I ever thought possible. I have struggled with the questions of ethics and goodness that are paramount in Jewish tradition, learned the ancient language of our people, met other Jewish students and formed a community more closely knit than I ever imagined."*
>
> **Heyden Graham, sophomore**

WHITTIER COLLEGE

Enrollment 1,000
Jewish 50

c/o Los Angeles Hillel Council
900 Hilgard Avenue
Los Angeles, CA 90024
(310) 208-6639

ON CAMPUS

At this time, a Jewish student organization is not active on campus. For further information contact the Los Angeles Hillel Council.

COLORADO

COLORADO COLLEGE

Enrollment 1,900
Jewish 150

The Colorado College Hillel
c/o Ofer Ben-Amots
14 E. Cache La Poudre
Colorado Springs, CO 80903
(719) 389-6555
Fax: (719) 389-6862
E-mail: hillel@coloradocollege.edu

Ofer Ben-Amots, Faculty Advisor

Jewish Studies

Colorado College's academic program includes Jewish Studies, Hebrew Language, Holocaust Studies, and Jewish Music. Three annual scholarships are also available through The Mitzvah Research and Travel Opportunity.

Study in Israel

Colorado College offers opportunities to study at Hebrew University and elsewhere in Israel.

Kosher Food

The College does not provide kosher food on campus. Students who keep kosher can be exempted from the meal plan.

ON CAMPUS

Hillel has office space in the College's multicultural buildiing. Students have opportunities for creative input into the Hillel program by becoming officers of the board. These positions include President of Hillel, Chairperson of Chaverim, Treasurer, Board Member for Membership, and Board Member for Programming.

COLORADO STATE UNIVERSITY

Enrollment 22,350
Jewish 750

Colorado State University Hillel
Lory Student Center
Box S1919
Colorado State University
Ft. Collins, CO 80523
(970) 491-2080
(970) 218-1461 Fax: (970) 204-6803
E-mail: hillel@lamar.colostate.edu/~hillel/

Hedy Berman, Advisor

 Study in Israel
Study abroad program.

 Kosher Food
Available at local supermarket or in Denver. Kosher meals also provided at special request of student.

ON CAMPUS

Colorado State has a vibrant, growing Hillel with a strong student board and opportunities for leadership. Activities include Shabbat dinners (at student's or director's home), holiday celebrations (including a Passover seder in the Student Center with more than 100 in attendance in 1999), guest lecturers/presentations, Holocaust Awareness Week, Torah study, and other Jewish learning programs. Hillel also sponsors social activities such as barbecues, ski trips, hikes, movie nights, etc. CSU students participate in statewide programs with campuses in Boulder and Denver, and in regional leadership retreats. The local Jewish community and synagogue Congregation Har Shalom are very welcoming and hospitable to students. Hillel students run the Har Shalom Purim carnival as a fun, fund-raising activity, and participate in other programs in cooperation with groups from the synagogue.

UNITED STATES AIR FORCE ACADEMY

Enrollment 4,200
Jewish 37

Jewish Chaplaincy
HQ USAFA/HCD
2348 Sijan Drive, Suite 100
U.S. Air Force Academy, CO 80840-8280
(719) 472-2636
(719) 472-2858

Rabbi Ira Flax, Advisor

 Jewish Studies
Every Monday evening 6:30–8:00 p.m.

 Study in Israel
3 weeks in Israel for entering seniors interested in Middle East policy.

 Kosher Food
Kosher food is available for holidays and occasional meals.

ON CAMPUS

Jewish cadets participate in Colorado regional retreats with Jewish students and have several events on campus, including weekly bagel brunches with a speaker, a seder retreat weekend, and Sunday morning study in Basic Judaism. The local community offers home hospitality for High Holidays and Passover. The Jewish Cadet Choir sings throughout the United States.

UNIVERSITY OF COLORADO

Enrollment 23,100 (UG 18,100; GR 5,000)
Jewish 1,800 (UG 1,200; GR 600)

 CU Boulder Hillel
2795 Colorado Avenue
Boulder, CO 80302
(303) 442-6571
Fax: (303) 442-6941
E-mail: hillecu@colorado.edu
Web: www.hillel.colorado.org/cuindex.html

Marcia Seigal, Director
Wendy Aronson, Program Director
Pat Blumenthal, Executive Director, Hillel Council of Colorado

 Jewish Studies
6 courses through the Religious Studies program.

 Study in Israel
Junior year abroad at Hebrew University.

 Kosher Food
Kosher meals available upon request. Hillel offers Shabbat and holiday dinners. Some residence halls provide kosher food for Passover.

ON CAMPUS

The Boulder Hillel House, recently renovated, is located on the corner of campus with a lounge, kosher kitchen, library, small sanctuary, and multipurpose room.

A wide range of social, volunteer, community service, educational, and religious programming is offered, as well as outdoor events and Holocaust Awareness Week. Students have the opportunity to participate in statewide events each year.

"Hillel has been a great outlet for me both socially and spiritually. It has allowed me to continue the religious traditions of my family and create a few of my own."

Melanie Ogin, Student Leadership Board

Boulder Hillel is served by the Hillel Council of Colorado.

UNIVERSITY OF DENVER

Enrollment 6,280 (UG 2,780; GR 3,500)
Jewish 900

Denver Hillel
Jewish Student Center
2240 East Wesley Avenue
Denver, CO 80210
(303) 777-2586
Fax: (303) 777-2773
E-mail: hillelcu@colorado.edu
Web: www.hillelcolorado.org/cuindex

Pat Blumenthal, Executive Director
Jennifer Serey, Program Director

Jewish Studies
35 courses; B.A., M.A.; Jewish studies minor.

Kosher Food
Hillel offers kosher meals to students on request. Kosher Shabbat and holiday meals are also available.

ON CAMPUS
Denver Hillel is located at the southern edge of Denver University's campus and serves students and young adults from the entire metropolitan Denver area.

Students enjoy a wide variety of programs, including social, political, social action/Tzedakah projects, educational, Holocaust Awareness Week, and religious activities. Denver Hillel works closely with the Center for Judaic Studies. Students also have the opportunity to meet with students from Colorado campuses at statewide retreats and parties throughout the year. The Denver Jewish community is supportive of Hillel and welcomes students at its many events and activities.

Denver Hillel is served by the Hillel Council of Colorado.

UNIVERSITY OF NORTHERN COLORADO

Enrollment 10,000
Jewish 200

c/o Hillel Council of Colorado
2795 Colorado Avenue
Boulder, CO 80302
(303) 442-6571
(303) 871-3402
Fax: (303) 871-4488
E-mail: hillel@lamar.colostate.edu
Web: www.hillelcolorado.org/cuindex

Hedy Berman, Advisor

ON CAMPUS
There is currently no Hillel or other campus organization for Jewish students at the University of Northern Colorado. Some students participate in Hillel activities at Colorado State University, which is approximately a half-hour drive northwest of Greeley in Fort Collins. Contact the Hillel Council of Colorado for specific information.

CONNECTICUT

CENTRAL CONNECTICUT STATE UNIVERSITY

Enrollment 12,000
Jewish 250

Hillel
200 Bloomfield Avenue
GSU 153
West Hartford, CT 06117
(860) 768-4987
(860) 768-4059
Fax: (860) 768-5008
E-mail: terdiman@mail.hartford.edu

David Terdiman, Director

ON CAMPUS
Hillel meets on campus once a week, and co-sponsors events with the University's Program Council, student government, and NAACP Chapter. Activities also include trips to the U.S. Holocaust Memorial Museum in Washington, DC, and other major Jewish points of interest.

Jewish students at CCSC are served by the Hillel Foundation at the University of Hartford.

CONNECTICUT COLLEGE

Enrollment 1,800 (UG 1,600; GR 200)
Jewish 200 (UG 180; GR 20)

Hillel
270 Mohegan Avenue
New London, CT 06320
(860) 439-2453
(860) 439-5175
Fax: (860) 439-2463
E-mail: aros@conncoll.edu

Rabbi Aaron Rosenberg, Associate Chaplain
Karla Bendor, Advisor

 Jewish Studies

2 courses, including Hebrew language; endowed Elie Wiesel Chair in Jewish Studies; instructor in Department of Religious Studies.

 Study in Israel

Yes.

Kosher Food

Vegetarian dining alternatives.

ON CAMPUS

Connecticut College's weekly Shabbat Dinner Experience is enhanced by blessings, songs, and guest speakers. Hillel also sponsors other events, according to student interest, such as bagel brunches, holiday celebrations, and field trips.

> *"Hillel is a great place to meet . . . other Jewish students, and the three or four congregations in nearby New London are open to the college community. We have fun on Hillel's annual trip to New York City, to the Carnegie Deli and to the Jewish Heritage Museum and to the Jewish Museum."*
>
> *Daniel J. Burns, junior*

QUINNIPIAC COLLEGE

Enrollment 5,780 (UG 3,780; GR 2,000)
Jewish 350

Quinnipiac Hillel
PO Box 264
Hamden, CT 06518
(860) 288-5251 ext. 8206
Fax: (860) 281-8654

Rabbi Stephen J. Steinberg, College Rabbi

Study in Israel

Program with Hebrew University in Jerusalem for the exchange of faculty and students.

 Kosher Food

Kosher foods are available in Hamden and New Haven.

ON CAMPUS

Hillel offers a wide range of activities including Shabbat services, Passover meals, Hanukkah celebrations, Holocaust remembrances, and cultural and social activities such as speakers, trips, brunches, and mixers.

TRINITY COLLEGE

Enrollment 2,000
Jewish 150

Trinity College Hillel
300 Summit Street
PO Box 702577
Hartford, CT 06106
(860) 297-2280
Fax: (860) 548-7797
E-mail: bellkrieg@aol.com

Nancy Beller-Krieger, Director

Jewish Studies

8 courses plus Hebrew. B.A. with major in religion or major in Middle Eastern Studies. Joint degree is available from area schools. Courses are offered in religion, history, philosophy, literature, and political science.

Study in Israel

Students participate in semester, year-long and summer programs at Israeli universities. Trinity also participates in the Wesleyan University Israel Consortium, a 6-month program in Jerusalem, affiliated with Hebrew University. Curricula include Hebrew language and literature, as well as the history and politics of the Middle East.

 Kosher Food

The Hillel House has a kosher kitchen. Students are welcome to prepare kosher meals at the house. All Hillel events with food are kosher or vegetarian, including monthly Friday night dinners, Sunday brunches, and student/faculty lunches. Vegetarian options are available through the dining service.

Housing

Hillel's new house will have space for 2 students.

ON CAMPUS

The Hillel House, which is a half-block from campus, is a comfortable place to hang out for study or socializing. It has a large-screen TV, a VCR, and a kosher kitchen. Student initiative for projects is strongly encouraged and essential to their success. Hillel sponsors a wide range of social, educational, cultural, and religious programming on campus, including guest lectures, films, concerts, parties, and trips, as well as Shabbat services and holiday dinners. Trinity faculy are highly supportive of Hillel and are regular participants in many events, including monthly student/faculty lunches. Faculty members have led trips to New York and the U.S. Holocaust Museum in Washington, DC.

Hillel also co-sponsors a number of programs with other campus groups, including cultural programs, and a monthly forum on religious tolerance. Students have many opportunities to connect to the Greater Hartford Jewish Community, and have served as interns at the Jewish Federation and the Jewish Community Center and as teachers at local religious schools. Through Hillel and Federation support, students can attend leadership conferences in the U.S. and Israel.

A new Hillel house is planned for the near future.

UNITED STATES COAST GUARD ACADEMY

Enrollment 900
Jewish 5

c/o Jewish Federation of Eastern CT
28 Channing Street
PO Box 1468
New London, CT 06320
(860) 443-8062
Fax: (860) 443-4175
E-mail: jefis@conncoll.edu

Karla Bendor, Advisor

UNIVERSITY OF CONNECTICUT

Enrollment 15,500 (UG 11,000; GR 4,500)
Jewish 1,600 (UG 1,200; GR 400)

Hillel at the University of Connecticut
54 North Eagleville Road
Storrs, CT 06268
(860) 429-9007
Fax: (860) 429-2344
E-mail: uconnhil@neca.com
Web: www.users.neca.com/uconnjil/

Debbie Rubenstein, Director
Nicole Uritz, Jewish Campus Service Corps Fellow
Rachel J. Gurshman, Program Director

Jewish Studies
15–20 courses per year taught by 6–8 faculty members. B.A., through individualized major program in the College of Liberal Arts and Sciences; M.A. in Judaic Studies. Ph.D. in related fields. Scholarships and stipends are available. The Center also organizes a Yiddish Tish (Table) discussion luncheon, with discussion

in Yiddish, as well as other lectures and colloquia. Professor Arnold Dashsefsky, Director, The Center for Judaic Studies and Contemporary Jewish Life, Thomas J. Dodd Research Center, (860) 486-2271.

Study in Israel
Junior/senior year abroad at major universities in Israel in cooperation with the UConn Study Abroad office. The Center for Judaic Studies and Contemporary Jewish Life sponsors a yearly archaeological dig in Israel at Sepphoris in conjunction with Duke University and Hebrew University at Jerusalem. Scholarships are available through the Center.

Kosher Food
Hillel offers bi-weekly Shabbat dinners, and Passover and holiday meals; frozen meals are available in the dining hall on request; vegetarian dining alternatives.

ON CAMPUS
The University of Connecticut distributes lists of holiday dates and asks that professors not schedule exams at these times. The atmosphere is friendly and comfortable for Jewish students.

Hillel is an active campus-recognized student group offering a wide variety of activities including dances, brunches, model weddings, trips, intergroup dialogue, lectures, classes, dorm programs, and Israel and Holocaust programs. Hillel offers many opportunities for student leadership ranging from social action to entertainment. Committees include community service, environment, Israel programming, women's issues, and UJA. And Hillel's Jewish Theatre Ensemble provides non-drama students with an opportunity to act in, produce, and direct productions. Hillel, AEPi, and Chabad work closely together on many projects, and Hillel co-sponsors many events with various campus organizations, including the cultural centers, the environmental group, and the Women's Center. The Hillel building has a large-screen TV/VCR, stereo, piano, Judaica library, sanctuary, and lounge.

"Over my four years at UConn, Hillel has become the social center for Jewish students on campus—many people tend to hang out for hours of socializing."

Elizabeth Lehmann, senior

"No matter how bad you feel or what kind of day you're having, going to Hillel always makes you feel better. You're always greeted with a smile."

Mara Goldstein, sophomore

UNIVERSITY OF HARTFORD

Enrollment 7,000 (UG 5,000; GR 2,000)
Jewish 1,500 (UG 1,200; GR 300)

Hartford Hillel Foundation
200 Bloomfield Avenue
GSU #153
West Hartford, CT 06117
(860) 768-4987
(860) 768-4059
Fax: (860) 768-5008
E-mail: hillel@mail.hartford.edu
Web: uhavax.hartford.edu/~hillel

David Terdiman, Director
Stephanie Melofsky, Jewish Campus Service Corps Senior Fellow
Melissa Freeman, Program Director

Jewish Studies

B.A., M.A. available through joint programs. Maurice Greenberg Center for Judaic Studies offers more than 20 courses; Hebrew and Yiddish are taught by 8 faculty members. Three interdisciplinary majors, in Jewish Studies, Jewish Education, and Judaic Studies and Voice (a pre-cantorial program), and a minor are offered. Additional courses are available through Hebrew College—Hartford branch and an area consortium. The Greenberg Center annually sponsors approximately a dozen lectures and symposia, which bring some of the world's leading scholars to the campus to speak and meet with students. Professor Jonathan Rosenbaum, Director, Maurice Greenberg Center for Judaic Studies; (203) 768-4964; rosenbaum@uhavax.hartford.edu.

Study in Israel

Junior year at the Hebrew University with opportunity to receive the University of Hartford's Trachtenberg Scholarship for support. Students may also study at Tel Aviv, Ben-Gurion, and Bar-Ilan Universities, and the University of Haifa.

Kosher Food

Pareve meals available through university dining services. Upperclassman may live in campus apartments and kosher kitchens. Kosher food locally available in West Hartford.

Housing

Although first- and second-year students usually reside in dorms, apartments are generally available to those who wish to observe kashrut.

ON CAMPUS

Situated on a 320-acre campus in a residential section of West Hartford, the University is less than a quarter mile from Greater Hartford's Jewish Community Center and Federation Campus, and within walking distance of many of Hartford's 25 synagogues. Hillel is based in its own campus center amid the residential complexes as well as in an office in the Student Union. Hillel at the University of Hartford provides a pluralistic environment for Jewish students of all backgrounds and denominations. Jewish students find it easy to celebrate Judaism on or off campus. Many of Hartford's faculty and staff are Jewish.

A very active Hillel offers a wide range of social, cultural, educational, social action, and religious activities, and students are also involved in many aspects of the broader Hartford community. Hillel works with all fraternities and sororities on campus to foster social action and community service—Tikkun Olam ("Repairing the World"). Some of the most popular activities are the Hanukkah bash, Greek events, Leadership Luncheons, and Heart and Soul, an evening of the arts. Jewish students at Hartford also enjoy an active Jewish Outdoor and Adventure Club, Black/Jewish Dialogue, the Jewish Freshman Council, the Jewish Athletic Club, an Israeli Dance Troupe, the Jewish-Greek Council, and the Mitzvah Corps.

WESLEYAN UNIVERSITY

Enrollment 3,400 (UG 2,700; GR 700)
Jewish 700

Havurah
c/o Department of Religion
Wesleyan University
Middletown, CT 06459-0029
(860) 685-2278
E-mail: ikramer@wesleyan.edu

Rabbi Ilyse Kramer, Director
Peter Salzman, Jewish Campus Service Corps Fellow

Jewish Studies

Courses available in religion, contemporary civilization, German, government, and history departments; additional credit/non-credit courses available through Jewish Chaplain's office; Lishmah Institute—4 week-long adult education seminars on topics of Judaica.

Study in Israel

Wesleyan-run spring semester in Israel program based in Jerusalem. Curriculum includes seminars, tutorials, cultural programs, and intensive field studies. Weekly discussion with prominent Israeli writers, artists, and religious and political leaders. The program is intended for both religion majors and non-majors, and no prior Hebrew training is required. Director, Professor Jeremy Zwelling, (860) 685-2296.

Kosher Food

The Kosher Kitchen, located in the Butterfield A dormitory, is open for lunch and dinner Monday-Friday and is on the university meal card plan. Shabbat meals (kosher) are prepared by a student co-op every week. All prepared meals have a vegetarian/meat option.

Housing

The Bayit, located in the center of campus, houses 26 students.

"The Jewish students who are active are very Jewish, positive, active, and exciting. Random classes are offered on Judaism. We do have a fabulous rabbi and she is very approachable and supportive."

Ilana Sumka, senior

"Excellent example for pluralistic Jewish communities! We have many Jewish groups and everything is student-run. A real place for learning about all Jewish flavors!"

Katherine Goldberg, junior

YALE UNIVERSITY

Enrollment 10,000
Jewish 3,000 (UG 1,500; GR 1,500)

The Joseph Slifka Center for Jewish Life
80 Wall Street
New Haven, CT 06511
(203) 432-1134
Fax: (203) 432-8690
E-mail: hillel@yale.edu
Web: www.yale.edu/hillel

Rabbi James E. Ponet, Director
Rabbi Sharon Cohen-Anisfeld, Associate Rabbi
Ari Gauss, Program Coordinator
Amy Aaland, Managing Director
Rabbi Michael Whitman, Director, Young Israel House at Yale

Jewish Studies

25 courses; B.A., Ph.D. The Program in Judaic Studies includes 6 permanent full-time faculty and 4 visitors annually from Israel, who teach about 400 students. Organized as an interdepartmental program, the Program in Judaic Studies has 5 endowed chairs. It offers courses in Hebrew Bible, rabbinics, Jewish history, Jewish thought, and Jewish Women's Studies and regularly sponsors lecturers and conferences. Students benefit from one of the largest university collections of Judaica in the United States. Professor Paula Hyman, Chair, Program in Judaic Studies; (203) 432-0843.

Study in Israel

Students make individual arrangements through programs with Israeli universities.

Kosher Food

Students can take out membership in the newest dining room at Yale, which is under the rabbinic supervision of the Director of Young Israel House at Yale.

Lunch, dinner, and a continental breakfast are served daily except on Sundays. This dining room is integrated into the University Dining Halls but run separately, and meals are transferable among them.

ON CAMPUS

The Joseph Slifka Center for Jewish Life at Yale provides exceptional opportunities to discover the best that Jewish college life has to offer. The Slifka Center, home of Yale Hillel and Young Israel at Yale, provides undergraduates and graduate students, faculty, alumni, and members of the greater New Haven community with a wide range of educational, religious, cultural, and social programs in a pluralistic setting. The Center is at the heart of the Yale campus and features a kosher dining facility, computer center, Jewish library, music listening library, Beit Midrash, student lounge with a fireplace, piano, TV and VCR, and several multi-purpose rooms used for a variety of programs.

An abundance of committees and groups fill each academic year with events. The Hillel Faculty Fellowship brings together Yale faculty with Jewish students for informal lunchtime conversations and mentoring opportunities. Garin explores the connection between Judaism and the environment. Urim v' Tumim (Uv'T), the student quarterly of Yale's Jewish community, publishes fiction, poetry, essays, opinion pieces, book reviews, and original art. Magevet, Yale's Jewish *a cappella* group, performs English, Hebrew, and Yiddish songs on campus and often tours during vacations. Yale Friends of Israel offers programs that delve into the political educational, social, and cultural aspects of Israel. It has hosted the Yale Model Israel Knesset and the Yale Model Peace Accords. Sherut (Students of Hillel Empowered to Renew Urban Ties) sends Yale students to tutor at a local New Haven Middle School. The Yale Klezmer Band plays across campus, in the community, and all over the east coast. Jewish Women at Yale meets weekly for study and discussion and has hosted two national student conferences on Women and Judaism. The Sunday Evening Soup Kitchen serves kosher food to those in need. Rabbis of three different denominations provide counseling and advice to individuals and student-led worship groups. Rotating art exhibitions, lectureships, film festivals, social gatherings, and formal and informal classes, in topics from Yiddish to Talmud to Midrash, ensure that Jewish life at Slifka Center grows daily.

The nationally recognized Holocaust video archives are housed at Yale's Sterling Library.

UNIVERSITY OF DELAWARE

Enrollment 21,350
Jewish 2,000

Abe and Pearl Kristol Hillel Student Center
47 West Delaware Avenue
Newark, DE 19711
(302) 453-0479
Fax: (302) 453-0629
E-mail: rbshatz@udel.edu

Renee Schatz, Director

Jewish Studies

The Frank and Yetta Chaiken Center for Jewish Studies offers several courses and a minor in Jewish Studies. The Director and Chair of the Jewish Studies Program is Dr. Sara Horowitz.

Study in Israel

Every second winter session the Jewish Studies Program sponsors a semester of study in Israel, for which students may earn 3 credits toward the minor.

Kosher Food

Hillel's student-run kosher kitchen serves meat, dairy, and vegetarian dinners at Shabbat and Holiday celebrations, and weekly Bagel Brunches. A full Passover meal plan is available at Hillel.

ON CAMPUS

Hillel's Abe and Pearl Kristol Student Center is located directly across from the University of Delaware's new Student Center at the hub of the campus. The building includes a large multipurpose room, lounge, and library.

Hillel-UDel works cooperatively with many other campus organizations, including all Jewish groups on campus, such as the Jewish Heritage Program, DIPAC (AIPAC) group, Chabad House, the Jewish Studies Department, AEPi, AEPhi, TEP, and others. Social action programs are undertaken in conjunction with other member organizations of the University Religious Leaders Organization.

"UD Hillel is not the center of Jewish religion on campus, but the center of Jewish life on campus. Whether it is celebrating Shabbat, dancing away at a semi-formal, making food for the homeless, or playing racquetball, UD Hillel allows each person to enjoy being Jewish in his or her own way."

Matt Schwartz, junior

AMERICAN UNIVERSITY

Enrollment 10,149 (UG 5,149; GR 5,000)
Jewish 2,200 (UG 1,100; GR 1,100)

American University Hillel
Kay Spiritual Life Center
4400 Massachusetts Avenue
Washington, DC 20016
(202) 885-3322
Fax: (202) 885-3317
E-mail: hillel@american.edu

Rabbi Toby Manewith, Director
Sara Kovensky Kalt, Program Director
TBA, Jewish Campus Service Corps Fellow

Jewish Studies

B.A., minor. 25 courses. The Jewish Studies Program, an interdisciplinary program in the College of Arts and Sciences, offers more than a dozen courses a year in Jewish Studies and the departments of History, Literature, Philosophy and Religion, and Language and Foreign Studies. Ten full-time faculty with international reputations in such areas as Holocaust Studies and Israeli politics are affiliated with the Program. Students who major in Jewish Studies write a senior thesis. Majors or minors may plan an internship in more than 60 metropolitan Washington agencies, including the Anti-Defamation League, AIPAC, and the US Holocaust Memorial Museum, or take a joint course with Howard University's Department of Afro-American Studies on Black/Jewish relations. Professor Pamela Nadel; (202) 885-2425.

Study in Israel

American University has a semester program with Hebrew University.

Kosher Food

Hillel has weekly Shabbat dinners, occasional Sunday bagel brunches, and holiday meals. Vegetarian alternatives are available through the University's meal plan. Passover food is available through the dining service.

ON CAMPUS

The Washington area has a vibrant Jewish community, offering students a wide variety of cultural, social, educational, and political opportunities. Students engage in political activism and intern in local and national Jewish organizations, and there are opportuniies to get involved in the area through community service projects.

AU Hillel publishes a monthly newsletter and maintains an electronic mailing list, and offers a wide range of programs as well as educational and counseling services. Hillel helps students locate internships and job opportunities, and helps students plan for Israel trips with programs and financial aid information. It also involves students with regional programming in the Washington area including social events, evenings at the Embassy of Israel, and programs of social and political interest.

Hillel works with a number of active student groups. The American Students for Israel sponsor speakers, social programs, and cultural events including the annual Israel Fair. The student UJA campaign has raised several thousand dollars over the past few years. Jewish law and graduate students regularly meet for social and educational programs. The Jewish women's group holds monthly Rosh Hodesh discussions and brings speakers of interest to campus. Weekly Reform and Conservative services are student-led. The Jewish Student Association plans social events where students can relax and celebrate together as well as community service projects.

Hillel is part of the Kay Spiritual Life Center, which fosters a sense of community and common interest with other religious groups on campus. It also has close relationships with the various offices within Student Services, and programs are often co-sponsored by other campus offices and groups.

Find AU Hillel's Web site through www.hillel.org.

CATHOLIC UNIVERSITY

Enrollment 7,000
Jewish 250 (UG 50; GR 200)

Catholic University Jewish Students
Hillel of Greater Washington
6101 Montrose Road, Suite 201
Rockville, MD 20852
(301) 468-3422
E-mail: bscheink@gmu.edu

Professor Clifford Fishman, Advisor
Bonnie Scheinker, Assistant Director, Hillel of Greater Washington

Catholic University is served by the Hillel Regional Center, Hillel of Greater Washington.

GALLAUDET UNIVERSITY

Enrollment 2,070
Jewish 125 (UG 75; GR 50)

Gallaudet Jewish Student Association
c/o Hillel of Greater Washington
6101 Montrose Road, Suite 201
Rockville, MD 20852
(301) 468-3422
E-mail: bscheink@gmu.edu

Bonnie Scheinker, Assistant Director, Hillel of Greater Washington

ON CAMPUS

JSA sponsors programs, holiday-related activities, and guest speakers on Jewish topics.

Gallaudet is served as an outreach program of the Regional Center, Hillel of Greater Washington.

GEORGE WASHINGTON UNIVERSITY

Enrollment 16,800 (UG 6,800; GR 10,000)
Jewish 3,200 (UG 1,700; GR 1,500)

George Washington University Hillel
2300 H Street, NW
Washington, DC 20037
(202) 994-5090
Fax: (202) 994-5027
E-mail: gwhillel@gwu.edu
Web: www.gwu.edu/~gwhillel/

Rabbi Gerald Serotta, Director
Amy Bebchick, Acting Director
Greg Schofer, Assistant Director
Aimee Weinstein, Director of Operations

Jewish Studies

30 courses; B.A., minor. Courses in Hebrew language (full 4-year sequence), literature in translation, Jewish history, Jewish philosophy, ethics and mysticism, Yiddish, Israeli politics, Arab-Israel conflict, and Hebrew Scriptures. Courses may be combined with major in Middle East affairs. Some credit internships are available as Service-Learning programs with local Jewish museums and organizations. Endowed Chair. Extensive library holdings, including large I. Edward Kiev Judaica Collection, which includes more than 10,000 volumes, many out-of-print, primarily from the 18-20th centuries. 4 full-time Jewish studies faculty; 4 interdisciplinary. Professor Marc E. Saperstein, Director; Professor Max D. Ticktin, Associate Director, The Charles E. Smith Program in Judaic Studies, 2142 G Street NW, Washington, DC 20092; (202) 994-6325.

Study in Israel

Full-year, semester, and summer programs; fully accredited.

Kosher Food

Hillel provides 5 lunches and 5 dinners (includes Friday night Shabbat dinner) on a contract basis; vegetarian dining alternatives available at the Marvin Center's J Street; cooking facilities in some residence halls.

ON CAMPUS

Hillel is very conveniently located close to the White House, the State Department, Kennedy Center, and the Mall, and only 1 block from the Foggy Bottom Metro station and 2 blocks from GW's student center. Because of this central Washington site, Hillel at GW facilitates many Public Policy internships with national Jewish organizations, and on Capitol Hill.

Life at GW is multifaceted, and the programs Hillel offers are as diverse as the University. Hillel is the center for a wide range of social, educational, cultural, and political action programs, including an active Student Alliance for Israel group, a campus UJA campaign, a graduate and professional students group, and community service projects. You can enroll in a mini-course on Judaism and the environment, attend a reception at the Israeli Embassy, listen to a Congressman speak on current issues, or hang out at a coffeehouse and relax to the sounds of local entertainers. Hillel also has a wealth of up-to-date information on opportunities for studying abroad, traveling to Israel, and finding summer jobs and internships, and has a housing board to help students with special roommate requirements.

The Hillel staff sits on the Board of Chaplains to help facilitate communication among student religious groups. Many programs are also co-sponsored with various other campus groups to promote diversity and reach out to other Jewish students with similar interests.

"Hillel provides a welcoming environment where students can explore and strengthen their Jewish identity."

Shoshana Isaac, sophomore

"There's something for everyone at GW—it may be an internship on the Hill or study abroad in Israel or Friday night Shabbat or coming to Hillel's social events."

Lee Lubarsky, sophomore

GEORGETOWN UNIVERSITY

Enrollment 12,400 (UG 6,000; GR 6,400)
Jewish 2,800 (UG 800; GR 2,000)

Jewish Student Association
1314 36th Street, NW
Washington, DC 20007
(202) 687-3480
(202) 687-4383
Fax: (202) 662-9297
Web: www.georgetown.edu/users/kassa/jsa

Rabbi Harold White, Director
Judy Wendkos, Program Director
Julie Reisler, Professional Schools, Law Center, and Medical School
Alexis Kilstein, GAP Coordinator
Mark Robbins, Georgetown University Ministry

Jewish Studies

12 courses. Yearly visiting Israeli professor. 3 levels of Hebrew language. Students currently take courses at the Center for Muslim and Christian Understanding and the Center for Arab Studies. Professor Jeffrey Peck, Center for German and European Studies, is directing the Jewish Studies initiative.

Study in Israel

Junior year abroad at Tel Aviv University and Hebrew University. Joint program with American University in Cairo and Hebrew University.

Kosher Food

Weekly Shabbat dinners and occasional holiday meals. Frozen meals available at dining hall on request. Vegetarian dining alternatives. Dormitory cooking facilities.

Housing

4 kosher kitchen apartments.

ON CAMPUS

Jewish student organizations exist at both the undergraduate and law centers. The Jewish Student House offers a kosher kitchen for students wishing to prepare their own meals. Programs and clubs include the Georgetown Israel Alliance, the Hebrew Language Club, a Hebrew Choir, and an active Shabbaton program.

HOWARD UNIVERSITY

Enrollment 10,000
Jewish 50

Howard University Jewish Community
c/o Hillel of Greater Washington
6101 Montrose Road, Suite 201
Rockville, MD 20852
(301) 468-3422
Fax: (301) 468-3641
E-mail: bscheink@gmu.edu

Bonnie Scheinker, Assistant Director, Hillel of Greater
Washington

 Study in Israel
Students may receive credits for study abroad in Israel.

 Housing
Yes

ON CAMPUS

There is no Jewish student life as such at Howard, although the area offers numerous opportunities for Jewish involvement. Jewish students in the Professional Schools participate in the regional Graduate and Professional (GAP) program organized by the Hillel Regional Center, Hillel of Greater Washington. Jewish undergraduates participate in programs at other Hillels in the region.

The University sponsors a course in Black/Jewish relations with American University.

The Howard University Jewish community is served as an outreach program of Hillel Regional Center, Hillel of Greater Washington.

MOUNT VERNON COLLEGE

Enrollment 460
Jewish 30

Jewish Student Association
c/o The American University Hillel
Kay Spiritual Life Center
Washington, DC 20016
(202) 885-3322
Fax: (202) 885-3317
E-mail: rabbi@american.edu

Rabbi Toby Manewith, Director

ON CAMPUS

Students at Mount Vernon College are invited to Hillel programs at American University.

See listing for American University.

BARRY UNIVERSITY

Enrollment 7,500
Jewish 150

Greater Miami Hillel Jewish Student Center
Barry University Programs
1100 Stanford Drive
Coral Gables, FL 33146
(305) 665-6948
Fax: (305) 661-8540
E-mail: hillel@miami.flahillel.org

Rabbi Jeffrey L. Falick, Director
TBA, Program Associate, Commuters/Graduate Students
Nancy Lipp, Jewish Student Career Network
Heather Storch Grosz, Public Relations

 Study in Israel
Summer program at Hebrew University offered through the Business School.

 Kosher Food
Vegetarian dining alternatives. Greater Miami Hillel offers 7–8 Shabbat dinners each semester, dinners for holidays, and a complete meal plan for Passover.

ON CAMPUS

Jewish students in the greater Miami area are served by the Greater Miami Hillel Jewish Student Center. Professionals from Greater Miami Hillel work actively on the campus of Barry University.

See listing for University of Miami.

BROWARD COMMUNITY COLLEGES

Enrollment 28,000
Jewish 1,500

Broward/Palm Beach Hillel Foundation
7200 Griffin Road, Suite 3E
Davie, FL 33314
(954) 327-8677
Fax: (954) 327-8614
E-mail: bpbhillel@flahillel.org

Nicole Rosen Packer, Director
Melanie Woodard, Program Director
Shoshana Kapnik, Jewish Campus Service Corps Fellow

 Jewish Studies
4 courses.

Kosher Food

2 Shabbat dinners a month; holiday meals. Local kosher markets and restaurants available.

ON CAMPUS

Hillel of Broward and Palm Beach serves BCC students on the North, Central, and South Campuses. Hillel holds meetings on campus, with social, recreational, and cultural programming to suit the commuter population. Activities include participation in national conferences and area retreats, happy hour, community service programs, Jewish learning opportunities, and a UJA campus campaign. There is also joint programming with area schools.

Israel scholarships are available. An Israeli Student Network works with Hillel, serving the needs of the Israeli population at Broward Community College.

FLORIDA ATLANTIC UNIVERSITY

Enrollment 17,500
Jewish 1,500

Broward/Palm Beach Hillel Foundation
7200 Griffin Road, Suite 3E
Davie, FL 33314
(954) 327-8677
Fax: (954) 327-8614
E-mail: bpbhillel@flahillel.org

Nicole Rosen Packer, Director
TBA, Program Director
Shoshana Kapnik, Jewish Campus Service Corps Fellow

Jewish Studies

B.A. in Jewish Studies; 15 courses. CSUN also houses an extensive Judaic library. For more information, contact Dr. Alan Berger, Director of Judaic and Holocaust Studies, 777 Glades Rd., Boca Raton, FL 33431; (561) 297-2979.

Study in Israel

Year abroad.

Kosher Food

2 Shabbat dinners a month; holiday meals. Local kosher markets and restaurants available.

ON CAMPUS

Florida Atlantic serves as a center for programming for Jewish students throughout the Broward and Palm Beach area. Social, recreational, and cultural programming is planned with and includes students from these schools. Activities include monthly "eat and learn" lunches, happy hour, community service programs, a UJA campaign, Israel activism, Holocaust programming, and participation in national conferences and area retreats. Hillel also provides information about Israel and Israel scholarships.

The Broward/Palm Beach Hillel Foundation serves all campuses in the Broward and Palm Beach area, including Broward Community College(s), Nova University, Florida Atlantic University, Lynn University, and Palm Beach Community Colleges.

FLORIDA INSTITUTE OF TECHNOLOGY— MELBOURNE

Enrollment 4,500
Jewish 50

Hillel Jewish Student Organization
F.I.T. Hillel
150 West University Boulevard
Melbourne, FL 32901
(407) 768-8104

Professor Arthur Gutman, Advisor

FLORIDA INTERNATIONAL UNIVERSITY—NORTH

Enrollment 6,500
Jewish 500

Greater Miami Hillel Jewish Student Center
FIU Programs
1100 Stanford Drive
Coral Gables, FL 33146
(305) 665-6948
Fax: (305) 661-8540
E-mail: hillel@miami.flahillel.org
Web: www.miami.flahillel.org

Rabbi Jeffrey L. Falick, Director
TBA, Wide Program Director
Nancy Lipp, Jewish Student Career Network
Heather Storch Grosz, Public Relations

Jewish Studies

12 courses; Certificate in Jewish Studies, which may be taken as a minor or independently. Interdisciplinary program. Dr. Stephen M. Fain, Director, Institute for Judaic Studies, DM290, FIU; (305) 348-3225; fains@fiu.edu. M.A. in Religious Studies. Dr. Lesley A. Northup, Graduate Program Director, Dept. of Religious Studies; (305) 348-2956; northupl@servax.fiu.edu.

Study in Israel

Junior year/semester abroad; winter and summer programs.

Kosher Food

Vegetarian food is available on campus. At the Greater Miami Hillel Center in Coral Gables, kosher Shabbat dinners are served every other week during the fall and spring semesters. Hillel offers a complete meal plan during Passover. Kosher restaurants are in the vicinity.

ON CAMPUS

Jewish life at FIU is growing rapidly. The Greater Miami Hillel Jewish Student Center in Coral Gables serves Jewish students on both FIU campuses. Hillel maintains two satellite offices—one on FIU's South Campus and another 3 miles north of the North Campus in a local JCC.

See listing for University of Miami.

FLORIDA INTERNATIONAL UNIVERSITY— UNIVERSITY PARK SOUTH

Enrollment 17,000
Jewish 1,000

Greater Miami Hillel Jewish Student Center
1100 Stanford Drive
Coral Gables, FL 33146
(305) 665-6948
Fax: (305) 661-8540
E-mail: hillel@miami.flahillel.org
Web: www.miami.flahillel.org

Rabbi Jeffrey L. Falick, Director
Rachel Levine, Program Associate, Commuters/Graduate Students
Nancy Lipp, Jewish Student Career Network
Heather Storch Grosz, Public Relations
Robyn Fryer, KOACH/Jewish Campus Service Corps Fellow

Jewish Studies

12 courses; Certificate in Jewish Studies, which may be taken as a minor or independently. Interdisciplinary program. Dr. Stephen M. Fain, Director, Institute for Judaic Studies, DM290, FIU, (305) 348-3225; fains@fiu.edu. M.A. in Religious Studies. Dr. Lesley A. Northup, Graduate Program Director, Dept. of Religious Studies; (305) 348-2956; northup@servax.fiu.edu.

Study in Israel

Junior year/semester abroad.

Kosher Food

Vegetarian food is available on campus. At the Greater Miami Hillel Center in Coral Gables, kosher Shabbat dinners are served every other week during the fall and spring semesters. Hillel also offers a complete meal plan for Passover.

ON CAMPUS

Jewish life at FIU is growing rapidly. Jewish students on both FIU campuses are served by a full-time Hillel professional through the Greater Miami Hillel Jewish Student Center in Coral Gables. In addition, Hillel main-

tains two satellite offices—one on FIU's South Campus and another 3 miles north of the North Campus in a local JCC.

See listing for University of Miami.

FLORIDA STATE UNIVERSITY

Enrollment 31,159 (UG 27,159; GR 4,000)
Jewish 3,000 (UG 2,500; GR 500)

Florida State University Hillel Foundation
843 West Pensacola Street
Tallahassee, FL 32304
(850) 222-5454
Fax: (850) 222-8679
E-mail: fsuhillel@talstar.com
Web: www.members.tripod.com/fsuhillel

TBA, Director
Andy Carrol, Jewish Campus Service Corps Fellow

Kosher Food

Hillel offers kosher monthly Shabbat dinners, Passover seder, break-the-fast, and other holiday food opportunities.

ON CAMPUS

Jewish students who wish to explore their Jewish identity can feel comfortable doing so at Florida State. Tallahassee, the state capital, is located in North Florida's panhandle, a land of rolling hills and lakes, and has 2 universities. Approximately 155,000 residents are in the city, which is home to 2 synagogues and Hillel.

Hillel runs a variety of weekly social programs and has a volleyball court and outdoor deck and patio for student recreation. A computer room maintains a connection to the FSU Internet system. The lox and bagel brunches twice a month on Sunday mornings have now become a Tallahassee tradition. The FSU Student Government sponsors the Jewish Student Union that runs educational programs on campus as well as serving as an advocacy group for Jewish students. There are no membership fees at Hillel. Jewish Greek life at FSU is on the rise. The Council of Jewish Student Organizations coordinates the activities of the various organizations, such as Big Bend Israel Committee, the Jewish fraternities and sororities, the Jewish Student Union, and the Jewish Law Students Association.

JACKSONVILLE UNIVERSITY

Enrollment 2,600
Jewish 120

Hillel at Jacksonville University
Box 837
Jacksonville, FL 32211
(904) 745-7557
(305) 661-8549
Fax: (305) 661-8540

Jem Golden, Advisor

Kosher Food
Vegetarian dining alternatives; dormitory cooking facilities.

ON CAMPUS
The group meets regularly for social and educational activities. Significant commuter population.

Hillel at Jacksonville is an outreach program of the Florida Hillel Council in Miami.

JOHNSON AND WALES UNIVERSITY

Enrollment 800
Jewish 40

Greater Miami Jewish Student Center
Johnson & Wales Programs
1100 Stanford Drive ·
Coral Gables, FL 33146
(305) 665-6948
Fax: (305) 661-8540
E-mail: hillel@miami.flahillel.org
Web: www.miami.flahillel.org

Rabbi Jeffrey L. Falick, Director
Nancy Lipp, Director, Community and Career Network
Heather Storch Grosz, Communications Coordinator

Study in Israel
The UM Study Abroad Office offers semester and junior year abroad opportunities.

Kosher Food
Vegetarian food on campus. Greater Miami Hillel offers 7–8 Shabbat dinners each semester, dinners for holidays, and a complete meal plan for Passover.

ON CAMPUS
Jewish students in the Greater Miami area are served by the Greater Miami Hillel Jewish Center. Professionals from Greater Miami Hillel work actively on the campus of Johnson & Wales, and Jewish faculty act as advisors.

See listing for University of Miami.

LYNN UNIVERSITY

Enrollment 1,100
Jewish 120

Broward/Palm Beach Hillel Foundation
7200 Griffin Road, Suite 3E
Davie, FL 33314
(954) 327-8677
(305) 661-8540
Fax: (954) 327-8614
E-mail: bpbhillel@flahillel.org

Nicole Rosen Packer, Director
Shoshana Kapnik, Jewish Campus Service Corps Fellow

Kosher Food
2 Shabbat dinners a month; holiday meals. Local kosher markets and restaurants available.

ON CAMPUS
Social, recreational, and cultural programming jointly with students from Florida Atlantic University and Palm Beach Community College. Weekly meetings on campus, and participation in national conferences and area retreats. Israel scholarships are available.

The Broward/Palm Hillel Foundation serves Jewish students at all area schools.

MIAMI-DADE COMMUNITY COLLEGES

Enrollment 12,000
Jewish 1,000

Greater Miami Hillel Jewish Student Center
Miami-Dade Community College Programs (Four Campuses)
1100 Stanford Drive
Coral Gables, FL 33146
(305) 665-6948
Fax: (305) 661-8540
E-mail: hillel@miami.flahillel.org
Web: www.miami.flahillel.org

Rabbi Jeffrey L. Falick, Director
Raina Goldberg, UM Program Director
Nancy Lipp, Director, Community and Career Network
Heather Storch Grosz, Communications Coordinator
TBA, Countywide Program Director

Jewish Studies
Courses vary.

Kosher Food
The Greater Miami Hillel Center in Coral Gables offers kosher Shabbat dinners every other week during the fall and spring semesters. In addition, full kosher Passover menus are offered.

ON CAMPUS

Jewish students in the greater Miami area are served by the Greater Miami Hillel Jewish Center.

See listing for University of Miami.

NEW COLLEGE OF THE UNIVERSITY OF SOUTH FLORIDA

Enrollment 586
Jewish 150

Hillel
PO Box 163235
Orlando, FL 32816-3235
(407) 262-1330
(305) 661-8549
Fax: (407) 647-5364
E-mail: hillel@pegasus.cc.ucf.edu
Web: www.pegasus.cc.ucf.edu/~hillel

Mimi Zimmerman, Director

 Jewish Studies
1 course.

 Study in Israel
Credits accepted for study in Israel.

 Kosher Food
Vegetarian alternatives.

ON CAMPUS

Guest speakers come to campus.

Hillel at New College is served as part of the outreach program of the Florida Hillel Council.

NOVA SOUTHEASTERN UNIVERSITY

Enrollment 12,700 (UG 2,400; GR 10,300)
Jewish 2,500 (UG 500; GR 2,000)

Broward/Palm Beach Hillel Foundation
7200 Griffin Road, Suite 3E
Davie, FL 33314
(954) 327-8677
(561) 395-9765
Fax: (954) 327-8614
E-mail: bpbhillel@flahillel.org

Nicole Rosen Packer, Director
Shoshana Kapnik, Jewish Campus Service Corps Fellow

 Kosher Food
2 Shabbat dinners a month; holiday meals. Local kosher markets and restaurants available.

ON CAMPUS

Hillel holds weekly meetings on campus, with social, recreational, and cultural programming to suit the commuter population. Activities include participation in national scholarship conferences and area retreats, an Israel Awareness Week, and a UJA campus campaign, as well as other programs held jointly with area schools. Israel scholarships are available. Nova has a high percentage of Jewish students in its graduate and professional programs. A Jewish Law Student Association, a Jewish Medical Student Group, and a Jewish Graduate Network coordinate social, professional, and cultural programs.

The Broward/Palm Beach Hillel Foundation serves Jewish students at all area schools.

PALM BEACH COMMUNITY COLLEGES

Enrollment 16,000 (4 campuses)
Jewish 1,500

Broward/Palm Beach Hillel Foundation
7200 Griffin Road, Suite 3E
Davie, FL 33314
(954) 327-8677
(561) 395-9765
Fax: (954) 327-8614
E-mail: bpbhillel@flahillel.org

Nicole Rosen Packer, Director
Shoshana Kapnik, Jewish Campus Service Corps Fellow

 Kosher Food
2 Shabbat dinners a month; holiday meals. Local kosher markets and restaurants available.

ON CAMPUS

Social, recreational, and cultural programming jointly with students from area schools. Weekly meetings on campus, and participation in national conferences, area retreats, and community service programs, as well as opportunites for Jewish learning.

The Broward/Palm Beach Hillel Foundation serves Jewish students at Broward Community Colleges, Nova University, Florida Atlantic University, Lynn University, and Palm Beach Community Colleges. See listing for Florida Atlantic University.

ROLLINS COLLEGE

Enrollment 1,300
Jewish 120

Jewish Student League
PO Box 163235
Orlando, FL 32816-3235
(407) 262-1330
Fax: (407) 823-5336
E-mail: hillel@pegasus.cc.ucf.edu

Janette Weiss, Area Coordinator
Professor Yudit Greenberg, Advisor
Linda Levin, Assistant Director, Florida Hillel Council

 Jewish Studies
6 courses through the Religion Department.

 Study in Israel
Not sponsored by the College, but possible through accepted programs.

 Kosher Food
Locally available: kosher market, kosher foods in local supermarket and deli.

ON CAMPUS

Jewish students at Rollins enjoy a variety of social activities, including movie and pizza evenings.

Rollins College is served by the Florida Hillel Council.

SAINT THOMAS UNIVERSITY

Enrollment 2,400
Jewish 150

Greater Miami Hillel Jewish Student Center
St. Thomas University Programs
1100 Stanford Drive
Coral Gables, FL 33146
(305) 665-6948
Fax: (305) 661-8540
E-mail: hillel@miami.flahillel.org
Web: www.miami.flahillel.org

Rabbi Jeffrey L. Falick, Director
Nancy Lipp, Director, Community and Career Network
Heather Storch Grosz, Communications Coordinator
TBA, Countywide Program Director

 Study in Israel
Junior year/semester abroad; winter and summer programs.

 Kosher Food
The Greater Miami Hillel in Coral Gables offers kosher Shabbat dinners every other week during the fall and spring semesters, as well as a complete meal plan for Passover.

ON CAMPUS

Jewish students at Saint Thomas are primarily in the Law School. They are integrated into regional activities by, and receive programming service from, the Greater Miami Hillel Jewish Student Center.

See listing for University of Miami.

UNIVERSITY OF CENTRAL FLORIDA

Enrollment 28,000
Jewish 1,500

Jewish Student Union/Hillel
PO Box 163235
Orlando, FL 32816-3235
(407) 262-1330
(407) 823-5336
Fax: (407) 647-5364
E-mail: hillel@pegasus.cc.ucf.edu
Web: www.pegasus.cc.ucf.edu/~hillel

Professor Moshe Pelli, Advisor
Janette Weiss, Area Coordinator

Jewish Studies
24 courses. Minor and certificate in Judaic Studies.

Kosher Food
Locally available in kosher market, supermarket, and deli.

ON CAMPUS

Distinguished lecture series in Judaic Studies; social and cultural activities on campus and participation in weekend retreats for area students. Commuter campus.

Jewish students at UCF are served through the outreach program of the Florida Hillel Council.

UNIVERSITY OF FLORIDA

Enrollment 40,500 (UG 31,500; GR 9,000)
Jewish 4,300 (UG 3,400; GR 900)

Hillel Foundation
16 Northwest 18th Street
Gainesville, FL 32603
(352) 372-2900
Fax: (352) 376-8374
E-mail: hillel@gnv.fdt.net
Web: http://gnv.fdt.net/~hillel/

Rabbi Andy Koren, Director
Keith Dvorchik, Assistant Director
Courtney Wegweiser, Administrative Assistant
Eliot Sokalsky, Jewish Campus Service Corps Fellow

 Jewish Studies
16 courses per semester; B.A. and M.A. in Jewish Studies; B.A. in Hebrew soon available.

 Study in Israel
Florida summer, semester, and year abroad with Hebrew University and Tel Aviv University. Florida March of the Living College Trip.

 Kosher Food
Hillel offers weekly Shabbat dinner and lunch with vegetarian option; occasional other dinners; brunches, and cookouts. Kosher butcher store at Hillel; daily Passover and holiday meals.

ON CAMPUS

The University of Florida Hillel is committed to creating opportunities for all types of Jewish life to flourish on campus. Hillel at Florida is located conveniently 1 block from campus near the most popular campus restaurants and stores. Major programs co-sponsored with the Jewish Student Union (JSU) include the annual campuswide Jewish New Year's party at a local club, Hanukkah Celebration and Spring Jewish Awareness Month, which features artists from around the world plus vintage and new Jewish and Israeli films. Hillel works closely with the JSU, which receives funding from student government for 12 Jewish student groups at UF, including Graduates and Professionals, and the Jewish Law Students Association. Undergraduate groups focus on special interests, such as community service, social activities, women, campus intergroup relations, Jewish culture, religion, Israel, and Holocaust awareness. Hillel offers non-credit classes in Basic Judaism, Talmud, Israeli dance, Jewish cooking, and other areas of student interest.

Hillel is powerfully integrated into campus life and frequently co-sponsors events with University departments and campus student organizations, such as the Student Union Program Council and Hispanic Student Association. Hillel also works closely with other national Jewish organizations, including AIPAC, UJA, the World Zionist Organization, Hadassah/Young Judea, USY, NFTY, and BBYO. Jewish students are well represented in fraternity and sorority life, with 5 "Jewish" houses and significant numbers in others. Jewish students are prominent in student government and other campus organizations.

Gainesville is centrally located between Orlando, Tampa, and Jacksonville, and offers many outlets for student recreation. Hillel programming takes advantage of the area's many lakes, springs, campsites, and other outdoor attractions. UF, home of the National Championship football team, offers a full range of sports, concerts, and physical recreation facilities for the campus community.

UF Hillel is working with the Florida Hillel Council and the state's Jewish leadership to build a new facility to better serve student, faculty, alumni, and parents, and to proudly represent the Jewish community on campus.

"This is a comfortable place for a Jewish student because there are members from every Jewish group (i.e., Reform, Conservative, Orthodox, etc.) and everyone is welcome. Also, we have a dedicated group of people behind us to help us feel more at ease. Our three main groups—the Jews in Residence Halls, Jews in Greek Life, and Jews Off-campus—each aim to carve niches for students and to engage them actively in the campus community. Hot programs are: Student-Professional Mentor Program, Jewish Awareness Month, and a women's group. The Jewish faculty is somewhat involved with dinners, various programs and ties to students, but we're always hoping for more interest."

Amy J. Kolodny, recent graduate

UNIVERSITY OF MIAMI

Enrollment 13,500 (UG 9,000; GR 4,500)
Jewish 2,000 (UG 1,600; GR 400)

Greater Miami Hillel Jewish Student Center
1100 Stanford Drive
Coral Gables, FL 33146
(305) 665-1407
Fax: (305) 661-8540
E-mail: info@miami.flahillel.org
Web: www.miami.flahillel.org

Rabbi Jeffrey L. Falick, Director
Nancy Lipp, Director, Community and Career Network
Raina Goldberg, Program Director
TBA, Countywide Program Director
Heather Grosz, Communications Coordinator
Sara Marion and Andrea Karpel, Jewish Campus
Service Corps Fellows

 Jewish Studies
20 courses annually, with 50 in the catalog. B.A. organized as an interdisciplinary program, with courses

offered by 14 faculty members in nearly every field of study: Religion, Philosophy, Literature, Language, Political Science, Sociology, History, Geography, Film, Music, and Art. The program also offers conferences, lectures, symposia, concerts, and film festivals. More than 500 students take classes annually. The program hosts one of the only Sephardic Studies Programs in the world, offers Ladino, and is endowed by the Littauer Foundation. Holocaust and Israel Studies are especially prominent and endowments support student scholarships and cultural programs. Professor Henry Green, Director; (305) 284-4375; hgreen@umiami.ir.miami.edu.

Study in Israel
Junior year/semester abroad; winter and summer programs. The UM Study Abroad Office offers semester and junior year abroad opportunities.

Kosher Food
Hillel offers kosher Shabbat dinners every other week during the fall and spring semesters. Kosher meals are also provided for all Jewish holidays, including a full kosher-for-Passover menu.

ON CAMPUS
Jewish life at the University of Miami is vibrant and diverse, and often celebrated around the greater Miami area. Miami, a place that is filled with an abundance of opportunities for social, educational, and other opportunities, serves as the playground for Hillel. Greater Miami Hillel also serves as the center for Jewish student life throughout Greater Miami.

Hillel facilitates groups and programs focusing on social activities, sports, Israel, Jewish culture, religious participation, and education. There are also opportunities to become involved in the Greek Jewish Council, environmental work, and community service. Graduate student programming is coordinated by the Director of Student Activities for Commuters/Graduate Students through a number of city-wide events. Medical students at the University's downtown medical campus enjoy activities planned with the Maimonides Society, while UM's law students participate in the highly visible and active Cardozo Legal Society. Finally, Greater Miami Hillel features the prestigious Jewish Career Network, which offers mentor opportunities, career exposure, and networking for Jewish students in Miami.

During winter break, Hillel offers a very special opportunity for Jewish students at all colleges and universities throughout the Miami area. The Schatz Family Foundation Hillel Israel Brithright Mission to Israel is a 10-day trip that offers students an opportunity to connect with their heritage, with the land of Israel, and with other Jewish students at their home university as well as at other Miami-area universities.

Greater Miami Hillel also serves as the center for Jewish student life throughout greater Miami, at Johnson and Wales University, Miami-Dade Community Colleges, Florida International University, and Saint Thomas University.

"Hillel is probably the most welcoming building on campus. It's a place to relax with other people with similar backgrounds."

Jenny Polonsky, sophomore

"The Jewish Greek Council allows Jewish men and women in UM's Greek system to come together and create Jewish social and philanthropic programs outside of their chapters."

Karen Maerovitz, junior

Find UM's Web page through www.hillel.org.

UNIVERSITY OF NORTH FLORIDA

Enrollment 10,000 (UG 4,100; GR 5,900)
Jewish 34

UNF Hillel c/o Florida Hillel Council
1100 Stanford Drive
Coral Gables, FL 33146
(904) 620-5362
(305) 661-8549
Fax: (305) 661-8540
E-mail: filch97@aol.com

Marc Blatt, Student Representative
Robyn Fryer, KOACH/Jewish Campus Service Corps Fellow

ON CAMPUS
Jewish students at UNF are served through the outreach program of the Florida Hillel Council in Miami.

"Because I am one of a few students who is active and Jewish, I am comfortable at my school. For those who don't participate and make an effort to 'be Jewish,' UNF is a lonely, Christian place to be. We are not really big enough to have much weight on campus but we have become adept at finding outside resources."

Melissa Fand, sophomore

UNIVERSITY OF SOUTH FLORIDA

Enrollment 35,000 (UG 13,000; GR 22,000)
Jewish 2,000

USF Hillel Foundation
14240 North 42nd Street, #1301
Tampa, FL 33613
(813) 972-4433
Fax: (813) 972-1882
E-mail: bjoc23@aol.com
Web: www.coedu.usf.edu/~hillel

Daniel Berman, Director
Missy Dobbins, Program Director

 Jewish Studies

10 courses; also joint master's in Religious Studies and Education, Ph.D.

Study in Israel

Student exchange program with Haifa University, and summer archaeological digs at Sepphoris. Student programs with other Israeli universities also available.

Kosher Food

Hillel offers Shabbat and Holiday dinners and occasional lunches; vegetarian dining alternatives are available on campus. Kosher food is locally available.

Housing

Fontana Hall.

ON CAMPUS

Hillel at the University of South Florida offers a full range of social, cultural, educational, and religious programming, including the Jewish Adventures Club, which sponsors many events such as camping, hiking, and out-of-state trips. Hillel's weekly Sunday bagel brunches are a tradition at USF. Hillel also has a strong Grads and Young Professional group for students 21 and over. Team Hillel participates in college campus intramural sports such as softball, basketball, volleyball, and bowling. Hillel also participates in the Tampa Rabbinical Association, and works in cooperation with the Campus Ministry Association at USF to co-sponsor programs on campus.

Hillel operates out of a townhouse just off campus. An on-campus building is currently being planned.

"The University of South Florida has provided me with a broad perspective of the real world. Hillel has helped to give me a stepping stone to my scholastic and social life while I am at the University. Hillel offers many different ways for students to be active and to interact with other Jewish students. I've participated in Team Hillel Sports, the Jewish Adventures Club, and in many other activities. I have enjoyed my experience here and I know I have gained vast knowledge that will help me for the rest of my life."

William Korenvaes, junior,

"USF really brings to life the concept of Hillel being the foundation for Jewish campus life. Hillel provides students with a home away from home. From the first day I arrived at orientation, until graduation day, USF Hillel has been there for me. The Foundation has something for everyone, ranging from Friday night services, bagel

brunches, and High Holidays, to the Jewish Adventurers Club, Grad groups and award winning programs like 'Havdalah Under the Stars.'"

Rony Keller, graduating senior

UNIVERSITY OF TAMPA

Enrollment 2,000
Jewish 250

Hillel Jewish Student Union
18820 Arbor Drive
Lutz, FL 33549
(813) 972-4433
Fax: (813) 972-1882
E-mail: berman@soleil.acomp.usf.edu

Dan Berman, Director
Dr. Helene Silverman, Advisor

 Jewish Studies

2 courses.

 Kosher Food

Vegetarian dining alternatives; dormitory cooking facilities.

ON CAMPUS

Joint program with Hillel at University of South Florida.

GEORGIA

AGNES SCOTT COLLEGE

Enrollment 800
Jewish 10

c/o Atlanta YAD
1767 Haygood Drive
Atlanta, GA 30322
Web: www.agnesscott.edu

Rabbi Louis Feldstein, Executive Director
Jessica Klein, Program Director

ON CAMPUS

Atlanta YAD is a recognized organization on campus and works with Agnes Scott students to connect them to citywide and regional events and to assist them in developing programs (such as a women's seder) they wish to sponsor on campus.

See listing for Emory University.

DEKALB UNIVERSITY

Enrollment 15,000
Jewish 650

> Atlanta YAD: The Jewish Young Adult Agency
> 1767 Haygood Drive
> Atlanta, GA 30322
> (404) 727-6490
> Fax: (404) 727-2087
> E-mail: metro-yad@atlantayad.org
>
> **Rabbi Louis Feldstein**, Executive Director
> **Jessica Klein**, Program Director

See listing for Emory University.

EMORY UNIVERSITY

Enrollment 7,500 (UG 3,500; GR 4,000)
Jewish 1,800 (UG 1,000; GR 800)

> Atlanta YAD: The Jewish Young Adult Agency
> 1767 Haygood Drive
> Atlanta, GA 30322
> (404) 727-6490
> (404) 727-CHAI
> Fax: (404) 727-2087
> E-mail: metro-yad@atlantayad.org
> Web: www.emory.edu
>
> **Jessica Klein**, Program Director
> **Heidi Berger**, Campus Rabbi

 Jewish Studies
14 courses; B.A., M.A.

Study in Israel
2 6-week summer programs for credit; junior year abroad. Israel Program Intern Debbie Cohn; (404) 727-6490.

Kosher Food
The University has had a kosher meal plan, which may be revived. The Atlanta YAD offers Shabbat dinners and Passover meals. Nearby kosher restaurant delivers pizza, etc., to campus. Presently, frozen kosher meals are available.

ON CAMPUS

Various student groups are active in Atlanta YAD: Hillel, the Jewish Educational Alliance (Orthodox), the Reform Jewish Student Committee, UJA, AIPAC, and ESI (Emory Students for Israel) groups, and graduate student groups. Atlanta's very supportive Jewish community provides home hospitality. The University respects the Jewish calendar in scheduling events. The activities hotline will tell you what's current: (404) 727-CHAI.

Atlanta YAD, which is housed at Emory, also serves students at Georgia Tech, Georgia State, Oglethorpe, Kennesaw, Life, and DeKalb Colleges, and postcollege single young adults.

GEORGIA INSTITUTE OF TECHNOLOGY

Enrollment 12,000 (UG 8,820; GR 3,180)
Jewish 400

> Atlanta YAD: The Jewish Young Adult Agency
> 1767 Haygood Drive
> Atlanta, GA 30322
> (404) 727-6490
> Fax: (404) 727-2087
> E-mail: metro-yad@atlantayad.org
> Web: www.gatech.edu
>
> **Rabbi Louis Feldstein**, Executive Director
> **Jessica Klein**, Program Director

 Jewish Studies
Students may take classes at Emory University.

 Study in Israel
The university accepts credit for study at Israeli universities.

 Kosher Food
Dormitory cooking facilities; kosher food locally available.

ON CAMPUS

Events are held regularly on campus, with programs coordinated with the Atlanta YAD at Emory, including services, Shabbat and Pesach meals, and social events. For latest information, call the activities hotline: (404) 727-CHAI.

See listing for Emory University.

GEORGIA PERIMETER COLLEGE

Enrollment 14,000
Jewish 600

> c/o Atlanta YAD
> 1767 Haygood Drive
> Atlanta, GA 30322
> E-mail: metro-yad@atlantayad.org
> Web: www.dc.peachnet.edu
>
> **Rabbi Louis Feldstein**, Executive Director
> **Jessica Klein**, Program Director

ON CAMPUS

Jewish students at Georgia Perimeter receive programming guidance from Atlanta YAD, and participate in citywide and regional events coordianted by Atlanta YAD.

Served by Atlanta YAD. See listing for Emory University.

GEORGIA SOUTHERN UNIVERSITY

Enrollment 14,000
Jewish 150

Georgia Southern Hillel
c/o Dr. William Becker
PO Box 8077
Statesboro, GA 30460
(912) 681-5311
Fax: (912) 681-0386
E-mail: hillel@gsaixz.gasou.edu
Web: www.gasou.edu

Dr. William Becker, Advisor
Paula Solomon, Advisor

Kosher Food

Vegetarian alternatives available through Food Services. Kosher meat available in Statesboro and Savannah (55 miles).

ON CAMPUS

Georgia Southern's Jewish students get together for social events, Shabbat dinners, Passover seder, and holiday celebrations. Events and Shabbat services are sometimes held in conjunction with the Statesboro Hebrew Congregation. Students also attend regional Hillel events.

Georgia Southern Hillel also reaches out to Jewish students at Armstrong State College and the Savannah College of Art and Design.

GEORGIA STATE UNIVERSITY

Enrollment 22,000 (UG 16,000; GR 6,000)
Jewish 1,000

Atlanta YAD: The Jewish Young Adult Agency
1767 Haygood Drive
Atlanta, GA 30322
(404) 727-6490
Fax: (404) 727-2087
E-mail: metro-yad@atlantayad.org
Web: www.ksu.edu

Rabbi Louis Feldstein, Executive Director
Jessica Klein, Program Director

Jewish Studies

1 course.

ON CAMPUS

Atlanta YAD is a recognized organization on campus and works with GSU students to connect them to citywide and regional events and to assist them in developing programs, such as monthly lunches and educational programs, they wish to sponsor on campus.

See listing for Emory University.

KENNESAW STATE UNIVERSITY

Enrollment 12,200 (UG 11,000; GR 1,2 00)
Jewish 200

Atlanta YAD: The Jewish Young Adult Agency
1767 Haygood Drive
Atlanta, GA 30322
(404) 727-6490
Fax: (404) 727-2087
E-mail: metro-yad@atlantayad.org
Web: www.ksu.edu

Rabbi Louis Feldstein, Executive Director
Jessica Klein, Program Director

ON CAMPUS

Atlanta YAD is a recognized organization on campus and works with KSU students to connect them to citywide and regional events and to assist them in developing programs they wish to sponsor on campus. The school has a very supportive administration, faculty, and student body.

See listing for Emory University.

LIFE UNIVERSITY

Jewish 300

Atlanta YAD: The Jewish Young Adult Agency
1767 Haygood Drive
Atlanta, GA 30322
(404) 727-6490
Fax: (404) 727-2087
E-mail: metro-yad@atlantayad.org
Web: www.life.edu

Rabbi Louis Feldstein, Executive Director
Jessica Klein, Program Director

ON CAMPUS

Atlanta YAD is a recognized organization on campus and works with Life students to connect them to citywide and regional events and to assist them in developing programs they wish to sponsor on campus.

See listing for Emory University.

OGLETHORPE UNIVERSITY

Enrollment 1,230
Jewish 25

Atlanta YAD: The Jewish Young Adult Agency
1767 Haygood Drive
Atlanta, GA 30322
(404) 727-6490
Fax: (404) 727-2087
E-mail: metro-yad@atlantayad.org
Web: www.oglethorpe.edu

Rabbi Louis Feldstein, Executive Director
Jessica Klein, Program Director

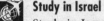 **Study in Israel**
Study in Israel for credit is supported by the university.

ON CAMPUS

Atlanta YAD works with Oglethorpe students to connect them to citywide and regional events, as well as giving them an opportunity to plan programs on campus.

See listing for Emory University.

UNIVERSITY OF GEORGIA

Enrollment 29,000
Jewish 1,450 (UG 1,300; GR 150)

 Georgia Hillel/Atlanta YAD
1155 South Milledge Avenue
Athens, GA 30605
(706) 543-6393
(404) 727-6490
Fax: (706) 543-2542
E-mail: hillel@arches.uga.edu

Phil Schlossberg, Director
Eileen Shuman, Program Director
Drew Burns, Jewish Campus Service Corps Fellow

Jewish Studies
The University offers several courses including a Holocaust class and Biblical Hebrew.

Kosher Food
Hillel has a kosher kitchen. Hillel offers holiday, Shabbat evening, and other occasional meals. Kosher food is locally available. There are also several restaurants in Atlanta, which is an hour and a half from Athens.

ON CAMPUS

UGA Hillel is an umbrella group supporting several constituent groups that include GeorgiaPAC on campus, UJA, and Hamagshimim. Traditionally Jewish Greek houses on campus are AEPi, DPhiE, SDT, and TEP. The Hillel House, a beautiful modern building within walking distance of campus, has a kosher kitchen, a library, a study room, a TV lounge, traditional southern porches, and a deck with a BBQ. Hillel sponsors an array of activities throughout the school year, which offer opportunities for student leadership through social, cultural, religious, political, educational, and community service projects. Hillel co-sponsors many events with other campus groups and facilitates strong community service programs, such as PB Jam and Habitat for Humanity. In conjunction with Chabad and the Atlanta Scholars Kollel, Hillel facilitates numerous educational and religious programs, such as Lunch 'n' Learn, evening study programs, and speakers on various subjects.

The Hillel program at the University of Georgia is a division of Atlanta YAD: The Jewish Young Adult Agency, based in Atlanta at Emory Universtiy.

HAWAII

UNIVERSITY OF HAWAII—HILO

Enrollment 3,000
Jewish 35

University of Hawaii at Hilo Hillel Affiliate
c/o Dr. Melissa Scott
Humanities Division
University of Hawaii at Hilo
200 W. Kawili Street
Hilo, HI 96720
(808) 974-7474
E-mail: mscott@hawaii.edu

Dr. Melissa Scott, Contact

Jewish Studies
There are religious studies courses that give Jewish students opportunities to study Jewish issues.

Kosher Food
Some frozen kosher food is locally available, but it is difficult to maintain a traditional lifestyle in Hawaii.

ON CAMPUS

Located on the Big Island of Hawaii, about 240 air miles from Honolulu, the school has several Jewish faculty members. The students who attend the University of Hawaii at Hilo are mostly local residents.

Students interested in studying at other campuses in Hawaii—the University of Hawaii in Honolulu, Chaminade University, or Hawaii Pacific University—should contact the Jewish Federation of Oahu in advance for specific information: 2550 Pali Highway, Honolulu, HI 96817; (808) 595-5225; fax: (808) 595-5220. Jewish faculty are at all of these colleges. The local communites welcome students to homes and services, and students attend Federation-sponsored Shabbatons, classes, and other events. Many Jews in the area are from Pacific rim countries.

On Oahu, religious services are held at Temple Emanu-el (Liberal and Traditional); Congregation Sof Ma'ariv (Conservative), 2550 Pali Highway; Chabad; and at the Aloha Chapel at Pearl Harbor.

IDAHO

UNIVERSITY OF IDAHO

Enrollment 8,000
Jewish 25-50

Hillel Foundation
c/o Professor Michael L. Kahn
Institute of Biological Chemistry
Washington State University
Pullman, WA 99164-6340
(509) 335-8327
Fax: (509) 335-7643
E-mail: kahn@wsu.edu
Web: www.uidaho.edu/~mschreck/jcp.html

Professor Michael L. Kahn, Advisor
Professor David Stiller, Advisor

ON CAMPUS

Activities for Jewish students at Idaho are held jointly with the Jewish Student Organization and Jewish Community of the Palouse (adult) at Washington State University.

ILLINOIS

BRADLEY UNIVERSITY

Enrollment 6,000
Jewish 400

Bradley University Hillel
Hillel House
1410 West Fredonia
Peoria, IL 61606
(309) 676-0862
(309) 677-3140
Fax: (309) 677-2797
E-mail: seth@bradley.edu

Seth Katz, Advisor

 Jewish Studies
Hebrew language, Holocaust, and History, as well as 2 courses in Religious Studies and 1 in Middle Eastern Studies.

 Study in Israel
1–2 semesters at Hebrew University.

 Kosher Food
Kosher food is available in Peoria, but kosher dining is not available on campus.

Housing
Rooms available at Hillel.

ON CAMPUS

Bradley University Hillel offers weekly Friday night services and dinners that are warm, crowded, and lively. Other popular events include breakfast, a Passover seder, and the 24-hour reading of names at Yom Hashoah, as well as karaoke. Students also participate in the UJA campaign.

CHICAGO KENT SCHOOL OF LAW

Enrollment 1,200
Jewish 400

Jewish Law Student Association—Decalogue
Hillels of Illinois Graduate and Professional Division (GAP)
1 South Franklin Street
Chicago, IL 60606
(312) 357-4702
(312) 444-2868
Fax: (312) 855-2479
E-mail: kfarkas@juf.org

Karen Farkas-Cohen, Director, GAP

Kosher Food

Two kosher restaurants in downtown Chicago are open for lunch during the week.

ON CAMPUS

Occasional events on campus with participation in citywide graduate programs through the Graduate and Professional Division of the Hillel Regional Center, the Hillels of Illinois. On-campus activities include speakers, the annual law student Shabbat dinner, and other social events. The Chicago Torah Network offers classes on campus at lunchtime.

DEPAUL UNIVERSITY

Enrollment 17,000 (UG 10,000; GR 7,000)
Jewish 1,000

DePaul University Hillel
c/o Rabbi Roy Furman
University Ministry
2312 N. Clifton Avenue
Munroe Hall, Room 100
Chicago, IL 60617
(773) 325-1186
Fax: (773) 325-7901
E-mail: ifrid@shrike.depaul.edu.
Web: shrike.depaul.edu/~croots/hillel/hillel.html

Rabbi Roy Furman, Advisor

Jewish Studies

The Jewish Experience; Modern Judaism; Holocaust Theology; and Joint Program with Spertus College.

Study in Israel

Arrangements can be made; credit and scholarships are available.

Kosher Food

Limited; packaged foods available. Contact Food Service Director for information.

ON CAMPUS

Small, active Hillel and Students for Israel groups plus independent Jewish student activities, together with college-wide, student life, and University Ministry programs of interest to Jewish students, faculty, and staff; cooperative events with other area Hillel groups. Rabbi Furman teaches in the Religious Studies department and is a part-time member of University Ministry staff.

DEPAUL UNIVERSITY LAW SCHOOL

Jewish Law Student Association—Decalogue
c/o Graduate and Profession Division (GAP)
The Hillels of Illinois
1 South Franklin Street, Suite 2528
Chicago, IL 60606
Phone: (312) 357-4702
(312) 444-2868
E-mail: kfarkas@juf.org

Karen Farkas-Cohen, Director, GAP

Kosher Food

Two kosher restaurants in the downtown area are open for lunch during the week.

ON CAMPUS

Occasional cultural, social, and social action events are held on campus, and students participate in citywide graduate and professional programs coordinated by the GAP division of The Hillels of Illinois.

Served by The Hillels of Illinois: Graduate and Professional Division (GAP).

HARPER COMMUNITY COLLEGE

Enrollment 10,000
Jewish 500

Harper Hillel
Student Activity Center
1200 W. Algonquin Road
Palentine, IL 60067
(847) 925-6242
Fax: (312) 855-2479
E-mail: spergric@harper.cc.il.us
Web: www.juf.org

Ammi Field, Director of Commuter Campus Services
Shari Pergricht, Faculty Advisor

Served by the Commuter Service Division of The Hillels of Illinois.

ILLINOIS INSTITUTE OF TECHNOLOGY

Enrollment 2,000
Jewish 100

IIT Hillel
c/o Student Activities
Illinois Institute of Technology
3300 S. Federal
Chicago, IL 60016
Phone: (312) 567-7043
Fax: (312) 855-2479
E-mail: afield@juf.org
Web: www.juf.org

Ammi Field, Director, Commuter Campus Services

ON CAMPUS

Jewish students at ITT receive programming assistance and guidance from the Commuter Campus Services division of The Hillels of Illinois, 1 S. Franklin St., Chicago.

Served by The Hillels of Illinois: Commuter Campus Services.

ILLINOIS STATE UNIVERSITY

Enrollment 20,000
Jewish 500

Hillel—Jewish Student Union
c/o Dr. Michael J. Stevens, Faculty Advisor—Hillel
4620 Psychology
Illinois State University
Normal, IL 61790
(309) 438-5700
Fax: (309) 438-5789
E-mail: mjsteven@ilstu.edu
Web: www.ilstu.edu

 Study in Israel
Transfer credits may be accepted pending transcript review.

ON CAMPUS

Jewish students at Illinois State have occasional programs, such as social action or community service, and celebrate all holidays with the local Jewish community. Faculty are very supportive of Jewish campus activities, serve as advisors and mentors to Jewish students, and sponsor brunches for visiting parents. Hillel also sponsors Holocaust Remembrance Week. Students at ISU often join with students at Bradley University and Illinois Wesleyan for special programs, and AEPi at ISU also holds events jointly with the fraternity's other chapters at nearby universities.

Served by The Hillels of Illinois.

ILLINOIS WESLEYAN UNIVERSITY

Enrollment 2,000
Jewish Few

ISU/IWU Hillel
c/o Moses Montefiore Congregation
102 Robinhood Lane
Bloomington, IL 61701
(309) 662-3182

Rabbi John Spiro, Advisor

Kosher Food
Dormitory cooking facilities.

ON CAMPUS

Joint programming with Illinois State University.

JOHN MARSHALL LAW SCHOOL

Enrollment 1,000
Jewish 150

Jewish Law Student Association—Decalogue
1 South Franklin Street
Chicago, IL 60606
(312) 357-4702
(312) 444-2868
Fax: (312) 855-2479
E-mail: kfarkas@juf.org

Karen Farkas-Cohen, Director, GAP

 Kosher Food
In the downtown area, 2 kosher restaurants are open for lunch during the week.

ON CAMPUS

Occasional events are held on campus, and students participate in citywide events for graduate students organized by the Graduate and Professional Division (GAP) of The Hillels of Illinois.

KNOX COLLEGE

Enrollment 1,100
Jewish 70

Jewish Student Association
Department of History
Knox College
Galesburg, IL 61401
(309) 341-7328
Fax: (309) 341-7090
E-mail: pgold@knox.edu

Professor Penny S. Gold, Advisor

Jewish Studies

4 courses including Judaism, Christianity, and Islam, The Holocaust, and Jews in America. In addition, each year a visiting scholar from Israel teaches a course. Other activities in Jewish Studies (guest lecturers, artistic performances, faculty and student research) are supported by the Rose L. and Mitchell Rudman Endowment Fund for Judaic Studies and the Max and Dora Barash Endowment Fund for Judaic Studies.

Kosher Food

No kosher meal plan available; vegetarian dining alternatives. Students wishing to keep kashrut live off campus in apartments where they prepare their own food.

Housing

No special housing, but students can propose new themes for a cluster, so a housing unit focusing on Jewish issues would be possible.

ON CAMPUS

Knox College is located about 200 miles west of Chicago, and is easily accessible by train, rail, or plane. There has been a Jewish community in Galesburg since shortly after the founding of the town and college in the 1830s. Temple Sholom, founded in the early 1950s, was the result of a merger between Reform and Orthodox groups in the city. It is now affiliated with the Union of American Hebrew Congregations. Knox students are welcome to participate in all Temple events, and students sometimes teach in the religious school. The Jewish Student Club has sponsored various activities including talks on Israeli-Palestinian relations; leading Shabbat services at the local synagogue; holding a Havdalah service on campus; and films, speakers, and discussion groups.

phy, theology, and literature departments. The theology department has 1 full-time professor of Jewish Studies.

Study in Israel

Formal relationship with Hebrew University in Jerusalem, including transferrable credit options and financial aid. Credits are also accepted on a case-by-case basis for students returning from yeshivot, seminaries, or other Israeli universities.

Kosher Food

Kosher snacks available on campus and at Hillel. Students have an option to store food for daily use in Hillel's section of the Ministry Center.

Housing

Most Jewish students commute to campus.

ON CAMPUS

Hillel, located in the Ministry Center at Loyola University, Chicago, is an integral part of university life and one of the most active groups on campus. Hillel sponsors a formal program at least once a week, and many of its programs, such as lectures and holiday celebrations, are campuswide, major events. Loyola is very supportive of Jewish life and sensitive to Jewish needs.

"Loyola is a great place to be Jewish! The University fosters a sense of diversity that enables Hillel to work with the widest variety of campus groups. From a Hanukkah party in the middle of the Student Union to a Mideast Dialogue with Muslim and Christian students, Hillel has given me the opportunity to grow as a Jew, a person and a leader."

Heather Meyers, senior

LOYOLA UNIVERSITY

Enrollment 12,000 (UG 5,450; GR 6,550)
Jewish 800 (UG 300; GR 500)

Hillel at Loyola
Ministry Center
1058 W. Loyola Avenue
Chicago, IL 60626
(773) 508-2193
(312) 444-2868
Fax: (773) 508-8509
E-mail: pray@orion.it.luc.edu
Web: www.luc.edu

Patti Ray, Director

Jewish Studies

Individual courses in Judaica are offered through an interdisciplinary program, in the history, philoso-

LOYOLA UNIVERSITY LAW SCHOOL

Enrollment 600
Jewish 150

Hillels of Illinois Graduate and Professional Division (GAP)
1 South Franklin Street
Chicago, IL 60606
(312) 444-2868
Fax: (312) 855-2479
E-mail: gap@cyberconnect.com
Web: www.cyberconnect.com/GAP

Karen Farkas-Cohen, Coordinator

ON CAMPUS

Occasional events on campus with participation in citywide graduate programs.

NATIONAL LOUIS UNIVERSITY

Enrollment 1,300 (UG 450; Gr 850)
Jewish 100

NLU Hillel
c/o Student Activities
National Louis University
2840 Sheridan Road
Evanston, IL 60201
(312) 357-4703
Fax: (312) 855-2479
E-mail: afield@juf.org
Web: www.juf.org

Ammi Field, Director, Commuter Campus Services
Dr. June Steinberg, Faculty Advisor

Served by The Hillels of Illinois: Commuter Campus Services.

NORTHEASTERN ILLINOIS UNIVERSITY

Enrollment 10,000
Jewish 500

Northeastern Illinois University Hillel
c/o Office of Student Activities
5500 N. St. Louis
Chicago, IL 60625
(773) 583-4050, ext. 2793
(312) 357-4703
Fax: (312) 855-2479
E-mail: afield@juf.org
Web: www.juf.org

Ammi Field, Director, Commuter Campus Services
Dr. Elaine Koffman, Faculty Advisor

 Jewish Studies
4 courses.

ON CAMPUS

Northeastern Illinois University is close to a Jewish neighborhood. Activities on campus are designed to accommodate the commuter campus population.

NIU is served by the Commuter Campus Services division of The Hillels of Illinois.

NORTHERN ILLINOIS UNIVERSITY

Enrollment 22,000 (UG 15,800; GR 6,200)
Jewish 300

NIU Hillel
820 Russell Road
DeKalb, IL 60115
(847) 459-4376
E-mail: Bisacovi@niu.edu

Joan Greening, Faculty Advisor

 Jewish Studies
Comparative religion courses.

 Kosher Food
Hillel offers seders and all Passover meals.

ON CAMPUS

Regular bagel brunches. Local congregation houses the Hillel and welcomes students.

NORTHWESTERN UNIVERSITY

Enrollment 12,450 (UG 7,800; GR 4,650)
Jewish 1,750 (UG 1,100; GR 650)

 Louis and Saerree Fiedler Hillel Center
629 Foster Street
Evanston, IL 60201
(847) 467-4455
Fax: (847) 467-4445
E-mail: balinsky@nwu.edu
Web: www.studorg.nwu.edu/hillel/

Rabbi Michael Balinsky, Director
Rachel Spiro, Program Director
Jen Lacoff, Jewish Campus Service Corps Fellow

 Jewish Studies
Undergraduate minor.

 Study in Israel
Junior year abroad possible.

 Kosher Food
Hillel offers 5 dinners; Kosher dinners and vegetarian options in the university cafeterias. Passover meals are available at Hillel with a university rebate.

ON CAMPUS

A new building, which puts Hillel in the center of the NU campus, has created many new opportunities for exciting Jewish programming. Hillel serves as the dynamic center of the campus Jewish community, supporting and working with numerous groups and organizations that focus on specific student interests. A wonderfully diverse group of Jewish students are active in leadership positions. Hillel sponsors excellent freshman programming, first-rate theater, student-organized Jewish learning opportunities, an annual Hillel formal, and activities for all Jewish religious denominations. Graduate students also participate in citywide programs.

NORTHWESTERN UNIVERSITY— PROFESSIONAL SCHOOLS

Enrollment 2,500
Jewish 500

Jewish Law Student Association/Jewish Medical Student Organization
1 South Franklin Street
Chicago, IL 60606
(312) 357-4702
Fax: (312) 855-2479
E-mail: gap@cyberconnect.com

Karen Farkas, GAP Coordinator

 Kosher Food
Two kosher restaurants in the immediate area are open for lunch only during the week.

ON CAMPUS
Joint programs with Northwestern University Law and Medical Schools: monthly Shabbat dinner club, monthly bagel brunches, Passover seders, Jewish lecture series.

The JLSA/JMSO is served by he Graduate and Professional Division (GAD). Students participate in citywide events.

OAKTON COMMUNITY COLLEGE

Enrollment 10,000
Jewish 1,000

Oakton Community College Hillel
c/o Student Activities Oakton Community College
1600 East Golf Road
Des Plaines, IL 60016
(847) 635-1697
(312) 357-4703
Fax: (847) 635-1764
E-mail: afield@juf.org
Web: www.juf.org

Ammi Field, Director, Commuter Campus Services
Joseph Kraus, Faculty Advisor

 Jewish Studies
1 course (Hebrew).

ON CAMPUS
On-campus programming includes lunchtime Table Talks, a campuswide interfaith Holocaust memorial program, holiday programs, and speakers. Off-campus social programs are held in cooperation with metropolitan Chicago campuses. Oakton's events are supported by an active Faculty Friends of Hillel group.

Oakton Community College is served by The Hillels of Illinois: Commuter Campus Services.

SOUTHERN ILLINOIS UNIVERSITY— CARBONDALE

Enrollment 19,807 (UG 16,078; GR 3,729)
Jewish 700 (UG 500; GR 200)

Hillel Foundation at SIUC
913 South Illinois Avenue
Carbondale, IL 62901
(618) 529-7260
(618) 549-5213
Fax: (618) 453-7388
E-mail: izabelle@siu.edu

Betsy Herman, Advisor

 Jewish Studies
Beginning Hebrew classes.

 Study in Israel
SIUC accepts credits from accredited Israeli institutions.

 Kosher Food
Some kosher food is available at the local supermarkets and can be ordered from St. Louis. Hillel provides occasional kosher meals.

 Housing
Thompson Point, Brush Towers, and quads.

ON CAMPUS
The campus is located in a rural community 6 hours from Chicago. There is a small Hillel, with a supportive Jewish faculty and community. Events throughout the year include a community seder, Shabbat dinners, lectures, films, exhibits, performances, and a Jewish/Christian dialogue. There are also opportunities for outdoor activities in the nearby Shawnee national forest.

UNIVERSITY OF CHICAGO

Enrollment 9,774
Jewish 1,350

Newberger Hillel Center
5715 South Woodlawn Avenue
Chicago, IL 60637-1602
(773) 752-1127
Fax: (773) 752-2460
E-mail: hillel@uchicago.edu
Web: www.juf.org

Rabbi David Rosenberg, Director
Dana Rubin Winkelman, Assistant Director
Shayna Klopott, Leni and Peter May Jewish Campus
Service Corps Fellow

Jewish Studies

Undergraduate concentrations and master's degree offered by the new Committee on Jewish Studies. Students may also take Jewish Studies courses through the Department of Near Eastern Languages and Civilizations.

Study in Israel

Students may petition for credit.

Kosher Food

Hillel offers a weekly Kosher Lunch and Dinner Plan. First-year students can transfer the university meal plan money toward the Hillel Kosher Lunch Plan. Friday evening dinner weekly; Passover and full High Holiday meals. Vegetarian dining alternatives are available, as are dormitory cooking facilities. Kosher food is available locally.

ON CAMPUS

Hillel's busy program reflects the diversity of life at the University of Chicago. The dynamic student body actively supports more than 20 student groups with special interests. Hillel provides a variety of classes, student-to-student discussions, and graduate brown bag discussions; coffeehouses, guest performers, and guest speakers; Israel programs, student-led holiday and Shabbat services and celebrations, student cooperative Shabbat cooking, Kosher Meal Plan, films, and parties; creative arts and music programming; and community service activities. Groups include Shircago, the Jewish *a cappella* group; Jews on Campus, a Jewish first-year group; and the Jewish Student Union. The campus Jewish community is rounded out by a strong Jewish graduate student body, Law Students Association, Jewish Medical Students Association, Council of Jewish Social Service Students, and Jewish Business School Students.

Several endowments support a variety of Hillel projects. The Rabbi Maurice and Nell Pekarsky Endowment provides funding for outstanding speakers and performers and scholarships to University of Chicago students attending Jewish leadership or educational conferences. The Rabbi Daniel I. Leifer Endowment supports programming in social justice, Jewish culture,

and religious pluralism. The Joan and James Shapiro Endowment annually enables 1 University of Chicago student to work on a social justice project in Israel for a quarter as a Leifer Fellow. The Sidney and Freda Davidson Library Endowment supports Hillel's 12,000-volume Davidson Library. The Davidson Library is the largest Hillel library and it contains Judaica in a variety of media available for browsing or research.

The Newberger Hillel Center is conveniently located 1 block east of the university's central quadrangle. In 1904, this warm Georgian mansion was designed by one of Chicago's most prominent architects, Howard Van Doren Shaw. In addition to the library, the Center has a new lounge with a television, and a chapel/auditorium. The University is very supportive of Jewish students and there is active faculty involvement in the Hillel program. Hillel is also well known for convening Chicago's annual Latke-Hamantash Symposium, which began at the university more than 50 years ago and has since been replicated on other American and Israeli campuses. The symposium, on the Tuesday before Thanksgiving, draws hundreds of students and faculty to a mock debate by faculty, using the language of their professional disciplines, about the comparative merits of these favorite Jewish foods.

"Newberger Hillel shares many of the wonderful aspects of the University of Chicago. Hillel's enthusiastic Jewish students come together for song, prayer, food, discussion, learning and schmoozing. Newberger Hillel combines religion, an intellectual environment and a warm social atmosphere."

Arielle R. Lutwick, '02

UNIVERSITY OF ILLINOIS—CHICAGO

Enrollment 23,000
Jewish 1,100

UIC Hillel
Levine Hillel Center
924 S. Morgan Street
Chicago, IL 60607
(312) 829-1595
Fax: (312) 829-1597
E-mail: marlabaker@aol.com

Marla Baker, Director
Debra Feld, Program Director

Jewish Studies

Minor, coordinated by Dr. Frank Tachaw. Beginning and Intermediate Hebrew language, with supplemental Chug Ivrit at Hillel.

Study in Israel

Opportunities for study abroad in Israel are available for credit. Credit status should be cleared in advance. Hillel maintains an Israel Resource Center to help students determine the right short- or long-term Israel program for them.

Kosher Food

The student-run Miriam's Timbrel Cafe provides kosher sandwiches in a cafe atmosphere. Passover lunches provided.

ON CAMPUS

Housed in a beautiful new building adjacent to campus, UIC Hillel is a lively on-campus meeting place (or home-away-from-home) for commuter and residential Jewish students from all backgrounds. The Jewish Student Council plans social, cultural, and social action activities throughout the year, both on campus and in students' home communities. Hillel's study space and computers for student use are popular, and the building's recreational facilities (pool, Ping-Pong, TV, games) are well used.

Especially attuned to the needs of commuter students, UIC Hillel maintains 17 parking spaces, which can be rented on a semester basis, and serves as a clearing house for carpooling. The bulletin board keeps students abreast of the happenings of the Jewish community and other job opportunities and activities. The Jewish Education Resource File is maintained for and by those teaching Sunday or Hebrew School. Lockers and showers are also available at Hillel.

Annual on-campus Hillel programming includes Jewish Awareness Week, Holocaust Remembrance Day activities, the Peanut Butter and Jam project for the hungry, and a Jewish Medical Ethics Symposium on the Medical Center Campus. Hillel actively participates in other campus cultural activities throughout the year, and there are many opportunities for building relationships and working with other groups on the diverse campus.

UIC also participates in citywide Hillel programming, which includes Jewish students at campuses throughout metropolitan Chicago. In addition to social events throughout the year, the Great Escape spring retreat is an annual highlight.

UNIVERSITY OF ILLINOIS — URBANA-CHAMPAIGN

Enrollment 36,800 (UG 25,800; GR 11,000)
Jewish 3,000 (UG 2,500; GR 500)

University of Illinois Hillel Foundation
503 East John Street
Champaign, IL 61820
(217) 344-1328
Fax: (217) 344-1540
E-mail: alanpotash@yahoo.com
Web: www.prairienet.org/hillel/

Alan E. Potash, Director
Shana Cohn, Program Director
Erin Boxt, Jewish Campus Service Corp Fellow

Jewish Studies

More than 20 courses; concentrations in Hebrew Studies and Jewish Culture and Society. Jewish studies are coordinated by the interdisciplinary Committee on Jewish Culture and Society.

Study in Israel

Study abroad, including in Israel, is highly supported by the University and full credit is possible.

Kosher Food

Hillel offers 3 dinners weekly, High Holiday meals, and lunch and dinner throughout Passover. Strictly kosher food is served at all Hillel meals, onegs, and parties.

ON CAMPUS

The University of Illinois is the home of the first Hillel, which was established in 1923. It also has the largest fraternity and sorority presence in the country. The campus's extensive Jewish Greek system mantains close ties with Hillel, sharing programming and resources. The university is home to more than a dozen Jewish student groups, many of which are housed at Hillel, representing a broad range of social, political, cultural, religious, educational, and Zionist concerns.

Hillel also offers opportunities to participate on sports teams, a campus Jewish journal, graduate programs, and women's programs. The many student organizations provide numerous opportunities for students to develop their leadership skills. The campus is home to an interdisciplinary Committee on Jewish Culture, whose faculty members are active with Hillel and the student community. Hillel works with the committee as well as other campus units to bring speakers to campus, and provides other formal and informal opportunities in Jewish education and development. Several rabbis from Chicago routinely visit and teach.

The Hillel building is located close to the main campus quad. It includes study areas, a Judaica library, an auditorium in which theatrical and musical productions are held, student offices, a 6-foot projection television, 2 synagogues, and a large dining facility.

"A large percentage of Jews from the North Shore suburbs of Chicago attend the U of I The Greek system on our campus is one of the biggest. There are four Jewish fraternities and two sororities so there is a large Jewish Greek life and community. The Jewish faculty is involved in campus life. The Hebrew program is excellent."

Samantha Lazarus, junior

"The great thing about Hillel at the University of Illinois is that it brings together Jews of very diverse backgrounds."

Aaron Benson, senior

INDIANA

WESTERN ILLINOIS UNIVERSITY

Enrollment 10,573 (UG 8,064; GR 2,509)
Jewish 25 (UG 20; GR 5)

Western Illinois University Hillel
c/o Prof. Sheldon Gary, Advisor
Graduate and International Studies
Memorial Hall
Macomb, IL 61455
(309) 298-1806
(309) 833-4231
Fax: (309) 298-2245

Professor Sheldon Gary, Advisor

ON CAMPUS

WIU Hillel is a student organization recognized by the University Student Government. Its programs reflect the interests and commitments of the members. The Jewish adults of the city of Macomb and neighboring areas also plan events in which the students are invited to participate.

WIU Hillel holds lox and bagel brunches, an autumn picnic, a Purim party, a Jewish foods theme dinner, and a potluck dinner on the theme of "Fruit from the Trees" for Tu B'Shevat. The Conservative rabbi from Springfield has visited to discuss being Jewish in a rural setting.

WILLIAM S. SCHOLL SCHOOL OF PODIATRY

Enrollment 800
Jewish 300

Hillels of Illinois Graduate and Professional Division (GAP)
1 South Franklin Street
Chicago, IL 60606
(312) 444-2868
(312) 357-4702
Fax: (312) 855-2479
E-mail: kfarkas@juf.org
Web: www.cyberconnect.com/gap

Karen Farkas-Cohen, Director, GAP

ON CAMPUS

Occasional events on campus, with participation in citywide graduate programs.

BALL STATE UNIVERSITY

Enrollment 20,000
Jewish 100

Hillel at Ball State University
c/o Susan Rubin Weintrob
Department of English
Muncie, IN 47306
(765) 285-8399
(765) 286-3026
Fax: (765) 285-3765 attn: Susan Weintrob
E-mail: srweintrob@bsuvc.bsu.edu

Professor Susan Rubin Weintrob, Advisor

Jewish Studies

The Hillel advisor offers an annual course in Holocaust, Genesis, and Basic Judism. Other courses are occasionally offered.

Kosher Food

Wellness Dorm offers more choices in food, which is easier for those selecting kosher food.

ON CAMPUS

Ball State Hillel, established in 1991, offers religious, social, and cultural activities for all Jewish students on campus. There are 2–3 activities a month, featuring Jewish movies, holiday and Shabbat dinners, speakers, and social events. Hillel is warmly supported by Jewish faculty and community members. The Jewish fraternity, SAM, is on campus.

BUTLER UNIVERSITY

Enrollment 3,300
Jewish 75

Jewish Student Union
4600 Sunset Avenue
Indianapolis, IN 46208
(317) 940-9910
Fax: (317) 940-9970
E-mail: rmarcus@butler.edu

Robert J. Marcus, Advisor

Jewish Studies

Introduction to Judaism is offered annually. Occasional offerings include Jewish-American Literature, The Jews of Germany, and The Changing Role of Women in Judaism.

Study in Israel
Study abroad in Israel is offered and encouraged.

 Kosher Food
Kosher meals are provided upon request.

ON CAMPUS

Butler University contains a small but growing Jewish presence. Indianapolis has a thriving Jewish community with opportunities for college students to explore spiritual matters and to get involved in social action and other areas of interest. Monthly, informal Shabbat dinners on campus are popular and participative, and Hillel also sponsors occasional other programs according to student interest.

> *"At Butler University the Jewish Student Union gets together for Shabbat dinners, holiday celebrations and community service. Although the Jewish population is small, the administration is supportive. At last year's commencement, a local rabbi was the guest speaker. Butler has a beautiful campus located in a nice part of Indianapolis."*
>
> *Martin McKenney, sophomore*

DEPAUW UNIVERSITY

Enrollment 2,090
Jewish 35

Jewish Fellowship Group: Havurah
Dept. of Jewish Study and Life
302 D. Harrison Hall
DePauw University
Greencastle, IN 46135
(800) 447-2495
(765) 658-4565
Fax: (765) 658-4120

TBA, Director

 Jewish Studies
A selection of courses is offered, and there are other options for study under consideration. Religious Studies Department offers a variety of courses that include aspects of Judaism. Religious Studies major.

 Study in Israel
Winter term in Israel.

Kosher Food
Kosher meals by arrangement; vegetarian meals in the dining halls.

ON CAMPUS

The University sponsors the DePauw Judaic Fellows Scholarship program; incentive and merit scholarships are renewable annually. The University supports a generous guest speakers program, and leadership training opportunities and offers strong institutional support for Judaic life and consideration of Jewish issues on campus.

Indiana University Hillel in Bloomington, as well as the synagogues in Indianapolis, offer additional Jewish resources for students at DePauw.

EARLHAM COLLEGE

Enrollment 1,200
Jewish 120

Jewish Student Union/Cultural Center
Earlham College
Richmond, IN 47374
(317) 973-2968
E-mail: bobs@earlham.edu

Professor Gordon Thompson, Advisor
Professor Robert Southard, Advisor

 Jewish Studies
8 courses in religion, literature, and history; 3 courses in Hebrew language study.

 Study in Israel
Jerusalem program.

 Kosher Food
Vegetarian dining alternatives; kosher food is available in Indianapolis.

 Housing
Jewish Cultural Center houses 9 students.

ON CAMPUS

The JSO's Shabbat dinners are popular with students; activities also include speakers and other events. Earlham's Jerusalem Program studies the Palestinian-Israeli conflict. Students serve the local synagogue, Beth Boruk, by teaching in its Sunday school and performing cantorial services.

INDIANA UNIVERSITY

Enrollment 33,100 (UG 26,100; GR 7,000)
Jewish 3,200 (UG 3,000; GR 200)

Helene G. Simon Hillel Center
730 E. Third Street
Bloomington, IN 47401
(812) 336-3824
Fax: (812) 339-1949
E-mail: hillel@indiana.edu
Web: www.indiana.edu/~hillel

Rabbi Susan Shifron, Director
Paul Alan Rosen, Program Director
Margo Hamburger, Outreach/PR Director
Rony Keller, Jewish Campus Service Corps Fellow

Jewish Studies

40 courses annually; 70 in catalog. B.A., undergraduate certificate, Ph.D., minor. 17 full-time faculty members. Interdisciplinary studies with the departments of Anthropology, English, History, Near Eastern Languages and Cultures, Philosophy, and Religious Studies. Wide range of courses on Jews and Judaism, including instruction in biblical studies, modern Jewish history and culture, Jewish thought, Holocaust studies, and Israel studies.

The $2,500 Glazer Scholarship is available to an incoming freshman (January 15 deadline); more than $65,000 in Jewish Studies scholarships have been awarded in the past 4 years to IU Jewish studies students. Annual undergraduate administrative internship and research internship; conference funding available to students; honors programs. The Jewish Studies Student Association sponsors regular student-faculty gatherings—dinner, monthly lunches, career mentor programs. Six ongoing endowed lectures bring distinguished scholars and writers regularly to campus. The Program regularly invites distinguished scholars from other universities to teach at Indiana University. Dr. Carolyn Lipson-Walker, Director, The Robert A. and Sandra S. Borns Jewish Studies Program, Indiana University, Goodbody Hall 308, Bloomington, IN 47405-2401; (812) 855-0453; clipson@indiana.edu.

Study in Israel

Summer archaeological field school at Tel Bet Schemesh in Israel; junior year program at Hebrew University in Jerusalem.

Kosher Food

Hillel offers Shabbat evening (weekly) and holiday dinners; kosher-for-Passover lunches and dinners; vegetarian dining alternatives; dormitory cooking facilities.

ON CAMPUS

Indiana offers a wide range of social and educational opportunities for Jewish students through its very active Hillel program and its excellent Jewish studies program. Hillel has extensive social, cultural, educational, and religious programming, including trips, parties, retreats, Bagel Talks, TV and movie nights, and Israel programs. Students can also participate in the Mitzvah Corps, Outdoor Adventure Club, Intramural Sports, or First-Year-Students-Only club.

Hillel's Haver Program welcomes new first-year students to campus, and the Discover Hillel card gives students program discounts and exercise room privileges. Very active student board. The Jewish Studies program also offers a wide variety of cultural activities, including major lectures. Hillel holds a Jewish Career Day in conjunction with the Jewish Studies program. There are five Jewish fraternities and sororities on campus. Find Indiana University's Hillel Web site through www.hillel.org.

"Indiana University is a comfortable place for a Jewish student. From the first moment I arrived, I became involved in Hillel, AIPAC, and other organizations. Now, I am going to be an AIPAC intern. I am the Public Relations Vice President of Hillel, and am the Student Cantor for High Holiday services in the IU auditorium. The IU faculty has been supportive for the most part. The Jewish Studies faculty is wonderful."

Melissa Dobbins, sophomore

PURDUE UNIVERSITY

Enrollment 35,000
Jewish 650

Purdue Hillel: Foundation for Jewish Campus Life
912 West State Street
West Lafayette, IN 47906
(765) 743-1293
Fax: (765) 743-0014
E-mail: hillel@expert.cc.purdue.edu
Web: expert.cc.purdue.edu/~hillel

Lee Koch, Director
Jonathan Stern, host/Shammas

Jewish Studies

33 courses; minor available. The Jewish department publishes *Shofar, An Inter-disciplinary Journal of Jewish Studies*. A minor in Hebrew is available with courses in Modern and Biblical Hebrew. The University library maintains a large Judaica collection.

Study in Israel

Study in Israel is available through many programs.

Kosher Food

Weekly Shabbat dinner, Passover meals and seders, cafe and deli-style meals, and BBQs throughout the semester.

ON CAMPUS

Hillel provides a warm environment where Jewish students can explore their Jewish identity, celebrate Jewish life, and build the community. The local community is very supportive of student activities. Hillel and the community have co-sponsored a committee on Human Rights in the Soviet Union, a Holocaust remembrance, Friends of Israel Action Committee, Student UJA Campaign, AEPi, a Jewish fraternity, and many more activities.

UNIVERSITY OF EVANSVILLE

Enrollment 2,870
Jewish 30

University of Evansville Hillel
1800 Lincoln Avenue
Evansville, IN 47722
(812) 479-2754
Fax: (812) 479-2101
E-mail: as7@evansville.edu
Web: www.evansville.edu

Professor Alan L. Solomon, Advisor

 Kosher Food
Vegetarian menu available.

ON CAMPUS

The University administration and the Chaplain are very supportive of Hillel. There is a campuswide Passover seder.

UNIVERSITY OF NOTRE DAME

Enrollment 7,600
Jewish 20

c/o Rabbi Michael Signer
Theology Department
University of Notre Dame
Notre Dame, IN 46556
(219) 631-7635
(219) 631-7811
Fax: (219) 631-8209
E-mail: michael.a.signer.1@nd.edu

Rabbi Michael Signer, Advisor

ON CAMPUS

Rabbi Signer is Abrams Professor of Jewish Thought and Culture.

CORNELL COLLEGE

Enrollment 1,140
Jewish 30

Jewish Student Organization
c/o Dr. Bernoff, Dept. of Religion
600 1st Street
Mt. Vernon, IA 52314
(319) 895-4373
Fax: (319) 895-5237
E-mail: thomas@cornell-iowa.edu

Reverend Dick Thomas, Chaplain
Dr. Charles Bernoff, Advisor

 Jewish Studies
6 courses in Judaic Studies; minor. Major available in Religious Studies.

 Study in Israel
Semester/year programs provided through University of Iowa (full credit).

 Kosher Food
Vegetarian dining alternatives.

ON CAMPUS

Cornell's Jewish population is small but very active. The University and Chaplain's Office are very supportive of Jewish activities and sponsor various events such as monthly Jewish/Christian Dialogue Groups (with 3 campuses and the local synagogue), annual Yom HaShoah commemoration, and an annual community seder. Cornell students have access to all programs and events at nearby University of Iowa Hillel.

DRAKE UNIVERSITY

Enrollment 3,800
Jewish 300

 Alliance of Jewish Student Students
Student Life Center
2507 University
Des Moines, IA 50312
(515) 277-5566

Allen Scult, Advisor

 Jewish Studies
3 courses.

 Kosher Food
Vegetarian dining alternatives.

ON CAMPUS

The Alliance of Jewish Students holds monthly programs. Also, the Des Moines Jewish community enjoys student involvement in community events. The community also offers home hospitality and arranges "open university" non-credit Judaica courses.

GRINNELL COLLEGE

Enrollment 1,300
Jewish 160

Chalutzim
Grinnell College
1127 Park Street
Grinnell, IA 50112
(515) 269-4981
Fax: (515) 269-4321
E-mail: brin@grinnell.edu

Rabbi Deborah Brinn, Associate Chaplain

Jewish Studies

7 courses; majors in Religious Studies with a concentration in Jewish Studies.

Study in Israel

Grinnell College gives academic credit for study abroad.

Kosher Food

Vegetarian dining alternatives; frozen kosher meals are available upon request; dairy kosher kitchen served for Shabbat and holidays.

ON CAMPUS

Chalutzim, the Jewish Student Organization, provides a community in which students can learn about and celebrate their Judaism. The Jewish student community is small, very diverse, and very active. All events sponsored by Chalutzim are student-generated and depend upon the interests and ideas of the membership. Chalutzim provides religious services as well as educational and cultural programming for students as well as the larger campus community. Chalutzim holds a weekly Shabbat Table, celebrates the holidays, sponsors a Jewish Cultural Week, and brings speakers and performers to the college campus. The group also holds informal discussions, sponsors informal classes, participates in interfaith dialogue, and is very involved in issues of multiculturalism and diversity on campus.

IOWA STATE UNIVERSITY

Enrollment 25,000
Jewish 250

Hillel, Iowa State University
633 Ross Hall
Iowa State University
Ames, IA 50011
(515) 294-0122
Fax: (515) 294-6390
E-mail: abix@iastate.edu

Amy Bix, Faculty Advisor

Jewish Studies

A few Jewish Studies courses are offered through the Department of Philosophy and Religious Studies.

Study in Israel

Students may participate in programs offered by other universities.

Kosher Food

Vegetarian dining alternatives.

ON CAMPUS

Hillel sponsors social and cultural events, such as speakers, special Shabbat and Jewish holiday celebrations, social action and community service programs, sports, and pizza get-togethers and similar social activities. The Holocaust Memorial Lecture draws a large crowd. Hillel sponsors celebrations for major holidays and works with the local synagogue to promote Jewish life in the community.

The Ames Jewish Congregation and the faculty are very supportive of Hillel activities. The Federation of Greater Des Moines also supports Hillel-sponsored speakers and other activities. Residence halls promote ethnic/cultural/religious diversity with awareness programs.

"The Jewish student group Hillel provides an excellent medium for the relatively small population of Jewish students here to meet and socialize with one another."

Adam Oris, Hillel president

PALMER COLLEGE OF CHIROPRACTIC MEDICINE

Enrollment 1,700
Jewish 35

Jewish Student Association
c/o Craig Mekow
Anatomy Department
1000 Brady Street
Davenport, IA 52803
(319) 884-5693
Fax: (319) 884-5692
E-mail: anatcraig@aol.com

Craig Mekow, Advisor

ON CAMPUS

Jewish students get together approximately once a month for social, cultural, and religious events.

The metro area (Quad cities of Illinois and Iowa) is served by a Reform and a Conservative synagogue.

UNIVERSITY OF IOWA

Enrollment 24,500
Jewish 800–900

Aliber/Hillel Jewish Student Center
122 East Market Street
Iowa City, IA 52245
(319) 338-0778
Fax: (319) 338-1482
E-mail: hillel@blue.weeg.uiowa.edu

Gerald Sorokin, Director
David Leventhal, Jewish Campus Corps Fellow
Meems Ellenberg, Development Director

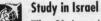 **Jewish Studies**
20 courses in School of Religion on Judaic and Comparative Topics. Holder of Jewish Studies Chair is most popular speaker on campus.

Study in Israel
The University accepts credit for study at Israeli universities.

Kosher Food
Hillel has a kosher kitchen and provides meals for holidays and bi-weekly Shabbat dinners.

ON CAMPUS

Aliber/Hillel's comfortable building provides study space, a TV lounge, a Judaica library, and a place for informal socializing and recreation. Hillel collaborates with Jewish student organizations at other Iowa campuses for joint events. Students participate in a variety of social and holiday activities, including sukkah-build-

ing, latke party, study breaks, Passover seders and meal services, student-cooked dinners, and High Holidays meal. For Grads Only group meets periodically for social/cultural events. Only Jewish Greek house is Sigma Alpha Mu; Jewish men and women are accepted in other fraternities and sororities.

Many leading members of the faculty are Jewishly identified, and the University administration is sympathetic to Jewish student interests. The local synagogue works closely with Hillel, and Iowa's Jewish students teach in its Sunday-Hebrew school.

KANSAS

KANSAS STATE UNIVERSITY

Enrollment 20,000 (UG 15,000; GR 5,000)
Jewish 150

Hillel
c/o Manhattan Jewish Congregation
1509 Wreath Avenue
Manhattan, KS 66503
(785) 532-4709
(785) 776-0597
Fax: (785) 532-6232
E-mail: andreab@ksu.edu

Dr. David Margolies, Advisor
Andrea Blair, Program Director

 Jewish Studies
4 courses; Literature and History of the Holocaust, Jewish American Literature and Theater.

Study in Israel
KSU sponsors the Israel Theater Program each summer, which offers American students the opportunity to understand Israeli society through its theater. Nine undergraduate and graduate credits are available. Contact Dr. Norman Fedder at (785) 532-6875.

Kosher Food
Will assist students who require kosher food.

ON CAMPUS

Jewish students at Kansas State meet for coffee and informal discussions weekly, hold monthly meetings showing films, and host guest speakers of Jewish interest, etc. Diverse group with students from Brazil, Costa Rica, Israel, and Russia. Services, all holiday celebrations, and monthly Sunday morning brunches are held in conjunction with the highly supportive and welcoming Jewish community. Kansas State activities, through the University's committee on religion, include a campus Holocaust remembrance ceremony, a Martin Luther King, Jr., commemoration, Racial and Ethnic Harmony week activities, and interfaith dialogues. Students also attend Hillel events at the University of Kansas, one and a half hours away.

UNIVERSITY OF KANSAS

Enrollment 25,300 (UG 18,000; GR 7,300)
Jewish 1,500 (UG 1,200; GR 300)

Univ. of Kansas Hillel Foundation
Kansas Union, Room 429
Lawrence, KS 66045
(785) 749-5390
Fax: (785) 749-5397 (Administration)
E-mail: hillel@ukans.edu
Web: www.ukans.edu/~hillel

Steve Jacobson, Director
Susan Shafer-Landau, Interim and Development Director
Dana Blecher, Jewish Campus Service Corps Fellow

 Jewish Studies
6 courses.

 Study in Israel
Study abroad credit available; Jerusalem Fellowships available.

 Kosher Food
Holidays, occasional Shabbat dinners, and vegetarian dining alternatives throughout Lawrence. Kosher meat available in Kansas City (40 minutes).

 Housing
Jewish Residence: Hillel House (6 students).

ON CAMPUS

Jewish students are very actively involved on the KU campus. Hillel works with the Jewish Student Council, HawkPac, the Jewish Students Artist coalition, the Jewish Law Student Association, the Jewish Graduate Association, Jewish Feminists of KU, KU Jewish Appeal, KU Tzedakah Project, Koach (Conservative), KU Chai (Chabad), and Eco-Jews. Three Jewish fraternities are on campus, and KU students participate in national Jewish student conferences.

Hillel's very active program includes political and social activity on campus and in the community, holiday celebrations, graduate social events, a community seder, and programs co-sponsored with other groups and academic departments. Hillel co-sponsored a discussion by author Grace Paley, with the Hall Center for the Humanities, and an Israeli Film Festival with Linguistics Department, among other such endeavors.

The Lawrence and Kansas City Jewish communities are very supportive, and there is strong faculty support for the program. Hillel has a good relationship with the campus ministries.

"The Hillel at KU is a comfortable and open community and operates with a variety of interest groups. There is something for everyone, and activities every week. Hillel takes advantage of relations with other groups on campus and co-sponsors many programs. The university administration is supportive of Jewish interests, as are the professors and the community as a whole. Jewish faculty are very involved in Hillel and in Jewish campus life."

Beth Ackerman, recent graduate

WICHITA STATE UNIVERSITY

Enrollment 17,000

Hillel at Wichita State University
c/o Department of Psychology
1845 N. Fairmount, Box 34
Wichita, KS 67260
(316) 689-3823

Professor Gary Greenberg, Advisor

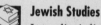

KENTUCKY

UNIVERSITY OF KENTUCKY

Enrollment 24,000
Jewish 200

Jewish Student Organization/Hillel Foundation
Box 613, University Station
Lexington, KY 40506
(606) 257-7531
(606) 278-2530
(606) 269-0908
Fax: (606) 323-1027
E-mail: acantor@ca.uky.edu

Dr. Austin Cantor, Director
Jerry Guttman, Program Coordinator

 Jewish Studies
Interdisciplinary minor in Jewish studies. Courses include Hebrew language, literature, religion, history, culture, and philosophy.

Study in Israel
Summer interships.

ON CAMPUS

The UK JSO/Hillel provides services to students enrolled in the several universities in the central Kentucky area. Most programming is social and educational.

Home hospitality is offered in the local Jewish community. Students are welcome to attend services and events at the local Reform and Conservative synagogues and in the events sponsored by the Central Kentucky Jewish Federation.

UNIVERSITY OF LOUISVILLE

Enrollment 22,000
Jewish 300

Hillel Foundation
University of Louisville
Interfaith Center
Louisville, KY 40292
(502) 852-6598
E-mail: armich01@ulkyvm.louisville.edu
Web: www.louisville.edu/interfaith/hillel/

Adrienne Michels, Director

 Jewish Studies
Some religious courses and a Holocaust class.

 Kosher Food
Kosher food is available locally.

ON CAMPUS
The local Jewish community is very supportive and provides home hospitality for Shabbat and High Holidays. Good relationship with the campus ministry. Commuter campus.

LOUISIANA

LOUISIANA STATE UNIVERSITY

Enrollment 40,000 (UG 30,000; GR 10,000)
Jewish 130

Hillel at LSU
c/o Jewish Federation of Greater Baton Rouge
3354 Kleinert Avenue
Baton Rouge, LA 70806
(225) 387-9744
Fax: (225) 387-9487
E-mail: lsuhillel2@aol.com

Barbara Minsky, Director
Professor Paul Aahron, Faculty Advisor

Jewish Studies
Minor. Interdisciplinary within the College of Arts and Sciences, requiring 12 hours of course work. Courses have included: Introduction to Judaism, Intro-

duction to the Holocaust, Introductory Hebrew, and Seminar in Literature of the Holocaust. Through a grant from the Louisiana Higher Educational Quality Support Fund, the Jewish Studies minor has added to the LSU library more than $40,000 worth of Judaica, making it the largest collection in the state; it has also sponsored a conference on Louisiana diaspora peoples (Jews, Cajuns, and African Americans). Speakers have included writer Steve Stern, folklorist Howard Schwartz, and Professor Nehemia Polen. Professor Rodger Kamenetz, Director; (504) 388-2984; kamenetz@aol.com.

 Kosher Food
Locally available.

ON CAMPUS
Hillel holds weekly lunchtime meetings. The local Jewish community is very supportive of Jewish student activities and provides home hospitality. Louisiana State's program for Jewish students is a service of the local Federation.

LOUISIANA TECHNICAL UNIVERSITY

Enrollment 10,000
Jewish 16

Jewish Student Organization
c/o Department of Physics
Louisiana Technical University
Ruston, LA 71272
(318) 257-4670
(318) 257-3293
E-mail: witriol@latech.edu

Professor Norman Witriol, Advisor
Professor Bill Friedman, Advisor

LOYOLA UNIVERSITY

Enrollment 5,600
Jewish 75

New Orleans Hillel Center
912 Broadway
New Orleans, LA 70118
(504) 866-7060
Fax: (504) 861-8909
E-mail: hillel@mailhost.tcs.tulane.edu
Web: www.tulane.edu/~hillel/

Rabbi Jeffrey Kurtz-Lendner, Executive Director
Ashley Klapper, Program Director
Scott Pranis, Jewish Campus Service Fellow

Jewish Studies
1–2 courses a year.

 Kosher Food
At Tulane.

ON CAMPUS

Loyola's Jewish students are served by the New Orleans Hillel Center based at Tulane University.
See listing for Tulane University.

NORTHEAST LOUISIANA UNIVERSITY

Enrollment 11,000
Jewish 15

Jewish Student Organization
c/o Rabbi David Kline
B'nai Israel Congregation
2400 Orell Place
Monroe, LA 71201
(318) 387-0731
Fax: (318) 387-0730
E-mail: hikline@alpha.nlu.edu
Web: www.shamash.org/reform/uahc/la/la002

Rabbi David Kline, Advisor

Jewish Studies

Introduction to Old Testament courses taught by Rabbi Kline and others; Legal Material in Old Testament taught by Rabbi Kline.

ON CAMPUS

The local community is very supportive of Jewish students at NLU, offers home hospitality for holidays, and can provide teaching positions for qualified students.

TULANE UNIVERSITY AND NEWCOMB COLLEGE

Enrollment 11,265 (UG 6,627; GR 4,638)
Jewish 2,500 (UG 2,000; GR 500)

 New Orleans Hillel Center
912 Broadway
New Orleans, LA 70118
(504) 866-7060
Fax: (504) 861-8909
E-mail: hillel@mailhost.tcs.tulane.edu
Web: www.tulane.edu/~hillel/

Rabbi Jeffrey Kurtz-Lendner, Executive Director
Ashley Klapper, Program Director
Scott Pranis, Jewish Campus Service Fellow

Jewish Studies

B.A., 15 courses annually, plus independent studies in Jewish Studies and Hebrew; 24 classes listed in the catalog. The Tulane Jewish Studies Program is an interdisciplinary program offering courses in Jewish history, religious thought, literature, language, and culture. The program is guided by two principles: that the critical study of Jewish text and culture is integral to a liberal arts education, and that a student who completes a major in Jewish studies gains a broad knowledge of the Jewish tradition and the precise thinking skills needed for further education and career goals. Special guest lecturers. 2 full-time Jewish studies faculty, plus faculty in other departments. Jewish Studies, Jones Hall 210, Tulane University, New Orleans, LA 70118; (504) 865-5349; Jewishst@mailhost.tcs.tulane.edu.

The Tulane Howard-Tilton Memorial Library houses the Archives of the American Southern Jewish Community, which contains manuscripts and materials of the New Orleans Jewish community and other southern communities.

Study in Israel

Junior year/semester abroad at Hebrew University; Tulane Law School offers summer classes at Hebrew University.

Kosher Food

Hillel offers strictly kosher Shabbat and High Holiday dinners. Tulane University offers kosher-style meals, which are provided by the kosher division of Sodexho-Marriott Food Services located at Woldenberg Living Centre in New Orleans. However, while the Woldenberg Living Centre houses the entire operation in a kosher environment, and the food service staff is experienced in providing food service in accordance with strict Jewish dietary laws, there is currently no rabbinical supervision of the food preparation at Woldenberg Living Centre and therefore kashrut cannot be guaranteed.

The kosher meals are prepared and packaged at Woldenberg and presented in self-serve packages to Tulane. Once at Tulane, the rabbi of the New Orleans Hillel Center provides a rabbinical guarantee that the food supplied by Woldenberg is the food which is distributed as kosher by Sodexho-Marriott at Tulane University. Students are advised to consult with Hillel's rabbi for religious advice in regards to the optional supplementation with Tulane's standard food service.

ON CAMPUS

Tulane offers a comfortable atmosphere for Jewish students, with the entire campus closed on Yom Kippur. Students will also find a supportive local community.

Tulane Hillel welcomes Jewish undergraduate and graduate students from all backgrounds. Students lead a wide variety of programs including social, educational, cultural, social action, Holocaust commemoration, community service, and holiday programs at the Hillel center, on campus, and throughout the community. Groups affiliated with Hillel include TIPAC (Tulane Israel Public Affairs Committee), UJA (United Jewish Appeal), and JCRC (Jewish Community Relations Council), as well as Jewish law and medical student organizations. New Orleans Hillel offers a special leadership program for Jewish student leaders at Tulane through the Hillel National Campus Leadership Initiative, which is sponsored by Steven Spielberg's Righteous Persons Foundation. The Campus Leadership initiative offers special workshops on Jewish identity and leadership, professional mentorship opportunities, and other events for campus leaders who have not otherwise been involved in Jewish life on campus. Information about other programs and organizations on the local, national, and international levels is available at Hillel.

UNIVERSITY OF NEW ORLEANS

Enrollment 11,600 (UG 8,100; GR 3,500)
Jewish 200

New Orleans Hillel Center
912 Broadway
New Orleans, LA 70118
(504) 866-7060
Fax: (504) 861-8909
E-mail: hillel@mailhost.tcs.tulane.edu
Web: www.tulane.edu/~hillel/

Rabbi Jeffrey Kurtz-Lendner, Executive Director
Ashley Klapper, Program Director
Scott Pranis, Jewish Campus Service Fellow

Jewish Studies
1 or 2 courses offered annually.

Kosher Food
At Tulane.

ON CAMPUS
UNO is a public city university, and primarily a commuter campus. Most Jewish students are older, with families, and belong to local congregations. Jewish students are encouraged to join with Tulane Hillel students in a wide range of Jewish activities.

UNO is served by the New Orleans Hillel Foundation at Tulane University. See listing for Tulane University.

BATES COLLEGE

Enrollment 1,630
Jewish 100

B'nai B'rith Hillel
c/o Temple Shalom
74 Bradman Street
Auburn, ME 04210
(207) 786-4201
Fax: (207) 786-4202
E-mail: sberkowi@bates.edu

Rabbi Douglas D. Weber, Advisor

Jewish Studies
3 courses of related interest (Holocaust history, post-biblical Jewish literature, etc.) offered on an irregular basis.

Study in Israel
Permission to receive credit for Israel study from non-Bates programs must be granted by the individual department; some are flexible, some are not. Students must persevere.

Kosher Food
Frozen meals are available on request; vegetarian dining alternatives.

BOWDOIN COLLEGE

Enrollment 1,521
Jewish 150

Bowdoin Jewish Students Organization
Bowdoin College
Brunswick, ME 04011
(207) 725-3669

Howard Burgwell, Director of Student Activities

Jewish Studies
Courses in departments of Religion, English, and History.

Study in Israel
Junior year abroad.

Kosher Food
Vegetarian dining alternatives. BJO brunches on request.

ON CAMPUS
Bowdoin holds an annual designated lecture on any subject or issue of Jewish interest.

COLBY COLLEGE

Enrollment 1,800
Jewish 175

Colby Hillel
Student Activities Office
Colby College
Waterville, ME 04901
(207) 872-3183
Fax: (207) 872-3744
Web: www.colby.edu/hillel/

Howard Lupovitch, Advisor
Rabbi Raymond Krinsky, Advisor

Jewish Studies

A new department now offers a minor in Jewish Studies. This department will soon offer a major in Jewish studies as well.

Study in Israel

Junior year abroad; January program on Ancient and Modern Israel, in conjunction with Ben-Gurion University of the Negev.

Kosher Food

Frozen meals are available on request in dining hall; vegetarian dining alternatives; dormitory cooking facilities.

Housing

None. Provisions for housing can be made if necessary.

ON CAMPUS

Colby College is very supportive of Jewish campus life, and considers Jewish holy days in planning its academic schedule. The university provides funds for an annual lecture by a prominent Jewish speaker, such as Amos Oz and Ambassador Rabinovich, as well as for a speaker for the Holocaust. The president of the college and his wife often attend Colby Hillel programs. Colby Hillel sponsors a large Passover seder with students, professors and their families and kiddush on Friday evenings. Hillel also co-sponsors programs with Jewish students at Bates College and Bowdoin College.

"Colby's Jewish community is gaining strength with a new Judaic studies program and increased funding. As a student-led community, incoming freshman must be active and prepared to assume leadership roles."

Eric Lantzman, '01

UNIVERSITY OF MAINE

Enrollment 10,000
Jewish 150

Hillel Foundation
c/o Dr. William Small
Little Hall, Room 214
University of Maine
Orono, ME 04469
(207) 581-2095

Dr. William Small, Advisor

Study in Israel

The University will accept credits for study in Israel.

Kosher Food

Vegetarian dining alternatives.

ON CAMPUS

Jewish students meet for holiday, educational, and social activities according to interest. There is an active Jewish community in Bangor.

MARYLAND

BALTIMORE HEBREW UNIVERSITY

Enrollment 1,200
Jewish 1,000

5800 Park Heights Avenue
Baltimore, MD 21215
(410) 578-6900
Fax: (410) 578-6940
E-mail: bhu@bhu.edu
Web: www.bhu.edu

Dr. Robert O. Freedman, President
Dr. Barry M. Gittlen, Graduate Dean
Dr. George Berlin, Undergraduate Dean
Karen Bernstein, Director, Baltimore Institute of Jewish Communal Service

Jewish Studies

35 courses; B.A. The Joseph and Rebecca Meyerhoff Center for Jewish Studies includes 8 full-time professors, as well as part-time faculty, who teach approximately 1,000 students annually. The Center has 3 endowed Chairs and a program in Israel. Organized as an interdepartmental program, Jewish Studies offers courses in Hebrew language, Jewish history, Jewish thought, Bible, rabbinics, Jewish literature, and Yiddish. In addition, the Jewish Studies Program organizes regular conferences, lectures, and symposia on important issues in Jewish Studies.

Study in Israel

Full year, semester, and summer programs. The University of Maryland sponsors a spring semester in Israel at Tel Aviv University, which is open to students at colleges and universities in Maryland. Study Abroad Office: (301) 314-7746; studyabr@deans.umd.edu.

Kosher Food

Full kosher meal plan (19 meals) at Hillel Jewish Student Center. Shabbat and partial meal plans available.

Housing

University housing priority for dorms near Hillel for full-time participants in Hillel kosher meal plan. Hillel will help match students together by Jewish observance if requested.

ON CAMPUS

Jewish life at the University of Maryland is active, vibrant, and diverse. Administration and faculty are supportive of Jewish issues, and Jewish interests are addressed regularly in the campus newspaper and other public forums. The University's main library houses a vast Judaica collection, including more than 70,000 volumes, as well as a music, video, and art collection. The 7,000-volume collection of Rabbi Max Gruenewald, which was donated by the Leo Baeck Institute, were written by German Jewish scholars or are about German Jewry. Books are available on interlibrary loan to any library in the Maryland public university system. Proximity to Washington, D.C., enables students to participate in a variety of internships at national Jewish organizations, as well as in national conferences and other events.

Maryland Hillel is housed in the new, state-of-the-art Ben and Esther Rosenbloom Center for Jewish Life, which offers comfortable meeting and relaxation space for the thousands of Jewish students at Maryland and serves as a base of operations for the 16 Jewish student organizations on campus. The new Center, which was dedicated in fall 1998, has student offices, a coffee bar/cafe, a computer lab, a library, meeting rooms, a multipurpose room, a game room, an outdoor basketball court, a lounge with a large-screen cable TV, a chapel, and a kosher dining hall.

Hillel works closely with students in the Greek system, on North Campus, in the dorms, and in other places throughout the campus. Jewish students may take part in Jewish women's groups, an Israeli dance troupe, a Jewish *a cappella* singing group, and diverse social action, political, and cultural activities, as well as Reform, Conservative, and Orthodox student groups. Hillel offers classes of Jewish interest, from Torah and Talmud to Jewish philosophy and mysticism, as well as weekly speakers and an excellent Judaica library. A Chabad house is on campus. Hillel coordinates the Nathan and Pauline Mash Family Campus Leaders Initiative—a special, highly selective program for Jewish students who are campus leaders but who are not actively involved in Jewish campus life. This program provides discussions, retreats, and professional mentorship opportunities.

Maryland Hillel is 1 of 10 "Tzedek Hillel" Foundations across the country, an international public service effort devoted to transforming Hillel Foundations into campus communities focused on service, education, and social responsibility.

"My Big Brother, through the Hillel Big Brother, Big Sister program, helped me to find my way,.He pointed me towards the Greek Jewish Council (GJC), an organization for Jewish fraternity and sorority members, which he had helped to create with Hillel."

Dan Margolis, junior

"Hillel has given so much to me already. The leadership abilities I have acquired will be of great benefit for the future, and the friendships I have formed are priceless. Hillel does something indeed incredible: it plants the seeds for tomorrow's leaders."

Abbie Hirsh, sophomore

Served by Hillel of Greater Baltimore.

CATONSVILLE COMMUNITY COLLEGE

Enrollment 8,500
Jewish 800

Jewish Student Association
c/o Department of Sociology
Catonsville Community College
Catonsville, MD 21228
(410) 653-2265

Dr. Michael Sanow, Advisor

Kosher Food

Vegetarian dining alternatives.

ON CAMPUS

Students participate in Baltimore-area intercampus programming.

Catonsville Community College is served by Hillel of Greater Baltimore; David Raphael, Executive Director.

FROSTBURG STATE UNIVERSITY

Enrollment 5,300
Jewish 120

Hillel at Frostburg State University
c/o Lane Center
Frostburg, MD 21532
(301) 687-4117
Fax: (301) 687-4784
E-mail: eschlegel@frostburg.edu

Professor Keith Schlegel, Advisor
Professor Ellen Grolman Schlegel, Advisor

 Study in Israel
Frostburg does not have an established program to Israel, but study abroad in Israel can be arranged on an individual basis.

Kosher Food
Passover foods are available at the dining hall during Passover.

ON CAMPUS
Hillel on the FSU campus offers the resident students social and educational opportunities. The advisors open their home on holidays to ensure that the students who can't travel home have a place to observe the holidays with their campus family.

GOUCHER COLLEGE

Enrollment 1,000
Jewish 250

 Goucher College Hillel
1021 Dulaney Road
Baltimore, MD 21204
(410) 653-2265 ext. 14
Fax: (410) 653-7809

Rabbi Rachel Hertzman, Campus Rabbi
Joel Lynn, Director

Jewish Studies
5 courses. Joint program: Baltimore Hebrew University; minor in Judaic Studies.

Study in Israel
A program is in place with Hebrew University in Jerusalem.

Kosher Food
The new, completely refurbished kosher dining hall has become one of the most popular places on campus for dining.

ON CAMPUS
Goucher College has an active Jewish Student Association that offers a full range of social, cultural, political, and religious activities. The new Jewish Student Center opened in 1995, and is conveniently located on Goucher's beautiful suburban campus. The Center provides lounge space, a library, a patio, a fireplace, an audio-visual center, programming space, and the campus's kosher dining program.

The JSA office on campus coordinates programs with nearby colleges. The college is supportive of Jewish student activities.

Jewish students at Goucher College are served by Hillel of Greater Baltimore.

JOHNS HOPKINS UNIVERSITY

Enrollment 9,000 (UG 3,600; GR 5,400)
Jewish 800 (UG 600; GR 200)

 Hopkins Hillel
Hopkins Hillel Office
3301 W. Charles Street
Baltimore, MD 21208
(410) 516-0333
(410) 516-0774
Fax: (410) 516-0797 or 516-4703
E-mail: hophillel@jhunix.hef.jhu.edu

Rabbi Joseph Katz, Campus Rabbi
Stuart Diamonto-Cohen, Director
Shelly Richelson, Jewish Campus Service Corps Fellow

 Jewish Studies
19 courses; B.A., M.A., Ph.D.

Kosher Food
Jewish Student Center offers several meal plans, including daily and Shabbat meals at the same price as the regular dining program.

 Housing
No.

ON CAMPUS
Hopkins's very active Jewish Student Association offers a full range of social, political, cultural, and educational programs, including informal classes and programs coordinated with activities at nearby colleges. The Jewish Student Center, which is conveniently located on the campus, was recently renovated and now provides space for a lounge, a synagogue, a library, programming, an audio-visual center, a recreation area, and a kosher dining program.

Hopkins Hillel is served by the Regional Center, Hillel of Greater Baltimore (bhillel@erols.com).

LOYOLA COLLEGE

Enrollment 3,075
Jewish 35

> Hillel of Greater Baltimore
> 1515 Reisterstown Road
> Baltimore, MD 21208
> (410) 653-2265
> E-mail: abujake@juno.com

> **David Raphael,** Director, Hillel of Greater Baltimore

 Jewish Studies
1 course.

ON CAMPUS

Occasional on-campus programming. Students participate in Baltimore-area intercampus programming as well as some on-campus programming.

Loyola's Jewish students are served by Hillel of Greater Baltimore.

MONTGOMERY COLLEGE

Enrollment 22,000
Jewish 2,000

> Jewish Student Association
> Montgomery College
> Psychology Department
> Rockville, MD 20850
> (301) 279-5238

> **Professor Len Rosenbaum,** Advisor

Jewish Studies
2 courses on the Holocaust from the History and English Departments, respectively, History of the Holocaust, and Literature of the Holocaust. Each spring, to commemorate the Holocaust, the College sponsors a 2-hour program featuring a survivor panel, a candlelighting ceremony, and remarks on the theme of the program. Themes have included "Resistance" and "Children During the Holocaust." Dr. Myrna Goldenberg, Department of English; (301) 279-7417; myrnag@umd5.umd.edu.

ON CAMPUS

Weekly programming. 2-year commuter college.

PEABODY INSTITUTE OF MUSIC

Enrollment 625
Jewish Few

> Hillel of Greater Baltimore
> 1515 Reisterstown Road
> Baltimore, MD 21208
> (410) 516-8439
> (410) 653-2265

ON CAMPUS

While pursuing their studies at this world-renowned institute, Jewish students are able to maintain a quality Jewish life through Peabody's proximity to Johns Hopkins University and its active Jewish student community.

See listing for Johns Hopkins University.

PRINCE GEORGE'S COMMUNITY COLLEGE

Enrollment 12,500
Jewish 20

> c/o University of MD Hillel
> 7612 Mowett Lane, Box 187
> College Park, MD 20740
> (301) 422-6200
> Fax: (301) 468-3422
> Web: www.tamos.net/~hillel

> **Professor Alan Schultz,** Advisor

Prince George's CC is served by an outreach program of Hillel of Greater Washington—Hillel at the University of Maryland, under the auspices of the Washington, D.C., Regional Center, Hillel of Greater Washington.

SALISBURY STATE UNIVERSITY

Enrollment 6,048
Jewish 100

> Jewish Student Association
> Box 3032
> Salisbury State University
> Salisbury, MD 21801-6860
> (410) 548-2883
> (410) 542-4900 ext. 21

> **Dean Mescon,** Advisor

ON CAMPUS

The active and growing Jewish Student Association participates in Baltimore intercampus programming.

Jewish students at Salisbury State University are served by Hillel of Greater Baltimore.

ST. MARY'S COLLEGE OF MARYLAND

Enrollment 1,400
Jewish 100

Hillel
c/o Dr. Rachel Myerwitz
St. Mary's College
Department of Biology
St. Mary's, MD 20686
(301) 862-0373
E-mail: rmyerwitz@osprey.smcm.edu

Dr. Rachel Myerwitz, Advisor

TOWSON STATE UNIVERSITY

Enrollment 15,400 (UG 9,500; GR 5,900)
Jewish 1,500

Hillel of Towson University
Media Center, Room 203
Towson University
Towson, MD 21252
(410) 830-4671
Fax: (410) 830-4364
E-mail: brenner@saber.towson.edu

Becky Brenner, Director
Joseph Katz, Campus Rabbi

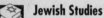 **Jewish Studies**
10 courses; Jewish Studies minor; several Hebrew courses offered each semester. 1 course a semester taught by a faculty member from Baltimore Hebrew University.

 Study in Israel
Credits accepted for study in Israel.

 Kosher Food
A kosher meal plan is available at the same cost as the regular meal plan.

ON CAMPUS
Towson State has a very active group, offering a wide variety of social, cultural, and political programming. By far the most popular event at Towson is the biweekly coffeehouse known as the B-Scene. Students have also enjoyed outdoor nature hikes, a Shabbat in the woods, and periodic Shabbat dinners in students' apartments. Although there is no Hillel building, Hillel participates in many campuswide events in order to be more visible and more accessible to all students.

"Hillel has allowed me to socialize with other Jewish students on campus and the [Hillel] board members that I work with may well become friends of mine for life. It's been the first group that I have been a part of in which everyone wants to work to make it a success."

Paul Snyder, junior

Jewish students at Towson State are served by Hillel of Greater Baltimore.

UNITED STATES NAVAL ACADEMY

Enrollment 4,040
Jewish 60

Office of the Chaplain
US Navy United States Naval Academy
Mitscher Hall
Annapolis, MD 21402
(410) 293-1100
Fax: (410) 293-4809
E-mail: elson@nada.navy.mil

Rabbi Irving A. Elsom, Jewish Chaplain

 Jewish Studies
Hebrew classes. Bar/bat mitzvah training.

 Study in Israel
Summer tour.

Kosher Food
Jewish Midshipmen's Club provides kosher food for holidays and occasional meals.

ON CAMPUS
The Jewish Midshipmen's Club is a highly active student-led group. Jewish midshipmen gather weekly to meet and have dinner. Programming includes speakers, professional development, concerts, Shabbatonim (retreats), and festival celebrations. Some midshipmen perform community service locally and in the D.C. area (including the U.S. Holocaust Memorial Museum). Students plan an annual Dance Extraordinaire in late autumn around a football game, with a tailgate party, a dance, and speakers. The event is well attended by students from other colleges and universities in the region. Other annual events include a large Passover seder, which is open to Academy and community members, and educational programs that cover topics such as the Holocaust and Israel. The Club also sponsors and conducts a trip to Israel every spring break. This trip is open to all students and it offers a unique opportunity for interfaith dialogue.

The Naval Academy has a full-time rabbi and a very supportive local community. Students may elect to participate in a program that matches each student with a local sponsor family. Religious services are offered on Sunday mornings during the summer for students.

The chapel also houses an educational display, which boasts a Holocaust sefer Torah and mementos from the careers of prominent Jewish Navy officers, including Commodore Uriah P. Levy (who, in the 19th century, was instrumental in outlawing flogging), Academy alumni Admiral Hyman Rickover (father of the nuclear navy), and Albert Michelson (who accurately measured the speed of light, thus becoming the first American to win the Nobel Prize in physics).

UNIVERSITY OF MARYLAND—BALTIMORE

Enrollment 4,560
Jewish 800

Hillel of Greater Baltimore
1515 Reisterstown Road
Baltimore, MD 21208
(410) 653-2265
(410) 706-8044
Fax: (410) 653-7809
E-mail: rkatz@umbc.edu

Rabbi Joseph Katz, Campus Rabbi
Judith Geller, Director, Graduate and Professional
Services (GAP)

ON CAMPUS

UMAB students may participate in one of the three professional student groups—the Jewish Law Students Association, the Jewish Medical Students Association, or the Jewish Social Work Students Association—or in joint Jewish Graduate Network programs. The Network sponsors monthly student dinners, a Graduate Chavurah the first and third Friday of every month, and a number of social programs.

Jewish students at the University of Maryland—Baltimore are served by Jewish College Services through the intercampus Jewish Graduate Network at 1515 Reisterstown Road, Baltimore; David Raphael, Executive Director.

UNIVERSITY OF MARYLAND—BALTIMORE COUNTY

Enrollment 7,739 (UG 6,300; GR 1,439)
Jewish 1,000

Hillel Jewish Student Community
University of Maryland—Baltimore County
Baltimore, MD 21250
(410) 455-1329
Fax: (410) 455-1097

Jeremy Benjamin, Campus Director
Shira Korman, Jewish Campus Service Corps Fellow
Rachel Hertzman, Campus Rabbi
Joseph Katz, Campus Rabbi

 Jewish Studies
7 or more courses offered each semester from among 20+ Judaic Studies and Hebrew courses; Jonathan Finkelstein, Director, Judaic Studies Program.

 Study in Israel
The University offers credits for study in Israel.

Kosher Food
Vegetarian dining alternatives; dormitory cooking facilities. Kosher deli available in campus pub.

ON CAMPUS

Informal classes and social, educational, religious, and cultural activities. Weekly Beit Cafe program. Students participate in Baltimore-area intergroup programming.

Jewish students at University of Maryland, Baltimore County are served by the Hillel of Greater Baltimore; David Raphael, Executive Director.

UNIVERSITY OF MARYLAND—COLLEGE PARK

Enrollment 27,000 (UG 21,000; GR 6,000)
Jewish 6,000

Ben and Esther Rosenbloom Hillel Student Center
7612 Mowatt Lane, Box 187
College Park, MD 20740
(301) 422-6200
Fax: (301) 422-4455
E-mail: info@hillelmd.org
Web: www.hillelmd.org

Scott Brown, Executive Director
Michael Scheinberg, Program Director
Jennifer Zukerman, Development Director
Katy Goldwater, Jewish Campus Service Corps Fellow
Stacy Blumenthal, Jewish Campus Service Corps Fellow
Roz Kram, Dining Coordinator

Jewish Studies
35 courses; B.A. The Joseph and Rebecca Meyerhoff Center for Jewish Studies includes 8 full-time professors, as well as part-time faculty, who teach approximately 1,000 students annually. The Center has 3 endowed chairs and a program in Israel. Organized as an interdepartmental program, Jewish Studies offers courses in Hebrew language, Jewish history, Jewish thought, Bible, rabbinics, Jewish literature, and Yiddish. In addition, the Jewish Studies Program organizes regular

conferences, lectures, and symposia on important issues in Jewish Studies. Contact Professor Bernard Cooperman, the Director of the Program, at (301) 405-4975.

Study in Israel

Full year, semester, and summer programs. The University of Maryland sponsors a spring Semester in Israel at Tel Aviv University, which is open to students at colleges and universities in Maryland. Study Abroad Office: (301) 314-7746; studyabr@deans.umd.edu.

Kosher Food

Full kosher meal plan (19 meals) at Hillel Jewish Student Center. Shabbat and partial meal plans available.

Housing

University housing priority for dorms near Hillel for full-time participants in Hillel kosher meal plan.

ON CAMPUS

Jewish life at the University of Maryland is active, vibrant, and diverse. Administration and faculty are supportive of Jewish issues, and Jewish interests are addressed regularly in the campus newspaper and other public forums. The University's main library houses a vast Judaica collection, including more than 70,000 volumes, as well as a music, video, and art collection. The 7,000-volume collection of Rabbi Max Gruenewald, which was donated by the Leo Baeck Institute, consists of works written by German Jewish scholars and books about German Jewry. Books are available on interlibrary loan to any library in the Maryland public university system. Proximity to Washington, D.C., enables students to participate in a variety of internships at national Jewish organizations, as well as in national conferences and other events.

Maryland Hillel is housed in a modern building that offers a dining hall with a full kosher meal plan, a game room, outdoor basketball and volleyball courts, an auditorium, a sukkah, and a small synagogue. A new, state-of-the-art Jewish student center on campus will be constructed in the immediate future, with the support of the Ben and Esther Rosenbloom family.

Some 15 Jewish student groups are on campus. Hillel works closely with students in the Greek system, on North Campus, in the dorms, and in other places throughout the campus. Jewish students may take part in Jewish women's groups, an Israeli dance troupe, and diverse social action, political, and cultural activities, as well as Reform, Conservative, and Orthodox student groups. Hillel offers classes of Jewish interest, from Torah and Talmud to Jewish philosophy and mysticism, as well as weekly speakers and an excellent Judaica library. A Chabad house is on campus. Hillel's Nathan and Pauline Mash Family Campus Leaders Initiative is a special, highly selective program for Jewish campus life. The program provides discussions, retreats, and professional mentorship opportunities.

"You can be Jewish on campus and feel good about it."

Jared Farber, junior

"It's easy to be Jewish here if you want to be. There are readily accessible ways to get involved."

David Plotinsky, senior

WASHINGTON COLLEGE

Enrollment 900
Jewish 30

Hillel
Washington College
300 Washington Avenue
Chestertown, MD 21620
(410) 778-7886
Fax: (410) 810-7108
E-mail: steven-cades@washcoll.edu

Dr. Steven Cades, Advisor

Kosher Food

A vegetarian menu is available for all dining service meals. Kosher-for-Passover meals are provided on request by prior arrangement.

ON CAMPUS

Washington College is a private, nonreligious 4-year liberal arts school located on Maryland's eastern shore. It is equidistant from Philadelphia, Baltimore, and Washington, D.C., and from the smaller communities of Easton and Annapolis, Maryland, and Newark and Dover, Delaware. Students may participate in the Jewish life of any of these cities. The most frequent off-campus events include trips to the U.S. Holocaust Memorial Museum in Washington and social gatherings of the larger Hillels at the University of Maryland and the University of Delaware.

Hillel at Washington College is necessarily small and largely student-driven. Students with leadership skills will find ample opportunity to be of service to the student body, Jewish and otherwise.

The annual Hillel-sponsored community seder is attended by Jewish students and faculty, and by many members of the larger college and local communities as well. Hillel is well supported by the college and its alumni, and sponsors occasional other social and cultural events as its members wish.

WESTERN MARYLAND COLLEGE

Enrollment 1,700 (UG 1,200; GR 500)
Jewish 50

Jewish Student Union
Western Maryland College
2 College Hill
Westminster, MD 21157
(410) 653-2265
E-mail: abujake@juno.com

David Raphael, Director, Hillel of Greater Baltimore

Kosher Food

A vegetarian menu is available for all dining service meals. Kosher-for-Passover meals are provided on request, by prior arrangement.

Jewish students at Western Maryland College are served by Hillel of Greater Baltimore.

MASSACHUSETTS

AMHERST COLLEGE

Enrollment 1,600
Jewish 250

Amherst Hillel Foundation
108 Chapin Hall
Amherst, MA 01002
(413) 542-8270
(413) 585-2754
Fax: (413) 585-2754

Rabbi Edward Feld, Director
Louise Krieger, Coordinator

Jewish Studies

10 courses; B.A. available as part of Five College Consortium.

Study in Israel

Students may participate in a variety of programs at Israeli universities.

Kosher Food

Amherst's Food Services provides full vegetarian dining options. Students prepare weekly Shabbat meals. Kosher meat dinners may be ordered through Dining Services.

ON CAMPUS

Amherst has a small but active Jewish campus community that works in close cooperation with campus groups at Smith and other area schools. Students and faculty actively shape the program, which includes an arts festival, classes, films, and an active program on behalf of Israel and oppressed Jewry. Amherst Hillel participates in the area's Five College Hillel Program. Strong links are maintained with nearby synagogues and Jewish communities.

BABSON COLLEGE

Enrollment 3,050 (UG 1,700; GR 1,350)
Jewish 800 (UG 550; GR 250)

Hillel Council of New England
233 Bay State Road
Boston, MA 02215
(617) 353-7210
(617) 239-4446
Fax: (617) 353-7214
E-mail: sandersj@babson.edu

Patti Sheinman, Assistant Director, Hillel Council
Janet Sanders, Advisor

ON CAMPUS

Jewish students at Babson participate in citywide programming with other Boston-area schools. The Hillel Council of New England runs the College Bond Program, which pairs Jewish college students with high school–aged students who have special needs, and developmentally delayed young adults. The program helps foster mutual understanding and encourages the spirit of Tzedakah. Students also participate in the Family Table, the first Jewish food pantry, also run by the Hillel of Greater Boston. Students help drive food to needy Jewish families and participate in benefits to collect food.

Babson College is served by the Hillel Council of New England.

BENTLEY COLLEGE

Enrollment 4,600 (UG 3,100; GR 1,500)
Jewish 200

Hillel Council of New England
233 Bay State Road
Boston, MA 02215
(617) 353-7210
Fax: (617) 353-7214
E-mail: psheinman@wn.net

Patti Sheinman, Assistant Director, Hillel Council

Kosher Food

Dormitory cooking facilities and monthly Shabbat dinners.

ON CAMPUS

Jewish students at Bentley participate in citywide programming with other Boston-area colleges.

Bentley College is served part-time by the Hillel Council of Greater New England. See listing for Babson College.

BOSTON COLLEGE

Enrollment 12,500 (UG 9,000; GR 3,500)
Jewish 150

Hillel Council of New England
233 Bay State Road
Boston, MA 02215
(617) 353-7210
Fax: (617) 353-7214

Patti Sheinman, Assistant Director, Hillel Council
Dr. Daniel Kirschner, Faculty Advisor

 Jewish Studies

11 courses. Jewish Studies courses are offered at Boston College through its Theology Department. All undergraduates are required to take a 2-semester sequence of Theology core courses. Options of interest to Jewish students include sections of Religious Quest, which compare Judaism to other religions, or of Biblical Heritage. Hebrew and upper-level courses specifically in Jewish Studies are taught by Prof. Ruth Langer and others. Professor Ruth Langer, Theology Department; (617) 551-8492; langerr@bc.edu.

Kosher Food
None.

ON CAMPUS

Monthly meetings, monthly bagel brunches, and interfaith seder. Regular activities with regional student council. Jewish students also participate in citywide programming with other Boston-area colleges through the Hillel Council of New England.

See listing for Babson College.

BOSTON UNIVERSITY

Enrollment 20,276 (UG 14,916; GR 5,360)
Jewish 4,000 (UG 3,000; GR 1,000)

 Boston University Hillel Foundation
233 Bay State Road
Boston, MA 02215
(617) 353-7200
Fax: (617) 353-7660
E-mail: rjp@bu.edu; jody@bu.edu
Web: www.web.bu.edu/HILLEL

Rabbi Joseph Polak, Executive Director
Nora Abrahamer, Assistant Director
Orna Siegel, Director of Student Activities
Michael Silbert, Development Associate

Jewish Studies

20–25 courses offered annually, 35–40 courses in catalog; B.A., M.A., Ph.D. Full range of Judaica courses, including Hebrew language and foreign study in Israel. Teaching in the Judaic Studies Program are two Nobel Prize winners: Elie Wiesel and Saul Bellow. Full range of lectures, symposia, conferences, and publications. Center for Judaic Studies, 745 Commonwealth Avenue, Boston, MA 02215; (617) 353-8096; stkatz@bu.edu.

Study in Israel

Junior year abroad, BU's program at Haifa University for undergraduates, and BU's master's programs in management at Ben-Gurion University. Students may also participate in year and summer programs in Israel and all over the world through BU or on independent programs. Hillel serves as a resource for hundreds of Israel tours, programs, internships, and volunteer/job opportunities.

Kosher Food

6 dinners and 6 lunches weekly. The University provides kosher meals at Hillel as part of the regular food plan. Vegetarian food and vegan options are also offered.

ON CAMPUS

Jewish students at Boston University are well integrated into all aspects of university life, and the university is generally supportive of religious needs. Students of all faiths are excused from class on holy days.

The University also sets a positive tone concerning relationships among the diverse campus groups. About 15 percent of the campus participates in fraternity/sorority life.

Boston University Hillel's very active, comprehensive program is based in a facility that is well located on campus, but events may take place anywhere on campus or in the community. Hillel facilitates strong community service programs, Israel action groups, a Holocaust Education Committee, 3 Graduate Student Groups, and the Hillel Student Board (social activities), as well as independent Orthodox, Conservative, Reform, and Sephardic groups.

Hillel regularly co-sponsors major conferences on social and ethical issues and on literature with the University. Several of these events have received national awards. Jewish faculty at BU include Elie Wiesel, Alicia Borinsky, Nancy Harrowitz, Steven Katz, Hillel Levine, Jeffrey Mehlman, Poet Laureate Robert Pinsky, and Uri Raanan, among others.

"BU is a welcoming and diverse community where many different racial and religious groups coexist with little difficulty."

Stephanie Berkowitz, senior

"Hillel has a very strong voice on campus. In 1994, classes were supposed to start on Rosh Hashanah and through the efforts of Hillel school was delayed until after the holiday. Many faculty are Jewish and are very understanding and accomodating about the Sabbath and holidays."

Melissa Zimmern, SMG '97

BRANDEIS UNIVERSITY

Enrollment 3,800 (UG 3,000; GR 800)
Jewish 2,350 (UG 2,000; GR 350)

Brandeis University Hillel Foundation
133/148 Usdan Student Center
Brandeis University
Waltham, MA 02254
(781) 736-3580
Fax: (781) 736-3582
E-mail: gladstone@brandeis.edu
Web: www.brandeis.edu/hillel/INDEX

Ora Gladstone, Associate Director
Cindy Spungin, Director of Student Activities

Jewish Studies
60 courses; B.A., M.A., Ph.D./Near Eastern and Judaic Studies Department. The Hornstein Graduate Program in Jewish Communal Service offers a 2-year master's degree program. Courses of Jewish content and interest are offered in other departments as well, including American Studies, Sociology, and Politics.

Study in Israel
Junior year abroad.

Kosher Food
The University provides full kosher board/vegetarian dining as part of the meal plan.

ON CAMPUS
Brandeis is the only Jewish-sponsored, non-sectarian, secular university in this hemisphere, and is closed for all major holidays, including all of Passover. Much of the student body is actively Jewish. Hillel offers a full range of social, cultural, educational, political, social service, and religious activities. More than 250 students attend the weekly communal Shabbat dinner. Currently there are 6 social service projects, an *a cappella* chorus (Manginah), an Israeli dance troupe (B'Yachad), the Hillel Theatre Group, a Jewish Women's Group (Nashim), the daily Beit Midrash, the weekly Study with a Buddy (chevruta) Program, the Brandeis Zionist Alliance, BIPAC, 2 newsletters, Holocaust Remembrance Week, 4 annual Shabbatonim, weekly Ongei Shabbat lectures, dances, parties, and much more! The Brandeis Jewish Education Program (an on-campus, independent Sunday school) and local congregations employ Brandeis students as teachers and bar/bat mitzvah tutors.

"I think that Brandeis University Hillel is a wonderful blanket organization that encompasses many clubs and activities that represent and service the entire Brandeis community, both Jewish and non-Jewish."

Eli Freedman, '02

"Even on a campus like Brandeis, Hillel has played an important role here. Between all the service coordination, social action projects, and social events, I've really enjoyed all of the activities that I've participated in."

Joshua Trunof, '99

"You can do anything here. There is such a wide range of opportunities to get involved; religiously, educationally, socially, and culturally. I've loved getting to know Jews from a variety of backgrounds. Regional Hillel events are great too; you get to meet students from colleges all over New England."

Sarah Chandler, '01

CLARK UNIVERSITY

Enrollment 1,900
Jewish 400

Clark University Hillel
950 Main Street, Box B28
Worcester, MA 01610-1477
(508) 793-7296
(508) 756-1543
Fax: (508) 798-0962
E-mail: hillel@black.clarku.edu

David Coyne, Advisor

Jewish Studies
20 courses; minor. Endowed Chair, the Sidney and Ralph Rose Professorship in Holocaust Studies and Modern Jewish History and Culture. Clark's Center for Holocaust Studies is in the process of developing the first doctoral program in Holocaust history in the United States, as well as an undergraduate program in Holocaust and genocide studies.

Study in Israel
Study abroad programs available.

Kosher Food
A kosher meal plan is being considered.

ON CAMPUS
Group meets weekly; joint programming with other groups on campus. Clark Hillel is strongly supported by the local community.

CURRY COLLEGE

Enrollment 1,210
Jewish 500

Hillel Council of New England
233 Bay State Road
Boston, MA 02215
(617) 353-7210
Fax: (617) 353-7214
E-mail: psheinman@wn.net

Patti Sheinman, Assistant Director, Hillel Council

 Kosher Food
Passover: by request only.

ON CAMPUS
Curry's learning disability program is a very important aspect of the college. Jewish students at Curry participate in citywide programming with other Boston-area colleges, and Curry College students have an opportunity to participate in the Regional Student Council.

Curry College is served as an outreach program of the Hillel Council of New England. See listing for Babson College.

EMERSON COLLEGE

Enrollment 2,200
Jewish 500

Hillel Council of New England
233 Bay State Road
Boston, MA 02215
(617) 824-8698
(617) 353-7210
Fax: (617) 353-7214
E-mail: psheinman@wn.net

Shayna Alexander, Director of Jewish Student Programming
Patti Sheinman, Assistant Director, Hillel Council

 Jewish Studies
2 courses. Independent study option.

 Study in Israel
Credit available for study in Israel.

 Kosher Food
Available by special arrangement.

ON CAMPUS
Emerson College Hillel is part of a consortium of service with Berklee School of Music and New England Conservatory of Music. Internships in Jewish media are available: Jewish cable TV, newspapers, magazines, theater, music, and advertising. Jewish students at Emerson also participate in citywide programming with other Boston-area colleges.

Emerson College is served part-time by the Hillel Council of New England. See listing for Babson College.

FITCHBURG STATE COLLEGE

Enrollment 3,400
Jewish 100

Jewish Student Union
Fitchburg State College
Percival Hall
Fitchburg, MA 01420
(508) 665-3244
E-mail: abernstein@fscvax.fsc.mass.edu

Professor Alan Bernstein, Advisor
Rabbi Miriam Spitzer, Advisor

 Study in Israel
Can be arranged.

 Kosher Food
Holidays: Daily kosher food can be arranged. Some dorm rooms have kitchen facilities.

ON CAMPUS
Nearby Boston and Boston-area campuses provide opportunities for FSU students to find Jewish community and activities. Limited program on campus.

See listing for Babson College.

FRAMINGHAM STATE COLLEGE

Enrollment 3,400

Hillel Club at FSC
100 State Street
Framingham, MA 01701
(508) 877-7875
(508) 626-4877

Professor Miller, Advisor
Cantor Scherr, Advisor

ON CAMPUS
Temple Israel in Natick, Massachusetts, is supportive of Jewish students at Framingham.

Served by Hillel Council of New England.

HAMPSHIRE COLLEGE

Enrollment 1,150
Jewish 200

Keshet
c/o Leadership Center
Box S.A.
Hampshire College
Amherst, MA 01002
(413) 582-5751
Fax: (413) 582-5584
E-mail: jducharme@hampshire.edu
Web: www.hampshire.edu

Jayne Ducharme, Advisor

Jewish Studies
5 courses at Hampshire; B.A. available as part of Five College Consortium.

Hampshire College formed a partnership with the National Yiddish Book Center in 1990 and provided land for the Center's new headquarters. The College and the Center have created a partnership to provide undergraduates with 1-year visiting fellowships—The Jeremiah Kaplan Fellowships—to study Jewish history and culture, drawing on the resources of both institutions. Kaplan Fellows take courses at any of the colleges in the Five College Consortium, and undertake a weekly 10-hour internship at the National Yiddish Book Center.

Study in Israel
Hampshire encourages international study and will easily incorporate study abroad into a student's academic program.

Kosher Food
Approximately half of Hampshire's students cook all meals for themselves in their living area where students will sometimes form groups to cook kosher meals together. Vegetarian dining alternatives are available.

ON CAMPUS
Keshet, like all student organizations at Hampshire College, is directed by students. This student interest changes the direction of the group each year. Recently, Keshet has sponsored weekly Erev Shabbat services on campus and the celebration of significant Jewish holidays, including a campuswide Passover seder. Jewish students also get support for their activities by working with students and staff at the nearby colleges.

HARVARD UNIVERSITY & RADCLIFFE COLLEGE

Enrollment 17,200 (UG 7,100; GR 10,100)
Jewish 4,500 (UG 1,500; GR 3,000)

Riesman Center for Harvard-Radcliffe Hillel
Rosovsky Hall
52 Mount Auburn Street
Cambridge, MA 02138
(617) 495-4696
Fax: (617) 864-1637
E-mail: hrhillel@hcs.harvard.edu
Web: www.hcs.harvard.edu/~hrhillel/

Dr. Bernard Steinberg, Director
Eva Gumprecht, Program Director

Jewish Studies
30 courses; B.A., M.A., Ph.D. Contact Professor Ruth R. Wisse, Director, Center for Jewish Studies, 6 Divinity Avenue, Cambridge, MA 02138; (617) 495-4326. Students may also take courses at the Harvard Divinity School.

Study in Israel
Junior year abroad.

Kosher Food
Harvard-Radcliffe Hillel offers 6 dinners and 1 lunch (no extra charge for undergraduates on board plan), as well as holiday meals. The kosher dining facilities serve more than 100 students each evening. Vegetarian dining alternatives are available, and kosher food is available locally. In addition, the freshman dining hall and many of the upper-class dining halls feature kosher refrigerators, toasters, and microwaves. There are also many kosher restaurants in Boston.

Housing
There is no special housing for observant Jewish students at Harvard, but the University makes provisions for students whose religious observance prohibits them from using the electronic entry system on Shabbat and holy days.

ON CAMPUS
The Harvard-Radcliffe Hillel community offers a very active social, cultural, educational, and religious program in a new facility well located on campus, Rosovsky Hall.

Harvard/Radcliffe Hillel's commitment to Building Unity Through Diversity, is reflected throughout its varied activities, which range from social events, study groups, and political activism to religious observance, faculty lectures, and graduate student programming.

Harvard-Radcliffe Hillel strives to be: 1) a community of inclusion, welcoming Jews of all backgrounds and enriching that community by enabling very different kinds of people to understand each other's points of view, clarify and deepen their own positions, and foster friendships that transcend personal ideology; 2) a community of learning, understanding the quest of Jewish identity as a lifelong process of learning and personal growth; 3) a community that cultivates leaders who love learning; and 4) a community that fosters a vital relationship to Israel as the most intense experiment in contemporary Jewish living.

The Coordinating Council, a 60-member, student-run group, governs undergraduate activities, and shapes programs and policies for Hillel. The council is comprised of 16 diverse committees, which create and assume responsibility for individual programs and events. Activities include drama and choir groups, a literary magazine and a newspaper, and Zionist groups as well as a broad spectrum of special-interest support groups and social action committees. Hillel often hosts four to five student-led programs each evening. Hillel also holds weekly events such as Israeli folk dancing, philanthropic activities for the homeless, and student-led discussions on current events. The Chai Graduate Student Council ensures that graduate students contribute to Hillel activities. Community building also occurs in the popular student lounge, where students study and relax among friends.

The pursuit of learning on all levels is an integral part of the program. Noncredit courses offered at Hillel's Institute of Jewish Studies range from 5 different levels of Talmud study to Hebrew and contemporary history and art. Distinguished teachers lead the courses each semester. Students also run a Beit HaMidrash program, where study partners meet weekly to examine and discuss Jewish texts. The Hillel Forum provides speakers who address current events and concerns. Finally, the Hillel library holds a rich collection of Jewish literature and maintains a Judaic reading room for the entire campus.

Harvard-Radcliffe Hillel offers a special, highly selective program for Jewish students who are campus leaders, but who have not been actively involved in Jewish campus life. The Gruss Leadership Development Project provides interactive lectures, a retreat, professional mentorship opportunities, and a seminar in Israel. JAGSS (the Jewish Adult and Graduate Student Society) is a vibrant and growing community that sponsors social events, outings, holiday celebrations, group learning sessions, and a variety of social action projects for those aged 22–30. Its members are an integral part of life at Hillel.

Religious activities reflect Harvard-Radcliffe Hillel's commitment to pluralism and tolerance. Rabbis from each movement are on the Hillel staff. Shabbat meals tie the 5 communities together. Holiday celebrations, often held in unison, also contribute to the sense of a single, united Jewish community.

Rabbi Ben-Zion Gold, Rabbi Harry Sinoff, and Rabbi David Starr serve as rabbinic advisors.

"Harvard-Radcliffe Hillel offers a rich and meaningful Jewish experience for students of all backgrounds. The University ensures that no student will be forced to take exams on their religious holiday. The Jewish Studies program is outstanding, with many prominent faculty in history, philosophy, literature, archaeology and theology offering courses on all levels. Many professors also teach classes, give lectures, or come to dinner as guests at Hillel."

David Andorsky, recent graduate

Served by Hillel Council of New England.

HEBREW COLLEGE

Enrollment 250
Jewish 238

Office of the President
43 Hawes Street
Brookline, MA 02446
(617) 278-4948
Fax: (617) 264-9264
E-mail: admissions@hebrewcollege.edu

Ilana Kobrin, Admissions and Recruitment Coordinator

Jewish Studies
All courses at Hebrew College are Jewish Studies courses. B.A., M.A., M. Jewish Studies, B.J.Ed., and M.J.Ed. in Jewish Education offered.

Study in Israel
Semester or summer study encouraged (appropriate credit will be granted).

Kosher Food
Dairy cafeteria open afternoons and evenings when classes are in session.

Housing
The College assists students in locating summer housing. Dormitory space is available for selected summer programs. Hebrew College is a commuter school. Most students live close to campus. The Registrar's Office assists students who are looking for housing.

ON CAMPUS

Located in the heart of Jewish Boston, Hebrew College is the home of the Jewish Music Institute and Wilstein Institute of Jewish Policy Studies. The 100,000-volume library includes a significant Japanese Judaica collection. The Hebrew College Student Organization plans programs during the academic year to enrich student life.

See listing under Specialized Educational Programs.

LESLEY COLLEGE

Enrollment 500
Jewish 200

Hillel Council of New England
233 Bay State Road
Boston, MA 02215
(617) 349-8929
Fax: (617) 353-7214
E-mail: psheinman@wn.net
Web: www.lesley.edu

Patti Sheinman, Assistant Director, Hillel Council
Dr. Carol Brandon, Faculty Advisor

 Jewish Studies
Occasional courses; Hebrew can be studied at an accredited institution and credits transferred.

Study in Israel
Credit granted for study in Israel/graduate program. Graduate program in Tel Aviv is in Expressive Arts Therapy.

Kosher Food
Vegetarian dining alternatives.

ON CAMPUS

Special Oneg Shabbats, with discussion of interesting topics. Jewish students at Lesley College participate in citywide programming with other Boston-area colleges.

Lesley College is served part-time by the Hillel Council of New England. See listing for Babson College.

MASSACHUSETTS BAY COMMUNITY COLLEGE

Enrollment 4,000
Jewish 200

Hillel
50 Oakland Street, Office 437
Wellesley, MA 02181
(617) 237-1100 ext. 2233
(508) 879-4879

Professor Myrna Jaspan, Advisor

 Jewish Studies
Integrated in other religious courses.

 Study in Israel
Individually arranged.

ON CAMPUS

Massachusetts Bay Community College has a small Jewish population with an active Hillel. Many of the students are Russian immigrants, both older and younger. All students are welcome at Brandeis, Wellesley College, and Babson Hillel events.

See listing for Babson College.

MASSACHUSETTS INSTITUTE OF TECHNOLOGY

Enrollment 9,800 (UG 4,500; GR 5,300)
Jewish 850

 MIT Hillel
Leventhal Center for Jewish Life at MIT Hillel
40 Massachusetts Avenue (W11)
Cambridge, MA 02139-4301
(617) 253-2982
Fax: (617) 253-3260
E-mail: hillel@mit.edu
Web: www.web.mit.edu/hillel/

Miriam Rosenblum, Director
Rabbi Joshua E. Plaut, Chaplain
Lisa Katz, Jewish Campus Service Corps Fellow

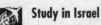 **Jewish Studies**
Joint program: Hebrew College; credit with Harvard and Wellesley.

Study in Israel
Summer, January intersession, and year programs.

Kosher Food
5 dinners and 1 lunch in Kosher Kitchen. Vegetarian dining alternatives as well as dormitory cooking facilities and kosher restaurants in area. Hillel sponsors Shabbat dinners and holiday meals.

Housing

Kosher living suites or groups in several dormitories.

ON CAMPUS

The Massachusetts Institute of Technology, situated on the banks of the Charles River in Cambridge, is known for its plethora of Nobel laureates, student hacks, and demanding academic environment. The Hillel at MIT acknowledges its special environment by encouraging students to participate in a stimulating social, cultural, and educational program as well as to develop Jewish applications to their work.

Hillel's test tube menorah and award-winning, student-designed sukkah are 2 examples of the unique community on campus.

The MIT Hillel Center, dedicated in 1994, provides a student lounge, classrooms, and a Judaic library and sanctuary. The Hillel Center is located in MIT's Religious Activities Center, which offers two kosher kitchens and dining and meeting rooms.

The student community is warm, supportive, and pluralistic. Active student leadership, the Jewish Learning Academy (which offers 6–8 courses a term), a strong program of community service, and several religious communities are highlights of the program. MIT's Israeli dancing attracts enthusiasts from throughout greater Boston. Since graduate students comprise more than half of the MIT population, the Hillel's "Graduate Hillel" group schedules its own diverse events, year-round, for these students. An annual feature of Hillel's program is the January Independent Activities Period, a 4-week term at MIT devoted to alternative learning. In past years Hillel has offered everything from pickle tastings to Yiddish, from shofar blowing lessons to bagel bakery tours.

MIT Hillel has received Hillel's national William Haber Award for Programs of Quality for the Jewish Campus Community, for "Electronic Communication and the Hillel Program: Prototype for Enhancing a Campus Hillel." This electronic communications system reaches Jewish students throughout the campus and serves as a network for discussion of topics of Jewish interest. Hillel cooperates with other Jewish student organizations on campus, such as MIT Students for Israel, the Sloan Student Organization, and the Israeli Student Government.

MIT excuses students for religious holidays. A number of Jewish staff and faculty are involved in Jewish campus life. There is 1 Jewish fraternity and 1 Jewish sorority.

"MIT is very comfortable, Hillel is well established, and the participation is generally good. Jewish campus activities are always well attended."

Michael Altman, junior

Served by Hillel Council of New England.

MOUNT HOLYOKE COLLEGE

Enrollment 1,850
Jewish 100

Jewish Student Union
Eliot House—Jewish Chaplaincy
Mount Holyoke College
South Hadley, MA 01075
(413) 538-2792
Fax: (413) 538-2127
E-mail: djacobso@mhc.mtholyoke.edu

Rabbi Devorah Jacobson, Jewish Chaplain

Jewish Studies

Special B.A.; 10 courses; Endowed Chair in Jewish Studies, joint program with U. Mass, Amherst, Smith, and Hampshire College; informal connection with Oxford Center for Hebrew Studies.

Study in Israel

Credit given for studies abroad.

Kosher Food

Kosher kitchen: food available at all times; dinners served on Wednesdays and Fridays.

ON CAMPUS

The Jewish students are an integral part of the larger multicultural, multifaith community on campus. The Jewish Student Union is a very active group with involvement in every aspect of Jewish life, whether social, spiritual, political, etc.

"The Jewish community at MHC is pretty small but extremely strong. We do a lot of activities (social and religious) and feel almost like a family. A large number of Jewish and Muslim students come every week to our Kosher/Hallal kitchen (to fit Jewish and Muslim dietary laws), but the delicious food attracts many students from other backgrounds as well. Usually, but not always, the Wednesday night speaker talks abut a topic related to Judaism or Islam. Our Jewish Student Union is part of the coalition of various cultural groups on campus.

"The administration is definitely supportive of Jewish interests and concerns. Our small Jewish Studies program offers a few classes each semester, but because of the Five College Consortium we can easily take classes at Smith, Amherst, Hampshire and UMass. About five Jewish faculty or staff are extremely involved in campus Jewish life. They are really friendly with students and make sure we have places to go for holidays. One dean hosts a wonderful break-the-fast every year for Yom Kippur, a woman in admissions invited all the Jewish stu-

dents to a party in her sukkah, and several professors have invited me to their seders.

"Mount Holyoke does a lot of work on being part of a multicultural community and differences are appreciated rather than devalued. I've found everyone I've met to be very interested in learning more about Judaism."

Natasha Domina, recent graduate

NEW ENGLAND CONSERVATORY OF MUSIC

Enrollment 750
Jewish 150

Hillel Council of New England
233 Bay State Road
Boston, MA 02215
(617) 353-7210
E-mail: psheinman@wn.net

Patti Sheinman, Assistant Director, Hillel Council

 Jewish Studies
Joint program with Tufts University.

 Kosher Food
Kosher food is available.

ON CAMPUS

The Conservatory is the home of the well-known Klezmer Conservatory Band. Jewish students at the New England Conservatory of Music are served as part of a consortium that includes Emerson College and Berklee College of Music. Part-time program.

Served by the Hillel Council of New England. See listing for Babson College.

NORTHEASTERN UNIVERSITY

Enrollment 17,400 (UG 11,000; GR 6,400)
Jewish 1,200

 Northeastern University Hillel
456 Parker Street
Boston, MA 02115
(617) 353-3937
(617) 353-3936
Fax: (617) 353-4231
E-mail: bmeltzer@lynx.neu.edu
Web: www.dac.neu.edu

Eydie Lieberman, Program Director
Adam Bovilsky, Jewish Campus Service Corps Fellow

 Jewish Studies
Minor available through Program of Jewish Studies; cross-registration with Hebrew College.

 Study in Israel
Junior year abroad. Co-op Education Department offers an Israel option.

 Kosher Food
Shabbat dinners and holiday meals. Kosher meals available in freshman dorms. Kosher food available locally.

 Housing
Limited housing at Hillel building. Kosher living arrangements can be made in university apartments.

ON CAMPUS

Hillel at Northeastern is the Jewish address on campus. Many programs are co-sponsored with the Spiritual Life Office, International Student Center, Diversity Committee, such as Walk for Hunger, AIDS Walk, Holocaust Awareness Week, and Diversity and Wellness Weeks. Hillel sponsors Friday night services with home-cooked dinners, holiday parties, social events, weekly meetings, dances, movie nights, visits to nursing homes, Israel programs, Passover meals, and much more. A pool table, Ping-Pong, 46" projection TV, VCR, and stereo in the Hillel building make it the place to hang out for both resident and commuter students.

SALEM STATE COLLEGE

Enrollment 6,400 (UG 5,600; GR 800)
Jewish 150

Hillel
Interfaith Center
Salem, MA 01970
(508) 741-4880
(508) 741-6000

Rabbi Samuel Kenner, Advisor

ON CAMPUS

Student-run program on campus. Temple Shalom in Salem welcomes students.

SIMMONS COLLEGE

Enrollment 1,200
Jewish 400

Hillel at Simmons
c/o Hillel Council of New England
233 Bay State Road
Boston, MA 02115
(617) 353-7210
Fax: (617) 353-7214
E-mail: psheinman@wn.net

Patti Sheinman, Assistant Director, Hillel Council

 Jewish Studies
2 courses/Joint Program: Hebrew College.

 Study in Israel
Credit for study in Israel.

 Kosher Food
Kosher kitchen, student-run co-op, on college board plan; part-time plans also available.

 Housing
Observant students live in Simmons Hall where special arrangements have been made for them.

ON CAMPUS

Students are active through bi-weekly meetings alternating with bi-weekly educational and social programs. Shabbat dinners, holiday parties, cooking classes, Israel week, dances, billiard parties, and Holocaust programming are all part of the ongoing Jewish life on campus.

Simmons College is served part-time by the Hillel Council of New England.

SMITH COLLEGE

Enrollment 2,800
Jewish 230

 Smith Hillel Foundation
Helen Hills Chapel
Northampton, MA 01063
(413) 585-2754
Fax: (413) 585-2794
E-mail: lkrieger@sophia.edu
Web: www.smith.edu/chapel/hillel

Rabbi Edward Feld, Director

 Jewish Studies
33 courses; minor; B.A. available as part of joint program with the Five College Consortium. The Program in Jewish Studies offers a range of courses in Jewish history, literature, thought, politics, and classical Hebrew language and literature. Special topics include regular offerings in mysticism, philosophy, and spirituality; the Holocaust; Israel, Zionism, and Middle Eastern Politics; women in Jewish history and rabbinic literature; contemporary Jewry; and Jewish-Christian and Black-Jewish relations.

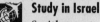 **Study in Israel**
Smith grants full credit for courses taken at all the major universities in Israel and has endowed funding for study in Israel.

Kosher Food
A kosher kitchen serves Friday night dinner and Passover meals. There is a kosher kitchen and dining area in one of the residence halls.

ON CAMPUS

Friday night dinners are special and popular at Smith, where there is a strong sense of community and a feeling of mutual support. Smith's active Jewish campus community works in close cooperation with campus groups at Amherst and other area schools. Students and faculty shape the program, which includes Shabbat dinners, holiday observances, lectures with major Jewish figures, discussions, classes, and many other activities. Every Tuesday the Hillel at Noon program provides an opportunity for informal discussion. Students also participate in an active interreligious program on campus. Smith students participate in programs of the area's Five College Hillel Foundation consortium, and there are strong links with nearby synagogues.

SUFFOLK UNIVERSITY

Enrollment 3,350 (UG 2,200; GR 1,150)
Jewish 250

Hillel Council of New England
233 Bay State Road
Boston, MA 02215
(617) 353-7210
Fax: (617) 353-7214
E-mail: psheinman@wn.net

Patti Sheinman, Assistant Director, Hillel Council

Jewish Studies
Courses in Holocaust studies.

ON CAMPUS

Suffolk's Jewish students are served part-time by the Hillel Council of New England, and participate in citywide activities with other Boston-area colleges.

See listing for Babson College.

TUFTS UNIVERSITY

Enrollment 6,400 (UG 4,800; GR 1,600)
Jewish 2,500 (UG 2,000; GR 500)

Tufts University Hillel Foundation
Granoff Family Hillel Center
Medford, MA 02155
(617) 627-3242
Fax: (617) 627-3044
E-mail: jsummit@emerald.tufts.edu
Web: www.tufts.edu/~hillel/

Rabbi Jeffrey Summit, Director
Debra Feldstein, Director of Development
Julie Roth, Program Director
Ari Gauss, Jewish Campus Service Corps/
Granoff-Steinhardt Fellow

 Jewish Studies

12 courses annually; 17 in catalog; B.A.; minor. Endowed Chair. The program in Judaic Studies is a full interdisciplinary program dealing with many aspects of the Jewish experience, from Sephardic tradition to Yiddish culture, from Talmud to the Holocaust, from ancient synagogues and Dead Sea Scrolls to music and film, from Genesis to Jewish women. The variety of offerings reflects the diversity of the core faculty, whose areas of expertise include German, English, and archaeology, as well as Hebrew and Judaic Studies. Selected courses in history, religion, political science, classics, Spanish, and world literature have been approved for the major and the minor. 7 full-time Jewish Studies faculty, all interdisciplinary except for the Hebrew instructor. Full range of courses in Hebrew language are available, taught by native Israeli instructors. Each year the program honors a student with the Joseph and Sara Stone Prize for excellence in Judaic Studies. Prof. Gloria J. Ascher and Prof. Joel Rosenberg, Directors, Program in Judaic Studies, Olin Center; (617) 628-5000 (Ascher), 2037 (Rosenberg); gascher@emerald.tufts.edu; jrosenbl@emerald.tufts.edu.

 Study in Israel

Study abroad is encouraged and credit is given for study in Israel.

 Kosher Food

Shabbat and Holiday dinners served at Hillel.

Housing

Jewish residence: Bayit-Jewish Culture House.

ON CAMPUS

Tufts has a very active Hillel Foundation and is housed in a beautiful, new building in the center of campus. Hillel offers a full range of social, cultural, educational, and religious programming, and has been honored several times by the Hillel International Center for its creative programming. Hillel is made up of more than 20 student-led groups, including: Tufts Friends of Israel, the Social Action Committee, a Jewish *a cappella* group, the Hillel Lecture Series, the Social/Cultural Committee, the Holidays Committee, the Jewish Women's Collective, and a Jewish Theater Troupe. Throughout the week, students can be found in the Hillel Center enjoying programs, talking with friends, meeting with committees, or just hanging out. Approximately 150 students gather each Friday evening for the Shabbat dinner and the 2 student-led services that follow (Reform and Conservative).

The University is especially supportive of Hillel activities, and Hillel is very involved with other campus groups, co-sponsoring programs with the University Chaplaincy, the African-American Center, and the Women's Center, among others. Recent programming highlights have included a Hanukkah Semi-Formal, an Interethnic Service Project, a dialogue between a child of a Holocaust survivor and the child of a Nazi, a Mock Jewish Wedding, a First Year Student Retreat, a Regional Reform Shabbaton, and a Jazz and Fondue Reception.

Served by Hillel Council of Greater New England.

UNIVERSITY OF MASSACHUSETTS—AMHERST

Enrollment 23,000 (UG 17,000; GR 6,000)
Jewish 3,000

Hillel House
University of Massachusetts—Amherst
388 N. Pleasant Street, #15
Amherst, MA 01002
(413) 549-1710
Fax: (413) 549-0329
E-mail: saulp@external.umass.edu
Web: www-unix.oit.umass.edu/~umhillel/

Paul Entis, Interim Director
TBA, Program Director
Cheryl Gordon, Jewish Campus Service Corps Fellow

Jewish Studies

15–20 courses; B.A./Joint Program: Five College Consortium.

Study in Israel

Junior year abroad; summer field program; annual Israel trip.

Kosher Food

The University provides 5 dinners (surcharge). Vegetarian dining alternatives.

Housing

Jewish Living Community in Hillel House for 26 students; coed with kitchen and laundry facilities. Chabad House near campus.

ON CAMPUS

UMass has a strong, vibrant, and diverse Jewish student community. Hillel plays an important role on the campus as a whole through initiating a Jewish Affairs Editorship in the campus newspaper, a University-funded Jewish Affairs Office, and large-scale programs such as the Elie Wiesel–Maya Angelou dialogue that attracted an audience of 6,000. UMass Hillel is a 4-time winner of International Hillel's William Haber Award for Programs of Quality for the Jewish Campus Community.

Hillel is located in the 15,000-square-foot Grinspoon Hillel House, which includes comfortable lounges and meeting rooms, a library, a residence for 26 students on the top floor called the Jewish Living Community, a kosher kitchen with a university-sponsored meal plan, and a Scholar-in-Residence Suite.

Hillel sponsors a wide variety of social, cultural, religious and social action programming. Special-interest groups include First Year Student Group, Israeli folk dancing, intramural sports teams, Rosh Hodesh Women's Group, Kolot *a cappella* singers, Kesher, AIPAC, Hamagshimim, and others. Hillel offers courses that students can take for 1 University credit such as Jewish Christian encounter, Yiddish, Judaism and Social Issues, Jewish Women's Spirituality, Torah and Haftarah Cantillation, and Israel and the Media.

UMass Hillel has a Jewish Campus Service Corps Fellow who connects with Jewish students throughout the campus, organizing events and meeting with individuals in residence halls and the fraternity-sorority system, and meeting especially with new students.

UMass Hillel has sent some of the largest student delegations to national conferences such as the AIPAC Policy Conference and the UJA Student Mission to Israel. Hilllel encourages this participation by offering subsidies for students to attend conferences that include leadership training opportunities.

UNIVERSITY OF MASSACHUSETTS— BOSTON HARBOR

Enrollment 5,350
Jewish 90

U. Mass Boston Harbor Hillel
156 McCormick Building, 4th floor
Univ. of Mass., Boston Harbor
Boston, MA 02125
(617) 353-7210
E-mail: smendales@wn.net

Samuel Mendales, Director, Hillel Council

 Jewish Studies
Usually 1 course per term.

ON CAMPUS

Programming includes activities for seasonal holidays, lectures, and seminars.

Boston Harbor Hillel is served part-time by the Hillel Council of New England. See listing for Babson College.

UNIVERSITY OF MASSACHUSETTS—DARTMOUTH

Enrollment 5,000
Jewish 100

UMass Dartmouth Hillel
UMD Hillel/Student Activities
285 Old Westport Road
N. Dartmouth, MA 02747
(508) 999-9241
(617) 353-7210
E-mail: psheinman@wn.net

Ailene Gerhahrdt, Director of Regional Services, Hillel Council of New England
Professor Janet Freedman, Advisor

 Jewish Studies
Minor.

 Study in Israel
Study in Israel (through Hillel Council).

ON CAMPUS

With part-time staffing from Hillel Council of New England, UMD Hillel has expanded its activities in the past few years. Programs include an annual Chocolate Passover seder, bagel brunches, and joint Shabbat services with other nearby campuses. The UMD Center for Jewish Culture offers cultural activities for both the campus and the greater community.

Served by Hillel Council of New England.

UNIVERSITY OF MASSACHUSETTS—LOWELL

Enrollment 6,000 (UG 5,700; GR 300)
Jewish 300

Jewish Students Organization
c/o Temple Beth El
105 Princeton Boulevard
Lowell, MA 01851
(508) 453-0073
(508) 453-7744

Rabbi Leslie Gordon, Advisor
Professor Jay Weitzen, Advisor

ON CAMPUS

Jewish students meet frequently, with activity varying according to the interest of the students, many of whom commute. The local Jewish community is supportive of Jewish students, offers home hospitality, and invites them to participate in Jewish education courses and attend services at the local synagogue.

Served by Hillel Council of New England. See listing for Babson College.

WELLESLEY COLLEGE

Enrollment 2,100
Jewish 180

Hillel Foundation
106 Central Street
Wellesley, MA 02181
(781) 283-2687
Fax: (781) 283-3676
E-mail: ibogosian@wellesley.edu
Web: www.wellesley.edu/Hillel/hillel.html

Rabbi Ilene Lerner Bogosian, Director

 Jewish Studies
Jewish studies program and cross-registration with Brandeis University.

 Study in Israel
Wellesley winter session in Israel.

 Kosher Food
Kosher vegetarian dining room; kosher kitchen next to the Hillel lounge.

ON CAMPUS

Wellesley has an active Hillel program, with strong co-operation by the college. In addition to social, religious, and educational programming, Hillel participates in local and Boston-area social action programs and the Northern New England Regional Hillel Council. Wellesley College Hillel offers a special, highly selective program for Jewish students who are campus leaders, but have not been actively involved in Jewish campus life. The Gruss Leadership Development Project provides interactive discussions, a retreat, professional mentorship opportunities, and a seminar in Israel.

Served by Hillel Council of New England.

WESTERN NEW ENGLAND COLLEGE

Enrollment 3,000
Jewish 250

Western New England Havurah
1215 Wilbraham Road
Springfield, MA 01119
(413) 782-1508
(413) 782-1346
Fax: (413) 796-2007
Web: www.wnec.edu

Rabbi Jerome S. Gurland, Advisor

 Jewish Studies
4 courses.

 Kosher Food
Kosher food is brought in for religious holy days.

ON CAMPUS

The local Jewish community is very supportive, and provides home hospitality for Shabbat and holidays. There is a good relationship with the campus ministry. Major lectures of Jewish interest are held annually on campus. The law school has many Jewish students. Programming includes Weekly Bagel Schmoozes with rabbi, faculty, and administrators, and occasional Shabbat dinners and programs. Guests are often university community members from a variety of religious and social groups.

WESTFIELD STATE COLLEGE

Enrollment 3,000
Jewish 50

Jewish Student Organization
c/o Department of History
Westfield State College
Westfield, MA 01086
(413) 568-3311
Fax: (413) 562-3613

Professor Martin Kaufman, Advisor

 Kosher Food
Frozen; on request in dining hall. Vegetarian dining alternatives and dormitory cooking facilities are available.

ON CAMPUS

The Jewish community is supportive. Students share a Hanukkah dinner, a second Passover seder, and other holiday meals.

Served by Hillel Council of New England. See listing for Babson College.

WHEATON COLLEGE

Enrollment 1,500
Jewish 150

Wheaton College Hillel
Wheaton College
26 East Main Street
Norton, MA 02766
(508) 286-5070
(508) 286-3694
Fax: (508) 285-3830
E-mail: hillel@wheatoncollege.edu

Dr. Jonathan Brumberg-Kraus, Faculty Advisor
David Dudek, Student Contact

Jewish Studies

Wheaton College offers a Judaic Studies minor options and Jewish Studies courses: Introduction to the Hebrew Bible, Judaism: Faith and Practice, Scripture in Judaism, Christianity, and Islam, Faith After the Holocaust, and others. Independent study courses in Judaica are also available, such as advanced Hebrew readings in Tanakh or Kabbalah, Judaism and Sexuality.

Study in Israel

The International Relations Junior Year Abroad program in Rehovot, Israel. Students may also participate in Hebrew University's Rothberg Program for Overseas Students.

Kosher Food

Vegetarian options available at every meal and extensive salad bar available in the dining halls. Hillel uses outside kosher catering options for its events.

ON CAMPUS

Wheaton College Hillel is a very active group involved in campus affairs and Regional activities. Located near Boston, Jewish students travel to area Hillel events in addition to sponsoring activities on campus. The students enjoy the mixture of the on- and off-campus activities that Wheaton College Hillel provides.

"Wheaton College Hillel provides students with a rich and growing presence on its campus. Hillel works together with other college Hillels in the Boston Area and Southeastern New England to integrate the Wheaton and regional Jewish experiences. Our Hillel no longer consists of a certain number of students on campus but extends to the entire region."

David Dudek, junior

"Under the guidance and inspiration of Professor (Rabbi) Jonathan Brumberg-Kraus, Wheaton College Hillel offers an authentic, vibrant and evolving Jewish communal existence on campus."

Joshua Levin-Epstein, sophomore

Served by Regional Student Board of the Hillel Council of New England.

WHEELOCK COLLEGE

Enrollment 700
Jewish 70

Hillel Council of New England
233 Bay State Road
Boston, MA 02215
(617) 353-7210
Fax: (617) 353-7214
E-mail: psheinman@wn.net

Patti Sheinman, Assistant Director, Hillel Council

Kosher Food

Kosher food is available at Simmons College. Vegetarian dining alternatives; dormitory cooking facilities.

ON CAMPUS

Jewish students at Wheelock participate in citywide activities with other Boston-area colleges.

Wheelock College is served part-time by the Hillel Council of New England. See listing for Babson College.

WILLIAMS COLLEGE

Enrollment 2,000
Jewish 240

Williams College Jewish Association
Student Union Box 1006
Baxter Hall
Williamstown, MA 01267
(413) 597-2483
Fax: (413) 597-2061
E-mail: djacobso@mhc.mtholyoke.edu

Rabbi Deborah Zecher, Chaplain
Rabbi Devorah Jacobson, Associate Chaplain
Professor Lawrence J. Kaplan, Advisor

Jewish Studies

4–5 courses/tutorials in Jewish studies and Hebrew language. An additional 2–5 courses related to Jewish Studies are taught in various departments of the College.

Study in Israel

Junior year abroad/winter study program.

Kosher Food

Jewish Center: daily lunch and dinner; vegetarian dining alternatives.

ON CAMPUS

The Williams College Jewish Religious Center is equipped with all facilities for student relaxation and observance, including a kosher kitchen, a library, a complete Torah scroll set, and a sanctuary with seating for up to 300.

Williams offers an extensive annual series of lectures and cultural activities of Jewish interest, as well as many opportunities for student initiative and leadership. Williams also sponsors a bi-weekly dinner discussion series relating to Jewish life as well as cultural topics. Students teach Hebrew school at the local synagogues.

"The Jewish community at Williams has made me feel very much at home. We are comprised of Jews of all types of backgrounds. We pride ourselves on being able to integrate all people's needs. The organization is student-run, so anyone wishing to express an idea is able to take steps to make their idea a reality."

Amy Sprengelmeyer, '00

WORCESTER POLYTECHNIC INSTITUTE

Enrollment 2,700
Jewish 100

Hillel at Worcester Polytechnic Institute
Club Box 2497
100 Institute Road
Worcester, MA 01609
(508) 831-5416
Fax: (508) 831-5776
E-mail: dfinkel@cs.wpi.edu

Dr. David Finkel, Advisor

 Kosher Food
Kosher food is available for Passover.

ON CAMPUS

A small but active Jewish campus community organizes social activities, films, classes, and discussions. The local community offers home hospitality for the holidays. There is a good relationship with the campus ministry.

CENTRAL MICHIGAN UNIVERSITY

Enrollment 16,000
Jewish 120

c/o Jewish Students Organization
Department of Geography/CMU
Mt. Pleasant, MI 48859
(517) 774-3032

Professor Robert Aron, Advisor

Jewish Studies
3 courses: Introduction to Bible, Introduction to Judaism, and the Holocaust.

Study in Israel
Study abroad programs with Haifa, Ben-Gurion, and other universities.

Kosher Food
Vegetarian dining alternatives. Kosher food is available locally.

ON CAMPUS

CMU is a very welcoming environment for Jewish students. Although Jews make up a small proportion of the student body, the University is highly supportive of programs sponsored by the Jewish Student Organization, and provides substantial support and funding to ensure their success. The Jewish faculty and the local Jewish community are very warm and welcoming to Jewish students on campus.

The JSO meets periodically for program planning and occasional Shabbat dinners. Last spring, Hillel sponsored Holocaust Awareness Day, a successful event in which more than 450 Jewish and non-Jewish students attended a talk given by a Holocaust survivor.

EASTERN MICHIGAN UNIVERSITY

Enrollment 23,000
Jewish 1,000

 EMU Hillel of HMD
965 Washtenaw
Ypsilanti, MI 48197
(734) 482-0456
(734) 483-6210
Fax: (313) 577-3461
E-mail: hillel@online.emich.edu
Web: www.emich.edu

Alissa Parker, Campus Director
Professor Jessica Alexander, Faculty Advisor

Study in Israel
Credit for university study in Israel.

 Kosher Food
Kosher food can be available. Kosher for Passover food must be ordered in advance and is paid for by EMU Hillel.

ON CAMPUS
EMU Hillel offers a variety of student-run programs on campus and in the metropolitan Detroit area. EMU also is home to a Jewish fraternity and many supportive and caring Jewish faculty. EMU Hillel is an affiliate of Hillel of Metro Detroit, based at Wayne State University. H.M.D. provides community-wide social, social action, Jewish awareness, Israel-related, and sporting events for Jewish students and young adults, aged 18–30, throughout the metropolitan Detroit area, including Wayne State University, Oakland University, and Oakland Community College.

FERRIS STATE UNIVERSITY

Enrollment 8,019

Jewish Student Union
Ferris State University
901 S. State
Big Rapids, MI 49307
(616) 592-2769

Dr. Lynn Bartholome, Advisor

HILLSDALE COLLEGE

Enrollment 1,100
Jewish 10-15

Jewish Students Association
c/o Dr. Robert Eden
Hillsdale College
Hillsdale, MI 49242-1298
(517) 437-7341
(517) 437-2487
Fax: (517) 437-3923
E-mail: bob.eden@ac.hillsdale.edu

Dr. Robert Eden, Advisor

 Jewish Studies
Classes offered in the Department of Religion in Biblical Hebrew or Old Testament Studies, depending on student interest.

ON CAMPUS
Hillsdale College is a small, traditional liberal arts school 80 miles outside Ann Arbor, Michigan. The students are serious academically, and the university and faculty are very active in fostering understanding among different racial and religious groups. The school has a very strong Public Affairs Department. The Jewish students at Hillsdale are few in number, but the atmosphere at the University is very supportive. Dr. Eden actively encourages Jewish students to participate, whenever possible, in social, cultural, and religious events at the University of Michigan Hillel.

LAWRENCE TECHNOLOGICAL UNIVERSITY

Enrollment 4,100
Jewish 100

Jewish Student Association/Hillel
Hillel of Metro Detroit (H.M.D.)
667 Grosberg Religious Center
Wayne State University
Detroit, MI 48202
(313) 577-3459
Fax: (313) 577-3461
E-mail: hillel@wayne.edu
Web: www.hillel-detroit.org

Miriam Starkman, Director
Sharon Wise, Program Director
Professor Gloria Rivkin, Advisor

ON CAMPUS
The JSA/Hillel at Lawrence Technological University is part of Hillel of Metro Detroit, based at Wayne State University. H.M.D. provides community-wide social, social action, Jewish awareness, UJA, and sporting events for Jewish students and young adults, aged 18–30, throughout the metropolitan Detroit area, including Wayne State University, Oakland University, Eastern Michigan University, and Oakland Community College.

MICHIGAN STATE UNIVERSITY

Enrollment 40,000
Jewish 2,000

Hillel Jewish Student Center
402 Linden Street
East Lansing, MI 48823
(517) 332-1916
Fax: (517) 332-4142
E-mail: hillel@pilot.msu.edu
Web: pilot.msu.edu/user/hillel

Rabbi Philip Cohen, Ph.D., Executive Director
Bryan Abramson, Program Director
Michelle Acosta, Jewish Campus Service Corps Fellow

Jewish Studies
15 courses; thematic program available.

Study in Israel
Archaeology summer program at Haifa University.

Kosher Food
Hillel co-op. Vegetarian dining alternatives.

Housing
Limited arrangements in the Hillel building.

ON CAMPUS

Activities for Jewish students at MSU include Hillel's social, cultural, educational, social action, and religious programs, as well as the Jewish Student Union, SpartiPac (the Israel advocacy coalition), and the Reform Chavurah program. Hillel's student-initiated projects include an *a cappella* group, Kolechad, and popular Israel-related activities. Hillel's theater group, newspaper, and social action program have grown during the past academic year. Hillel also sponsors a weekly Torah study class and an active CLI group. The campus has 3 predominately Jewish fraternities and 1 sorority. Several students work with dorm-based representatives to stimulate the development of Jewish community within many of the residence halls. Hillel also serves Cooley Law School, the fourth-largest law school in the country.

> *"I am from a primarily Jewish area, and when I moved to a school where the Jewish population is minimal, I learned firsthand about the ignorance that exists once one leaves the 'bubble' of Jewish suburban life. Hillel at Michigan State offered me something I could still belong to, something I was proud of. Once I began going, I acted on the leadership roles that became available to me. Hillel restored a lot of faith that I could continue the values, morals, and traditions I grew up with. I am eager to continue my sophomore year with Hillel, and introduce its legacy to the new freshmen."*
>
> **Rachel Wright, sophomore**

OAKLAND COMMUNITY COLLEGE— ORCHARD RIDGE

Enrollment 6,000
Jewish 600

Jewish Student Association/Hillel
27055 Orchard Lake Road
Farmington Hills, MI 48334
(248) 577-3459
Fax: (248) 577-3461
E-mail: hillel@wayne.edu
Web: www.hillel-detroit.org

Miriam Starkman, Director
Sharon Wise, Program Director
Professor Harvey Bronstein, Advisor

Kosher Food
Community availability.

ON CAMPUS

Oakland's JSA/Hillel has its own student board and programs on campus. The JSA/Hillel is part of Hillel of Metro Detroit, based at Wayne State University. H.M.D. provides community-wide social, social action, Jewish awareness, UJA, and sporting events for Jewish students and young adults, aged 18–30, throughout the metropolitan Detroit area, including Wayne State University, Oakland University, Eastern Michigan University, and Lawrence Technological University.

OAKLAND UNIVERSITY

Enrollment 13,600
Jewish 200

Jewish Student Organization/Hillel
Hillel of Metro Detroit (H.M.D.)
19 Oakland Center
Rochester Hills, MI 48309-4401
(248) 370-4257
(248) 577-3459
Fax: (248) 577-3461
E-mail: hillel@wayne.edu
Web: www.hillel-detroit.org

Miriam Starkman, Director
Sharon Wise, Program Director
Professor Robert Stern, Advisor

Kosher Food
Vegetarian dining alternatives; kosher food locally available.

ON CAMPUS

The JSO/Hillel at Oakland University is part of Hillel of Metro Detroit, based at Wayne State University. H.M.D. provides community-wide social, social action, Jewish awareness, UJA, and sporting events for Jewish students and young adults, aged 18–30, throughout the metropolitan Detroit area, including Wayne State University, Eastern Michigan University, Oakland Community College, and Lawrence Technological University.

UNIVERSITY OF DETROIT LAW SCHOOL

Enrollment 700
Jewish 50

Jewish Law Students Association
Hillel of Metro Detroit (H.M.D.)
667 Grosberg Religious Center
Wayne State University
Detroit, MI 48202
(313) 577-3459
Fax: (313) 577-3461
E-mail: hillel@wayne.edu
Web: hillel-detroit.org

Miriam Starkman, Director
Sharon Wise, Program Director

ON CAMPUS

University of Detroit Law School is part of Hillel of
Metro Detroit, based at Wayne State, H.M.D. provides
community-wide social, social action, Jewish awareness, UJA, and sporting events for Jewish students and
young adults, aged 18–30, throughout the metropolitan
Detroit area, including Wayne State University, Eastern
Michigan University, Oakland Community College, Oakland University, and Lawrence Technological University. The JLSA collaborates on programs with the Wayne
State University Jewish Law Students Association.

UNIVERSITY OF MICHIGAN

Enrollment 35,000 (UG 24,000; GR 11,000)
Jewish 6,000 (UG 4,000; GR 2,000)

University of Michigan Hillel
1429 Hill Street
Ann Arbor, MI 48104
(734) 769-0500
Fax: (734) 769-1934
E-mail: umhillel@umich.edu
Web: www.umich.edu/~umhillel

Michael Brooks, Executive Director
Rabbi Richard Kirschen, Assistant Director
Shani Lasin, Program Director
Sallie Abelson, Director of Development
Rabbi Rod Gloglower, Staff Associate
Megan Nesbit, Jewish Campus Service Corps Fellow

Jewish Studies

90 courses in catalog. B.A., M.A., Ph.D. Endowed
Chair. The Frankel Center for Judaic Studies, an interdisciplinary program, offers more than 30 courses each
semester. Fifteen faculty teach Jewish history, culture,
thought, and literature; Hebrew; Yiddish; law, political
science, rabbinics; religious studies; social work; and
sociology; reaching 1,500 students annually. Students
can pursue a B.A. in Judaic Studies, an M.A. in affiliated
departments, or a certificate in Jewish Communal Ser-

vices with an MSW. (See listing for University of
Michigan's Project STAR program in Schools of Jewish
Communal Service section.) The Center sponsors sev-
eral annual lectures and prizes, including the David W.
Belin Lecture in American Jewish Affairs; the Derrow
Lecture in Judaic Studies and Anthropology; and the
Weinberg Prize for Excellence in Judaic Studies.
Frankel Center for Judaic Studies, 3302 Frieze Building;
Ann Arbor, MI 48109-1285; (313) 763-9047;
amybeth@umich.edu.

Study in Israel

Junior year abroad/summer seminar. Hillel sponsors a 6-week, 6-credit archaeological dig in Israel.

Kosher Food

Hillel offers 7 dinners, 6 lunches; vegetarian dining alternatives; kosher food available locally.

ON CAMPUS

UM Hillel, the second largest student programming orga-
nization on the University of Michigan campus, plays a
vital role not only in the campus Jewish community, but
in the life of the entire University. Throughout the year
Hillel sponsors services and classes, top-flight cinema
and theater, major speakers and entertainers (Chaim
Potok, Adam Sandler, Oliver Stone, Art Spiegelman, Elie
Weisel, Adrienne Rich, etc.), publications (*Prospect*, the
UM Hillel's Jewish student journal, and *Consider*, the
University's award-winning weekly issues forum), meals,
counseling, a Jewish feminist group, 2 theater compa-
nies, the annual Golden Apple Award for outstanding
university teaching, 2 Israel affairs groups representing
every political stripe, the UJA Half Shekel Campaign, and
many more activities.

*"I can't imagine the University of Michigan
without Hillel."*

**Royster Harper, UM Vice President for
Student Affairs**

UNIVERSITY OF MICHIGAN—DEARBORN

Enrollment 3,503
Jewish N/A

Hillel at U of M, Dearborn
667 Grosberg Religious Center
Wayne State University
Detroit, MI 48202
(313) 577-3459
Fax: (313) 577-3461
E-mail: hillel@wayne.edu

Richard Adler, Advisor

WAYNE STATE UNIVERSITY

Enrollment 32,000
Jewish 600

Hillel of Metro Detroit (H.M.D.)
667 Grosberg Religious Center
Wayne State University
Detroit, MI 48202
(313) 577-3459
Fax: (313) 577-3461
E-mail: hillel@wayne.edu
Web: www.hillel-detroit.org

Miriam Starkman, Director
Sharon Wise, Program Director

 Jewish Studies
Hebrew language major/minor. The University Center for Judaic Studies brings scholars to campus. The Department of Near Eastern and Asian Studies offers Hebrew classes and other Judaic studies classes.

Kosher Food
At Hillel: lunch, fall and winter semesters.

ON CAMPUS

Hillel at Wayne State provides a comfortable atmosphere for its commuter students, activity on campus during weekdays, and programs with other Hillel of Metro Detroit participants on weeknights and weekends. Wayne State Hillel has representation on the Detroit Metro Council. Wayne State is 20 minutes from a sizable Jewish community.

Hillel of Metro Detroit, based at Wayne State, organizes community-wide social, social action, Jewish awareness, UJA, and sporting events for Jewish students and young adults, aged 18–30, throughout the Detroit metropolitan area, including the University of Detroit, Oakland University, Oakland Community College and Lawrence Technological Institute.

WESTERN MICHIGAN UNIVERSITY

Enrollment 25,000
Jewish 80

WMU Hillel
1304 Faunce, WMU
Kalamazoo, MI 49008
(616) 384-6643
(616) 387-2089
E-mail: jweiss@fmd.org

Jan Lyddon, Faculty Liaison
Gillian Beaty, Advisor

 Jewish Studies
5 courses.

 Study in Israel
Study abroad through Hillel.

 Kosher Food
Students who require kosher food may be able to board with local families.

ON CAMPUS

The small local Jewish community is very receptive to students. Hillel sponsors occasional programs and meals each month.

MINNESOTA

CARLETON COLLEGE

Enrollment 1,800
Jewish 200

Jewish Students of Carleton
100 North Union Street
Northfield, MN 55057
(507) 646-4003

Carolyn Fure-Slocum, Chaplain

 Jewish Studies
5 courses; major in religion with Jewish concentration.

 Kosher Food
Interest House has a kosher kitchen available; regular Shabbat dinners; vegetarian dining available.

 Housing
Reynold House houses 3 Jewish students, a library and a Torah, and a kosher kitchen.

ON CAMPUS

Jewish Students of Carleton, an organization led by Jewish students, serves Jewish students, faculty, and staff on Carleton's campus. The JSC's events are open to anyone from the outside community with an interest in Judaism. The JSC celebrates festivals, holds Passover seders, and organizes, in cooperation with the Office of the Chaplain, High Holiday services. The JSC has close ties with the large Jewish community in the Twin Cities Metro area. The organization brings diverse speakers and films to campus and enjoys contact with Jewish students from the U of M and Macalester College.

MACALESTER COLLEGE

Enrollment 1,600
Jewish 100

Macalester Jewish Organization
1600 Grand Avenue
St. Paul, MN 55105
(651) 696-6117
E-mail: idelson@macalester.edu

Shirley Idelson, Associate for Jewish Life

 Jewish Studies
8 courses.

 Kosher Food
The Hewbrew House is a residence hall for 11 students and has a kosher kitchen.

ON CAMPUS

Jewish students at Macalester College enjoy The Hebrew House, open Shabbat, Torah study, Jewish studies, Hebrew language instruction, and the archaeology dig in Israel. The Macalester Jewish Organization sponsors events September through May.

The Macalester Jewish Organization also served by the Twin Cities Hillel at the University of Minnesota.

UNIVERSITY OF MINNESOTA

Enrollment 37,000
Jewish 1,200

 Hillel Foundation
1521 University Avenue, SE
Minneapolis, MN 55414
(612) 379-4026
Fax: (612) 379-9004
E-mail: bbhf@tc.umn.edu
Web: www.umn.edu/nlhome/g014/bbhf/

Amy Olson, Director
Rabbi Sharon Stiefel, Associate Director

 Jewish Studies
12 courses; B.A.

 Kosher Food
A kosher vegetarian restaurant is opening at Hillel in the fall of 1999; Hillel offers Friday evening meals; vegetarian dining alternatives are available.

Housing
Hillel has very limited housing available.

ON CAMPUS

Hillel at the University of Minnesota is a friendly meeting place for commuter and residential students from all backgrounds. Hillel provides a warm environment where Jewish students can explore their Jewish identity, celebrate Jewish life, and build community. Student interest and initiative determine Hillel's programming. In recent years, students have established an outdoor adventure program, a monthly women's Rosh Hodesh group, a Hebrew conversation group and a beit cafe/coffee house. Hillel activities occur not only in Hillel's building but in different locations throughout the campus and the Twin Cities. Activities include barbecues, community service projects, Shabbat dinners, weekly Israeli folk dancing, graduate student potluck dinners, weekly Torah study, and an annual Hanukkah lunch, allowing students to enjoy a wide range of Jewish social, cultural, educational, activist and religious interests.

Hillel's large building is a comfortable place to hang out and study, and has many amenities: computers, a big screen TV and VCR, a Ping-Pong table, a pool table, a library, and a copy machine.

Hillel works closely with several other campus groups and regularly co-sponsors events with them. Students take advantage of the many cultural, social, and employment opportunities in the Twin Cities and the general community.

The University of Minnesota's policy is to honor all religious observances. Alternative arrangements may be made for exams or homework due on religious holidays such as Yom Kippur. Students are required to inform their instructor prior to their absence.

"Coming from a Jewish community in Milwaukee, WI, I was unsure how I would express my Jewish identity in a new environment. Thankfully, Hillel made my transition easier by introducing me to a vibrant Jewish community. My leadership at Hillel has given me the opportunity to interact with the president of the university and serve on campus-wide committees. I have grown both as a Jew and a leader through Hillel."

Renata Batuner, senior

MISSISSIPPI

UNIVERSITY OF MISSISSIPPI

Enrollment 9,000
Jewish 20

> Office of International Programs
> and Religious Activities
> University, MS 38677
> (601) 232-7404
> Fax: (601) 232-7486

ON CAMPUS

There is no organized campus activity at this time. Some Jewish faculty are on campus. The closest rabbi is in a town 80 miles away.

MISSOURI

ST. LOUIS UNIVERSITY

Enrollment 11,000 (UG 6,497; GR 4,533)
Jewish 100 (UG 40; GR 60)

> St. Louis Hillel Center Extension
> 6300 Forsyth Boulevard
> St. Louis, MO 63105
> (314) 935-9040
> Fax: (314) 935-9041
> E-mail: hillel@rescomp.wustl.edu
> Web: www.stlouishillel.org
>
> **Robert Goldberg**, Director
> **Rabbi Hyim Shafner**, Campus Rabbi
> **Nina Sackheim**, Jewish Campus Service Corp Fellow

 Jewish Studies
3 courses.

 Kosher Food
Available locally. Passover meals at Hillel.

Jewish students in the St. Louis metropolitan area are served by St. Louis Hillel. See listing for Washington University.

STEPHENS COLLEGE

Enrollment 500
Jewish 25

> Hillel Foundation for Jewish Campus Life
> 1107 University Avenue
> Columbia, MO 65201
> (573) 443-7460
> Fax: (573) 499-1773
> E-mail: khhillel@mail.socket.net
> Web: www.students.missouri.edu/~jso
>
> **Kerry Hollander**, Director
> **Gabe Bodzin**, Jewish Campus Service Corps Fellow

 Study in Israel
The College accepts credits from Israeli institutions.

 Kosher Food
Vegetarian options.

ON CAMPUS

Stephens College Jewish students are encouraged to participate in activities at Hillel at the University of Missouri, which is 4 blocks from the Stephens campus. Mikreh, the Jewish student organization at Stephens, meets according to student interest and need.

See listing for University of Missouri, Columbia.

TRUMAN STATE UNIVERSITY

Enrollment 6,000
Jewish 20

> Truman State University Hillel
> c/o Division of Social Sciences
> Truman State University
> Kirksville, MO 63501
> (660) 785-4690
> (660) 785-1810
>
> **Professor Jerrold Hirsch**, Advisor
> **Sherry Palmer**, Advisor

 Jewish Studies
Several courses on Judaism offered, as well as Hebrew and ancient Hebrew history.

 Study in Israel
Study tour options in Haifa and Jerusalem, archaeological digs.

UNIVERSITY OF MISSOURI—COLUMBIA

Enrollment 21,300
Jewish 600

Hillel Foundation for Jewish Campus Life
1107 University Avenue
Columbia, MO 65201
(573) 443-7460
Fax: (573) 499-1773
E-mail: khhillel@mail.socket.net

Kerry Hollander, Director
Gabe Bodzin, Jewish Campus Service Corps Fellow

 Jewish Studies
1 course.

 Study in Israel
The University accepts credits for study at israeli universities with prior approval.

 Kosher Food
Hillel offers 1 dinner weekly, as well as holiday and occasional meals; full week of Passover meals.

ON CAMPUS

The Columbia Jewish community is very supportive of Jewish student life. Hillel sponsors programs of special interest to the University's many journalism students. Social events, a campus Jewish newspaper, a UJA campus campaign, an active Israel program, Judaica courses, and Holocaust memorial month activities are part of Hillel's programming. Students also enjoy alternative-style Shabbat services which are often held at campsites and students' apartments. Swing dances, which are held almost weekly, bring together undergraduate and graduate students. Hillel sponsors community services projects on a regular basis. These projects frequently impact the entire campus. Hillel's activities are well respected and well attended by the campus community.

"Our Hillel building lies in a strategic position on our campus in midwestern Missouri. As part of a small Jewish population at a Midwest Big 12 school, many of my friends told me I was the first Jew they had ever met. While most students were very receptive to this diversity, minority status was something new for me. Our Hillel provides a concentrated Jewish atmosphere figuring prominently on our campus, which made me proud as I walked to Shabbat services from my dorm freshman year. Hillel also provided me the opportunity to be a part of the 1997 UJA

Winter Student Mission and helped fund my first, but hopefully not my last, trip to Israel."

Leon Mendlowitz, veterinary medicine student

Hillel at Columbia also serves Stephens College.

UNIVERSITY OF MISSOURI—ST. LOUIS

Enrollment 16,094 (UG 13,558; GR 2,536)
Jewish 100

St. Louis Hillel Extension
6300 Forsyth Boulevard
St. Louis, MO 63105
(314) 935-9040
Fax: (314) 935-9041
E-mail: hillel@rescomp.wustl.edu

Robert Goldberg, Executive Director
Nina Sackheim, Jewish Campus Service Corps Fellow

 Jewish Studies
3 or 4 courses.

 Study in Israel
The UMSL Center for International Studies refers students to programs in Israel. Credit is generally accepted.

 Kosher Food
Vegetarian dining alternatives.

Jewish students in the St. Louis metropolitan area are served by St. Louis Hillel. See listing for Washington University.

WASHINGTON UNIVERSITY

Enrollment 11,430 (UG: 5,723; GR: 5,707)
Jewish 4,000

St. Louis Hillel Center
6300 Forsyth Boulevard
St. Louis, MO 63105
(314) 935-9040
Fax: (314) 935-9041
E-mail: hillel@rescomp.wustl.edu
Web: www.stlouishillel.org

Robert Goldberg, Executive Director
Laurie Goldberg, Associate Director

Jewish Studies
B.A., M.A. The Jewish and Near Eastern Studies Program offers 63 courses annually, with 106 courses listed in the catalog. The program features close cooperation be-

tween the Islamic studies faculty and those who work on Jewish materials. Four years of Hebrew language and literature are offered, in addition to Arabic, Persian, and Turkish. Jewish and Near Eastern Studies, One Brookings Drive, Campus 1121, St. Louis, MO 63130; (314) 935-8567; rabuska@artsci.wustl.edu.

Study in Israel
Spring semester or academic year programs at Hebrew University in Jerusalem. Contact Office of Overseas Programs at (314) 935-6151.

Kosher Food
University dining services offers kosher meal options prepared under supervision in all major dining facilities. Hillel provides kosher Friday night and holiday meals. The campus student center offers kosher meals to go, as well as a kosher lunch cart. Vegetarian food is available at all dining centers. Kosher butchers, delis and bakeries are within driving distance.

Housing
There is often a Hillel suite in the dorms, made up of 6 sophomores.

ON CAMPUS
Washington University is an inviting and comfortable campus for Jewish students. With a significant Jewish population, Jewish students are active in all areas of the University, including student government, performing arts, journalism, Greek life and leadership programs. The Jewish Student Council is composed of over 20 student-led project teams. As a registered student group, JSC receives significant support from the student government to allocate to its project teams. These teams include: community service groups, Jewish Theatre Group, Israeli Dancing, Campus Jewish Relations Council, Women's Forum, Israel Committee, Holocaust Awareness and Education, TEVA (Environmental Group), Graduate and Young Professionals, and more. Students plan trips and retreats, classes, parties, and lectures.

St. Louis Hillel Center at Washington University offers a special, highly selective program for Jewish students who are campus leaders, but who have not been actively involved in Jewish campus life. Sponsored by Steven Spielberg's Righteous Persons Foundation, the Campus Leadership Initiative program offers interactive discussions, visits to various sites in the local Jewish community, and a trip to Israel.

The spacious Hillel Center is available to students for studying, watching TV, or just hanging out. It includes a library, living room, den, kitchens, conference rooms, and auditoriums.

The University is sensitive to Jewish religious concerns, and most professors excuse students from class for Jewish holidays. Graduation events are held during the week and do not conflict with Shabbat. Hillel enjoys a close and interactive relationship with other campus organizations, including the Catholic Student Center, student government organizations, the Performing Arts Department, the Jewish and Near Eastern Studies Department, Residential Life, Campus Y, and the University's administration. The Greek system is strong, and many of the houses have a considerable number of Jewish students.

St. Louis is home to more than 60,000 Jews. Many students find jobs at local synagogues teaching religious school, advising youth groups, and working in summer camps. There are also opportunities to gain professional experience, mentoring, and internships through the organized Jewish community. St. Louis Hillel Center provides limited programming for other Jewish college students in St. Louis.

"Washington University has a warm and enthusiastic Jewish community. Hillel is bursting with a variety of programs from "Black Women/Jewish Women Dialogue" to Israeli dance to Jewish dramatic performances. The Jewish community is pluralistic and welcoming. Students have incredible opportunities for leadership and involvement with all aspects of Hillel."

Kara Jacobson, junior

"There is a wonderful and warm community on campus which is run and nurtured by the students and supported by the Jewish community as a whole. The Wash U Hillel and Jewish Campus Religious Council have many wonderful programs with the other cultural and ethnic groups on campus. The administration and faculty support but are not involved in Hillel. The Jewish and Near Eastern Studies Program is very good."

Danny Sherwinter, sophomore

WEBSTER UNIVERSITY

Enrollment 11,401
Jewish 150 (UG 100; GR 50)

St. Louis Hillel Center Extension
6300 Forsyth Blvd.
St. Louis, MO 63105
(314) 935-9040
Fax: (314) 935-9041

Robert Goldberg, Executive Director
Nina Sackheim, Jewish Campus Service Corps Fellow

Jewish Studies
1–6 courses.

Kosher Food
Dormitory cooking facilities.

Jewish students in the St. Louis metropolitan area are served by St. Louis Hillel. See the listing for Washington University.

NEBRASKA

CREIGHTON UNIVERSITY

Enrollment 5,760 (UG: 3,360; GR: 2,400)
Jewish 50

Administration Building 333
2500 California Plaza
Creighton University
Omaha, NE 68178
(402) 280-2303/2304
Fax: (402) 280-1454
E-mail: ljgrn@creighton.edu.

Prof. Leonard J. Greenspoon, Advisor

ON CAMPUS

Creighton University is a coeducational, independent Catholic university operated by the Jesuits. To enhance Jewish student enrollment, the University has established the A.A. and Ethel Yossem Scholarships, 2 annual $7,000 scholarships (renewable up to 4 years) awarded to entering Jewish undergraduate students. Further information can be obtained from the University Department of Admissions, 2500 California Plaza, Omaha, NE 68178; (800) 282-5835; (402) 280-2703.

Creighton University now has an officially recognized Jewish student organization, and the Jewish community of Omaha is unusually supportive and offers a wide variety of educational, social, and religious opportunities that are open to Creighton students.

UNIVERSITY OF NEBRASKA—LINCOLN

Enrollment 24,000
Jewish 100 (UG 70; GR 30)

Hillel at University of Nebraska, Lincoln
c/o Norman & Bernice Harris Center for Judaic Studies
107 Bessey Hall
Lincoln; NE 68588-0346
(402) 472-2343
Fax: (402) 472-1123

Professor Alan Steinweis, Advisor

Jewish Studies

12–14 courses annually; 20 in catalog; minor. Endowed Chair. The Norman and Bernice Harris Center for Judaic Studies was established by the University's Board of Regents in 1993 "to educate Nebraskans and the wider

Great Plains community about Judaism and Jewish traditions, Jewish contributions to other traditions, the influence of other traditions on Jewish life and culture, and the origins and effects of anti-semitism." 9 faculty, from the departments of History, Modern Languages, English, Philosophy, Classics, Political Science, the College of Law, and the University Library. The program hopes to have an undergraduate major in place by the end of the decade. The program also sponsors frequent guest lecture and special programs. Professor Alan E. Steinweis, Director, Harris Center for Judaic Studies, Bessey Hall 107, Lincoln, NE 68588-0346; (402) 472-9561; aes@inlinfor.unl.edu.

Study in Israel

Junior year abroad can be taken in Israel.

Kosher Food

Available in Omaha, an hour away.

ON CAMPUS

Stimulating speakers on a wide variety of topics of Jewish interest come to campus. The Lincoln Jewish Community is very hospitable and supportive of Jewish initiatives on campus.

UNIVERSITY OF NEBRASKA—OMAHA

Enrollment 9,800 (UG 7,300; GR 2,500)
Jewish 150 (UG 100; GR 50)

Hillel
University of Nebraska
60th and Dodge Streets
Omaha, NE 68182
(402) 554-3349
Fax: (402) 554-3349

Professor Richard A. Freund, Advisor

Jewish Studies

6 courses, including Jewish Ethics, Modern Judaism, Holocaust, History of Judaism, and Women and Judaism; full Hebrew program.

Study in Israel

Summer program, archaeological dig at Beth Saida.

Kosher Food

Vegetarian dining alternatives.

ON CAMPUS

The Omaha Jewish community is very supportive of Jewish student life, with activities in the local synagogues and JCC. A few activities per semester are held on this primarily commuter campus. The annual major Holocaust commemoration involves the campus and the community in symposia.

NEVADA

UNIVERSITY OF NEVADA—LAS VEGAS

Enrollment 22,000
Jewish 1,000

Hillel at UNLV
4765 Brussels Avenue
Las Vegas, NV 89119
(702) 736-0887
Fax: (702) 891-0615
E-mail: hillel@nevada.edu
Web: www.hillelunlv.org

Melanie Greenberg, Director
Shari Schaeffer, Program Director

 Study in Israel
The Hotel Administration Department allows for training in Israel. Additional Israel programs are offered by the Jewish Federation of Las Vegas. The International Studies Department has developed a new exchange program with Ben-Gurion University.

Kosher Food
Hillel provides a monthly Shabbat dinner and holiday celebrations. Kosher food is available locally.

ON CAMPUS
The Las Vegas Jewish community is very supportive of Jewish students. The campus is centrally located in the city.

"We are excited by the growth of our Hillel. We're known on campus for our Welcome Back Limo Scavenger Hunt, Holocaust Program, and Interfaith/Multicultural Passover Seder."

Stephanie Lehrner, senior

UNIVERSITY OF NEVADA—RENO

Enrollment 11,000
Jewish 300 (UG 250; GR 50)

Jewish Student Union
c/o Professor Victoria Hartling
Center for Holocaust and Genocide Studies
1048 N. Sierra Street
Reno, NV 89557-0200
(775) 784-6767
E-mail: hertling@scs.unr.edu

Professor Victoria Hertling, Advisor

 Jewish Studies
Minor in Holocaust, Genocide, and Peace Studies.

 Study in Israel
Contact Advisor, Office of International Education, or University Studies Abroad Consortium on campus.

 Kosher Food
Available locally.

ON CAMPUS
University of Nevada—Reno is a small multi-college land grant state university. Jewish campus programming is expanding through the Center for Holocaust, Genocide, and Peace Studies, the Western Traditions Program, and other programs.

NEW HAMPSHIRE

DARTMOUTH COLLEGE

Enrollment 5,270 (UG 4,200; GR 1,070)
Jewish 500 (UG 450; GR 50)

 Dartmouth Hillel
Roth Center for Jewish Life
5 Occum Ridge Road
Hanover, NH 03755
(603) 646-3782
(603) 646-1288
Fax: (603) 646-0362
E-mail: hillel@dartmouth.edu

Rabbi Edward Boraz, Director

Jewish Studies
Major in Jewish Studies.

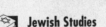 **Study in Israel**
Transfer program with University of Tel Aviv.

Kosher Food
Kosher frozen meals and kosher deli sandwiches are available in all Dartmouth dining halls. Packaged kosher food is available on the meal plan.

Housing
Dartmouth provides 2 apartments for students who wish to keep kosher or speak Hebrew.

ON CAMPUS
The Dartmouth Hillel Intercollegiate Ski Shabbaton, which is now in its fourth year, draws students from all over the Northeast. Dartmouth Hillel relies heavily on its beautiful surroundings for programming, and events such as the Multicultural Sukkot Celebration at the Dartmouth Organic Farm are very successful.

"When I first came to Dartmouth Hillel, I found a group of people who were surprisingly different from each other. Students who are Jewishly active at Dartmouth participate in a panoply of other activities on campus, from the Student Assembly to the Dartmouth Outing Club to Greek houses to the Dartmouth Organic Farm. As a result, the Jewish experience at Dartmouth is not only pleasant but is invaluably rewarding. I am confident that many of the friendships I have made through Hillel will last for the rest of my life."

Jesse Cook-Dubin, junior

KEENE STATE COLLEGE

Enrollment 4,000
Jewish 150

Jewish Students Association
c/o Dr. Howard Bohm
Science Center
Keene, NH 03431-4183
(603) 358-2572

Dr. Howard Bohm, Advisor

ON CAMPUS
Keene State is witnessing growth in Jewish life on campus. This year, students took a trip to New York City to visit the Museum of Jewish Heritage. Keene State has a Holocaust Center on campus.

NEW ENGLAND COLLEGE

Enrollment 1,000
Jewish 275

Jewish Student Organization
New England College
Henniker, NH 03242
(603) 428-2337
Fax: (603) 428-7230

A.A. Metzegen-Bundiy, Advisor

 Study in Israel
Occasional travel and study programs.

ON CAMPUS
New England College is a small liberal arts college with specialities in education and the performing arts. The College is located about an hour and a half from Boston, which enables Jewish students to participate in the Boston Hillel Intercampus Council. There are several Jewish congregations in Concord (20 minutes away) and Manchester (40 minutes away).

UNIVERSITY OF NEW HAMPSHIRE

Enrollment 12,300
Jewish 400

Hillel Student Activity Office
University of New Hampshire
Durham, NH 03824
(603) 862-4120
(617) 353-7210

Ailene Gerhardt, Director of Regional Student Services, Hillel Council of New England
Rabbi Lev Ba'Esh, Jewish Chaplain

 Jewish Studies
1 class in Jewish Literature; 1 class in Politics of the Middle East.

 Study in Israel
Students may study at UNH-approved universities.

Kosher Food
Vegetarian dining alternatives; dormitory cooking facilities.

ON CAMPUS
There is increasing Jewish life at UNH. Recent activities have included a standing-room-only campuswide lecture by a Holocaust survivor, trips to D.C. (U.S. Holocaust Memorial Museum), Israel Day, International Food Day, Israeli dance, and a campuswide Hanukkah dinner. The local rabbi is supportive of Jewish students at the University and encourages participation.

Served by Hillel Council of New England.

NEW JERSEY

ATLANTIC COMMUNITY COLLEGE

Enrollment 1,500
Jewish 150

Association of Jewish Students
5100 Black Horse Pike
Mays Landing, NJ 08330
(609) 343-4989
(609) 822-1167

Professor Yechiel Lehavy, Advisor

ON CAMPUS
An active Jewish club meets weekly.

BERGEN COMMUNITY COLLEGE

Enrollment 12,000
Jewish 300

> Jewish Student Association
> c/o Prof. Susan Klarreich
> Bergen Community College
> 400 Paramus Road
> Paramus, NJ 07652
> (201) 447-7904/7906
> Fax: (201) 488-1507
> E-mail: mgisser@compuserve.com
>
> **Professor Susan Klarreich**, Advisor
> **Professor Ruth Feigenbaum**, Advisor
> **Michael Gisser**, Director

Jewish Studies
1–2 courses per year through the Philosophy and Religion Department.

Housing
Local synagogues and UJA Federation (201-488-6800) will help place students in kosher homes or help find housing close to campus.

ON CAMPUS

The Jewish Students Association runs a combination of cultural and religious events, including trips, lectures, holiday celebrations, and historical commemorations. The group is known for its efforts in reaching out to the greater community by working with the homeless, Jewish high school students, and Jewish elderly. The College's location easily lends itself to trips to New York City (Ellis Island, Lower East Side) and Washington, D.C. (U.S. Holocaust Memorial Museum). In addition, the JSA works closely with the Hillels at Fairleigh Dickinson University and Ramapo College of New Jersey and runs events in conjunction with Hillels throughout the state of New Jersey.

Bergen Community College is located in northern Bergen County, NJ, an area extremely rich in Jewish culture and presence, and supportive of BCC's Hillel. Numerous synagogues (Reform, Conservative, and Orthodox) blanket the area and open their doors to students.

COUNTY COLLEGE OF MORRIS

Enrollment N/A
Jewish 100

> Jewish Student Organization
> 760 Northfield Avenue
> West Orange, NJ 07052
> (201) 736-3200 ext. 285
> Fax: (201) 736-6871
> E-mail: tfeller@ujfmetrowest.org
>
> **Toby Feller**, Director
> **Leslie Morris**, Campus Advisor

ON CAMPUS

Students enjoy a significant collaborative program with the Alliance of Jewish Student Organizations, an umbrella group for all the college and university campuses in northern New Jersey. The advisor is on campus one day a week. Many students commute. This campus is served by Jewish Student Services of Metrowest.

DREW UNIVERSITY

Enrollment 1,400
Jewish 150

> Drew University Hillel
> Pat Glucksman
> Jewish Studies Program
> 119 Brothers College
> Madison, NJ 07940
> (973) 408-3270
> (973) 408-3711
> E-mail: aroth@drew.edu or pglucksm@drew,edu
> Web: www.users.drew.edu/~hillel
>
> **Akiva Roth**, Director
> **Peggy Samuels**, Faculty Advisor
> **Pat Glucksman**, Jewish Studies Adminstrator

Jewish Studies
2-track minor: general Judaic and concentration in Holocaust Studies. Endowed Professorship in Jewish studies, with 10 other faculty members contributing courses, such as Biblical and Modern Hebrew; Shoah; The Epic Film; Arab-Israeli Conflict in Literature; Meaning of Life in the Jewish Tradition; Patristic and Rabbinic Exegesis; Jewish Experience; Modern Jewish History; and Science, Religion, and the Holocaust. Drew Center for Holocaust Studies has courses, conferences, and film series. There is also a Middle East Studies program. Upper-level students may also take graduate-level courses.

Study in Israel
Drew International Seminars in Israel, and Middle East Region, and Holocaust Seminar to Eastern Europe.

Arrangements made for semester or year-long study. Scholarships are available annually for study or work/travel programs in Israel. Drew University accepts credits from Hebrew University, Tel Aviv University, and other institutions by petition.

Kosher Food

Vegetarian/dairy options at all meals; Shabbat and Holiday dinners from kosher caterer. Students may use the kosher cooking facilities in Religious Life Theme House.

Housing

Drew University does not have special housing for Jewish students, but the University has a "theme" house, the spirituality house, which houses students interested in inter-religious communication and experiences.

ON CAMPUS

Located in the vibrant Jewish community of Metrowest with dozens of synagogues and kosher restaurants, and less than an hour from New York City's many Jewish attractions, Drew provides many opportunities for a Jewish campus life. Hillel provides social, educational, religious, social action/community service, and sports programs for students, faculty, staff and local residents. Hillel is active in interfaith programming on campus. Local families host students for Jewish holidays. Hillel runs programs in conjunction with the New Jersey Alliance of Jewish Students Organizations, and with other Hillels.

ESSEX COMMUNITY COLLEGE

Enrollment N/A
Jewish 50

Jewish Student Union
760 Northfield Avenue
West Orange, NJ 07052
(973) 736-3200 ext. 285
Fax: (973) 736-6871
E-mail: tfeller@ujfmetrowest.org

Toby Feller, Director

ON CAMPUS

Students enjoy a significant collaborative program with the Alliance of Jewish Student Organizations, an umbrella group for all the college and university campuses in northern New Jersey. The advisor is on campus one day a week. There are many commuter students. This campus is served by Jewish Student Services of Metrowest.

FAIRLEIGH DICKINSON UNIVERSITY— MADISON

Enrollment 3,100 (UG 1,100; GR 2,000)
Jewish 400

Jewish Student Organization
285 Madison Avenue
Madison, NJ 07940
(201) 443-8505
(201) 736-3200
Fax: (201) 736-6871
E-mail: tfeller@ujfmetrowest.org

Toby Feller, Director
Dina Roher, Campus Advisor

Jewish Studies

4–6 courses annually. Holocaust Center, Comparative Religion courses.

Study in Israel

FDU Israel was established in 1996. U.S. students may study for a semester or year at FDU Israel; Hebrew fluency is required since most courses are in Hebrew. Israeli students can receive a full FDU degree in communications, hotel and restaurant management, psychology, and other fields; they must spend a full summer semester on the Teaneck campus. Dr. Leonard Grob, U.S. coordinator; (201) 692-2408.

Kosher Food

Frozen kosher meals and vegetarian meals are available through food services. Kosher-for-Passover meals are also available in the cafeteria. Packaged kosher sandwiches and pastries are available in the student lounge.

Housing

Local synagogues and UJA Federation (201-488-6800) will help place students in kosher homes or help find housing close to campus.

ON CAMPUS

Students enjoy a significant collaborative program with the Alliance of Jewish Student Organizations, an umbrella group for all the college and university campuses in northern New Jersey. The advisor is on campus one day a week. Many students commute. This campus is served by Jewish Student Services of Metrowest.

FAIRLEIGH DICKINSON UNIVERSITY— TEANECK AND HACKENSACK

Enrollment 4,500 (UG 3,800; GR 700)
Jewish 350

FDU Hillel/JSU
1000 River Road
Teaneck, NJ 07666
(201) 488-6800
(201) 692-2406
Fax: (201) 488-1507
E-mail: mgisser@compuserve.com

Michael Gisser, Director

Jewish Studies
4-6 courses annually. Holocaust Center, Comparative Religion courses.

Study in Israel
FDU Israel was established in 1996. U.S. students may study for a semester or a year at FDU Israel; Hebrew fluency is required since most courses are in Hebrew. Israeli students can receive a full FDU degree in communications, hotel and restaurant management, psychology, and other fields; they must spend a full summer semester on the Teaneck campus. Dr. Leonard Grob, U.S. coordinator; (201) 692-2408.

Kosher Food
Frozen kosher meals and vegetarian meals are available through food services. Kosher-for-Passover meals are also available in the cafeteria. Packaged kosher sandwiches and pastries are available in the student lounge.

Housing
Local synagogues and UJA Federation (201-488-6800) will help place students in kosher homes or help find housing close to campus.

ON CAMPUS
Hillel runs a combination of cultural and religious events, including trips, lectures, holiday celebrations, and historical commemorations. Hillel is known for its efforts in reaching out to the greater community by working with the homeless and Jewish high school students. FDU's location easily lends itself to trips to New York City (Ellis Island, Lower East Side) and Washington, D.C. (U.S. Holocaust Memorial Museum). In addition, FDU Hillel works closely with the Hillels at Ramapo College of New Jersey and Bergen Community College, and plans events in conjunction with Hillels throughout the state of New Jersey.

Teaneck is one of New Jersey's strongest and largest Jewish communities. Bergen County is rich in Jewish culture and presence, and supportive of FDU's Hillel in any way possible. Numerous synagogues of all denominations blanket the area and open their doors to students.

KEAN COLLEGE OF NEW JERSEY

Enrollment 12,800
Jewish 600

c/o Jewish Federation of Central New Jersey
843 St. Georges Avenue
Roselle, NJ 07203
(908) 298-8200
Fax: (908) 298-8220

Harry Glazer, Advisor

Kosher Food
Kosher restaurants and grocery stores located nearby.

ON CAMPUS
Kean College has a Holocaust Resource Center and an Oral Testimonies Project affiliated with Yale University. Nearby Elizabeth, NJ, offers kosher restaurants and food, as well as religious services. This is a part-time program of the Jewish Federation of Central New Jersey.

"I don't think most of the administration are supportive of Jewish life on campus. Yet, the Jewish faculty members are extremely supportive and helpful to our organization."

Robert Katz, senior

MONMOUTH UNIVERSITY

Enrollment 4,500
Jewish 400

JSU/Hillel
Monmouth University
West Long Branch, NJ 07764-1898
(732) 571-3487
Fax: (732) 263-5167
E-mail: lichter@monmouth.edu
Web: lichter@monmouth.edu

Lori Lichter, Student Development Counselor

Jewish Studies

1 senior level course: The Jewish Experience.

Study in Israel

Study abroad.

Kosher Food

Vegetarian options available.

ON CAMPUS
Jewish campus activities vary according to the interest of the students.

MONTCLAIR STATE UNIVERSITY

Enrollment 13,500
Jewish 450

Jewish Student Union
Student Center, Room 123
Montclair State University
Upper Montclair, NJ 07043
(201) 655-5280
(201) 736-3200
Fax: (201) 736-6871
E-mail: jsu@alpha.montclair.edu

Toby H. Feller, Director
Dina Roher, Campus Advisor

 Jewish Studies
Courses available through various departments.

 Study in Israel
Semester abroad.

ON CAMPUS

Students enjoy a significant collaborative program with the Alliance of Jewish Student Organizations, an umbrella group for all the college and university campuses in northern New Jersey. The advisor is on campus one day a week. Many students commute.

This campus is served by Jewish Student Services of Metrowest.

MORRIS COUNTY COMMUNITY COLLEGE

Enrollment N/A
Jewish N/A

Morris County CC Jewish Center
c/o Pearl Lebovic
7 Kissel Lane
Morristown, NJ 07960
(201) 285-1769
Fax (201) 267-6640
E-mail: ylebovic @juno.com
Web: www.Florida.com/shiduch/

Pearl Lebovic, Advisor

ON CAMPUS

Mrs. Lubovic facilitates home hospitality and other activities according to student interest.

NEW JERSEY INSTITUTE OF TECHNOLOGY— NEWARK

Enrollment 3,400
Jewish 50

Jewish Student Union
760 Northfield Avenue
West Orange, NJ 07052
(973) 736-3200 ext. 285
Fax: (973) 736-6871
E-mail: tfeller@ujfmetrowest.org

Toby Feller, Director
Leslie Morris, Campus Advisor

ON CAMPUS

Students enjoy a significant collaborative program with the Alliance of Jewish Student Organizations, an umbrella group for all the college and university campuses in northern New Jersey. The advisor is on campus one day a week. Many students commute. This campus is served by Jewish Student Services of Metrowest.

PRINCETON UNIVERSITY

Enrollment 6,300 (UG 4,600; GR 1,700)
Jewish 750 (UG 550; GR 200)

 Center for Jewish Life
70 Washington Road
Princeton, NJ 08540
(609) 258-3635
Fax: (609) 258-2884
E-mail: hillel@phoenix.princeton.edu

Rachel Rubenstein, Director
Amy Reisner, Program Director

Jewish Studies

12–15 courses per year. Program certificate. New program in process of ambitious full funding. Fully interdisciplinary program, involving junior independent work and senior thesis on a Jewish topic in the student's home department, with core courses and junior/senior seminar required. Courses in Hebrew; Jewish history; Bible; rabbinics; music; modern Middle East; Judaism ancient, medieval, and modern; Jewish literature; and other related fields in the humanities and social sciences. At present there are 4 full-time faculty; a new endowed chair to be filled, with several others expected; plus provision for visiting faculty. In addition to Religion and Near Eastern Studies, interdisciplinary faculty are in the Department of German, English, History, Music, Classics (and Ancient World), Sociology, Anthropology, and the Woodrow Wilson School. Annual senior thesis prize. Opportunities for summer study, conferences, and endowed lectures. Froma I.

Zeitlin, Dept. of Classics, Princeton University, Princeton NJ 08544; (609) 258-3951; 6201/3597.

Study in Israel

Princeton will accept transfer credits for a semester or a year of study in Israel. The course of study must be approved in advance by the academic advisor to assure that it meets university standards and furthers the student's academic major. While Princeton does not have a standing year abroad program with any Israeli university, a new, experimental program began in 1999 between the Woodrow Wilson School and Hebrew University: juniors majoring in politics or foreign affairs may study these subjects at Hebrew University under the guidance of Prof. Ehud Sprinzak, who conducts an exclusive seminar for them on international terrorism.

Kosher Food

The University operates a full kosher dining service housed in the Center for Jewish Life. This kosher dining option is an integral part of the University dining service. Students who purchase a dining service contract may eat at any of the University dining facilities, including the Center for Jewish Life. The CJL dining hall attracts a wide spectrum of Princeton students and faculty. Vegetarian meals and full salad bar are available at every meal. The After Hours Cafe offers kosher dessert and coffee 6 nights a week.

ON CAMPUS

Jewish life thrives at Princeton as never before. The Center for Jewish Life is a state-of-the-art facility located near the heart of the picture-book campus. The CJL is the fruit of a unique partnership between Princeton University and Hillel. The University owns the building and operates a superb dining hall in it that is a gathering place for Princeton students of all backgrounds. Hillel staffs the CJL and operates the program.

There are nearly 20 different groups and projects teams, including the Very Interesting Professors lunch time conversations series; Roots: A Week of Jewish Learning, which attracts a broad range of undergrads, grads, faculty, and community people; and Jewish Heritage Week, a springtime series of events such as a mock Jewish wedding and semi-formal, performances by Koleinu, Princeton's Jewish *a cappella* group, and discussions on Israel and world Jewry. Among the speakers the CJL has recently brought to campus are playwright Tony Kushner, Rabbi Adin Steinsaltz, Dr. Ruth Westheimer, editor of *The New Republic* Martin Peretz, and Rabbi Gunther Plaut. There is an annual Princeton student UJA campaign, and PIPAC focuses on Israeli political issues. Recent interfaith projects have included a lively conversation group on the Book of Genesis and an interfaith seder. Interethnic programs included a joint Black/Jewish student meeting. The Jewish Women's Connection explores feminist issues and holds Rosh Hodesh gatherings. CJL students participate in various community service projects such as toy drives and visits to a local Jewish senior citizen home. Princeton's excellent location makes possible CJL-spon-

sored trips to New York City and to Washington, D.C. Social events such as a "Jewish Singled Out" evening occur frequently.

The CJL offers special programs for upper-level students and grad students. The Covenant Club sponsors subsidized theater and movie trips, gourmet dinners, special clothing items, and an annual canoe trip.

The CJL building contains a comfortable lounge with an excellent collection of magazines, a reference library and Beit Midrash, a computer cluster, TV and billiards rooms, a piano, and several multipurpose rooms for programs, study, or lounging. The staff is always available for shmoozing and personal counseling.

Princeton University is well attuned to the needs and concerns of Jewish students. Scheduling and examination conflicts are easily resolved. The Jewish student body is large enough and talented enough to create a vast array of quality programming and yet is of a size where one can really feel part of a warm, friendly, and pluralistic community.

"Princeton is a terrific place for Jewish students. Jews from all kinds of backgrounds can thrive at Princeton, enjoying the benefits of a strong and active Hillel as well as participating in an enriching campus environment. Socially, academically, and religiously—Princeton is an excellent place to be."

Tzivia Friedman, '02

"Our community is incredibly unified—there is an atmosphere of mutual respect and understanding that makes me proud to be a Jew at Princeton."

Courtney Weiner, '01

"Singing in the Jewish a cappella group brings me to the CJL regularly. There are lots of things to love about the place: the building, the people, the big screen TV, and the pool table. Plus, students from all across campus, Jewish or not, prefer the CJL's food over the other dining halls.

Jason Kessler, '02

"Princeton has a wonderful, supportive, diverse community, filled with exciting people, where I can always be assured of having an interesting conversation."

Laura Saslow, '00

RAMAPO COLLEGE OF NEW JERSEY

Enrollment 4,700
Jewish 400

Hillel
Ramapo College Student Center
505 Ramapo Valley Road
Mahwah, NJ 07430
(201) 684-7292
Fax: (201) 529-7452
E-mail: hillel@ramapo.edu

Michael Gisser, Director
David I. Bacall, VP, Communication

Jewish Studies
3–4 courses per semester; minor in Jewish Studies; Holocaust and Genocide Studies Center on campus.

Study in Israel
Annual archaeological dig at Tel Hadar; credits accepted from most Israeli universities.

Kosher Food
Dormitory cooking facilities; boxed kosher and vegetarian meals available from campus dining service by special order.

Housing
On-campus housing option available for Jewish students who have kashrut requirements.

ON CAMPUS

Ramapo is located in Northern Bergen County, NJ, adjacent to Rockland County, NY. Both communities are rich in Jewish culture and presence and supportive of Ramapo's Hillel in every way possible. Numerous synagogues of all denominations in the community open their doors to students.

Hillel runs a combination of cultural and religious events, including trips, lectures, holiday celebrations and historical commemorations. Hillel is known for its efforts in reaching out to the greater community by working with the homeless and Jewish high school students. Ramapo's location easily lends itself to trips to New York City (Ellis Island, Lower East Side) and Washington, D.C. (U.S. Holocaust Memorial Museum). In addition, Hillel works closely with the Hillels at Fairleigh Dickinson University and Bergen Community College and runs events in conjunction with Hillels throughout the State of New Jersey. A Jewish fraternity and a Jewish sorority are on campus.

"The campus is very religiously friendly and fully supports various religious groups on campus."

Cindy D. Simon, recent graduate

RICHARD STOCKTON COLLEGE OF NEW JERSEY

Enrollment 5,900
Jewish 700

Jewish Student Union/Hillel
PO Box 195
Pomona, NJ 08240
(609) 652-4699

Gail Rosenthal, Advisor
Professor Yitzhak Sharon, Faculty Advisor
Mrs. Lynn Berkowitz, Advisor

Jewish Studies
15 courses; minor in Jewish studies. Internship programs are available at the Federation of Jewish Agencies, the Holocaust Resource Center, and through semesters in Washington, D.C. and independent studies.

Study in Israel
Junior year or semester abroad; summer Israel seminars; winter study tours in Israel; archaeological digs.

Kosher Food
Vegetarian dining alternatives; dormintory cooking facilities; kosher-for-Passover meals.

ON CAMPUS

The South Jersey Jewish Studies Library is housed on the Stockton campus. Jewish student activities at Stockton are supported by the Federation of Jewish Agencies of Atlantic and Cape May County. Scholarships are available for Stockton students to study and travel in Israel. Additional scholarships are offered yearly for full-time students who intend to obtain the Jewish Studies Certificate, plan a career in Jewish communal service, or pursue Holocaust Studies.

The regional Holocaust Resource Center, a joint project of the Jewish Federation of Atlantic and Cape May Counties and Richard Stockton College, is located in the library. The Ida E. King Distinguished Visiting Professorship of Holocaust Studies annually brings to Stockton a different scholar of international reputation to teach and do research about the Holocaust. Stockton's active student program also includes Purim and Hanukkah dinners, student-faculty conversations and dinners, and Israel days on campus. Each week, 35-40 students meet to socialize and plan future Hillel events.

RIDER UNIVERSITY

Enrollment 4,000
Jewish 400

Memorial Hall
Rider University
Lawrenceville, NJ 08648
(609) 896-4977
(609) 883-5000
(609) 219-0555 (Federation)

Howard Gases, Executive Director, Federation
Rabbi Daniel T. Grossman, Religious Advisor
Professor Albert Nissman, Faculty Advisor

ON CAMPUS

Rider has an active Hillel group, which is in close relationship with Adath Israel Congregation across the street. The program is supported by the Jewish Federation of Mercer and Bucks Counties, and the local community provides home hospitality. The new Koppelman Holocaust Center has just opened (609-896-5345).

ROWAN COLLEGE OF NEW JERSEY

Enrollment 10,000
Jewish 1,000

Rowan College Hillel
Jewish Federation, Regional Jewish Student Union
1301 Springdale Rd.
Cherry Hill, NJ 08003
(856) 424-4444 ext. 291
Fax: (856) 751-6804

Sara Geist, Adult Department Director

 Jewish Studies
1 course.

 Kosher Food
Frozen meals available on request in the dining hall; vegetarian dining alternatives.

ON CAMPUS

Rowan College has an active Jewish Student Union/Hillel. Activities include holiday celebrations, holiday gift packages, subscriptions to appropriate publications, and participation in Jewish community activities. The Hillel program at Rowan College is a service of the Jewish Federation of Southern New Jersey in conjunction with the efforts of the Continuity Commission.

RUTGERS UNIVERSITY—CAMDEN

Enrollment 4,500 (UG 3,500; GR 1,000)
Jewish 250

Jewish Student Union
Jewish Federation, Regional Student Union
1301 Springdale Road
Cherry Hill, NJ 08003
(856) 424-4444 ext. 291
Fax: (856) 751-6804
E-mail: scharme@camden.rutgers.edu

Sara Geist, Adult Department Director
Professor Stuart Charme, Advisor

 Jewish Studies
3 courses.

 Study in Israel
Junior year at Haifa University.

ON CAMPUS

Rutgers University—Camden has an active Jewish Student Union/Hillel. Activities include holiday celebrations, holiday gift packages, subscriptions to appropriate publications and participation in Jewish community activities. The program is supported by Jewish Federation of Southern New Jersey in conjunction with the efforts of the Continuity Commission.

RUTGERS UNIVERSITY— DOUGLASS-COOK-LIVINGSTON

Enrollment 34,000
Jewish 4,000

 Rutgers Hillel Foundation
93 College Avenue
New Brunswick, NJ 08901
(732) 545-2407
Fax: (732) 932-1063

Rabbi David Gutterman, Director
Rabbi Norman Weitzner, Director of Special Projects
Geoffrey Menkowitz, Jewish Campus Service Corps.
Fellow

 Jewish Studies
12 courses; B.A. Rutgers University's new Judaic Studies Center, The Bildner Center for the Study of Jewish Life, offers an undergraduate degree in Jewish Studies through an interdisciplinary curriculum.

 Study in Israel
Programs with Hebrew University, Haifa University, and Ben-Gurion University. The Hebraic Studies Department approves credit transfers from other Israeli intitutions.

Kosher Food

Hillel instituted a glatt-kosher plan through the dining services located on all campuses. Chabad also has a kosher meal plan in their building.

Housing

The "Hebrew House" coed dormitory offers housing for 17 students.

ON CAMPUS

For the past 3 years, Hillel has lead the campus in a host of relevant and exciting programming. Hillel has received the coveted Most Outstanding Student Group Award and the peer award for Excellence in Campus Programming, in recognition of its creative and dynamic programming. The Hillel Leadership Council, the student-empowered board, is at the heart of this renaissance in Jewish programming.

Hillel is creating Jewish conversation opportunities and social projects through its Mitzva Service Corps. A highlight of the year is the Israel Learning/Leadership Experience led by Rabbi Gutterman, which takes 18 students to Israel during winter break. Hillel's newly created "Emerging Leaders Grants Assistance" program seeks to identify and provide opportunities for students to develop leadership skills outside of campus. CUPA (Challenge Underwriting for Programming Alternatives) provides funds for students, whether active with Hillel or not, to develop, design and bring to campus unique and appealing Jewish programming.

RUTGERS UNIVERSITY— NEWARK CAMPUS

Enrollment 6,300 (UG 3,100; GR 3,200)
Jewish 50

Jewish Student Union
760 Northfield Avenue
West Orange, NJ 07052
(973) 736-3200 ext. 285
Fax: (973) 736-6871
E-mail: tfeller@ujfmetrowest.org

Toby Feller, Director
Leslie Morris, Campus Advisor

Jewish Studies

8 courses.

Study in Israel

Junior year abroad/summer seminar.

ON CAMPUS

Students enjoy a significant collaborative program with the Alliance of Jewish Student Organizations, an um-

brella group for all the college and university campuses in northern New Jersey. The advisor is on campus one day a week. Many students commute. This campus is served by Jewish Student Services of Metrowest.

RUTGERS UNIVERSITY LAW SCHOOL—NEWARK

Enrollment 800
Jewish 250

Decalogue Society
760 Northfield Avenue
West Orange, NJ 07052
(201) 736-3200
Fax: (201) 736-6871
E-mail: tfeller@ujfmetrowest.org
Web: www.jewishstudies.rutgers.edu

Toby Feller, Director

ON CAMPUS

The advisor is on campus one day a week to serve this mostly commuter population. This campus is served by Jewish Student Services of Metrowest.

STEVENS INSTITUTE OF TECHNOLOGY

Enrollment 3,100 (UG 1,600; GR 1,500)
Jewish 400 (UG 50; GR 350)

Stevens Hillel
c/o Math Department
Castle Point Station
Stevens Institute of Technology
Hoboken, NJ 07030
(201) 216-5000 ext. 5449

Professor Lawrence E. Levine, Advisor

Kosher Food

Frozen kosher meals available on request in the dining hall; dormitory cooking facilities.

ON CAMPUS

Programs include occasional lectures, a model seder, and various holiday activities. These events change from year to year depending upon student interest.

THE COLLEGE OF NEW JERSEY

Enrollment 6,000 (UG 5,000; GR 1,000)
Jewish 300

Jewish Student Union/Hillel
CDS Office—Brower Student Center
The College of New Jersey
Trenton, NJ 08650
(609) 771-2613
(609) 530-1005
E-mail: jsu@tcnj.edu
Web: www.tcnj.edu/~jsu

Magda Manetas, Advisor
Rabbi Joel D. Chernikoff, Religious Advisor

 Kosher Food
Kosher food is available locally.

ON CAMPUS

The College of New Jersey students mainly come from New Jersey, Pennsylvania, and the northeast Philadelphia areas. There is a strong Jewish community in the region.

WILLIAM PATTERSON COLLEGE

Enrollment 10,000
Jewish 900

Jewish Student Association at William Patterson
300 Pompton Road, Room 320
Student Center Building
Wayne, NJ 07470
(201) 942-8545
(201) 595-0100

Lisa Constants, Advisor

 Jewish Studies
2 courses.

Study in Israel
Israel semester.

 Kosher Food
The JSA and the University offer holiday and occasional meals; frozen meals available on request in dining hall; vegetarian dining alternatives; dormitory cooking facilities; kosher food is available locally.

ON CAMPUS

Students enjoy a variety of social and holiday activities, including lectures, films, a JSA sukkah, a Hanukkah toy drive, a Passover seder, Yom Ha' atzmaut observance, as well as teach-ins. This is a part-time program. Students are also welcome at the YM-YWHA of North Jersey. The supportive local community provides home hospitality for Shabbat and holidays. Most William Patterson students commute.

NEW MEXICO

NEW MEXICO STATE UNIVERSITY

Enrollment 16,000 (UG 9,100; GR 6,900)
Jewish 100

Jewish Student Association
c/o Temple Beth El
P.O. Box 1029001
Parker Road at Melendres
Las Cruces, NM 88005
(505) 524-0111
(505) 646-3724
Fax: (505) 646-1002
E-mail: arthur@cs.nmsu.edu

Rabbi Cy Stanway, Advisor
Professor Arthur Karshmer, Advisor

 Jewish Studies
1 course.

 Kosher Food
Dormitory cooking facilities; vegetarian dining alternatives.

ON CAMPUS

No formal Hillel group currently exists, but Professor Karshmer will assist any efforts to create a Jewish student presence on campus.

UNIVERSITY OF NEW MEXICO

Enrollment 22,000
Jewish 250

Hillel at UNM
The Aaron David Bram Hillel House
1701 Sigma Chi Road, NE
Albuquerque, NM 87106
(505) 242-1127
Fax: (505) 242-1127
E-mail: jhgaines@unm.edu
Web: www.unm.edu/~hillel/hillel.html

Dr. Janet Gaines, Director

Jewish Studies
Students may take Jewish studies courses through the English, History, and Continuing Education departments.

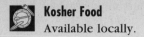 **Kosher Food**
Available locally.

ON CAMPUS

Hillel at UNM offers a variety of activities for Jewish students, faculty, and staff in the comfortable, home-like atmosphere of the Aaron David Bram Hillel House located on campus. Shabbat evening candle lightings and vegetarian meals; holiday observances; faculty-student lunches; social functions; retreats; Hebrew, Bible, and special topics courses; lectures and cultural events; community service opportunities; travel; public service opportunities, and inter-faith gatherings are offered. Hillel celebrates Jewish identity and builds leaders.

Shabbat meals and social events are popular the small Jewish student population on campus. Hillel has started a scholarship fund for Jewish students.

"There are very few young (college student) faces at synagogues, so our own center is invaluable."

Aaron Bernstein, graduate student

NEW YORK

ADELPHI UNIVERSITY

Enrollment 8,261
Jewish 600

Hillel at Adelphi
Religious Center—Earle Hall
Adelphi University
Garden City, NY 11530
(516) 877-3115
Fax: (516) 877-3039

Barry Dov Schwartz, Jewish Chaplain

 Jewish Studies
2 courses.

 Kosher Food
The University will provide frozen entrees to be cooked in kosher microwave and toaster ovens.

Adelphi is served as an outreach program of Hofstra University.

ALFRED UNIVERSITY

Enrollment 2,000
Jewish 200

Hillel at Alfred
c/o Prof. Arthur Greil
Alfred University
Alfred, NY 14802
(607) 871-2215
Fax: (607) 871-2114
E-mail: fgreil@alfred.edu

Professor Arthur L. Greil, Advisor

 Jewish Studies
Courses on Judaism and the Bible.

 Study in Israel
A number of students have studied abroad in Israel. Individual arrangements may be made through the Study Abroad Office.

 Kosher Food
Vegetarian dining alternatives; dormitory cooking facilities; kosher cooking facilities at Hillel House.

 Housing
Rooms are available for upperclassmen at Hillel House.

ON CAMPUS

Hillel serves as the center of Jewish life for both Jewish students and the surrounding Jewish community. The new Hillel House, opened in September 1994 with financial support from the University, has generated enthusiasm among students and has created new programming possibilities. The atmosphere on campus and in the community is one of mutual respect between Jews and non-Jews. Two of the seven fraternities on campus are historically Jewish houses.

"Hillel was a huge help in the transition between high school and college. The first time I went to Hillel, everyone was so friendly and warm which made it easy for me to get involved."

Naomi Manon, '00, Hillel President

"Hillel is always growing with new and exciting people each year. Many recent graduates also return to attend events, showing what a strong organization Hillel is. I enjoy the holidays even though I'm away from home, and the services are always fun and relaxing."

Adam Ostroff, '99

BARD COLLEGE

Enrollment 1,100
Jewish 175

Jewish Students Organization
Bard College
Annadale-on-Hudson, NY 12504
(914) 758-6822

Rabbi Jonathan Kligler, Jewish Chaplain

Jewish Studies

Students can create a Jewish Studies major through an interdisciplinary approach between the Department of Religion and other departments.

Kosher Food

The University provides "kosher style" Passover meals. At present, it is not possible to keep kosher unless you live off campus.

ON CAMPUS

The Jewish Students Organization is a relatively new feature on the Bard campus, and is quite small, but the size creates an intimate environment and the rabbi is very accessible. The Jewish Students Organization generally holds weekly Shabbat services and holiday celebrations and sponsors a variety of programs. Due to the JSO's small size, the intensity of Jewish activities varies from year to year depending on the student leadership. The Jewish chaplain teaches classes and is the rabbi of a nearby congregation where students are invited to participate, including involvement in the Hebrew School and youth group.

BINGHAMTON UNIVERSITY

Enrollment 12,000 (UG 10,000; GR 2,000)
Jewish 4,500

Binghamton University Hillel
Binghamton University
PO Box 6000
Binghamton, NY 13902-6000
(607) 777-4980
Fax: (607) 777-2679, c/o Judaic Studies Department
E-mail: bd24737@binghamton.edu
Web: www.sa.binghamton.edu/~hillel/hillpg.htm

Linda Salomons, Advisor

Jewish Studies

20 courses; B.A. in Judaic Studies and Hebrew. Minor also available.

Study in Israel

Exchange program with Haifa University. Many students go to Hebrew University or Tel Aviv University.

Kosher Food

The University provides 7 dinners and 7 lunches. The kosher dining hall is in the Student Union and is supervised mashgiach.

ON CAMPUS

Hillel and The Jewish Student Union have merged to form the only on-campus Jewish Organization. Now known as Hillel—The Jewish Student Union (Hillel-JSU), the organization seeks to serve Jewish students and those interested in Judaism, regardless of their background or religious affiliation. As a Student Association-funded organization, Hillel-JSU is entirely student-operated. Through the Hillel-JSU, all students have the power to plan any program and are only limited by their imaginations. Hillel-JSU conducts individual committee meetings and weekly General Board meetings.

Hillel-JSU is comprised of numerous active committees such as Social Action, Israel Action, United Jewish Appeal, Chug Ivrit (Hebrew speakers group), *Hatikvah* (JSU newspaper), a social committee, and a Jewish *a cappella* group, Kaskeset. Programming includes dances, barbecues, movies, Israeli programming, services, classes, Holocaust events, speakers, holiday events, a weekly radio program, sukkot building, bagel brunches, Israel fairs, Kristallnacht vigil, Yom Ha'Shoa commemoration, Yom Ha'atzmaut celebrations, and break-the-fast, and hosts numerous speakers and programs.

With the exception of the main library on campus, Hillel-JSU's library/resource center has the largest collection of Judaic resources on campus, including new books, current periodicals, and an interactive multimedia library. Hillel-JSU's library covers all historical, cultural, and religious aspects of Jewish life. The library's extensive collection of entertainment and educational videos and cassette tapes, its constantly expanding CD collection, and its weekly radio program, *Kol Yisrael*, enable students to keep up with the latest Jewish and Israeli music and news. The library's fully interactive multimedia library permits students to conduct class or personal research on subjects such as Israel, religion, the Holocaust, Jewish history, Bible, and Hebrew. The multimedia software includes the complete Encyclopedia Judaica and Jerusalem 3000. In addition, Hillel-JSU has recently purchased more than 200 new books to update its Judaic book section. Subjects include the Holocaust, anti-Semitism, archeology, art, history, philosophy, fiction, politics, Israel, and Hebrew, as well as biblical and religious books for all Jewish denominations. Subscriptions include *The Jerusalem Post* and *The Jerusalem Report*.

The University suspends classes for Rosh Hashanah, Yom Kippur, and Passover.

C.W. POST CENTER OF LONG ISLAND UNIVERSITY

Enrollment 8,000
Jewish 800

Jewish Student Union
CW Post/LIU, Box 333
Brookville, NY 11548
(516) 299-3111 (JSU)
(516) 299-2217 (Rabbi Gutoff)
Fax: (212) 299-2228
E-mail: jgutoff@liunet.edu
Web: www.cwpost.liunet.edu/cwis/stuart/interfaith

Rabbi Joshua Gutoff, Jewish Chaplain

 Jewish Studies
15 courses. Modern Hebrew.

 Study in Israel
Through LIU's "Friends World Program," full semester.

 Kosher Food
Shabbat Deli Dinner twice a month, and a kosher (though not shomer Shabbat) restaurant is 5 minutes from campus. Frozen packaged meals are available during Passover. Vegetarian selections are available at both cafeterias.

ON CAMPUS
The Jewish Student Association holds weekly meetings, at which are planned a variety of social and cultural events, such as parties, speakers, movie nights, and various excursions. AEPi, a predominantly Jewish fraternity, is also very active. The school itself is very supportive of Jewish life, and there are no classes on the High Holy Days or the first 2 days of Passover. In addition, special support is available for Jewish students with learning disabilities through ARC Plus, a program of the Jewish Child Care Association.

CLARKSON UNIVERSITY

Enrollment 2,750
Jewish 50

Clarkson Jewish Culture Club
Box 253
Potsdam, NY 13676
(315) 265-9242
E-mail: rosen@elum.clarkson.edu

Donald Rosenthal, Advisor
Judith Glassner, President, Congregation Beth El

ON CAMPUS
The Jewish Culture Club celebrates holidays, goes on trips to other schools, and participates in social activities. Most activities are held jointly with the SUNY Potsdam Jewish Culture Club.

COLGATE UNIVERSITY

Enrollment 2,885 (UG 2,870; GR 15)
Jewish 500

Colgate Jewish Union
Saperstein Jewish Center
Colgate University
Hamilton, NY 13346
(315) 228-7818
(315) 228-7150
Fax: (315) 228-7998
E-mail: cju@mail.colgate.edu

Rabbi Joan Friedman, Jewish Chaplain

 Jewish Studies
Approximately 12 courses available; Jewish studies is a 5-course minor concentration.

 Study in Israel
3-week summer program every other year in conjunction with Core 174: Multi-Ethnic Israel, offered every other spring. Students may go on other programs; credits may transfer, grades do not.

Kosher Food
Kosher kitchen facilities in the Saperstein Jewish Center; Shabbat dinners for up to 50 students are prepared there by students. Kitchens are available for individual use at other times. Kitchens are kashered for Pesach, and Pesach meals are available for all to prepare themselves. University dining service provides vegetarian alternatives at every meal.

ON CAMPUS
Colgate is a small and fairly isolated campus. The unofficial school motto, "Work hard, play hard!" indicates that academics, sports, and campus social life are intense. For Jewish students, the Colgate Jewish Union (CJU) is a non-pressured home away from home, not another demanding activity. In the past, Colgate was not the address of choice for many Jews, but the past decade has seen growth in both absolute numbers and the Jewish commitment of Jewish students. The Shabbat evening service and dinner remains the focus of Jewish life at Colgate. It is more than a religious observance: It is the community's social center, drawing more than 10 percent of the JSU membership each week. The monthly Sunday morning bagel brunches also draw large crowds. Holidays are observed with enthusiasm, and students participate actively in social events and Tzedakah projects.

Jewish life is organized jointly by the CJU, a student group that receives funding from the Student Association and the Jewish Chaplain, whose position is funded by the university. The Jewish Chaplain also teaches in the Philosophy and Religion Department. The Saperstein Jewish Center contains kitchens and a dining area, a synagogue, a library, and a lounge. Activities include a Jewish-Christian Dialogue group jointly sponsored by the University chaplains, a nascent Muslim-Jewish dialogue group, and a floating coffeehouse jointly sponsored by all the religious groups.

"Seeing a large Jewish center on the tour at Colgate helped make my decision when applying to colleges. Soon it became my second home!"

Joel Omansky, senior

COLUMBIA UNIVERSITY AND BARNARD COLLEGE

Enrollment 20,000
Jewish 5,000

The Jewish Office
Columbia University
105 Earl Hall
Mail Code 2002
New York, NY 10027
(212) 854-5111
Fax: (212) 854-3012
E-mail: jewish-office@columbia.edu
Web: www.columbia.edu/cu/jsu

Rabbi Charles Sheer, Chaplain
Rabbi Jennie Rossen, Associate Chaplain
Leora Shudofsky, C.S.W., Associate Director for Programming

Jewish Studies
25 courses; M.A., Ph.D. Columbia University offers courses in various departments in Jewish religion and history, Hebrew language and literature, rabbinics, philosophy, and Yiddish. The University offers several joint programs with Jewish Theological Seminary and Union Theological Seminary. The Columbia library has a world-renowned Judaica collection.

Study in Israel
Semester and year-long courses of study can be arranged at Israeli universities.

Kosher Food
A 7-day-a-week dining service is available on the Barnard College campus. Students may participate in a board plan or dine on a cash basis. Vegetarian alternatives and dormitory cooking facilities are available, as are kosher food products in many local stores. The Hartley Kosher Deli is conveniently located on campus.

Many kosher restaurants are a short subway ride away; the Jewish Theological Seminary cafeteria is a 5-minute walk from Columbia.

ON CAMPUS
Columbia has a large, diverse, and vibrant Jewish community, which looks forward to the opening of the Robert K. Kraft Family Center for Jewish Life in 2000.

The Jewish Student Union includes more than 30 groups and projects that sponsor cultural and educational programs, community service, Israel-focused events, and religious life. These groups include: Pizmon (Columbia/JTS *a cappella* group), various Israel groups, the Yiddish Club, Gayava, Haber Award-winning Annual Jewish Collegiate Festival of the Performing Arts, and an academic journal, magazine, dance troupe, and theatre ensemble. New groups and projects are added each year.

The Jewish Office offers educational courses on many levels and topics for the entire Columbia community each semester, in addition to the Jewish Studies courses offered by the University. A Beit Midrash is open daily for study. Many students gather each week for the award-winning Wednesday Night Learning Program.

The Jewish Graduate Student Program hosts a variety of cultural and educational programs such as monthly Shabbat dinners with speakers. A variety of social gatherings occur throughout the year including a kosher wine tasting and an annual Hanukkah party. Activities are organized within specific schools as well as for the entire graduate student population.

"The beauty of a community like ours at Columbia is that by respecting and admiring the plurality of Judaism, Jews with many different beliefs can still come together as one larger community."

Joshua Kunis, GS, JTS '01

COOPER UNION

Enrollment 950
Jewish 100

Kesher
Cooper Union
30 Cooper Union
New York, NY 10003
(212) 802-6808
(212) 696-1590
Fax: (212) 696-0964

TBA, Advisor

Jewish Studies
1 Hebrew class.

ON CAMPUS

All students are welcome at all New York University Jewish functions and all area events.

Students at Cooper Union are served by the Hillel Regional Center, Hillel of New York.

CORNELL UNIVERSITY

Enrollment 19,000 (UG 12,000; GR 7,000)
Jewish 3,500

Cornell Hillel
G-34 Anabel Taylor Hall
Ithaca, NY 14853
(607) 255-4227
Fax: (607) 255-8513
E-mail: hillel@cornell.edu
Web: www.hillel.cornell.edu

Vally N. Kovary, Executive Director
Judith F. Stauber, Director, Community Programs
Jeffrey Sultar, Campus Rabbi
Joanna Paley, Jewish Campus Service Corp Fellow

 Jewish Studies

Growing Jewish Studies department now with 5 endowment chairs. Call Cornell Hillel or Cornell's Jewish Studies Department for more information.

 Study in Israel

Programs with Hebrew University, Tel Aviv, Haifa, Ben-Gurion, and Bar Ilan available.

Kosher Food

Available on campus (sandwiches); full meal plan in the kosher dining hall.

Housing

The Center for Jewish Living (Young Israel House) is a residential facility for 30–35 students just off campus.

ON CAMPUS

Cornell Hillel is a very active and innovative Jewish community with major social, educational, and social action events, Israeli folk dancing every week, a performing dance troupe, Israel group, Mitzvah Corp., UJA, grad group classes, films, speakers, concerts, and other cultural events, as well as Jewish faculty-student programs. Hillel is located in the campus interfaith center and enjoys good relations with other campus ministries. Local Jewish families invite students for Passover. A Chabad House is also near campus. Additional Jewish groups affiliated with Hillel include Alpha Epsilon Pi fraternity, Chai Notes, Graduate and Professional Group, Hebrew Club, Jewish Law Student Association (JLSA), Jewish Business Students, Jewish Russian Club,

Jewish Women's Group, Kesher, KOACH, Lights in Action, Nitsots Dance Troupe, Women's Aerobics, and 3000 for Tomorrow.

The 2 local synagogues hire students as teachers. Cornell does not cancel classes on Jewish holidays, but a liberal attendance policy is in place. The University has an active Greek system that includes an Alpha Epsilon Pi chapter, a national Jewish fraternity, as well as several other predominantly Jewish houses.

CUNY—BARUCH COLLEGE

Enrollment 15,000 (UG 13,000; GR 2,000)
Jewish 2,000 (UG 1,000; GR 1,000)

Hillel at Baruch College
Box F-1511
17 Lexington Avenue
New York, NY 10010
(212) 802-6808
(212) 656-1590
Fax: (212) 802-6781
E-mail: hillel_foundation@scsu.baruch.cuny.edu
Web: www.geocities.com/baja/dunes/5383

Leonard Petlakh, Director

 Jewish Studies

10 courses; B.A.

 Study in Israel

Credit is accepted for study at Israeli universities.

 Kosher Food

Kosher restaurants are nearby.

ON CAMPUS

Hillel at Baruch College is a completely commuter school with a wide-ranging Jewish student body. Baruch students are part of the area-wide Hillel network facilitated by the Hillel Regional Center, Hillel of New York and based at Baruch. Baruch is the center of service for Jewish students at Pace—Manhattan, John Jay College of Criminal Justice, Cooper Union, Parsons School of Design/New School of Social Research, Pratt Institute, and Fashion Institute of Technology.

CUNY—BROOKLYN COLLEGE

Enrollment 14,000
Jewish 3,000

Hillel Foundation for Jewish Campus Life
2901 Campus Road
Brooklyn, NY 11210
(718) 859-1151
Fax: (718) 859-1165
E-mail: askenazil@juno.com

Linda Askenazi, Director
TBA, Program Director
Janine Okmin, Director, Center of Jewish Cultural and
   Artistic Expression
David Nekrutman, Social Work Intern/Theater Club
Nadya Drukker, Russian Outreach Coordinator
Avi Saiger, Jewish Campus Service Corps Fellow

 Jewish Studies
67 courses; B.A., M.A.

 Kosher Food
Hillel has a lunchtime dairy cafeteria, and a dinner program is being developed.

ON CAMPUS

The Brooklyn College Hillel, located in the middle of Brooklyn, serves commuter students from every Jewish background imaginable. In recent years, large numbers of immigrants from the former Soviet Union have become so active that Hillel has established a Center for Russian Jewish Life, which also serves students at Long Island University and Brooklyn Polytechnical University. Trips to Israel, educational activities, and social and cultural opportunities foster Jewish pride among these students.

The Hillel Council is comprised of students from Orthodox and non-Orthodox backgrounds, many from the Sephardic Jewish community, and some from other countries, including Israel. Activities abound throughout the week. Those that are offered in the evening and on weekends provide a "residential feel" to a community campus. Every Jewish interest group, club, or committee finds its home at the Hillel House, a facility that is currently undergoing renovations. An active Jewish newspaper, theater group, UJA committee, and Jewish community relations council, among others groups, offer something for everyone. Of particular interest is the program to reach students not engaged with their heritage, most notably through community service projects.

"The Brooklyn College Hillel arts program makes Jewish theater and other artistic opportunities more accessible to students. It's a different way to learn more about Jewish culture."

Lily Posner, sophomore

"The Russian Jewish Club is my friend, my Yiddishkeit, and the best four years of my life."

Roman Shmulenson, recent graduate

"Women's Rosh Chodesh Programs are great. They give women a chance to explore their own possibilities and situations."

Margo Menahem, senior

Brooklyn College Hillel also serves students at Kingsborough Community College. Also see Long Island University and Polytechnic University of Brooklyn for information about campuses served by the Center for Russian Jewish Life.

CUNY—CITY COLLEGE

Enrollment 14,000
Jewish 250

Hillel of New York
381 Park Avenue
New York, NY 10016
(212) 696-1590
E-mail: samiel@hillels-ny.org

Simon Amiel, Director

 Jewish Studies
5 courses per semester (20 in catalog); B.A.

 Study in Israel
Junior year abroad.

 Kosher Food
Nearby kosher restaurant.

CUNY—COLLEGE OF STATEN ISLAND

Enrollment 13,000
Jewish 1,300

Hillel at CSI
Multi Faith Center 3A-104
2800 Victory Boulevard
Staten Island, NY 10314
(718) 982-2650
(718) 982-2652
Fax: (718) 982-2673
E-mail: gidalowitzf.hillel@jon.cjfny.org
Web: www.nachas.org

Frances Gidalowitz, Director

Kosher Food

Prepackaged sandwiches offered under the supervision of Va'ad of Staten Island. Kosher restaurants locally available within a half-mile radius of the campus.

ON CAMPUS

Hillel at CSI is a student-run organization. Students meet weekly to plan activities, including social events and social action programs. Religious events and learning programs are especially popular on campus.

Served by Hillel of New York.

CUNY—HUNTER COLLEGE

Enrollment 23,000 (UG 19,000; GR 4,000)
Jewish 4,000 (UG 2,000; GR 2,000)

Hunter College Hillel Foundation
East Building, #1209 E
695 Park Avenue
Hunter East 1317A
New York, NY 10021
(212) 650-3568
(212) 696-1590
Fax: (212) 650-3544
E-mail: hillel@hunter.cuny.edu

Veronika Galperin, Director
TBA, Jewish Campus Service Corps Fellow

 Jewish Studies
17 courses (approximately); B.A.; Hebrew.

 Study in Israel
Program at Tel Aviv University.

 Kosher Food
Hillel offers a kosher lunch twice a week. Nearby restaurants. Vegetarian dining alternatives.

ON CAMPUS

Hunter College is a public commuter school with a very diverse student population. The College is best known for its undergraduate programs in English, Human Services, and Nursing. The graduate programs in Social Work and Education are considered the best in the city.

The students involved with Hillel range from Orthodox to "bagel and lox," and everyone is always welcome. Programs cover career planning assistance, academic and scholarship assistance, and mental health services, as well as holiday celebrations, Shabbatons, Jewish study, and more. Hunter College has a growing Russian Jewish population and an active Russian Jewish heritage club. The group meets several times each week in the afternoons and evenings. Hunter Hillel students often participate in intercollegiate activities with students from nearby universities.

"I have been a student at several universities in America but at Hunter Hillel I felt at home right away. Everyone was so warm and friendly. Even though I am from France and many students here are from Russia, I felt very comfortable and made many new friends. This has been a great year. I learned many new things about my Jewish heritage and truly enjoyed every moment I spent at Hillel. Too bad it was my senior year."

Ilana Abodia, recent graduate

Hillel at Hunter College is a service of the Hillel Regional Center, Hillel of New York.

CUNY—JOHN JAY COLLEGE
COLLEGE OF CRIMINAL JUSTICE

Hillel
445 West 59th Street
New York, NY 10019
(212) 237-8000
Fax: (212) 802-6781
E-mail: hillel_foundation@scsu.sitea.baruch.cuny.edu

Leonard Petlakh, Advisor

Students at John Jay College are part of the area-wide network served by the Hillel Center at Baruch College.

CUNY—KINGSBOROUGH COMMUNITY COLLEGE

Enrollment 14,000
Jewish 3,500

c/o CUNY—Brooklyn College
2901 Campus Road
Brooklyn, NY 11210
(718) 859-1151
Fax: (718) 421-4761

 Jewish Studies
Associate degree in Jewish Studies.

ON CAMPUS

This campus has a large Russian population and an active Russian club with special activities and holiday celebrations.

Kingsborough is served part-time as an outreach program of CUNY—Brooklyn College.

CUNY—QUEENS COLLEGE

Enrollment 16,000
Jewish 5,000

Hillel at Queens College
Student Union Building, #206
65-30 Kissena Boulevard
Flushing, NY 11367
(718) 793-2222
Fax: (718) 793-2252
E-mail: hillel@qcvaxa.acc.qc.edu
Web: www.gc.edu/~rmsgc

Rabbi Moshe Shur, Director
Ami Monson, Associate Director
Rosy Kimchi, Jewish Campus Service Corps Fellow
Meredith Farrell, Jewish Campus Service Corps Senior Fellow

Jewish Studies

40 courses annually; 65 in catalog. B.A.; minor. The aim of Jewish Studies is to provide students with an understanding of the history, philosophy, religion, politics, sociology, anthropology, folklore, languages, and literature of the Jewish people. The program is intensive yet flexible, tailored to a wide range of interests normally included in the broad concept of Jewish Studies. Approximately 500 students take courses in any given semester, and approximately 50 students are pursuing a baccalaureate degree in Jewish Studies. Queens College, Jewish Studies Program, 65-30 Kissena Boulevard, Flushing, NY 11367; (718) 997-4530.

Study in Israel

Study abroad: Hebrew, Tel Aviv, and Bar Ilan Universities.

Kosher Food

2 campus restaurants. Food at all Hillel activities is kosher.

ON CAMPUS

Queens College has one of the largest Jewish campus populations in the country. On this mostly commuter campus, Hillel facilitates a wide range of social, cultural, religious, and Israel programs in response to the interests and needs of the broad diversity of students at Queens. Students come to Hillel to hang out and talk, plan programs, and meet in the large lounge located on the second floor of the Student Union building.

The activities they organize include a Sephardic Club, a Russian Club, a Persian Club, and an Israeli Club, as well as a Reform Club, B'nai Akiva, and Koach, the Conservative Jewish program. Queens Hillel holds Tuesday evening jam sessions and has an *a cappella* choir, Tizmaret; it has a performing arts group and a performing arts night club, Coffee Talk, a men's learning group, Lilmod, a women's study group, Pa'am, and a women's club. Chaverim is a group that volunteers for hospital and nursing homes, and the Hillel Sports League not only meets to play basketball and volleyball, it also trav-

els to Mets, Yankees, Rangers, and Knicks games. Queens Hillel also sponsors non-Traditional Friday night dinners; Weekend in the Catskills Retreat; Hillel Goes to Broadway, *Smokey Joe's Cafe*; and PJC Jewish Heritage Program, and is home to numerous other Jewish campus organizations and interests, such as AIPAC, the Council of Jewish Organizations, and the United Jewish Appeal.

One of Queens College's Jewish Campus Service Corps Fellows also provides service to Jewish students at Queensborough Community College and St. John's University.

FASHION INSTITUTE OF TECHNOLOGY

Enrollment 4,200
Jewish 375

Jewish Student Association at FIT
Student Life Office
7th Avenue at 27th Street
New York, NY 10001
(212) 760-7887
(212) 696-1590
Fax: (212) 760-7144
E-mail: hillel-foundation@scsu.sitea.baruch.cuny.edu

Leonard Petlakh, Advisor

Kosher Food

Kosher restaurants in neighborhood.

Students at FIT are part of the areawide network served by the Hillel Center at Baruch College.

HAMILTON COLLEGE

Enrollment 1,600
Jewish 150

Hillel
c/o Dean of Students Office
Hamilton College
Clinton, NY 13323
(315) 859-4026
(315) 859-4011
E-mail: dreichler@hamilton.edu

Rabbi Deborah Reichler, Advisor

Jewish Studies

10 courses; B.A.

Study in Israel

Credit is accepted for study at Israeli institutions.

Kosher Food

Vegetarian dining alternatives. Some kosher-for-Passover food is available.

ON CAMPUS

Hamilton Hillel's close-knit group allows students to form long-lasting friendships. Hillel sponsors a different social, educational, or religious event every week, celebrates all holidays, and brings in a rabbi for High Holidays and Passover.

HEBREW UNION COLLEGE— JEWISH INSTITUTE OF RELIGION

Enrollment 164
Jewish 152

Brookdale Center
1 West 4th Street
New York, NY 10021-1186
(212) 674-5300
Fax: (212) 388-1720
E-mail: ncohen@huc.edu
Web: www.huc.edu

Rabbi Norman J. Cohen, Dean

See listing for HUC-JIR in Cincinnati, OH.

HOBART AND WILLIAM SMITH COLLEGES

Enrollment 1,750
Jewish 175

Hillel
c/o Department of Religious Studies
Hobart and William Smith Colleges
Geneva, NY 14456
(315) 781-3385
(315) 781-3671
Fax: (315) 781-3348
E-mail: lweinstock@hws.edu

Professor Michael Dobkowski, Advisor
Reverend Leslie Adams, College Chaplain
Lorinda Weinstock, Hillel Program Professional

Jewish Studies

10 courses.

Study in Israel

Credit program with Ben-Gurion University.

Kosher Food

Holidays; occasional meals; vegetarian dining alternatives. There is no formal kosher dining program, but student residences may provide kitchen facilities.

Housing

Students may choose to live in the Jewish Culture theme house.

ON CAMPUS

Hobart and William Smith Colleges are located 1 hour from Rochester, Syracuse, and Ithaca, and students are invited to participate in activities on campuses in these areas. HWS Jewish students are involved in all areas of campus life. On-campus activities include social programming and holiday observances, such as a Passover seder and Yom HaShoa Remembrance Week. They also sponsor occasional symposia on Jewish themes, including Middle East issues, Soviet Jewry, American Jewry, and Jewish-Christian relations. The Chaplain's Office provides memberships for all students at Temple Beth-El, a Reform congregation, which is located across the street from campus. The rabbi is available to students and is frequently involved in services and programs on campus.

HOFSTRA UNIVERSITY

Enrollment 12,800
Jewish 2,600 (UG 1,400; GR 1,200)

Hofstra Hillel
Student Center 213
200 Hofstra University
Hempstead, NY 11550-1022
(516) 463-6922
Fax: (516) 463-7439
E-mail: chamem@hofstra.edu; chaeip@hofstra.edu

Rabbi Meir Mitelman, Executive Director
Becca Maslow, Program Director
Alon Levkovitz, College Chaplain

Jewish Studies

10 courses; B.A.

Study in Israel

The University gives credit for study in Israel.

Kosher Food

The University provides frozen kosher meals, 7 lunches and 7 dinners, on request. Hillel offers one hot dinner and 1 bagel brunch per week in addition to Shabbat dinners following services every other week. Kosher restaurants are nearby.

ON CAMPUS

Hofstra Hillel, a 7-time winner of the New York metropolitan area's award for outstanding Jewish campus programs and a recipient of the International Hillel's William Haber Award for Programs of Quality for the Jewish Campus Community, is also a 2-time recipient of a UJA-Federation Continuity Grant to reach out to unaffiliated Jewish students and strengthen Jewish awareness.

As the Center for Jewish Life on Campus, Hofstra Hillel consists of a wide variety of student-led groups and projects. These include the Jewish Freshmen Council, Social Action Alliance, Israel Group, Kesher (Reform Student Group), KOACH (Conservative Student Group), Kol Isha (Women's) groups, UJA Campus Campaign, Intercollegiate Jewish Council, and the Jewish Law Students Association. Hillel also plays a prominent role in coordinating major campuswide community service projects. Hillel highlights include weekly dinner programs, social activities, celebrations of Shabbat and Jewish holidays, monthly visits to a nearby geriatric center, and trips to Broadway shows and sites of Jewish interest in New York City. Subsidies are always available for students' participation in national and regional conferences and Shabbatonim.

The University's location permits easy access to New York City and to other Hillel Foundations in the metropolitan area. The supportive local Jewish community provides home hospitality for Shabbat and holidays. University classes are not held on the High Holidays or the first 2 days of Passover.

"I think of Hofstra Hillel as a big family that is always attuned to the needs of Jewish students. Its resources are incredible. I and many of my friends have had wonderful, life-changing experiences because of the exciting opportunities Hillel has provided us."

Laurie Gewanter, senior

Hofstra Hillel also provides service to Jewish students, on a part-time basis, at Adelphi University and at Nassau Community College.

ITHACA COLLEGE

Enrollment 5,300 (UG 5,200; GR 100)
Jewish 800

Hillel Foundation at Ithaca College
1001 Muller Chapel
Ithaca, NY 14850
(607) 274-3323
Fax: (607) 274-1901
E-mail: faber@ithaca.edu
Web: www.ithaca.edu/orgs/hillel/hillel1/

Michael Z. Faber, Director
TBA, Program Director

 Jewish Studies
Hebrew (1 year); Jewish-content courses in Humanities Departments.

Study in Israel
Study abroad in Israel is accepted.

Kosher Food
Excellent glatt kosher dining at no extra charge includes 20 meals per week. There are no special sign ups for this option.

ON CAMPUS

Based at Ithaca's interfaith chapel, Hillel offers a full range of social, religious, cultural, and educational activities. Shabbat dinners are well attended by Jewish students of all denominations, and arts-related programming is popular. The Hillel Director also serves as advisor to other Jewish student groups on campus, such as Friends of Israel and UJA. Chabad is also on campus.

JEWISH THEOLOGICAL SEMINARY OF AMERICA

Enrollment 625

Albert A. List College of Jewish Studies
3080 Broadway, Box 32
New York, NY 10027-4649
(212) 678-8832
Fax: (212) 678-8947
E-mail: lcadmissions@jtsa.edu

Reena Gold, Director of Admissions

 Jewish Studies
284 courses; B.A., M.A., Ph.D., D.H.L., Rabbinic Ordination, and Diploma of Hazzan. JTS has the largest full-time faculty in Jewish Studies and the largest research library in Jewish Studies in North America. Majors include: Bible, Jewish History, Talmud, Jewish Literature, Midrash, Jewish Music, Jewish Philosophy, and Modern Jewish Studies.

 Study in Israel
Semester and year programs abroad.

Kosher Food
Kosher meal plan with vegetarian options; full kitchens in the residence hall; regularly sponsored community Shabbat and festival meals.

ON CAMPUS

List College students can pursue 2 undergraduate degrees simultaneously: a B.A. in a Jewish Studies major from JTS, and a second B.A. or B.S. in a liberal arts or science major at Columbia University or Barnard College. These dual-degree programs enable students to participate in a wealth of activities at each of these institutions, in addition to the limitless social and cultural opportunities of New York City.

In addition to need-based financial aid, List College offers a number of generous merit scholarships including Honors Fellowships, community service awards, and leadership awards. There are 2 5-week summer sessions, and a 3-week concentrated summer mini-semester for students who plan to work as counselors at a Ramah Camp for the remainder of the summer. A Visiting Student program is available for students who wish to study at List College for a semester or a year and transfer the credits to their own institution.

See listing for Columbia University.

LONG ISLAND UNIVERSITY — BROOKLYN CAMPUS

Enrollment 11,114
Jewish 1,000

Hillel and the Jewish Russian Culture Club of LIU
Office of Student Activities S-304
University Plaza
Brooklyn, NY 11201
(718) 780-4010
(718) 968-2179
E-mail: liuhillel@prodigy.net
Web: www.linet.edu

Roman Kalika, Director

 Jewish Studies
3-credit course on Jewish history; weekly non-credit Hebrew classes.

 Study in Israel
Winter and summer highly subsidized Israel programs.

 Kosher Food
Some kosher food available in the campus dining hall.

ON CAMPUS

Ongoing programs for all Jewish students include educational events, holiday celebrations, speakers, and films. LIU has a large number of Jewish faculty and administrators, and a very strong informal Jewish Faculty Association. Classes are not held on major Jewish holidays.

Long Island University is served as an outreach program of the Center for Russian Jewish Life at Brooklyn College Hillel.

MANHATTANVILLE COLLEGE

Enrollment 870
Jewish 40

Jewish Student Association
2900 Purchase Street
Purchase, NY 10577
(914) 251-6498
Fax: (914) 793-3222
E-mail: lgali64@aol.com

Lisa Galinson, Director

Kosher Food
Kosher frozen dinners are available through campus dining services.

The JSA is served on a part-time basis by Hillels of Westchester, which is affiliated with the Hillel Regional Center, Hillel of New York.

MARYMOUNT MANHATTAN COLLEGE

c/o Hillel of New York
695 Park Avenue South
Hunter East 1317A
New York, NY 10016
(212) 772-5563
Fax: (212) 650-3544

Nika Galperin, Director

ON CAMPUS

Marymount Manhattan is a Catholic school in New York famous for its arts programs. There is a small but very active Jewish presence on campus. With assistance from Hunter Hillel, students at Marymount's student-run Hillel Club plan programs for major holidays. Students attend events at nearby Hunter Hillel.

Hillel at Marymount Manhattan is a service of the Hillel Regional Center, Hillel of New York. See listing for CUNY—Baruch College.

MAX WEINREICH CENTER FOR ADVANCED JEWISH STUDIES

Enrollment 34
Jewish 34

> Max Weinreich Center
> YIVO Institute for Jewish Research
> 15 W. 16th Street
> New York, NY 10011
> (212) 246-6080
> Fax: (212) 292-1892
> Web: www.baruch.cuny.edu/yivo
>
> **Dr. Lisa Epstein**, Director of Research
> **Chava Boylan**, Dean's Assistant

ON CAMPUS

YIVO is the major resource for study of East European and American Jewish culture, with more than 22 million items in 750 archival collections and a 330,000-volume multilingual library. Graduate studies are available at the Max Weinreich Center. A 6-week summer intensive language program is offered through the Uriel Weinreich Program in Yiddish Language, Literature and Culture. The Max Weinrich Center, chartered and accredited by the New York State Department of Education, does not offer certificates or degrees. Credits from courses are transferrable under a formal course exchange program with major universities in the New York area.

NEW YORK CHIROPRACTIC COLLEGE

Enrollment 1,000
Jewish 100

> Hillel
> New York Chiropractic College
> 2360 St. Rt. 89
> Seneca Falls, NY 13148-0800
> (315) 568-3164
>
> **Dr. Steve Feldman**, Advisor

 Kosher Food
Kosher kitchen available on campus by request. Some kosher food is available locally.

ON CAMPUS

The campus of New York Chiropractic College is 296 acres in the Finger Lakes region. About half of the Jewish students on campus are connected with Hillel. The substantial Jewish community in neighboring towns welcomes Jewish students for holidays in Rochester, Syracuse, and Ithaca.

NEW YORK INSTITUTE OF TECHNOLOGY— METROPOLITAN CENTER

Enrollment 12,600

> Shalom Club
> 1855 Broadway, Room 402A
> New York, NY 10023
> (212) 399-8371
> (212) 696-1590

 Jewish Studies
2 courses.

ON CAMPUS

The Institute has many active Israeli students who participate with American students in cultural programming on campus, as well as in New York–area Jewish and Israeli-centered events.

Students at New York Institute of Technology are served by the Hillel Regional Center, Hillel of New York. See listing for CUNY—Baruch College.

NEW YORK UNIVERSITY

Enrollment 44,000 (UG 13,500; GR 30,500)
Jewish 14,000

> Edgar M. Bronfman Center for Jewish Life
> 7 East 10th Street
> New York, NY 10003
> (212) 998-4114
> Fax: (212) 995-4774
> E-mail: rabbi.bachman@nyu.edu
> Web: www.pages.nyu.edu/clubs/Bronfman
>
> **Rabbi Andrew Bachman**, Director
> **Sarah Gershman**, Assistant Director
> **Karyn Riegel**, Culture & Media Coordinator
> **Rena Dascal**, Senior Jewish Campus Corps Fellow
> **Randi Jaffe**, Administrator

Jewish Studies
40 courses offered annually; 100 listed in catalog. B.A., M.A., Ph.D.; minor. The Skirball Department of Hebrew and Judaic Studies offers a comprehensive program in Jewish Studies, ranging from Bible and the ancient Near East through the 20th century. Its doctoral program is one of the largest in North America. Staffed by a full-time faculty of 15, areas of strength include: Bible and ancient Near East, Second Commonwealth history, rabbinic literature, medieval history and thought, early modern history, modern European and American Jewry, and modern Hebrew literature. 7 Endowed Chairs. Skirball Department of Hebrew and Judaic Studies; (212) 998-8980.

Study in Israel

Study in Israel. Semester and year-long opportunities available.

 Kosher Food

Kosher dining room; vegetarian dining alternatives.

ON CAMPUS

The Edgar M. Bronfman Center for Jewish Student Life at NYU has now completed its second full year of programming. Endowed in affiliation with Hillel: The Foundation for Jewish Campus Life, with the mission of reaching the wide range of Jewish students on the NYU campus, the Bronfman Center has flourished as a place of social gathering, arts programming, learning, prayer, and community activism since its inception in December 1996. The Bronfman Center is a Tzekek Hillel. As such, programs are infused with the Jewish values of justice, kindness, and service.

The Center—a magnificent 5-floor townhouse with galleries, meeting rooms, sanctuaries, and a state-of the art computer center—serves as the central location for Jewish students to explore and enrich their Jewish identities. It is centrally located close to the array of Jewish institutions, community centers, museums, seminaries, and libraries that combine to make New York the most vibrant Jewish city in America.

Active clubs include Hillel, Chabad, Stars of David, NYU Jewish Film Series, Bronfman Galleries, Top of Bronfman, Kesher, Jewish Heritage Program, Israel Club, Sketch Comedy, Ani'v'Atah *a cappella* singing, GLBT, Association of Jewish Women, and Jewish Greeks.

PACE UNIVERSITY—MANHATTAN

Enrollment 14,000
Jewish 350

> Hillel-JSA at Pace
> c/o Student Life Office
> Pace University
> 41 Park Row, 8th Floor
> New York, NY 10038
> (212) 802-6808
> Fax: (212) 802-6781
>
> **Leonard Petlakh**, Advisor

ON CAMPUS

The Hillel-Jewish Student Association at Pace is an active group that helps spearhead areawide activities.

Students at Pace are part of the areawide network served by the Hillel Center at Baruch College.

PACE UNIVERSITY—PLEASANTVILLE

Enrollment 9,896
Jewish 250

> Jewish Student Association
> 861 Bedford Road
> Pleasantville, NY 10570
> (914) 251-6498
> E-mail: lgali64@aol.com
>
> **Lisa Galinson**, Director

 Study in Israel

Possible through study abroad program.

 Kosher Food

Kosher frozen dinners are available through dining services.

ON CAMPUS

The JSA has been most successful in coordinating holiday programming, Holocaust awareness, fundraisers, and intergroup relations.

Jewish students at Pace receive programming guidance from Hillels of Westchester, which is affiliated with the Hillel Regional Center, Hillel of New York.

PARSONS SCHOOL OF DESIGN

Enrollment 2,200
Jewish 100

> Parsons School of Design
> 66 Fifth Avenue
> New York, NY 10011
> (212) 802-6808
> (212) 656-1590
> Fax: (212) 802-6781
>
> **Leonard Petlakh**, Advisor

Students at Parsons and the New School are part of the areawide network served by the Hillel Center at Baruch College.

PLATTSBURGH STATE UNIVERSITY OF NEW YORK

Enrollment 5,800 (UG 4,800; GR 1,000)
Jewish 700

> Hillel
> c/o Temple Beth Israel
> 1 Bowman Street
> Plattsburgh, NY 12901

Jewish Studies
1 course taught by the rabbi per semester.

 Study in Israel
Junior year abroad.

ON CAMPUS

The very small local Jewish community is supportive of Jewish students, who meet for social and other activities according to interest. Students are always welcome at all Temple services and programs. Each year Hillel and the Temple hold a joint Passover seder.

POLYTECHNIC UNIVERSITY OF BROOKLYN

Enrollment 10,500
  Jewish 800

> Jewish Student Union, Wunsch Student Center
> 6 MetroTech, Room 205
> Brooklyn, NY 11201
> (718) 637-5905
> (718) 859-1151
> Fax: (718) 968-2179
> E-mail: jsu@students.poly.edu
>
> **Roman Kalika**, Russian Outreach Coordinator

 Jewish Studies
Weekly noncredit Hebrew classes at 2 levels; course on the Holocaust planned.

 Study in Israel
Seminar on High-Technology in Israel offered.

 Kosher Food
Off-campus restaurants within walking distance. Some kosher food available in the dining hall.

ON CAMPUS

Ongoing programs for all Jewish students include educational events, holiday celebrations, speakers, and films. Polytech is a very friendly environment. A large percentage of the faculty are Jewish. Classes are not held on Rosh Hashanah and Yom Kippur.

The campus is served as an outreach program of the Center for Russian Jewish Life at Brooklyn College Hillel.

PRATT INSTITUTE

Enrollment 4,000
  Jewish 600

> c/o Hillel of New York
> 381 Park Avenue South, Suite 613
> New York, NY 10016
> (212) 696-1590
> Fax: (212) 696-0964
>
> **Leonard Petlakh**, Advisor

ON CAMPUS

Hillel of New York provides professional advice, grants, and program information to Jewish students at Pratt Institute.

See listing for CUNY—Baruch College.

QUEENSBORO COMMUNITY COLLEGE

Enrollment 10,500
  Jewish 800

> The Hillel Club
> Student Activities Office—Hillel Club
> Queensborough Community College
> 222-05 56th Avenue
> Bayside, NY 11364-1497
> (718) 793-2222
> Fax: (718) 793-2222
>
> **Meredith Farrell**, Jewish Campus Service Corps
>   Senior Fellow
> **Reuvain Zahavy**, Faculty Advisor

 Jewish Studies
Some Jewish studies courses.

 Study in Israel
Credit is accepted from Israeli academic institutions.

ON CAMPUS

Hillel at Queensboro, a commuter college, holds weekly social and cultural events, some in conjunction with Jewish students from nearby colleges.

Queensboro's Jewish students receive programming advice and support from a Jewish Campus Service Corps Fellow based at Queens College. See listing for CUNY—Queens College.

RENSSELAER POLYTECHNIC INSTITUTE

Enrollment 6,329 (UG 4,260; GR 2,069)
Jewish 500

> RPI—Russell Sage Hillel
> Chaplain's Suite, Room 217
> Troy, NY 12180
> (518) 276-8621
> (518) 272-6151
> Web: www.albany.edu/~jss
>
> **Rabbi Aryeh Wineman**, Acting Advisor

Jewish Studies

Joint Program: SUNY—Albany.

Kosher Food

Frozen meals are available, on request, in the dining hall. Vegetarian dining alternatives; dormitory cooking facilities.

ON CAMPUS

The local community, both through the Student Services Committee of the United Jewish Federation of Northeastern New York and through local synagogues in Troy, is very helpful, providing funds, special programs, and holiday hospitality. Many programs are planned jointly with Jewish students at Russell Sage College, and activities are also coordinated with SUNY—Albany, Union, and Skidmore Colleges. RPI—Russell Sage Hillel serves students on both campuses.

ROCHESTER INSTITUTE OF TECHNOLOGY—NTID

Enrollment 13,500
Jewish 300

> Rochester Foundation
> Interfaith Center
> 40 Lomb Memorial Drive
> Rochester, NY 14623
> (716) 475-5171
> Fax: (716) 475-5485
> E-mail: mclcpm@rit.edu
> Web: www.rit.edu/~hillel
>
> **Rabbi Ari Israel**, Director
> **Michael Lombardo**, Program Director
> **Andrea Allmayer**, Jewish Campus Service Corps Fellow

Kosher Food

Kosher food is available by special arrangement through the university and/or Hillel. Hillel offers biweekly Shabbat dinners and holiday and other occasional meals; vegetarian dining alternatives. Passover meals are available. There is a self-service kosher kitchen.

ON CAMPUS

The Hillel House is on the residential side of campus. The kosher kitchen, couches, stereo, TV, and VCR are all open to students to meet, study, or schmooze. All cultural and religious activities are interpreted for the deaf and hard of hearing.

Hillel is part of a Center for Campus Ministries with outstanding interfaith relationships. Hillel sponsors a full range of social, cultural, religious, and educational programs, including an annual Israeli scholar-in-residence, intercampus events with other Rochester area universities, Bingo at the Jewish Home, parties, speakers, trips to Washington, D.C., and the U.S. Holocaust Memorial Museum, leadership training and conferences, Israeli nights, and bagel brunches. There is an annual interfaith Thanksgiving celebration and annual interfaith Yom HaShoah observance.

At RIT/NTID, deaf, blind, and learning-disabled students use their strengths as leaders in the campus Jewish community, thanks to RIT/NTID's Louis S. and Molly B. Wolk Center for Jewish Cultural Enrichment for the Deaf. The Wolk Center Home Page on the World Wide Web (www@infoshop.com/wolkcenter) links national Hillels, Jewish Web sites, and Web sites for the deaf to deaf students who can keep in touch by signing up on its guest page. They may also subscribe to an internet discussion list for the Jewish deaf.

RUSSELL SAGE COLLEGE

Enrollment 1,000
Jewish 45

> RPI—Russell Sage Hillel
> Chaplain's Suite, Room 217
> Student Union
> Rensselaer Polytechnic Institute
> Troy, NY 12180
> (518) 276-8621
> (518) 272-6151
> E-mail: www.albany.edu/~jss
>
> **Rabbi Aryeh Wineman**, Acting Advisor

Jewish Studies

Joint Program: SUNY—Albany.

Kosher Food

Passover food plan available at Rensselaer Polytechnic Institute.

ON CAMPUS

The local community, both through the Student Services Committee of the United Jewish Federation of Northeastern New York and through local synagogues in Troy, is very helpful, providing funds, special programs, and Holy Day hospitality. Many programs are planned jointly with Jewish student groups at other area schools including SUNY—Albany, and Union and Skidmore Colleges. RPI—Russell Sage Hillel serves students on both campuses.

SAINT LAWRENCE UNIVERSITY

Enrollment 2,100 (UG 2,000; GR 100)
Jewish 50

Jewish Students Union
c/o Chaplain's Office
Saint Lawrence University
Canton, NY 13617
(315) 229-5127
(315) 229-5388
Fax: (315) 379-5628
E-mail: mgre@music.stlawu.edu

Ellen Gallow, Acting Chaplain
Rabbi Michael Greenwald, Advisor

 Jewish Studies
2 courses.

 Study in Israel
By individual arrangement.

 Kosher Food
Frozen meals, on request in dining hall; vegetarian alternative, on request.

ON CAMPUS

The local Jewish community is very supportive. Activities have included the Jewish University Students Shabbaton and Conference, Hanukkah and Passover activities, and seder.

SARAH LAWRENCE COLLEGE

Enrollment 1,050
Jewish 325

Chavurah Jewish Student Union
Sarah Lawrence College
1 Mead Way
Bronxville, NY 10708
(914) 251-6498
Fax: (914) 793-3565
E-mail: lgali164@aol.com

Lisa Galinson, Director

 Jewish Studies
1 course.

 Study In Israel
Available and encouraged through Study Abroad Office.

 Kosher Food
Frozen dinners are available through dining services.

ON CAMPUS

Chavurah students are very involved in all aspects of planning and coordinating programs. Recent programs include discussion groups, Shabbat dinners, holiday celebrations, and other activities according to student interest.

The Chavurah is served by the newly formed Hillels of Westchester, which is affiliated with the Hillel Regional Center, Hillel of New York.

SKIDMORE COLLEGE

Enrollment 2,200
Jewish 450

 Jewish Student Union
c/o Chaplain's Office
Skidmore College
Saratoga Springs, NY 12866
(518) 580-5683
Fax: (518) 580-5556
E-mail: lmotzkin@skidmore.edu

Rabbi Linda Motzkin, Chaplain

 Jewish Studies
2 courses.

Study in Israel
Skidmore does not have an official program in Israel, but students have participated in other academic programs in Israel and received full credit from Skidmore.

 Kosher Food
Bi-weekly or monthly catered kosher Shabbat dinners on campus. Vegetarian dining alternatives.

ON CAMPUS

The Jewish Student Union sponsors social, cultural, and holiday programming. On-campus programming varies from year to year depending on student interest. The warm, hospitable local Jewish community hosts students for Shabbat and holidays. The local synagogues welcome Skidmore students, and opportunities exist for students to work with the religious school teaching staff.

STERN COLLEGE FOR WOMEN

Enrollment 810
Jewish 810

Midtown Center
245 Lexington Avenue
New York, NY 10016-4699
(212) 340-7700

Karen Bacon, Dean
Ethel Orlian, Associate Dean

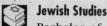 **Jewish Studies**

Bachelor of Arts and Associate in Arts degrees; Hebrew Teacher's Diploma.

ON CAMPUS

Stern College for Women provides liberal arts and sciences curricula and pre-professional programs. Students may pursue interdepartmental majors, honors work, independent study, and joint bachelor's-master's programs.

See listing for Yeshiva University.

SUNY—ALBANY

Enrollment 17,000
Jewish 5,000 (UG 3,500; GR 1,500)

Chapel House
SUNY Albany Station, Box 22225
Albany, NY 12222
(518) 489-8573 ext. 24
Fax: (518) 489-8975
E-mail: jssunya@crisny.org
Web: www.albany.edu/~jss/

Gary Metzger, Campus Director

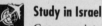 **Jewish Studies**

Department of Judaic Studies offers 41 courses (23 per semester); B.A. Major and minor in Judaic Studies and Hebrew. Graduation scholarships awarded biannually.

Study in Israel

Cross-registration programs with University of Haifa, Ben-Gurion University, Tel-Aviv University, and Bar-Ilan University.

Kosher Food

Vaad Hakashruth of the Capital District (Glatt); 7 dinners, 6 lunches (surcharge); vegetarian dining alternatives. Students prepare and serve free Shabbat dinners every other week after services in Chapel House. On alternating weeks, dinners are served at Shabbos House (Chabad) after services (within walking distance).

ON CAMPUS

The University at Albany has a diverse Jewish community. With a strong Judaic Studies Department, an extensive Jewish library (which includes the Kossover Collection of Jewish Books), and vibrant and active Jewish student organizations, this campus offers a strong Jewish lifestyle. Hillel provides social, educational, cultural, and religious programming year-round. There are also four additional Jewish groups on campus, which provide for a vast array of differing Jewish practices.

SUNY—BUFFALO

Enrollment 25,000
Jewish 3,000

 Hillel of Buffalo
Campus Center for Jewish Life
40 Capen Boulevard
SUNY at Buffalo, North Campus
Buffalo, NY 14214
(716) 639-8361
Fax: (716) 639-7917
E-mail: spando@buffalo.edu
Web: wings.buffalo.edu/~semintz

Susan Goldberg Pardo, Executive Director
Jamie Solomon, Program Director
Rabbi Shay Mintz, Campus Rabbi

Jewish Studies

18 courses; B.A., M.A.; courses in Jewish History, Introduction to Judaism, and Jewish Women in America as well as a course on kehilah (the Jewish community) and Israel are offered by Hillel staff through the Judaic Studies program. Bar/bat mitzvah class.

Study in Israel

Semester/year program at Hebrew University, Tel Aviv University, Haifa University, Ben-Gurion University, and Bar-Ilan University. Summer archaeological dig program.

Kosher Food

The University's kosher kitchen is open daily 11 a.m.–2 p.m. under Va'ad HaKashrut supervision. Vegetarian dining alternatives. Hillel has kosher Shabbat dinners every Friday, as well as holiday meals.

ON CAMPUS

Hillel of Buffalo recently moved to a new central location on campus. The Campus Center for Jewish Life is the base for a wide variety of social, cultural, political, educational, and religious events throughout the year. Friday morning Challah baking, and Shabbat services and dinner are increasingly well attended, and Hillel sponsors an annual spring conference, the Conference on Jewish Concerns, which is planned and executed by students for the university and the community at large.

A Student Leadership Council is being implemented that will further enable students to create a Jewish campus life that meets their interests and needs. Many students involve themselves with ARI, a student newspaper published 6 times a year. Students also come to the Campus Center for Jewish Life to socialize, relax, or get a snack. Hillel of Buffalo is growing and welcomes Jewish students from all backgrounds.

SUNY—STONY BROOK

Enrollment 17,600
Jewish 3,000

Hillel Foundation for Jewish Life
165 Humanities Building
Interfaith Center
SUNY at Stony Brook
Stony Brook, NY 11794-5335
(516) 632-6565
Fax: (516) 632-6576
E-mail: ksacks@notes.cc.sunysb.edu
Web: www.sunysb.edu/hillel

Rabbi Joseph S. Topek, Director
Rabbi Menachem Even-Israel, Assistant Director
Kohava Sacks, Assistant Director, Administration and
    Development
Rachel Jurisz, Jewish Campus Service Corps Fellow

Jewish Studies
6–9 courses offered annually; 21 courses in catalog; minor. Courses include 3 years of Hebrew and topics in Jewish history, religion, and literature. The Religious Studies major offers an emphasis in Judaism.

Study in Israel
SUNY system program for study at all Israeli universities.

Kosher Food
University/Hillel offer 5 lunches and dinners, some weekend meals when the University is in session, and Shabbat dinner every week. Kosher meal plan is part of University Food Service and has a nice private dining room. Vegetarian dining and dormitory cooking is also available.

ON CAMPUS

Hillel at SUNY—Stony Brook, located on the north shore of Long Island, sponsors a wide range of social, cultural, educational, social action, and religious activities. Programs include bi-monthly Shabbatonim, Welcome Back BBQ and Bonfire, High Holiday Services, Hanukkah Celebration, Israel Opportunities Fair, Annual Persian Purim Masquerade Party, and Yom Ha'atzmaut Festival. Other activities vary from year to year based on student interest and initiative. Recent student-initiated programming includes Shabbat Across Stony Brook, Seders on Wheels, '60s Flashback Tie-Dye Event, Havdalah at the Beach, Open Mic Coffee House Nights, and bringing Passover to local nursing homes. Programs occur on campus and in the local community. Hillel also offers periodic Israeli trips for Stony Brook students led by staff and designed for students' specific needs.

The coordinating body of Stony Brook Hillel, The Council of Jewish Student Organizations, is comprised of the Hillel Student Club, UJA Campus Campaign, Yavneh, the Traditional Club; Yisrael B'yachad, for Israel programming; the Graduate Organization for Jewish Life; *Stony Brook Shelanu*, the Jewish student newspaper; Chabad Student Club; Nashim Echad, the Jewish women's group; Koach, the Conservative group; Russian Club, and the Vaad Hakashrut.

Stony Brook Hillel is a multiple recipient of the Program of the Year Award from Hillel of New York and the William Haber Award from Hillel: The Foundation for Jewish Campus Life located in Washington, D.C. The University does not conduct class on the High Holy Days or the first 2 days of Passover. Stony Brook's many Jewish faculty members are active in and supportive of Jewish life on campus.

"Stony Brook Hillel rocks! Not only do we have great programs, but we are also great friends. I can't imagine Stony Brook without Hillel . . . and, we have Rabbi Joe!"

Josh Lipshitz, senior

SUNY COLLEGE—BROCKPORT

Enrollment 7,400
Jewish 100

Hillel
212 Seymour Union
SUNY College at Brockport
Brockport, NY 14420
(716) 395-5125
(716) 275-4323
E-mail: gmintz@brockvma.cc.brockport.edu

Rabbi Ari Israel, Director
Greg Mintz, Advisor

Jewish Studies
6 courses.

Study in Israel
Semester/year programs abroad at Tel Aviv University and Hebrew University.

Kosher Food

Hillel offers kosher bagel brunches, deli dinners, Shabbat dinners, and other occasional meals.

ON CAMPUS

SUNY College—Brockport is located in a village 30 miles northeast of Rochester, New York. Hillel at Brockport has an office in the Student Union and plans many social and cultural events during the academic year. As part of the Rochester Area Hillel Foundation, students from Brockport participate in intercampus events with students from SUNY College—Geneseo, University of Rochester, and Rochester Institute of Technology.

See listing for University of Rochester.

SUNY COLLEGE—BUFFALO

Enrollment 15,000 (UG 13,500; GR 1,500)
Jewish 1,000 (UG 800; GR 200)

Hillel Foundation at Buffalo
40 Capen Boulevard
Buffalo, NY 14214
(716) 835-3832

Susan Pardo, Director

Jewish Studies
10 courses; B.A.

Kosher Food
Hillel-JSU offers Friday night dinners. The University will provide frozen meals on request, and vegetarian dining alternatives are available.

Joint program with SUNY—Buffalo.

SUNY COLLEGE—CORTLAND

Enrollment 6,900
Jewish 600

Jewish Student Society at SUNY Cortland
Education Department
Box 2000
Cortland, NY 13045
(607) 753-4801
(607) 753-2065
E-mail: schafferl@syncortland.edu
Web: www.cortland.edu

Professor Sheila Cohen, Advisor
Professor Sanford J. Gutman, Advisor

Jewish Studies
Minor. Jewish Studies is supported by the Center for Multicultural and Gender Studies. Courses include Basic Judaism, Jewish Authors, Jews in the Ancient World, Jews in the Middle Ages, Holocaust, Modern Is-

rael, and Jews in the Modern World. There is a small section in the library dedicated to Judaica.

Study in Israel
Junior year abroad/summer seminar.

Kosher Food
Vegetarian dining alternatives.

ON CAMPUS

Cortland's Jewish students participate in a variety of cultural and social events, some with other nearby Hillel groups: skating parties, bagel brunches, Israeli dance, speakers, films, seder, and Yom Kippur breakfast. Some programs are held in cooperation with the campus ministry and interfaith center, and funding is received from the Student Government. This past year, popular activities included Passover seder, Hanukkah lighting, the Yom Hashoah recognition program, the Gruber lecture on Eastern European Jewish monuments, and the latke party for children and students. Hillel provides this programming on a bi-weekly basis and students meet with the advisor twice a month. Cortland has a supportive, if small, Jewish community.

SUNY COLLEGE—FREDONIA

Enrollment 4,800
Jewish 300

c/o Alumni Office
172 Central Avenue
SUNY Fredonia
Fredonia, NY 14063
(716) 673-3529
(716) 672-4049
Fax: (716) 673-4661
E-mail: steinberg@fredonia.edu

Theodore Steinberg, Advisor

Jewish Studies
2–3 courses.

Study in Israel
Credit is accepted for study at Israeli universities.

Kosher Food
Vegetarian alternatives available.

ON CAMPUS

The Jewish Student Union at SUNY College—Fredonia sponsors ongoing social and cultural activities, including Jewish History Month, in April, with a full program. The Jewish Student Union works closely with the local synagogue.

SUNY COLLEGE—GENESEO

Enrollment 5,600 (UG 5,200; GR 400)
Jewish 500

> Hillel
> Interfaith Center
> 11 Franklin Street
> Geneseo, NY 14454
> (716) 243-1460
> (716) 275-4323
> E-mail: mclcpm@rit.edu
> Web: www.rochesterhillel.org
>
> **Rabbi Ari Israel**, Director
> **Michael Lombardo**, Advisor
> **TBA**, Jewish Campus Service Corps Fellow

 Jewish Studies
Informal classes in modern Hebrew and Judaic workshops.

 Study in Israel
Summer and junior year abroad programs at Tel Aviv University and Hebrew University.

 Kosher Food
Vegetarian dining alternatives available. Kosher dining plan for Passover.

ON CAMPUS

SUNY College—Geneseo campus is located 30 miles south of Rochester. The University is supportive of Jewish campus life. There is a mural on campus during Holocaust Remembrance Week, a Holocaust service, Hanukkah decorations in the College Union, and modified foods during Passover. The on-campus program may include speakers, religious services, holiday celebrations, films, and discussion programs, often held in conjunction with the faculty. Students plan weekly events and a bi-weekly free Shabbat dinner. The Jewish fraternity, AEPi, is active on campus. Students also participate in monthly intercampus activities with the Hillels at SUNY College—Brockport, RIT/NTID, and University of Rochester. SUNY College—Geneseo Hillel is part of the Rochester Area Hillel Foundation.

See listing for the University of Rochester.

SUNY COLLEGE—NEW PALTZ

Enrollment 7,800
Jewish 1,000

> Jewish Student Union
> Student Union Building, Room 427
> SUNY College at New Paltz
> New Paltz, NY 12561
> (914) 257-3565

 Jewish Studies
4 courses per semester; 13 in all.

Study in Israel
Junior year and summer programs.

Kosher Food
Vegetarian dining alternatives upon request. Dormitory cooking facilities are available.

ON CAMPUS

The Jewish Student Union meets weekly to discuss topics of interest and to plan cultural and religious programs.

SUNY COLLEGE—ONEONTA

Enrollment 5,600
Jewish 2,000

> Jewish Cultural and Social Club
> c/o Temple Beth El, Box 383
> 83 Chestnut Street
> Oneonta, NY 13820
> (607) 432-5522

 Kosher Food
Locally available.

Rabbi Roberts at SUNY College—Oneonta also serves Jewish students at SUNY—Delhi and nearby Hartwick College.

SUNY COLLEGE—OSWEGO

Enrollment 6,500 (UG 6,000; GR 500)
Jewish 1,000

> Hillel
> Hewitt Union
> SUNY College at Oswego
> Oswego, NY 13126
> (315) 341-3277
>
> **Professor Steven Baron**, Advisor

 Jewish Studies
2 courses.

Kosher Food
Frozen food on request in dining hall.

SUNY COLLEGE—PLATTSBURGH

Enrollment 5,800 (UG 4,800; GR 1,000)
Jewish 700

Hillel
c/o Dr. Lynn Schlesinger
Dept. of Sociology
101 Broad Street
Plattsburgh, NY 12901
(518) 563-3343
(518) 564-3004
Fax: (518) 564-3333
Web: www.hillel.org/listings/hillel_schools/schools_static.htm

Lynn Schlesinger, Advisor

 Jewish Studies
1 course taught by the rabbi per semester.

 Study in Israel
Junior year abroad.

ON CAMPUS

The very small local Jewish community is supportive of Jewish students, who meet for social and other activities according to interest. Students are always welcome at all Temple services and programs. Each year Hillel and the Temple hold a joint Passover seder.

SUNY COLLEGE—POTSDAM

Enrollment 4,000 (UG 3,400; GR 600)
Jewish 150

Jewish Culture Club
Student Union
SUNY College at Potsdam
Potsdam, NY 13676
(315) 267-2505
(315) 265-9242

Aram Ayalon, Advisor
Mark Rubenstein, Advisor
Judy Glaser, Synagogue President

 Study in Israel
International Exchange Program.

 Kosher Food
Kosher food may be ordered from Syracuse.

ON CAMPUS

The very small local Jewish community is supportive of Jewish students, who meet for social and other activities according to interest. Students are always welcome at all Temple services and programs. Each year Hillel and the Temple hold a joint Passover seder.

SUNY COLLEGE—PURCHASE

Enrollment 2,500
Jewish 350

Jewish Student Coalition
Campus Center, North Room 0024
735 Anderson Hill Road
Purchase, NY 10577
(914) 251-6498
(914) 696-1590
Fax: (914) 251-6499
E-mail: lgali64@aol.com

Lisa Galinson, Director, Synagogue President

 Jewish Studies
6 courses.

 Study in Israel
Transfer credits are often accepted.

 Kosher Food
Kosher frozen dinners are available through dining services.

ON CAMPUS

Jewish students meet in the Jewish Student Coalition lounge in the students activities building, Campus Center North. The JSC often coordinates programming and holiday celebrations with students at nearby campuses; last year they celebrated Passover with a seder at the home of the president of Sarah Lawrence College. Activities have included discussion groups, Israel fairs, an *a cappella* group, poetry readings, intergroup programs, and social action programs such as feeding the NYC homeless. The JSC recently instituted an annual intercollegiate retreat with other Westchester County schools, conducted its first High Holiday services, built a sukkah, and sponsored a Purim Bash and Masquerade Ball.

"The Jewish Student Coalition at SUNY College—Purchase uses an acronym, EAST, to describe our group. It stands for "Education, Awareness, Support and Tolerance," and our motto is, "Turn to the EAST." We believe that Jewish campus life is not about how religious you are but more about exploring your Judaic heritage and finding out what Judaism has to offer you. It's about having fun and getting spiritual. The JSC is an educating, supportive and tolerant group on campus. No one is excluded from the group based on race, color or sexual orientation. Judaism is for everyone who wants to enjoy!!!"

Steve Sissleman, sophomore

Jewish students at SUNY College—Purchase are served by Hillels of Westchester, which is affiliated with the Hillel Regional Center, Hillel of New York.

SYRACUSE UNIVERSITY

Enrollment 16,000
Jewish 3,000

Hillel at Syracuse University
Hendricks Memorial Chapel
Syracuse, NY 13244
(315) 443-2904
(315) 443-5042
Fax: (315) 443-4128
E-mail: hillel@syr.edu
Web: www.web.syr.edu/~sujsu/

Sivan Kaminsky, Director
Philip Lambert, Program Director
Brian Cohen, Advisor

Jewish Studies

Minor. Core courses in history, religion and sociology are integrated by a senior seminar. Five core courses are augmented by 2 elective courses, for a total of 21 credit-hours. B.G. Rudolph, Chair in Jewish Studies in Department of Religion, 501 Hall of Languages; (315) 443-3861.

Study in Israel

Semester and year programs at Tel Aviv University, Ben-Gurion University, and Hebrew University. Financial assistance is available through the Edith and Jay B. Rudolph and the Elaine and Joseph Spector Scholarships, the Joseph S. Kalina Prize, the Benjamin Fellowship, and the Danziger Award. Jewish Studies also sponsors an essay contest.

Kosher Food

University Food Services operates a kosher kitchen in one of the residence halls on campus, serving meat lunches and dinners weekdays. The plan is provided at the same rate as other University meal plans. Vegetarian food is available at all dining centers. There is a kosher deli and a kosher bakery within driving distance.

ON CAMPUS

Jewish students at Syracuse will find a wide range of social, cultural, educational, and religious opportunities. Hillel is located on the Quad right in the center of campus, and sponsors events such as an annual major speaker, Holocaust Awareness Week activities, Graduate Student Vegetarian Pot Luck Shabbat dinners, and intramural sports and tournaments. It also sponsors speakers and educational events each semester, as well as a student-run UJA campus campaign. Within the strong Greek system at Syracuse are 2 historically Jewish fraternities—SAM and ZBT—and 2 historically Jewish sororities—AEPhi and SDT. Many of the other houses have considerable numbers of Jewish students.

Outstanding scholars of Judaism speak regularly at the University under the auspices of the B.G. Rudolph Lecture Series, the Arlene and R. Raymond Rothman Lecture in Judaica, and the Jewish Studies Department. Students also benefit from the Jerome and Arlene Gerber Judaica Collection in Bird Library. The Holstein Family Endowment supports visiting scholars in the senior seminar.

Hillel will facilitate volunteer experience with local Jewish agencies, as well as employment in area religious schools. Community members invite students to their homes for Shabbat and holidays. Close cooperation and joint activities characterize the relationship between Hillel and the other campus ministries and student groups. The vibrant Jewish Student Union on campus works out of the Hillel office; the two groups enjoy a cooperative and mutually supportive relationship. The Hillel Director is also the advisor to the JSU, which sponsors Jewish Identity Week, Holocaust Awareness Week, a Modern Jewish Ethics Symposium, and a major speaker each year. They also sponsor diverse interest groups such as Syracuse University Students for Israel (SUSI), a Jewish student newspaper, Hakol, a choir (Kol Simcha), an AIPAC chapter, a KOACH chapter, and a Reform Chavurah.

Syracuse University is fairly sensitive of Jewish religious concerns. Classes are not scheduled on Yom Kippur. Although classes are held on Rosh Hashanah, the Vice Chancellor for Academic Affairs circulates a memo each year which includes the dates of the fall Holy Days and asks faculty members to excuse students from classes these days and to offer make-up assignments. During finals week, Friday exams are scheduled to end by mid-afternoon. Graduation is held on a Sunday, but convocations for many of the individual schools are held on Saturday. In December, a large electric menorah is lit atop a building on the Quad. While speakers hostile to Jews occasionally appear on campus, the University has placed conditions concerning venue and security, as well as video and audio taping.

"The students at Syracuse University are very involved in Jewish life on campus and in the community. Whether students participate in a program to distribute food to the hungry, a Shabbat service, a dance, or a softball game, there is something at Syracuse University Hillel for everyone. Syracuse University professors often attend Hillel events, adding to the student-professor relationship. The Hillel lounge is a great place to relax between classes and the Friday night dinner is known for the great food."

Brian Cohen, senior

TOURO COLLEGE

Enrollment 9,600
Jewish 7,250

c/o Dean of Students
Touro College
27-33 W. 23rd Street
New York, NY 10010
(212) 463-0400, ext. 420, 419
Fax: (212) 627-9054

Dr. Stanley Boylan, Dean of Faculties
Robert Goldschmidt, Dean of Students

Jewish Studies

100 undergraduate courses and 120 graduate courses; B.A., M.A.

Study in Israel

Year abroad option enables students to earn up to 36 credits in Jewish Studies toward their bachelor's degree at Touro. Undergraduate courses in management, history, psychology, and related fields are offered at Touro's Israel Center in Jerusalem. The center also has its own self-contained School of International Business. The Israel campus of the Graduate School of Jewish Studies enrolls 300 students in the Master of Arts program.

Kosher Food

Dormitory cooking facilities; kosher food available at each campus and in local shopping areas.

ON CAMPUS

Touro is a multinational institution of higher and professional education under Jewish auspices. Touro encompasses the College of Liberal Arts and Sciences, with coordinate men's and women's divisions in Manhattan, Flatbush, and Brooklyn; School of Law; Allied Health Sciences (including physical therapy, occupational therapy, and physician assistant and featuring a cooperative MD program with the Technion in Israel); Jewish Studies Education and Psychology; Lifelong Education; and Applied Career Studies. Undergraduate co-curricular and social programming has a religious orientation. The main campuses are located in the heart of New York City's vibrant Jewish communities.

UNION COLLEGE

Enrollment 2,050
Jewish 360

Hillel
Religious Programs Office
Union College
Schenectady, NY 12308
(518) 388-6539
Fax: (518) 388-6529
E-mail: stroberg@aol.com
Web: www.albany.edu/~jss/

Margo Strosberg, Jewish Chaplain
Gary Metzger, JSS Director

Jewish Studies

10 courses: Jewish History in the Biblical and Post-Biblical Periods, The Holocaust, History of the Modern Middle East, Modern Jewish History, Hebrew I, II, and III, Literature of the Holocaust, The World of the Bible, and Modern Hebrew Literature. In addition, there is an annual Fred Miller lecture on the Middle East. The annual Hans Hainebach Memorial Prize in Judaica is given annually to a student who has offered the best performance in the field of Judaica. The Union College library has a good Judaica collection.

Study in Israel

Term abroad at Ben-Gurion University in Beer Sheva; other options.

Kosher Food

Tuesday and Friday night dinners; complete Passover 8-day meal plan; holiday meals; occasional special events. Kosher deli sandwiches available at regular dining halls upon request.

ON CAMPUS

Almost one-fifth of the declared Jewish students on campus are members of Hillel. Traditional Hillel events include a Break-the-Fast, a sukkah-building party, a Tu B'Shvat tree sale, a Yom Hashoah commemoration, a Yom Ha'atzmaut celebration, a student-faculty Shabbat dinner, a Parents Weekend brunch, and barbeques. Lunch 'n' Learns with the area rabbis have been well received. The Hillel lounge is located next to the kosher kitchen. Some students work at the local synagogues as youth group advisors or at the local JCC.

Although Union College holds classes on holidays, faculty are given a Jewish calendar, are notified that students may be absent, and are asked to make it possible for them to make up work missed. Some Jewish faculty are very actively involved in Jewish campus life.

"Hillel offers a warm, friendly environment where students and faculty can come together to enjoy home-cooked meals, socialize, debate current issues, or just relax and have a good

time. Our new lounge allows for movies and various other social events that appeal to many on campus. Both Jews and others participate in all of the various aspects of Hillel, and newcomers are always welcome."

Ali Baum

"Evenings at our kosher kitchen are truly refreshing, and make Hillel a true home."

Sofia Mazo

UNITED STATES MERCHANT MARINE ACADEMY

Enrollment 967
Jewish 5

United States Merchant Marine Academy
Steamboat Road
Kings Point, NY 11024
(516) 773-5365
Dr. Jane Brickman, Faculty Advisor

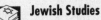 **Jewish Studies**
No formal courses. Accredited, independent study by arrangement.

 Kosher Food
Available by special arrangement with commissary.

ON CAMPUS

While Jewish enrollment is small, the Academy is a comfortable place to be Jewish. Classes are not cancelled for holidays, but Jewish midshipmen may be excused for observance. The administration does not schedule exams during holidays. There are many Jewish faculty and the Academy is located in the predominantly Jewish community of Great Neck, Long Island. Home hospitality is offered by the community on holidays.

UNITED STATES MILITARY ACADEMY

Enrollment 4,000
Jewish 55

United States Military Academy
USMA Jewish Chaplain
Building 750
West Point, NY 10996-1698
(914) 938-2766
(914) 938-2710
Fax: (914) 938-6519

Chaplain H. Richard White, Lt. Col., U.S. Army

Jewish Studies
3 courses: Modern Hebrew, History of Western Religions, and Holocaust.

 Study in Israel
Summer work/study program for 3 weeks in June.

 Kosher Food
Available at the Jewish Chapel.

ON CAMPUS

West Point offers a full and enriching Jewish program in a magnificent chapel facility. A U.S. Army rabbi leads the Jewish congregation. New York–area Jewish communities help support the program, which includes religious retreats, social functions, trips with the Jewish Cadet Choir, a summer trip to Israel, and other special programs.

The Jewish Chapel is open to the general public daily 9 a.m.–4 p.m.; weekends and holidays 12 p.m.–4 p.m. The Chapel houses a fine Judaica collection of close to 100 items. A Torah, rescued from destruction by the Nazis in Czechoslovakia, is on permanent loan at the Jewish Chapel from the Westminster Synagogue in London.

UNIVERSITY OF ROCHESTER

Enrollment 6,000
Jewish 1,080 (UG 800; GR 280)

 Rochester Area Hillel Foundation, University of Rochester
Interfaith Chapel
Wilson Boulevard
Rochester, NY 14627
(716) 275-4323
(716) 275-8525
Fax: (716) 442-4279
E-mail: ari@rochesterhillel.org
Web: www.rochesterhillel.org

Rabbi Ari Israel, Director
Jennifer King, Program Director
Lisa Sandler, Jewish Campus Service Corps Fellow

Jewish Studies
12 courses; minor in Judaic Studies along with classes in religion, philosophy, and history as well as a special track on Israeli archeology.

Study in Israel
The University of Rochester has reciprocal programs with Haifa University, Ben-Gurion University, and Hebrew University. In addition to these study abroad programs, students have the opportunity to participate in the Winter Mission to Israel as well as an archaeological dig offered each summer by the university.

Kosher Food

The University of Rochester has recently re-vamped its Glatt Kosher Deli, which is located in Douglass Dining Center, the main dining center on campus. In addition, vegetarian options are always available in all campus dining units. Provisions are made for kosher meals during holidays by Hillel. Passover seders and meals, including all lunches and dinners, can be deducted from the students regular meal plan and are served in the Interfaith Chapel on campus. Free Shabbat meals are also provided on a bi-weekly basis and an Oneg Shabbat is provided on the off-weeks.

ON CAMPUS

The University of Rochester is a very warm school and provides a continuously supportive environment for its Jewish students. The campus is virtually free of anti-Semitic and racial incidents, and the local community is very supportive of Jewish students and Jewish life on campus as well. Due to these positive factors, Jewish students tend to live anywhere on campus and are very integrated into all aspects of campus life. Many of the Jewish students at the University are involved in the Greek system; sororities are based in the residence halls, and fraternities either are based in residence halls or have their own houses.

The University of Rochester offers a full range of on-campus Jewish social, religious, community service, and educational programs initiated by many of the student groups that work through Hillel. Recently named a Tzedek Hillel, the University of Rochester Hillel is 1 of 4 schools in the country to focus their programming on community service and Tikkun Olam. Ongoing programs of this nature include Adopt-a-Grandparent, Big Brother/Big Sister, the Russian Family Program, and Project Assist, a program that allows students the opportunity to work with youth of the inner city.

In 1997, Hillel inaugurated a new and very popular "tradition": Shabbat 300 brought 300 students, faculty, staff, and community members together for a Shabbat meal and celebration; in 1998, the number increased to 500, and 1999's goal is to have 613 students celebrating Shabbat together. Hillel also prides itself on its annual bar/bat mitzvah program for a Russian immigrant who has not yet performed the mitzvah of becoming B'nai Mitzvah. Other ongoing programs include First Year Student Council and First Year Events, United Jewish Appeal.

Hillel sponsors a variety of intercampus events with the Hillels of SUNY College—Geneseo, SUNY College—Brockport, and Rochester Institute of Technology/National Technical Institute for the Deaf, and also supports GAP (Graduate and Professional) Hillel for graduates and professionals in their 20s.

"This is a very comfortable place for a Jewish student. We have a strong Hillel which includes a variety of community service programs, social, religious, Israel and other programs. The faculty is very supportive."

Laurie R. Krantz, sophomore

VASSAR COLLEGE

Enrollment 2,200
Jewish 600

Vassar Jewish Union
Vassar College
Office of Religious Activities
Box 488
Poughkeepsie, NY 12601
(914) 451-3920
Fax: (914) 437-5550
E-mail: shidelson@vaxsar.vassar.edu

Efraim Eisen, Advisor to Jewish Students

Jewish Studies

10 courses; B.A. Religion major with concentration in Jewish Studies. Correlate sequence in Jewish Studies also available.

Study in Israel

Junior year abroad.

Kosher Food

Frozen kosher meals are available, on request; vegetarian dining alternatives; dormitory cooking facilities; locally available. The Kosher Co-op provides student-cooked meals on Friday nights and during holidays.

ON CAMPUS

The Vassar Jewish Center, just beyond the campus gates, houses the Kosher Co-operative Kitchen, 2 student meeting rooms/lounges, the offices of the Advisor to Jewish students, the Vassar Jewish Union, and Ra'ashan: A Journal of Jewish Culture. Vassar has a Jewish *a cappella* group, Zimriah, and occasional other activities.

WESTCHESTER COMMUNITY COLLEGE

Jewish 50

Jewish Students Association
Westchester Community College
75 Grasslands Road
Valhalla, NY 10595
(914) 251-6498
Fax: (914) 793-3222
E-mail: lgali64@aol.com

Lisa Galinson, Director

Study In Israel
Possible through Study Abroad Office.

Kosher Food
Kosher frozen dinners are available through campus dining services.

The JSA is served on a part-time basis by Hillels of Westchester, which is affiliated with the Hillel Regional Center, Hillel of New York.

YESHIVA UNIVERSITY
STERN COLLEGE FOR WOMEN
SY SYMS SCHOOL OF BUSINESS

Enrollment 1,950

Yeshiva University
Joel Jablonski Campus
500 West 185th Street
New York, NY 10033-3201
(212) 960-5277
(212) 960-0845
Fax: (212) 960-0086

Michael Kranzler, Dean of Admissions
Norman Adler, Dean, Yeshiva College
Karen Bacon, Dean, Stern College for Women

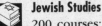

Jewish Studies
200 courses; B.A., M.A., Ph.D., Certificate, Professional Degrees. Joint Programs.

Study in Israel
Most undergraduates spend 1 year in Israel.

Kosher Food
The University provides 7 dinners and 7 lunches; vegetarian dining alternatives.

ON CAMPUS

Yeshiva University, in its second century, is the nation's oldest and largest university under Jewish auspices. An independent institution chartered by the state of New York, it is accredited by the Middle States Association of Colleges and Schools and by specialized professional agencies. With 16 undergraduate, graduate, and professional schools, divisions, and affiliates at 4 major campuses in New York City, and additional campuses in Los Angeles and Jerusalem, Yeshiva offers studies in liberal arts, business, health sciences, law, social work, psychology, Jewish education, and Jewish studies. YU conducts widespread programs of research and community outreach, issues publications, and is the home of the Yeshiva University Museum.

The arts and sciences and business curricula are supplemented with courses in Jewish learning, emphasizing original sources and tailored to individual needs and backgrounds. Joint bachelor's-master's programs are available with YU graduate schools and other institutions in engineering, Jewish education, Jewish studies, nursing (B.A.-B.S.N.), occupational therapy, podiatry (B.A.-D.P.M.), psychology, and social work. Independent study is offered.

"Yeshiva University is a great place for Jewish students, but it tends to be insular. The program is designed to provide strong Jewish learning with equally strong secular studies. The classes are small, and faculty-student interaction is fantastic. It is a great place if you are an Orthodox Jew or if you are looking for opportunities to openly express your Jewish heritage."

Ilan Haber, '96

"This is a comfortable place for a Jewish student as it is a Jewish college. But there are not many intergroup programs and there is no Jewish Greek life. There are many community service opportunities and programs. The academic program is excellent."

Penina Joel, Stern '97

APPALACHIAN STATE UNIVERSITY

Enrollment 12,500
Jewish 52

Appalachian Jewish Students Association
ASU PO Box 9052
Boone, NC 28608
(828) 262-6021
(828) 264-4576
Fax: (828) 262-4976
E-mail: hanfts@appstate.edu

Professor Sheldon Hanft, Advisor

 Jewish Studies
1 course.

 Study in Israel
Appalachian State University accepts credit from Israeli institutions.

 Kosher Food
Local community/holidays; occasional meals.

ON CAMPUS

On-campus activities include holiday celebrations, parties, films, and bi-monthly social action/community service programs as well as Israel-related activity. The local Jewish community is very supportive and provides home hospitality for Shabbat and holidays. ASU also has a Yom HaShoah commemoration, and the campus has speakers from the Jewish Chautauqua Society. The AJSA is active in the United Campus Ministries Association of ASU.

ASU is part of the outreach program of North Carolina Hillel at Chapel Hill.

DAVIDSON COLLEGE

Enrollment 1,600
Jewish 25

Jewish Students Organization
Davidson College
PO Box 1719
Davidson, NC 28036
(704) 892-2420
Fax: (704) 892-2005

Rob Spach, Chaplain
Deborah Hogg, Assistant Dean of Admissions

 Jewish Studies
Offered through the Religion Department.

 Kosher Food
Available in Charlotte (20 minutes away).

ON CAMPUS

Davidson College is located 20 miles north of Charlotte, and Jewish students from Davidson participate in events in the Charlotte community and with the Hillel at University of North Carolina, Chapel Hill.

Davidson College Hillel is served as an affiliate of Hillel at University of North Carolina—Chapel Hill.

DUKE UNIVERSITY

Enrollment 11,000
Jewish 1,800

 Freeman Center for Jewish Life
Campus Drive at Swift Avenue
PO Box 90936
Durham, NC 27708-0936
(919) 684-6422
(919) 684-1949
Fax: (919) 684-6451
E-mail: roger.kaplan@duke.edu
Web: www.duke.edu/hillel/

Dr. Roger Kaplan, Director
Nanci Steinberg, Jewish Campus Service Corps Fellow
Helena Lawrence, Program Director
Gretchen Codey, Assistant to the Dean

 Jewish Studies
34 courses; Certificate program.

 Study in Israel
Year/semester abroad at Hebrew, Tel Aviv, and Ben-Gurion Universities. Summer archaeological dig in the Galilee through the Department of Religion.

 Kosher Food
The Freeman Center for Jewish Life includes a kosher cafeteria serving kosher dairy and meat meals on a daily basis.

ON CAMPUS

With the opening of the Freeman Center for Jewish Life in May 1999, Jewish life on the Duke campus has increased and become more varied. The Freeman Center provides a wide range of social, cultural, educational, and religious programs, and has a student lounge, computer cluster, Judaica library, sanctuary, multipurpose room, and meeting rooms. The many activities include Israel-related programs, a Jewish women's network, community service projects, speakers, and Israeli dancing.

As a unit of the University's Division of Student Affairs, the Freeman Center is well integrated into campus life and maintains close ties with the University. The Center also has strong ties with the local Jewish community and nearby synagogues. Beginning in late fall, the Freeman Center will include a mikvah that will serve the students and the greater Durham—Chapel Hill community.

The University requires faculty to make accommodations for students observing religious holidays.

"The Jewish community at Duke has always been very accommodating toward every level of religious practice, and for all ages. It's the only place I know of where the formal barriers between faculty, graduate, and undergraduate students fade."

Jason Moss, senior

EAST CAROLINA UNIVERSITY

Enrollment 16,000
Jewish 21

Hillel at East Carolina University
c/o Rabbi Ed Elkin
North Carolina Hillel
210 W. Cameron Avenue
Chapel Hill, NC 27516
(919) 942-4057
Fax: (919) 967-4622
E-mail: nc.hillel@unc.edu
Web: www.unc.edu/student/orgs/nchillel

Debbie O'Neal, Faculty Advisor

East Carolina University is served by North Carolina Hillel in Chapel Hill.

ELON COLLEGE

Enrollment 3,845 (UG 3,641; GR 204)
Jewish 62

Elon Hillel
c/o Dr. Jimmie D. Agnew
Campus Box 2119
Elon College, NC 27244-2020
(336) 584-2398
(919) 942-4057
Fax: (336) 538-6933
E-mail: agnew@elon.edu
Web: www.elon.edu/agnewj/hillel

Dr. Jimmie D. Agnew, Advisor
Michael Zarkin, NC Hillel Greensboro Program
  Coordinator
Richard McBride, College Chaplain

 Jewish Studies
Jewish Studies, Holocaust Studies, and Hebrew.

 Study in Israel
Study abroad in Israel, for credit, is accepted.

 Kosher Food
Vegetarian options are available.

ON CAMPUS

Hillel is one of the most active organizations on the campus of this small, liberal arts college. Jewish students meet weekly on campus to socialize and plan activities. Activities include Family Weekend Shabbat Dinner; speakers such as an Israeli teacher in an Israel/Arab school, an expert on Jews in the media, and Holocaust survivors; Israeli dancing; Holocaust Remembrance Day; a Passover seder; and an annual retreat to Charleston, South Carolina. Each year there is a trip to a site of Jewish interest, such as to the U.S. Holocaust Memorial Museum in Washington, D.C., the Museum of Jewish Heritage in New York City, or the Jewish Museum in Atlanta, Georgia. Students also participate in Greensboro area events as well as in events at Hillel in Chapel Hill.

"I feel very lucky that I found a group on campus that does things together and celebrates being Jewish on the campus of Elon College. This group made me feel comfortable."

Adam Phillip Kriss, '99

"Elon College Hillel has really made me feel at home. Everyone is there for each other. We are a very close-knit group."

Erica Petersiel '99

Hillel at Elon College is served by Hillel at the University of North Carolina—Chapel Hill, and by the North Carolina Hillel Greensboro Regional Coordinator, The ACM Center, 500 Stirling Street, Greensboro, NC 27412; (336) 334-4500.

GREENSBORO COLLEGE

Enrollment 756
Jewish 10

Hillel
c/o The ACM Center
500 Stirling Street
Greensboro, NC 27412
(336) 334-4500
(919) 942-4057
E-mail: nchillel@unc.edu

Michael Zarkin, NC Hillel Greensboro Program
Coordinator

ON CAMPUS

Hillel programs take place at neighboring UNC—Greensboro. Events are planned jointly with other Greensboro-area schools, and statewide Hillel programs are sponsored by NC Hillel in Chapel Hill.

GUILFORD COLLEGE

Enrollment 1,100
Jewish 40

Guilford College Hillel
c/o The ACM Center
500 Stirling Street
Greensboro, NC 27412
(336) 334-4500
(919) 942-4057
E-mail: nchillel@unc.edu

Professor Jonathan Malino, Faculty Advisor
Max Carter, Campus Ministry Coordinator
Michael Zarkin, NC Hillel Greensboro Program
Coordinator

 Jewish Studies
Occasional courses.

ON CAMPUS

Guilford is a small Quaker school. Hillel programs take place at Guilford as well as jointly with Greensboro area schools, with program assistance by North Carolina Hillel Foundation at Chapel Hill. Students are warmly welcomed into Jewish homes for holiday and Shabbat celebrations.

HIGH POINT UNIVERSITY

Enrollment 2,411
Jewish 20

c/o The ACM Center
500 Stirling Street
Greensboro, NC 27412
(336) 334-4500
(919) 942-4057
Fax: (919) 967-4622
E-mail: nchillel@unc.edu

Michael Zarkin, NC Hillel Greensboro Regional
Coordinator

ON CAMPUS

Jewish students at High Point receive programming assistance from the NC Hillel Regional Program Coordinator in Greensboro, and are welcome to all statewide events coordinated by North Carolina Hillel and UNC—Chapel Hill.

Served by North Carolina Hillel.

NORTH CAROLINA STATE UNIVERSITY—RALEIGH

Enrollment 25,000
Jewish 200

Hillel
1200 Student Center
NCSU Box 7206
North Carolina State
Raleigh, NC 27695
(919) 515-4183
E-mail: ajcitrin@eos.ncsu.edu
Web: www.ncsu.edu/stud.orgs/hillel/

Adam Citrin, President
Ann Weingold, Raleigh Area Program Coordinator

 Jewish Studies
A local rabbi has offered to learn with students weekly on campus.

ON CAMPUS

Hillel at North Carolina State has monthly programs on campus, covering topics of Jewish interests and awareness. At least 1 event a week averages 15–20 students per event with about 50 active members.

Hillel at North Carolina State is served part-time by North Carolina Hillel Foundation at Chapel Hill.

UNIVERSITY OF NORTH CAROLINA — CHAPEL HILL

Enrollment 21,500
Jewish 1,000 (UG 600; GR 400)

North Carolina Hillel
210 West Cameron Avenue
Chapel Hill, NC 27516
(919) 942-4057
Fax: (919) 967-4622
E-mail: nchillel@unc.edu
Web: www.unc.edu/student/orgs/nchillel

Rabbi Edward Elkin, Director
Kes Spilker, Program Director

 Jewish Studies
10 courses; B.A., M.A., Ph.D./Joint Program: Duke University; Jewish courses and Biblical Hebrew offered through the Religious Studies Department.

Study in Israel
Year abroad at Hebrew University and Ben-Gurion University.

Kosher Food
Kosher kitchen at Hillel may be used by students; dormitory cooking facilities; weekly Shabbat dinners; monthly bagel brunches; Tu B'Shevat seder; and all holidays.

ON CAMPUS

The North Carolina Hillel Foundation functions as the Jewish community center for UNC. Special activities include GradsPlus, Mitzvah Corps, UJA Campaign, dialogues with other campus organizations, Israeli dancing, and modern Hebrew courses. UNC's annual Beach Retreat and Hanukkah dance attract Jewish students from all parts of North Carolina.

> *"Coming from New Jersey, I discovered an amazing Jewish community in Chapel Hill. North Carolina Hillel has enriched my life and helped shape my Jewish identity."*
>
> **Lauren Kwiat, junior**

North Carolina Hillel is the center of service to Jewish students throughout the state, including North Carolina State University, the Greensboro area (Guilford, Greensboro College, UNC—Greensboro, and Elon College), Wake Forest University, High Point University, Charlotte, and East Carolina.

UNIVERSITY OF NORTH CAROLINA — CHARLOTTE

Enrollment 12,000 (UG 10,000; GR 2,000)
Jewish 55

Jewish Students Organization
c/o Hillel—UNC
210 West Cameron Avenue
Chapel Hill, NC 27516
(919) 942-4057
E-mail: nchillel@unc.edu

The University of North Carolina—Charlotte is served by North Carolina Hillel in Chapel Hill, and students are invited to participate in Hillel regional events.

UNIVERSITY OF NORTH CAROLINA — GREENSBORO

Enrollment 10,000 (UG 7,300; GR 2,700)
Jewish 80

Greensboro Area Hillel
c/o The ACM Center
500 Stirling Street
Greensboro, NC 27412
(336) 334-4500
(919) 942-4057
E-mail: nchillel@unc.edu

Rabbi Edward Elkin, Executive Director
Michael Zarkin, NC Hillel Greensboro Outreach
    Coordinator

 Jewish Studies
Courses in Judaism are offered by the Department of Religious Studies.

ON CAMPUS

Located in the Associated Campus Ministries Center on the campus of UNC—Greensboro, Hillel offers a wide variety of social, cultural, political, and religious programs. Events are held with students from area colleges as well as statewide programming.

Greensboro is served by North Carolina Hillel in Chapel Hill.

WAKE FOREST UNIVERSITY

Enrollment 6,314
Jewish 50

WFU Jewish Student Organization/Hillel
PO Box 7345
Reynolda Station
Winston Salem, NC 27109
(336) 758-5368
(336) 758-5403
Fax: (336) 758-4935
E-mail: louieg@wfu.edu
Web: www.students.wfu.edu.jso

Louis Goldstein, Faculty Advisor
Andrew Ettin, Religious Advisor
Michael Zarkin, Greensboro Area Coordinator

 Jewish Studies
Some credit courses are available.

Study in Israel
The University accepts credits from Israeli universities on a case-by-case basis.

ON CAMPUS

The Wake Forest University Jewish Student Organization's goals are to provide for the religious and cultural needs of Wake Forest University students and faculty and their families while creating an open, comfortable religious environment for all. The JSO's mission includes raising awareness of Judaism and encouraging learning about and respecting the many religions of Wake Forest. The JSO is now in its third year as a bonafide university organization.

Among the JSO's recent activites have been a faculty/student dinner held at Dr. Andrew Ettin's home, which introduced upperclassmen to the incoming freshmen and to the new Jewish faculty, and a campuswide Passover seder, which brought together 40 students, faculty, administrators, and their families. All programs reflect the group's interest, and have included a variety of activities such as hosting New York State Supreme Court Justices and sponsoring race relation discussions, prayer groups, and bowling outings.

Jewish students at Wake Forest are served as part of the statewide outreach program of North Carolina Hillel in Chapel Hill, through the Greensboro Area Coordinator, and are welcome to participate in all regional activities. The ACM Center, 500 Stirling Street, Greensboro, NC 27412; (336) 334-4500.

NORTH DAKOTA

UNIVERSITY OF NORTH DAKOTA

Enrollment 8,123
Jewish 16

Jewish Stud. Assn./Org. Center
PO Box 8136 Center
University Station
Grand Forks, ND 58202
(701) 777-3215
(701) 772-5810

Professor Kitty Maidenberg, Advisor

ON CAMPUS

Jewish students at UND enjoy occasional meals together on campus, and have a good relationship with their local Jewish community.

OHIO

BALDWIN WALLACE UNIVERSITY

Enrollment 3,400 (UG 2,750; GR 650)
Jewish 20

Cleveland Hillel Foundation
11291 Euclid Avenue
Cleveland, OH 44106
(216) 231-0040
E-mail: axl24@cwru.edu
Web: www.cwru.edu/cwru/org/jsab/main.html

Amos Levi, Program Director
Gary Simon Shyken, Jewish Campus Service Corps Fellow

 Jewish Studies
1 course.

Jewish students at Baldwin Wallace are served part-time by the Cleveland Hillel Foundation.

BOWLING GREEN STATE UNIVERSITY

Enrollment 14,300 (UG 13,300; GR 1,000)
Jewish 250 (UG 150; GR 100)

Hillel at Bowling Green
Jewish Federation of Greater Toledo
6505 Sylvania Avenue
Sylvania, OH 43560
(419) 885-4461
Fax: (419) 885-3207
Web: www.bgsu.edu/studentlife/organizations/hillel/

Judy Stanton, Director
Alix Greenblatt, Federation Director

 Jewish Studies
1 course per year.

 Kosher Food
Available in Toledo, 20 minutes away.

ON CAMPUS

The Federation sponsors Bowling Green's program for Jewish students on this residential campus. Events vary according to student interest. Faculty and other local residents support and participate in programs, which have included holiday celebrations, Friday night Shabbat dinner, social activities, and Holocaust programming. There are no Jewish fraternities or sororities on campus.

CASE WESTERN RESERVE UNIVERSITY

Enrollment 8,300 (UG 3,200; GR 5,100)
Jewish 1,050 (UG 250; GR 800)

 Cleveland Hillel Foundation
11291 Euclid Avenue
Cleveland, OH 44106
(216) 231-0040
Fax: (216) 231-0256
Web: www.cwru.edu/cwru/org/jsab/main.html

Marcia Bloomburg, Executive Director
Rabbi Carie Carter, Assistant Executive Director
TBA, Program Director
Jill Ross, Director of Community Projects
Gary Simon Shyken, Jewish Campus Service Corps Fellow

 **Jewish Studies**
3 courses; 15 courses at Cleveland College of Jewish Studies.

 Study in Israel
CWRU accepts credit for study abroad at Israeli universities.

 Kosher Food
Hillel offers 5 dinners and 5 lunches; Shabbat and holiday dinners; occasional brunches and lunches on weekends; special arrangements with dining service during Passover. Vegetarian option in dorms. Kosher dairy restaurant.

ON CAMPUS

Case Western Reserve is located in the heart of a major cultural area. Cleveland's supportive local Jewish community offers home hospitality for Shabbat and holidays. Activities include weekly Israeli dancing, an active, friendly graduate student havurah, and Zionist, oppressed Jewry, and Tzedakah student groups. Lunch 'n' Learn sessions offer Jewish students an opportunity to learn with rabbis of all denominations. Students may also participate in the weekly Pizza Torah Association (PTA), the Intercultural Dialogue Group, and Kol Hashamayim, CWRU's *a cappella* group.

Case Western Hillel also serves nearby Cleveland Institute of Music, the Cleveland Institute of Art, and the Ohio College of Podiatry.

CLEVELAND STATE UNIVERSITY

Enrollment 11,600 (UG 7,600; GR 4,000)
Jewish 800 (UG 600; GR 200)

Cleveland Hillel Foundation
11291 Euclid Avenue
Cleveland, OH 44106
(216) 231-0040
Fax: (216) 231-0256
E-mail: mbb11348@aol.com
Web: www.csuohio.edu/hillel

Marcia Bloomburg, Executive Director

 Jewish Studies
A few courses are available on campus, and students may also take courses at the Cleveland College of Jewish Studies.

 Study in Israel
Study abroad in Israel is possible.

Kosher Food
Prepackaged kosher meals are available.

ON CAMPUS

The annual Yom Ha'atzmot and Yom Hashoah programs are the major on-campus events.

Cleveland State is served by the Regional Center, the Cleveland Hillel Foundation, at Case Western Reserve, which coordinates most activities on campus.

COLLEGE OF WOOSTER

Enrollment 1,644
Jewish 45

Hillel at the College of Wooster
Box C-3144
College of Wooster
Wooster, OH 44691
(216) 263-2298
(800) 877-9905
E-mail: sroot@acs.wooster.edu
Web: www.wooster.edu/inside/hillel.html

Dr. Samuel Root, Advisor
Dr. Peter Pozefsky, Advisor

 Jewish Studies
2 courses.

 Study in Israel
Junior year abroad.

 Kosher Food
Vegetarian dining alternatives.

ON CAMPUS

The College of Wooster is making a concerted effort to attract Jewish students and is very supportive of Jewish activities. Speakers and films of Jewish interest are sponsored by the college or the Jewish Student Association. Activities also include occasional brunches, a weekly dinner table, and an annual Holocaust program. The Jewish community is very supportive and welcomes students to Temple activities. Jewish students enjoy a good working relationship with the campus ministry.

CUYAHOGA COMMUNITY COLLEGE

Enrollment 23,000
Jewish 300

Cleveland Hillel Foundation
11291 Euclid Avenue
Cleveland, OH 44106
(216) 231-0040
E-mail: axl24@cwru.edu
Web: www.cwru.edu/cwru/org/jsab/main.html

Amos Levi, Program Director
Gary Simon Shyken, Jewish Campus Service Corps Fellow

Jewish students at Tri-C are served part-time by the Cleveland Hillel Foundation.

DENISON UNIVERSITY

Enrollment 1,900
Jewish 55

Denison Hillel
Denison University
Granville, OH 43023
(740) 587-6386

Darleen Girsh, Advisor

 Jewish Studies
2 courses.

Kosher Food
Kosher food is available for holidays and occasional meals. Vegetarian dining alternatives. Dormitory cooking facilities. Kosher food is also locally available.

ON CAMPUS

Hillel at Denison offers a full range of social, cultural, educational, and religious programs. Jewish faculty and staff are actively involved in the Hillel program, and Hillel has a very good relationship with the University and the larger community. Activities include bagel brunches, deli dinners, movie nights, Holocaust commemoration, speakers, Shabbat services, and an annual Passover seder held at the president's home.

HEBREW UNION COLLEGE— JEWISH INSTITUTE OF RELIGION

Enrollment 150
Jewish 110

3101 Clifton Avenue
Cincinnati, OH 45220-2488
(513) 221-1875
Fax: (513) 221-0321
E-mail: kehrlich@cn.huc.edu
Web: www.huc.edu

Rabbi Kenneth E. Ehrlich, Dean

Jewish Studies
More than 500 courses; Rabbinic ordination; Cantorial investiture; M.A. in Hebrew Literature, Bible and Cognate Studies, Jewish Education, Religious Education, Sacred Music (NY campus), and Jewish Communal Service; joint degrees of Master of Social Work or Master of Science in Gerontology and M.A. in Jewish Communal Service; Master of Public Administration; M.Phil.; Ph.D.; Ph.D. in Jewish Education; Doctor of Ministry, Doctor of Hebrew Studies, Doctor of Hebrew Letters. B.S. in Hebrew Education or Jewish Education and B.A. in Judaic Studies or Religion offered on limited basis. Certificate programs in Judaic Studies, Jewish Communal Service, and Synagogue Management. Post-

graduate studies in Bible, and archaeology and history of ancient Israel; postgraduate fellowships at School of Graduate Studies and American Jewish Archives.

ON CAMPUS

Founded in 1875, Hebrew Union College—Jewish Institute of Religion is the nation's oldest institution of higher Jewish education and the academic and professional leadership development center of Reform Judaism. HUC-JIR educates men and women for service to American and world Jewry as rabbis, cantors, educators, and communal workers and offers graduate and postgraduate degree programs to scholars of all faiths.

With centers of learning in Cincinnati, Los Angeles, New York, and Jerusalem, HUC-JIR's Skirball Cultural Center and Museums, Klau, Frances-Henry and Abramov Libraries, American Jewish Archives (10 million documents on Western Hemisphere Jewry and the Holocaust), and archaeological excavations in Israel provide extensive research opportunities for students in all programs and represent major centers of study, research, and publication.

HUC-JIR has a vibrant Jewish community on all of its campuses. Tikkun Olam and community outreach activities include the weekly Monday night dinners for the homeless in New York, home and hospital chaplaincy for people with HIV/AIDS, and Kollel—A Center for Liberal Study in New York; the shelter for battered women and children in Cincinnati; programs for the elderly and developmentally disabled in Los Angeles; and outreach to Ethiopian and Russian olim and weekly Israeli folk dancing in Jerusalem. Jewish holiday celebrations, cultural programs, faculty and student recitals, concerts, dance performances, lectures, and conferences (e.g., healing, spirituality) are offered at all the schools.

See also listing for the HUC-JIR Jerusalem campus under "Specialized Educational Opportunities & Experiences" in the Resources section of this guide.

HIRAM COLLEGE

Enrollment 900
Jewish 20

Hillel Extension
c/o Hillel at Kent State
202 North Lincoln Street
Kent, OH 44240
(330) 678-0397
Fax: (330) 678-1179
E-mail: dlettofs@kentvm.kent.edu
Web: www.kent.edu/stuorg/hillel

TBA, Director
TBA, Jewish Campus Service Corps Fellow

 Kosher Food

Kosher food is locally available and is provided for Hillel activities.

See listing for Kent State University.

JOHN CARROLL UNIVERSITY

Enrollment 4,000 (UG 3,000; GR 1,000)
Jewish 200 (UG 50; GR 150)

Cleveland Hillel Foundation
11291 Euclid Avenue
Cleveland, OH 44106
(216) 231-0040
E-mail: axl24@cwru.edu
Web: www.cwru.edu/cwru/org/jsab/main.html

Amos Levi, Program Director
Gary Simon Shyken, Jewish Campus Service Corps Fellow

 Jewish Studies

4 courses.

Jewish students at John Carroll are served part-time by the Cleveland Hillel Foundation.

KENT STATE UNIVERSITY

Enrollment 24,000 (UG 16,600; GR 7,400)
Jewish 1,200 (UG 1,000; GR 200)

Hillel Foundation
202 North Lincoln Street
Kent, OH 44240
(330) 678-0397
Fax: (330) 678-1179
Web: www.kent.edu-stuorg/hillel

TBA, Director
TBA, Jewish Campus Service Corps Fellow

 Jewish Studies

Certificate program in Jewish studies with courses in other departments. Freshman scholarships available.

Study in Israel

Year abroad program at Haifa University.

Kosher Food

Hillel offers weekly Shabbat dinners, occasional weekday meals, Sunday bagel brunches, Passover seder, and holiday meals. Passover lunches and dinners are also provided. Hillel has a kosher kitchen.

ON CAMPUS

Hillel offers a wide variety of cultural, artistic, social, educational, and religious activities. Leadership training, speakers, art exhibits, pizza parties, barbecues, UJA campaign, trips to Israel, and Sunday bagel brunches are just some highlights of what one can find at KSU Hillel. There is 1 Jewish fraternity, AEPi, on campus.

KENYON COLLEGE

Enrollment 1,500
Jewish 100

Kenyon College Hillel
Snowden Multicultural Center
209 Chase Avenue
Gambier, OH 43022
(740) 427-5228
Fax: (614) 427-5219
E-mail: cooperm@kenyon.edu

Michael Cooper, Director

Jewish Studies
3 courses. Jewish Studies courses are part of the Religious Studies Department.

Study in Israel
Junior year abroad.

Kosher Food
Vegetarian dining alternatives. Kosher food is available from Columbus (1 hour away). There is a limited supply of kosher food in the local grocery store.

ON CAMPUS

Hillel at Kenyon College is a student-run organization. Many opportunities exist for students to take on leadership roles, to plan programs, and to interact closely with the Hillel director, the Jewish faculty and staff, and the Jewish communities in Gambier and Mount Vernon.

Hillel organizes both the social and the religious elements of Jewish life at Kenyon, and many of the Jewish professors and their families participate in these events. Hillel has hosted its own catered Passover seders, as well as holiday parties, and social and cultural events. Activities have included deli dinners, bagel brunches, guest speakers, Hanukkah Latke Party, and a Halloween party. There is also a weekly Torah Reading Group, led by philosophy professor Andrew Pessin.

Hillel staff is on campus 2–3 days a week. Kenyon College Hillel also co-sponsors some events with other college Hillels in the area. Kenyon is served as an extension service of Hillel at Ohio State.

"I chose to come to Kenyon College for a few reasons. I loved the small, close-knit community that was offered both among students and between students and professors and their families. I also chose to come to Kenyon because of the Jewish life on campus. I liked the way that Hillel was set up and that it really was a student-run organization. I also liked the opportunity to become involved on the Board during my freshman year. The Hillel Board is an excellent opportunity for first-year students to become involved at Kenyon, obtain some leadership experience, and form some great friendships with other Jewish students."

Erin R. Shanahan, junior

MIAMI UNIVERSITY

Enrollment 15,000
Jewish 1,000

Hillel Foundation at Miami University
Beerman Jewish Student Center
11 East Walnut Street
Oxford, OH 45056
(513) 523-5190
E-mail: muhillel@aol.com
Web: www.muohio.edu/~hillel

Nicky Scott Spivak, Director
Ellary Spiezer, Jewish Campus Service Corps Fellow

Jewish Studies
Thematic Sequence in Judaic Studies; Hebrew.

Study in Israel
Long-standing, informal program with Israeli universities.

Kosher Food
Hillel offers Shabbat dinners, holiday meals, and brunches; Passover: seders, co-op (University will refund food costs to participants), matzah, and Passover menus in dorms.

ON CAMPUS

Miami University's Jewish students enjoy a wide variety of social and educational opportunities, including participation in on-campus diversity and community service projects and an active Greek/Jewish Council.

Hillel is located 1 block from campus, and has a highly enthusiastic and active student membership from the East and West Coasts, as well as from the Midwest. Warm family atmosphere; active UJA campaign, annual Holocaust memorial programs, and programs with other Ohio Hillels.

> *"Miami's Hillel is a wonderful place and I am very thankful to have had the opportunity to be a leader. I met so many people and made so many friends through Hillel."*
>
> **Cari Kramer, recent graduate**

> *"Miami's Hillel has been my home away from home for the past four years. I have found life-long friends and learned so much from my experience at Hillel."*
>
> **Faith Brodsky, recent graduate**

NOTRE DAME COLLEGE OF OHIO

Enrollment 810
Jewish 24

Jewish Students Association
c/o Multicultural Affairs Office
4545 College Road
South Euclid, OH 44121
(216) 381-1680
Fax: (216) 381-1680
E-mail: gss7@po.cwru.edu

Anne L. Lukas, Advisor
Gary Simon Shyken, Jewish Campus Service Corp Fellow

 Jewish Studies
Credit accepted from Cleveland College of Jewish Studies, just minutes away.

 Kosher Food
Available within minutes of campus.

Housing
Several opportunities in the area.

ON CAMPUS

Notre Dame College of Ohio welcomes Jewish students. The neighboring area has a large and active Jewish community.

OBERLIN COLLEGE

Enrollment 2,820
Jewish 800

 Oberlin Hillel Foundation
Wilder Hall, Room 219
Oberlin, OH 44074
(440) 775-8182
(440) 775-8103
Fax: (440) 775-8886
E-mail: shimon.brand@oberlin.edu

Rabbi Shimon Brand, Director
Peter Salzman, Program Director
Kate Palley, Jewish Campus Service Corp Fellow

 Jewish Studies
10 courses; B.A.

 Study in Israel
Junior year abroad.

Kosher Food
The Kosher-Halal Co-op is a student-run dining co-operative located in Talcott. The co-op is a member of Hillel and the Oberlin Student Cooperative Association. Before Passover, the co-op is cleaned thoroughly, and dishes are exchanged for those used only on Passover. The co-op changed its name from Kosher Co-op to Kosher-Halal Co-op, as a place where Muslim as well as Jewish dietary laws are observed. Both observant and non-observant Jews and non-Jews are drawn to Kosher-Halal's warm atmosphere, which is also the site of stimulating discussions.

On Friday nights, the co-op hosts the Shabbat meal. 7 dinners, 7 lunches. Vegetarian dining alternatives. Rabbi Shimon Brand is the Advisor to the Co-op.

ON CAMPUS

Oberlin Hillel is the foundation for Jewish student life on campus. Shabbat is the centerpiece of Jewish life at Oberlin. Every Friday evening, 50-80 students, faculty, staff, and townspeople come together to enjoy a Shabbat dinner featuring fresh-baked challah. Music from Conservatory students sets the festive mood, and participants join in the singing.

Social activism is the significant aspect of many Hillel programs, which reflect the broadest spectrum of Jewish life and experience. Jewish students at Oberlin are constantly challenged to explore and celebrate their similarities and differences. Hillel has comprehensive cultural, social, political, and religious programming as well as a diverse Zionist community and an active Jewish Women's Group. The Sunday Lox and Bagel Brunch, in Wilder Hall, offers a warm atmosphere for meeting people; it also is an opportunity to discuss ideas and feelings about politics, science, law, history, music, literature, and many other topics with outside speakers and Oberlin professors.

Hillel at Oberlin has recently hosted these outstanding Jewish personalities: Israeli poet Yehuda Amichai; writer Roger Kamenetz, author of *The Jew in the Lotus: A Poet's Rediscovery of Jewish Identity in Buddhist India*; writer and former civil rights leader Julius Lester, who discussed "Blacks and Jews: Where We Are and What We Can Do"; Tikva Frimer-Kinsky, on Jewish lesbian identity; author Laurie Gunst, who discussed her book, *A Southern Jewish Child in the Civil Rights South*; Israeli political scientist Shlomo Avineri; Israeli political commentators Ehud Yeari and Meron Benvenisti; and a panel on the Middle East, comprised of Jordanian, American, and Israeli students.

"Oberlin Hillel is a great place. I have learned a lot and feel very welcomed by the community."

Sally Neff, senior

OHIO STATE UNIVERSITY

Enrollment 48,500 (UG 30,500; GR 18,000)
Jewish 3,300 (UG 2,500; GR 800)

Hillel at Ohio State University
Wexner Jewish Student Center
46 E. 16th Avenue
Columbus, OH 43201
(614) 294-4797
Fax: (614) 294-4796
E-mail: hillel@osu.edu
Web: www.acs.ohio-state.edu/students/hillel/

Joseph Kohane, Executive Director
Rabbi Scott Aaron, Assistant Director
Miriam Benstein, Program Director
Liba Beyer, Program Director
Rena Gelb and Cydney Singer, Jewish Campus Service Corps Fellows
Susannah Sagan, Director of Development

Jewish Studies

60 courses annually; B.A., M.A., Ph.D. The Melton Center for Jewish Studies includes 23 full-time professors. Organized as an interdepartmental program, the Melton Center coordinates the various elements of Jewish Studies at Ohio State, with 80 courses in the catalog in Jewish history, philosophy, Hebrew language and literature, Yiddish language and literature, Bible, rabbinics, mysticism, and Holocaust studies. Two graduate fellowships in Jewish Studies are available for the M.A. and Ph.D. Undergraduate scholarships are available for qualified students majoring in Jewish Studies, Hebrew, or Yiddish. The Judaica collection, with more than 100,000 volumes, is one of the largest and finest Jewish studies libraries in the United States.

The Melton Center regularly sponsors lectures, symposia, conferences, and an annual Jewish film festival. Professor Tamar Rudavsky, Director, Melton Center, 306 Dulles Hall, 230 West 17th Ave., Columbus, OH 43210; (614) 292-0967; Fax: (614) 292-8838; tamar+@osu.edu.

Study in Israel

Israel summer-study tour for Ohio State credit.

Kosher Food

Hillel offers 5 dinners, 6 lunches. Hillel operates a full-menu bagel cafe Sunday through Friday 9:00 a.m.–7:00 p.m.

ON CAMPUS

Hillel at OSU is committed to nurturing and enabling all the expressions of Jewish life found on campus, as well as those expressions that are still waiting to be discovered. In recognition of the vast array of backgrounds of today's Jewish students, OSU Hillel strives to fashion as many attractive entry points as possible through the quality and quantity of its innovative and traditional programs.

Numerous student groups under Hillel auspices create and deliver an impressive number of services and initiatives in every dimension of Jewish life: communal, artistic, political, intellectual, and religious.

Hillel's beautiful new building, the Wexner Jewish Student Center, which opened its doors in December 1994, includes student offices, meeting areas, and even a fitness center. It represents the Columbus Jewish community's statement of confidence in the promise of its institution.

OHIO UNIVERSITY

Enrollment 18,000
Jewish 800 (UG 700; GR 100)

The Jewish Foundation of Southeastern Ohio
21 Mill Street
Athens, OH 45701
(740) 592-1173
(740) 592-5604
Fax: (740) 592-6279

Rabbi Elena Stein, Director
Rochelle Young, Jewish Campus Service Corp Fellow

Jewish Studies

Courses on the Holocaust and American Jewish history are offered through the History Department.

Study in Israel

OU accepts credit transfer from Israeli universities.

Kosher Food

Hillel offers a kosher dinner every other Friday during the quarter, and provides kosher lunches and dinners during Passover.

ON CAMPUS

The Jewish community at Ohio University consists of a unique blend of students and local residents. There are approximately 120 Jewish households in Athens. Programming includes a student-run planning board, a UJA campus campaign, Students for Israel, social, educational, and cultural events, an outdoor club, and Hebrew classes. Hillel at Ohio University has a relaxed, warm atmosphere and friendly community members.

> *"Hillel has become a wonderful Jewish home while I'm away from home. I've met some of my closest friends through Hillel's social programs. The Jewish population is small in Athens, but our spirit and reach is very powerful."*
>
> **Shanie Israel, sophomore**

> *"Hillel is a way for me to express my Jewish creativity as well as my spirituality. I have common ground with people at Hillel because we are all Jews. I can let a part of me come out that would otherwise be unexpressed."*
>
> **Jodi Jacobson, senior**

OHIO WESLEYAN UNIVERSITY

Enrollment 1,800
Jewish 50

Hillel Extension
c/o Prof. Robert J. Gitter
Department of Economics
Ohio Wesleyan University
Delaware, OH 43015
(740) 368-3536
Fax: (740) 369-5879
E-mail: rjgitter@cc.owu.edu

Prof. Robert Gitter, Advisor
Jon Powers, Chaplain

 Jewish Studies
4 courses; B.A. The University will assist students in designing an interdepartmental major in Jewish Studies.

 Kosher Food
Vegetarian dining alternatives. Kosher food is available in Columbus.

ON CAMPUS

Activities in past years have included speakers, brunches, and Holocaust commemoration, depending upon student interest each year. There is no active Hillel at this time.

Hillel at Ohio Wesleyan is served as an extension of Ohio State University.

UNIVERSITY OF AKRON

Enrollment 27,670 (UG 11,500; GR 16,170)
Jewish 300

Hillel
202 North Lincoln Street
Kent, OH 44240
(330) 678-0397
Fax: (330) 678-1179
E-mail: dlettofs@kentvm.kent.edu

TBA, Director
TBA, Program Director

 Study in Israel
Year abroad program at University of Haifa.

 Kosher Food
Kosher food is locally available and is provided for Hillel activities.

ON CAMPUS

Hillel Jewish Student Union has become very active in recent years. Hillel provides a wide array of programs including social activities, educational and cultural programs, and religious celebrations, both on and off campus. The Jewish Law Student Association is very active.

Jewish students are served part-time by Hillel at Kent State University and are welcome to participate in all Kent Hillel programs.

UNIVERSITY OF CINCINNATI

Enrollment 34,000
Jewish 1,500

 Hillel Jewish Student Center
Rose Warner House
2615 Clifton Avenue
Cincinnati, OH 45220
(513) 221-6728
Fax: (513) 221-7134
E-mail: uchillel@brugold.com
Web: www.brugold.com/uchillel/

Rabbi Abie Ingber, Executive Director
Stephanie Kaplan, Program Associate
Ryan Schultz, Jewish Campus Service Corps Fellow
Toby Warnick, Assistant to the Director
Vicki Tuckman, Rabbinic Intern

 Jewish Studies
36 courses offered annually. B.A.; minor. Enrolling about 700 students annually, UC Judaic Studies is an undergraduate, interdisciplinary program; its courses in Jewish history, literature and thought, and Hebrew language also fulfill University-wide curricular and general

education requirements. The program organizes annual lectures and culture series, arranges student internships in local Jewish agencies, confers several competitive awards for educational achievement, communal service, and study in Israel, and periodically publishes the student journal, *Cincinnati Judaica Review*. Professor Benny Kraut, Director, Judaic Studies Program, PO Box 210169, University of Cincinnati, Cincinnati, OH 45221-0169; (513) 556-2297; kraut@ucbeh.san.uc.edu.

Study in Israel
UC and Hillel work together with the community representative from Israel, the schlicha, to promote and arrange study in Israel.

Kosher Food
Hillel offers 2 dinners and 1 lunch a week, as well as Passover lunches and dinners. Hillel will work with students on campus who need to make special arrangements for kosher food services.

ON CAMPUS

The University of Cincinnati has an extremely varied and very visible Jewish presence. Among the numerous programs facilitated by Hillel are: FreshPoPs, a first-year student outreach program; Just Like Me, a social action project focusing on inner-city youth; Greek Link, activities of special interest to students in the Greek system; Jewish Folk Festival, an annual, award-winning, citywide celebration of Jewish culture that attracts up to 10,000 people; Big Jewish Ball, where Jewish students meet and dance to the music of a live band; Jewish Student Campaign, a leadership and educational opportunity for students to conduct a campuswide Tzedakah campaign; Jewish Affairs Committee, working for Israel awareness on campus; Shirley's Grill, a weekly buffet dinner; graduate and young professional programming; Feed the Homeless breakfast program; Operation Warm-up, creating care packages for those in need; weekly Shabbat dinners and programs; holiday celebrations; and summer programming.

Cincinnati Hillel's Big Jewish Bar Mitzvah is an annual event held during winter quarter at Hillel. At the Bar Mitzvah party, students relive their bar/bat mitzvah years with a traditional celebration, but without the stress that often accompanies these days. Jewish students from all area colleges—Northern Kentucky University, Xavier College, Raymond Walters College, Cincinnati State, Hebrew Union College, the University of Cincinnati professional schools, and the University of Cincinnati—dance together and enjoy the music.

Cincinnati Hillel is also well known for its impressive collection of architectural Judaica, which it has salvaged from synagogues throughout the United States and the world. Hillel's collection and art gallery are listed by the American Automobile Association as a significant Cincinnati tourist attraction.

"The Midwest is a great place to call home; Hillel is my Jewish home. Hillel is what you make it— a place to make friends and have fun."

Neil Aronson, junior, College of Business Administration

UNIVERSITY OF TOLEDO

Enrollment 17,000 (UG 13,600; GR 3,400)
Jewish 250 (UG 150; GR 100)

Hillel
Jewish Federation of Greater Toledo
6505 Sylvania Avenue
Sylvania, OH 43560
(419) 885-4461 (Federation)
Fax: (419) 885-3207

Marilyn Levine, Director
Alix Greenblatt, Federation Director

Jewish Studies
1 course each quarter.

Kosher Food
Kosher food is available locally.

ON CAMPUS
The Federation sponsors Toledo's program for Jewish students on this commuter campus. Events vary according to the interest of the students, who run a seder, the Yom Kippur break-the-fast, Oneg Shabbats, and other social activities. There are no Jewish fraternities or sororities on campus.

OKLAHOMA

UNIVERSITY OF OKLAHOMA

Enrollment 20,000
Jewish 400 (UG 300; GR 100)

OU Hillel Foundation
University of Oklahoma
494 Elm Avenue
Norman, OK 73069
(405) 321-3703
Fax: (405) 321-3705
E-mail: okhillel@flash.net
Web: www.ou.edu/student/hillel

TBA, Director

Jewish Studies
M.A. and Ph.D. through graduate interdisciplinary program; undergraduate minor. Courses in Jewish history and Hebrew language. Endowed Schusterman Chair in Jewish Studies. Scholarships available.

Study in Israel
Study abroad opportunities in Israel.

Kosher Food
Occasional meals at Hillel.

ON CAMPUS

Although a relatively small percentage of the overall student population, Jewish students at the University of Oklahoma are very active on campus. Jewish students participate in a wide range of Hillel-sponsored, campuswide events and programs on Israel, Jewish culture, the Holocaust, human rights, canned food drives, parties, mixers, and weekly kosher Shabbat dinners. In addition, the Judaic Studies program sponsors a monthly lunch lecture, Jewish film festivals, and cultural exhibitions.

The Hillel Jewish Student Center, conveniently located across the street from campus, is a comfortable place for students to relax between classes, watch TV or movies in a state-of-the-art entertainment center, play pool, or surf the Internet.

Hillel also serves as the focal point of Jewish activity for the local Jewish community of Norman. University students regularly interact with the local community by attending community-sponsored dinners and brunches, tutoring local children in Hebrew, teaching at the local religious Sunday school, and joining families for home hospitality for holiday meals.

The University administration is supportive of and sensitive to the needs of Jewish students and faculty on campus. An estimated 150 Jewish faculty and staff are at the University of Oklahoma.

UNIVERSITY OF TULSA

Enrollment 5,000
Jewish 50

University of Tulsa Jewish Association
c/o Jewish Federation of Tulsa
2021 E. 71st Street
Tulsa, OK 74136
(918) 495-1100
E-mail: tulsafed@jon.cjf.org

Martin Belsky, Jewish Student Advisor
Deborah Levine, Jewish Student Advisor

Jewish Studies
Hebrew is taught.

Study in Israel
Junior year abroad.

Kosher Food
Available locally. Kosher bakery and meat co-op at JCC; kosher kitchen at Congregation B'nai Emunah.

ON CAMPUS
The Tulsa Jewish Community is very supportive of efforts by students to establish a campus Jewish community at the University of Tulsa, more so than the University. The Tulsa community enables students to attend national conferences.

OREGON

LEWIS & CLARK COLLEGE

Enrollment 2,800 (UG 1,500; GR 1,300)
Jewish 75–100 (UG)

Jewish Student Union Lewis & Clark College
Lewis & Clark College
0615 Southwest Paltine Hill Road
Portland, OR 97219
(503) 768-7082
E-mail: duntley@lclark.edu
Web: www.lclark.edu/~chapel

Reverend Mark Duntley, College Chaplain

Jewish Studies
2 courses offered in the Religious Studies department: Introduction to Judaism and European Jewish History. 1 course offered on the Holocaust.

Study in Israel
Transfer credits available.

Kosher Food
Vegetarian options available.

ON CAMPUS
While the Jewish Student Union offers many activities on a regular basis, in general, religious groups on campus are relatively low-key. Student initiative plays a key role in fulfilling this aspect of student campus life. JSU-sponsored activities are well supported through school funding and student participation.

The JSU at Lewis & Clark College offers many activities, including community service programs, building a sukkah, Tu B'shvat tree planting events, a Passover Seder, Hanukkah activities, and a day of programming for Yom Hashoah. The JSU also sponsors speakers on campus throughout the academic year.

OREGON STATE UNIVERSITY

Enrollment 15,000
Jewish 250

OSU Hillel/Jewish Student Union
c/o Paul Kopperman
Department of History
Oregon State University
Corvallis, OR 97331-5104
(541) 737-1265
(541) 758-0501
Fax: (541) 737-1257
E-mail: pkopperman@orst.edu

Professor Paul Kopperman, Faculty Advisor
Cantor Lyle Rockler, Counselor

 Jewish Studies
2 courses on the Holocaust only.

Study in Israel
Opportunities for study in Israel and credit transfers from Israel institutions may be approved on an individual basis.

Kosher Food
The Jewish community will assist students in ordering kosher food from Portland. Vegetarian alternatives are available.

ON CAMPUS

For the most part, Jewish students at Oregon State participate in religious and social activities with the Corvallis Jewish community, off campus. On-campus programming focuses on speakers and films. Hillel is an active participant in the university's Holocaust Memorial Program.

PORTLAND STATE UNIVERSITY

Enrollment 16,000
Jewish 400

Jewish Student Union at Portland State, L&C, Reed College
c/o Jewish Federation of Portland
6651 Southwest Capitol Highway
Portland, OR 97219
(503) 245-6219
(503) 725-5652
Fax: (503) 245-6603

David Martinez, Advisor, Multicultural Student
Association

REED COLLEGE

Enrollment 1,300
Jewish 500

JSU at Portland State, Reed, Lewis & Clark College
c/o Jewish Federation of Portland
6651 Southwest Capitol Highway
Portland, OR 97219
(503) 245-6219
Fax: (503) 245-6603

Jill Adelman, Advisor

UNIVERSITY OF OREGON

Enrollment 15,830 (UG 12,000; GR 3,830)
Jewish 1,200

 Hillel at University of Oregon
1059 Hilyard
Eugene, OR 97401
(541) 343-8920
Fax: (541) 343-4552
E-mail: uohillel@efn.org
Web: darkwing.uoregon.edu/~hillel/

Rabbi Karen Landy, Director
Jeff Klein, Program Director

 Jewish Studies
Several courses; independent major possible; Jewish Studies program.

 Study in Israel
Hebrew University exchange program. Relationship with Arava Institute for Environmental Studies.

 Kosher Food
Hillel has a kosher kitchen and serves kosher meals for Friday Shabbat services and other holidays and events.

ON CAMPUS

Jewish campus life at the University of Oregon has expanded greatly in recent years. Students play a vital role in shaping the Jewish campus community, and activities and leadership opportunities abound. The Hillel board works closely with other student groups, including the campus Jewish Student Union, Jewish Law Students, and AEPi Jewish fraternity. Hillel has an excellent profile and is well received on campus as well as in the greater Eugene Jewish community. The University of Oregon works closely with Common Ground, an organization dedicated to Muslim-Jewish relations on campus.

The University of Oregon will make social action the focus of the 1999–2000 academic year. A conference will feature speakers who will discuss Tikkun Olam, social responsibility, and volunteerism.

The International Free University: Hillel students and staff collaborate with the University for a high-quality conference series. The first 3-day conference, Ethics After the Holocaust featured Elie Wiesel, Jewish theologian Emil Fackenheim, and Holocaust historians Deborah Lipstadt and Raul Hilberg, and other top scholars. The second brought Joseph Teluskin, Avivah Zornberg, and others to campus.

"The University of Oregon Hillel is a comfortable place for students with diverse Jewish backgrounds. Hillel at the University of Oregon provides a forum for spiritual, social and educational needs for all students. Hillel is active in both the campus and the Eugene community."

Jessica Elkan, president of Hillel at the University of Oregon

PENNSYLVANIA

ALBRIGHT COLLEGE

Enrollment 1,008
Jewish 50

> Hillel
> PO Box 15234
> Reading, PA 19612
> (610) 921-7708
> Fax: (610) 921-7530
> E-mail: incledonj@jalbright
>
> **Dr. John Incledon**, Advisor

Jewish Studies

Albright offers a number of courses in religion that include Understanding Judaism, Christianity, and Islam; History and Theology of Judaism; and the Study of the Hebrew Bible. Also, there is a Holocaust course offered through the History department.

Kosher Food

Vegetarian dining alternatives; dormitory cooking facilities.

Albright College is served by the local Jewish Community Center.

ALLEGHENY COLLEGE

Enrollment 1,900
Jewish 50

> Hillel
> Box 5, Allegheny College
> Meadville, PA 16335
> (814) 332-4351
> Fax: (814) 337-0431
> E-mail: mgoldber@admin.alleg.edu
>
> **Professor Martin A. Goldberg**, Advisor

Jewish Studies

3 courses.

Kosher Food

Kosher kitchen in the Hillel House.

ON CAMPUS

The Hillel house on campus is the center for Allegheny College's very active Jewish student group. Hillel is a visible presence on campus. All holidays are celebrated, and Jewish students erect a sukkah on campus as well as a 10-foot Hanukkah menorah, which is lit publicly each evening. Each year, Hillel sponsors trips to the U.S. Holocaust Memorial Museum in Washington, D.C.; last year the trip filled two buses. Hillel also brings speakers and klezmer bands to campus and holds bag lunch discussions. The College is very supportive of Jewish activities, and the Jewish Chautauqua Society provides a visiting rabbi to teach in the Religion Department. An endowed lectureship enables Hillel to sponsor major speakers for the entire college.

BEAVER COLLEGE

Enrollment 800
Jewish 150 (UG 110; GR 40)

> Hillel at Beaver College
> c/o Multi-Campus Hillel Center
> 2014 North Broad Street
> Philadelphia, PA 19121
> (215) 517-2454
> E-mail: marlaj@vm.temple.edu
> Web: www.beaver.edu
>
> **Marla Meyers**, Director
> **Hila Reichman**, Associate Director
> **Ken Krivitzky**, Program Director
> **Rachel Salis**, Jewish Campus Service Corps Fellow

Study in Israel

Junior year abroad.

Kosher Food

Frozen; on request in dining room.

ON CAMPUS

This is a small campus with a small Jewish population. Beaver's Jewish students are involved in activities with other Jewish students in the Philadelphia area through Philadelphia's Multi-Campus Hillel Center. Programs, which include Shabbat dinners, leadership seminars, and social events, are often held at Beaver College's beautiful castle.

See listing for Temple University.

BLOOMSBURG UNIVERSITY

Enrollment 6,000
Jewish 40

Hillel at Bloomsburg University
c/o Professor Neal Slone
Department of Sociology and Social Welfare
400 E. 2nd Street
Bloomsburg, PA 17815
(570) 389-4431
(570) 389-4432
Fax: (570) 389-2019
E-mail: slone@planetx.blumu.edu

Professor Neal Slone, Advisor
Gloria Cohen, Advisor

 Kosher Food
Vegetarian dining alternatives.

ON CAMPUS

Hillel at Bloomsburg University sponsors informal gatherings to celebrate holidays, and gathers for occasional cultural events. Faculty offer home hospitality for Shabbat dinners.

BRYN MAWR COLLEGE

Enrollment 1,200
Jewish 200

 Suburban Campus of Philadelphia Hillel
Bryn Mawr College
Bryn Mawr, PA 19010
(610) 526-5538
(610) 896-4988
E-mail: mpiknat1@swarthmore.edu
Web: students.haverford.edu/dsayres/jsu/jsu.html

Rabbi Marsha Pik-Nathan, Director
Jessica Cooper, Jewish Campus Service Corps Fellow

 Jewish Studies
The Department of Hebrew and Judaic Studies offers courses in the Hebrew language, conducted in Hebrew, on 3 levels. These courses focus on biblical,

rabbinic, and modern literary sources. Courses in Judaic Studies (1 course per semester) are theme-based, focusing on various subjects in Jewish philosophy, sociology, and history.

 Study in Israel
Junior year abroad.

 Kosher Food
Kosher co-op (part of meal plan option) and kosher-for-Passover co-op vegetarian dining alternatives.

 Housing
Hebrew Hall in Hafner Dorm.

ON CAMPUS

Bryn Mawr/Haverford Hillel is a bi-college student-run organization. Social, educational, political, and religious programs are planned by both board members and interested Jewish students. The monthly calendar is sent to all students on the mailing list. All holidays are celebrated. Holocaust Awareness Week includes a 24-hour reading of names, films, and talks by survivors. There are Jewish educational courses, speakers, and social action and Tzedakah activities.

The colleges' administrations and Jewish faculty are very supportive of Jewish life on campus. Both college presidents join Hillel for the first Shabbat of the year.

The faculty plan an annual Hamantashen/Latke Debate. Students are encouraged to attend national student conferences, and subsidies are usually available. Students also participate in citywide programming coordinated by the Hillel Regional Center, Hillel of Greater Philadelphia.

BUCKNELL UNIVERSITY

Enrollment 3,300
Jewish 175

Hillel
Owen 188—Department of Physics
Bucknell University
Lewisburg, PA 17837
(570) 577-1348

Professor Tom Solomon, Faculty Advisor

 Jewish Studies
4–5 courses in Judaism and Holocaust Studies. Additional courses of related interest are taught in the Departments of Religion and Philosophy. Bucknell plans to hire a scholar in Judaic Studies in the coming year.

 Study in Israel
Semester/year abroad at Tel Aviv and Hebrew Universities.

Kosher Food

Vegetarian dining alternatives. Friday evening Shabbat meals are kosher. During Passover, students can use their meal plan toward eating in the Hillel kitchen, which is made kosher for Passover.

Housing

Martin House, the Jewish Studies House, provides housing through the campus special-interest house program.

ON CAMPUS

Bucknell's administration is very supportive of and committed to Jewish life on campus and is increasing opportunities for Jewish programming. The University has a strong campaign to develop the Judaic Studies program, as well as a commitment to hire a full-time rabbi for the campus. Bucknell policy forbids the scheduling of exams on the High Holidays, and campus organizations work together to avoid conflicts between major Jewish holidays and Greek and multicultural events.

Jewish students are active in many campus organizations, creating ties among a diverse array of student groups. Bucknell Hillel is dedicated to fostering an open Jewish community on campus and to offering a variety of social, educational, and cultural programs. Students, faculty, and staff come together to celebrate Shabbat and holidays. Hillel staff and members also work to enrich the understanding of Jewish traditions and culture, and to promote the exchange of ideas and the enhancement of religious and cultural diversity in the broader campus community.

BUCKS COUNTY COMMUNITY COLLEGE

Enrollment 15,000
Jewish 750

Hillel at Bucks County Community College
Swamp Road
Newtown, PA 18940
(215) 769-1174
(215) 898-8265
Fax: (215) 763-9686
E-mail: hillel@vm.temple.edu

Marla Meyers, Director
Hila Reichman, Associate Director
Ken Krivitsky, Program Director

Kosher Food

Vegetarian alternatives in the dining hall.

ON CAMPUS

Jewish students at BCCC organize meetings and events throughout the semester. BCCC students also partici-

pate in citywide events and projects sponsored by Philadelphia's Multi-Campus Hillel Center.

See listing for Temple University.

CARNEGIE-MELLON UNIVERSITY

Enrollment 7,500 (UG 4,800; GR 2,700)
Jewish 1,000

Hillel Jewish University Center of Pittsburgh
4551 Forbes Avenue, 2nd Floor
Pittsburgh, PA 15213-3510
(412) 621-8875
(412) 621-8859
Fax: (412) 621-8861
E-mail: hillel@sgi.net
Web: www.cmu.edu

Daniel Wiseman, Director
TBA, Program Director
Alison Ross, Jewish Campus Service Corps Fellow

Jewish Studies

CMU offers a Holocaust course through the Humanities and Social Sciences College, and students can cross-register at the University of Pittsburgh.

Study in Israel

Students can receive credit for study in Israel through a variety of programs.

Kosher Food

On campus, Food Services offers 2 kosher meals a day, 6 days a week. The Hillel Foundation of Pittsburgh offers Shabbat dinners, holiday meals, and vegetarian dining alternatives. There is a kosher kitchen at the Jewish Student Association, and many residence halls contain cooking facilities.

Housing

A special-interest house, the Jewish Student Association, is located on campus; programs are open to all students.

ON CAMPUS

Hillel at Carnegie-Mellon University offers a wide range of social, cultural, Zionist, educational, and social action opportunities, with a strong emphasis on leadership development and student involvement. CMU has a Jewish Student Association House on campus. Hillel offers Reform, Conservative, and Orthodox services and programs.

The campus is located close to the geographic center of Pittsburgh's Jewish community, which has a Jewish Community Center, kosher restaurants, stores, and synagogues. The Pittsburgh community is very supportive of campus Jewish life and offers home hospitality and part-time and full-time employment opportunities.

The Hillel Foundation of Pittsburgh is the center for programming and service to Carnegie Mellon University, the University of Pittsburgh, Chatham College, Point Park College, and Duquesne University.

Served by Hillel Jewish University Center of Pittsburgh.

CEDAR CREST COLLEGE

Enrollment 818
Jewish 2

Hillel at Muhlenberg College
2400 Chew Street
Allentown, PA 18104
(215) 821-3244
(215) 432-7571
Fax: (215) 821-3234

Patti Mittleman, Director

Cedar Crest College is served by Hillel at Muhlenberg College. See listing for Muhlenberg College.

CHATHAM COLLEGE

Enrollment 300
Jewish 15

Hillel Foundation—Jewish University Center
4551 Forbes Avenue
Pittsburgh, PA 15213-3510
(412) 621-8875
Fax: (412) 621-8861

TBA, Director

Jewish Studies
1 course.

ON CAMPUS

A Jewish student group at Chatham runs yearly holiday celebrations and participates in annual community service events.

Chatham College is served as an extension program of the Hillel Foundation of Pittsburgh. See listing for University of Pittsburgh.

COMMUNITY COLLEGE OF PHILADELPHIA

Enrollment 11,000
Jewish 250

Multi-Campus Hillel Center
2014 North Broad Street
Philadelphia, PA 19121
(215) 769-1174
(215) 898-8265
Fax: (215) 763-9686
E-mail: hillel@vm.temple.edu

Marla Meyers, Director
Hila Reichman, Associate Director
Ken Krivitsky, Program Director

Support for Jewish student activities at Community College is provided by the Center for Commuter Service, Hillel of Greater Philadelphia. See listing for Temple University.

DELAWARE VALLEY COLLEGE

Enrollment 1,350
Jewish 50

Hillel at Delaware Valley College
700 East Butler Avenue
Doylestown, PA 18901-2697
(215) 489-2350
(215) 769-1174
Fax: (215) 345-5277

Professor Michael Tabachnik, Advisor

 Kosher Food
Vegetarian dining alternatives; kosher food locally available; Passover meals.

ON CAMPUS

DVC was founded by Rabbi Krauskopf as the National Farm School to educate poor Jewish immigrant boys. Now a full 4-year college with diversified majors, DVC retains the principle of hands-on education. Hillel at DVC is a small but active group, with hay rides, picnics, movies, and a seder. DVC participates in joint activities with other Hillels at small colleges in the Philadelphia area. The Doylestown Hadassah, which has "adopted" DVC Hillel, provides ongoing assistance, and the community offers home hospitality during the holidays. Three Hillel book scholarships are available to members of Hillel: 1 to an entering freshman and 2 to upperclassmen.

Support for Jewish student activities at DVC is provided by the Center for Commuter Service, Hillel of Greater Philadelphia. See listing for Temple University.

DICKINSON COLLEGE

Enrollment 1,789
Jewish 275

Hillel House
Dickinson College
PO Box 1773
Carlisle, PA 17013
(717) 240-3876
E-mail: vandoren@dickinson.edu

Fred Van Doren, Advisor

 Jewish Studies
12 courses; B.A.

 Study in Israel
Junior year abroad/summer seminar.

 Kosher Food
Frozen meals are available on request in the dining hall; vegetarian dining alternatives; Jewish holiday meals in the cafeteria.

 Housing
Jewish residence house.

ON CAMPUS

Dickinson has an active program, with an annual major lecture (Pincus Lecture), films, trips, seders, and social events. The Jewish community is very supportive and involved in the Hillel program. They provide home hospitality for Shabbat and holidays, and jobs for students to teach in the community Sunday School.

DREXEL UNIVERSITY

Enrollment 12,000
Jewish 800

Hillel at Drexel
232 Creese Student Center
Drexel University
3210 Chestnut Street
Philadelphia, PA 19104
(215) 895-2531
Fax: (215) 763-9686
E-mail: hillel@vm.temple.edu
Web: www.drexel.edu

Marla Meyers, Director
Hila Reichman, Associate Director
Ken Krivitzky, Program Director
Maureen Levinkron, Jewish Campus Service Corps Fellow

 Jewish Studies
Several courses available.

 Study in Israel
Cooperative program in Israel.

 Kosher Food
Students are released from Drexel's dining plan if they wish to eat at University of Pennsylvania Hillel (3 blocks from Drexel), where there is a full kosher dining program.

ON CAMPUS

Drexel Hillel has on-campus social, cultural, and political programming. Drexel University also has an active Jewish Greek Council. Both groups plan programs and Shabbat dinners often. Because of Drexel's co-op system, which means that half the students are away from campus at any one time, turnout for events varies. Students may also participate in a wide range of activities coordinated by the Multi-Campus Hillel Center of Hillel of Greater Philadelphia.

See listing for Temple University. Served by multi-campus Hillel Center.

DUQUESNE UNIVERSITY

Enrollment 9,500
Jewish 250

Hillel Foundation—Jewish University Center
4551 Forbes Avenue
Pittsburgh, PA 15213-3510
(412) 621-8875
Fax: (412) 621-8861

Dan Wiseman, Director

 Jewish Studies
1 course annually.

Duquesne University is served as an extension program of the Hillel Foundation of Pittsburgh. See listings for Carnegie-Mellon University and University of Pittsburgh.

ELIZABETHTOWN COLLEGE

Enrollment 1,550
Jewish 15-20

Hillel
c/o Social Work Program
Elizabethtown College
Elizabethtown, PA 17022
(717) 361-1446
Fax: (717) 361-1487

Dr. Vivian Bergel, Advisor
Dr. Joan Austin, University Chaplain

 Jewish Studies
1 course.

ON CAMPUS

Activities at Elizabethtown are held on campus and in cooperation with the Hillel groups at Franklin & Marshall College and Millersville University. The local Jewish community is very supportive and provides home hospitality for Shabbat and holidays. Jewish students at Elizabethtown find sympathetic support from the campus ministry.

FRANKLIN & MARSHALL COLLEGE

Enrollment 1,800
Jewish 220

Hillel
645 College Avenue
PO Box 3003
Lancaster, PA 17604-3003
(717) 291-4268
(717) 291-4390
Fax: (717) 399-4420
E-mail: r-taber@fandm.edu

Dr. Ralph S. Taber, Advisor

 Jewish Studies
Classes each semester plus modern Hebrew; independent study is possible.

 Study in Israel
Junior year abroad.

Kosher Food
Hillel offers Friday evening and holiday meals; Passover meal plan; vegetarian dining alternatives; residence hall cooking facilities. Kosher food store in the community.

ON CAMPUS

Franklin & Marshall has social, cultural, political, and religious activities according to student interest. All 3 local rabbis are on the college staff. The local community provides home hospitality for the holidays. There is a local Jewish Community Center and Jewish Day School.

GETTYSBURG COLLEGE

Enrollment 2,200
Jewish 45

Hillel
Gettysburg College
c/o Temona Berg
Department of English
Box 397
Gettysburg, PA 17325-1486
(717) 337-6753
E-mail: tberg@gettysburg.edu

Temona Berg, Advisor, Associate Professor of English

 Jewish Studies
1 course.

 Study in Israel
Semester or year at Hebrew, Tel Aviv, or Ben-Gurion University. Summer fellowship programs available.

 Kosher Food
Vegetarian dining alternatives.

ON CAMPUS

Hillel sponsors cultural events and museum trips, as well as hosting Shabbat and High Holiday meals. Hillel has also developed relationships with other minority campus organizations, whether ethnic, racial, or religious, and has worked with these groups to create joint projects and celebrations.

GRATZ COLLEGE

Enrollment 332
Jewish 295 (UG 204; GR 91)

Old York Road and Melrose Avenue
Melrose Park, PA 19027
(215) 635-7300
(800) 475-4635
Fax: (215) 635-7320

Evelyn Klein, Director of Admissions

Jewish Studies
150 courses; B.A., M.A. Gratz offers bachelor's and master's degree programs in Jewish studies, Jewish education, Jewish music, Jewish liberal studies; Certificate programs in Judaica librarianship, Jewish communal studies, Jewish education, Israel studies; and a Hebrew teacher's diploma.

 Kosher Food
Kosher cafeteria.

ON CAMPUS

Social and cultural programming. Gratz has many specialized resources, including a 100,000-item Judaica library.

HARCUM JUNIOR COLLEGE

Enrollment 700
Jewish 50

Harcum Junior College Hillel
Academic Building
Bryn Mawr, PA 19010
(610) 526-6064
(215) 769-1174

Marla Meyers, Director
Hila Reichman, Associate Director
Ken Krivitzky, Program Director
Judy Franklin, Faculty Advisor

Kosher Food
Vegetarian alternatives available.

Support for Jewish student activities at Harcum is provided by the Center for Commuter Service, Hillel of Greater Philadelphia. See listing for Temple University.

HAVERFORD COLLEGE

Enrollment 1,100
Jewish 300

Haverford College Hillel
Haverford College
Lancaster Avenue
Campus Center, Room 212
Haverford, PA 19041
(610) 896-4918
(215) 898-8265
Fax: (610) 896-1338
E-mail: mpiknat1@swarthmore.edu

Rabbi Marsha Pik-Nathan, Director
Jessica Cooper, Jewish Campus Service Corps Fellow

Jewish Studies
A few courses are offered each semester; major in religion; 2 Jewish Studies professors. Access to Hebrew and Judaic Studies Department at Bryn Mawr College. Students can also take classes at Swarthmore College and University of Pennsylvania.

Study in Israel
Junior year abroad.

Kosher Food
Kosher kitchen available for use on Friday nights and holiday services.

ON CAMPUS

Bryn Mawr/Haverford Hillel is a bi-college student-run organization. Social, educational, political, and religious programs are planned by the student organization, the Jewish Student Union, and other interested students. Recent programs include a Freedom seder, a Chocolate seder, a Jewish *a cappella* festival, and the national conference on Children of Interfaith Families, where Hillel served as the host. Hillel also sponsors cultural and social events, such as an opening barbecue, parties, speakers, and performances, as well as weekly Friday night Shabbat services, kosher Shabbat dinners, and observances for all Jewish holidays. Speakers and performers have included bioethicist Nancy Dubler; Jewish *a cappella* groups; and Holocaust Awareness Week, which features a 24-hour vigil where names of Holocaust victims are read, as well as films and talks. Other events include Israeli cafe nights, Jewish Awareness Week, the Yiddish Culture Festival, and visits to Philadelphia. Students also participate in citywide programming coordinated by both Hillel board members and interested Jewish students. There are Jewish educational courses, speakers, and social action and Tzedakah activities.

The Colleges' administrations are very supportive of Jewish life on campus, as are faculty. The faculty plans an annual Hamantashen/Latke Debate. Both college presidents join Hillel for the first Shabbat of the year. Students are encouraged to attend national student conferences, with subsidies often provided. The monthly calendar is sent to all students on the mailing list. Students participate in citywide programming coordinated by the Hillel Regional Center, Hillel of Greater Philadelphia.

INDIANA UNIVERSITY OF PENNSYLVANIA

Enrollment 13,000
Jewish 100

Hillel at Indiana University of PA
c/o Department of Criminology
Walsh Hall B210
Indiana, PA 15705
(724) 357-2707

Dr. Robert Mutchnick, Advisor

Jewish Studies
1 course (Philosophy and Religious Studies Department).

KUTZTOWN UNIVERSITY

Enrollment 6,065
Jewish Few

Hillel at Kutztown University
c/o Dr. Matt Nesvisky
English Department
Kutztown, PA 19530
(610) 683-4336

Dr. Matt Nesvisky, Advisor

ON CAMPUS

Hillel at Kutztown University is a new organization in contact with Jewish students at other schools in the region.

LA SALLE UNIVERSITY

Enrollment 3,200
Jewish 150

Jewish Student Union
c/o Multi-Campus Hillel Center
2014 North Broad Street
Philadelphia, PA 19121
(215) 769-1174
E-mail: hillel@vm.temple.edu

Marla Meyers, Director
Hila Reichman, Associate Director
Ken Krivitzky, Program Director

 Jewish Studies

1 course/Joint Program: Gratz College.

 Kosher Food

Frozen meals are available on request in University facilities.

ON CAMPUS

This is a Catholic university with a small Jewish population. The university is supportive of Jewish activities and interests, and a Jewish chaplain is on campus part-time. However, Jewish students should be prepared for Christian symbols in every classroom. The Jewish Student Union holds monthly Shabbat programs, an annual interfaith seder, and holiday celebrations, and brings in speakers occasionally. The Jewish Student Union has a small office and meeting space in the Interfaith Lounge. La Salle Jewish students find most of their Jewish activities by participating in citywide events sponsored by the Multi-Campus Hillel Center, Hillel of Philadelphia.

See listing for Temple University.

LAFAYETTE COLLEGE

Enrollment 2,000
Jewish 250

Hillel Society
520 Clinton Terrace
Easton, PA 18042
(610) 330-5174
Fax: (610) 250-5176
E-mail: weinerr@lafayette.edu
Web: www.lafayette.edu/~hillel/home.htm

Professor Robert Weiner, Co-Director
Professor Gary Gordon, Advisor
Professor Elizabeth McMahon, Advisor

Jewish Studies

15 courses. Minor; interdisciplinary B.A. possible. Several senior professors teach Jewish studies. Lafayette is part of the Berman Center for Jewish Studies based at Lehigh University. Students are encouraged to do individual study and honors with the Jewish Studies faculty advisor.

Study in Israel

Four professors lead seminars—1 seminar related to contemporary Israel, the other to the Jewish experience in antiquity. Credits accepted.

Kosher Food

Kosher food can be made available by special arrangement with the Hillel staff. Vegetarian alternatives also available.

Housing

Jewish Residence: Hillel.

ON CAMPUS

Lafayette has an active Jewish cultural and social campus life, with very strong faculty involvement in Hillel programs. The College respects all major religious holidays; absences are excused at these times. The College circulates a calendar and notice requesting faculty to respect Jewish holidays when composing class and examination schedules.

The Lafayette College Hillel is one of the most active student organizations on campus, and has recently won 3 Aaron O. Hoff Awards for outstanding contributions to the College. Hillel is well funded by the Student Government. Hillel sponsors a diverse series of cultural, social, and religious events throughout the course of the academic year. Major events have included concerts by Debbie Friedman, Doug Cotler, and Brave Old World. Hillel has instituted an Awareness Week, including 6 special, linked cultural and academic events.

Hillel events are held in a variety of settings, from the Hillel House (adjacent to the campus) to the interfaith chapel (on the quad) to the Williams Center for the Performing Arts. Strong student leadership plans regular events such as tri-weekly bagel brunches with speakers, Hillel-sponsored major campus-wide cultural events, interfaith activities and dialogues, and a popular interfaith seder. The local rabbis are also involved in Hillel and the local community offers home hospitality. Students work in the local synagogues as youth group leaders and teachers.

LEHIGH UNIVERSITY

Enrollment 6,300 (UG 4,300; GR 2,000)
Jewish 800 (UG 700; GR 100)

Lehigh University Hillel Society
Jewish Student Center
216 Summit Street
Bethlehem, PA 18015
(610) 758-4896
Fax: (610) 758-4897
E-mail: inhil@lehigh.edu

Gale S. Wachs, Director
Ron Ticho, Board President

Jewish Studies

24 courses; minor. The Philip and Muriel Berman Center for Jewish Studies at Lehigh University administers and coordinates Lehigh's strong Jewish Studies program. In addition to 3 full-time Berman Center faculty, a visiting Israeli scholar teaches at the Center each year. Courses include the Holocaust, Middle East politics, Hebrew language, Jewish thought, philosophy, history, religion, literature, and folklore. The Center's program is enhanced by films, lectures, cultural events, and international conferences. The Center provides Jewish study opportunities for Jewish students at other campuses in the region. Professor Laurence J. Silberstein, Director, Lehigh University, 9 W. Packer Ave., Bethlehem, PA 18015; (610) 758-4869.

Study in Israel

Summer, semester, or year programs at Tel Aviv University or the Hebrew University of Jerusalem, including kibbutz-study program and the Tel Miqne-Ekron archaeological excavation. Courses are taught in English and credits can be transferred. Partial scholarships are available to qualified students through the Berman Center.

Kosher Food

The Jewish Student Center maintains a kosher kitchen. The University offers vegetarian alternatives and provides frozen kosher meals by request.

Housing

Jewish Student Center has 5 private rooms; Jewish fraternity and sorority.

ON CAMPUS

The Jewish Student Center, built in the early 1990s, is located on campus and serves as one of the focal points for Jewish activity. The building features a kosher kitchen and dining area, a spacious living and family room, and Jewish student housing. The Center sponsors the Hillel Society, which offers a full gamut of cultural, social, and spiritual activities—from Sunday bagel brunches to Shabbat services, from kosher Chinese dinners to building the campus sukkah. The Center also sponsors the Israeli Culture Club, an organization that actively promotes and disseminates information pertaining to Israel, and the Jewish Graduate Student Union. A graduate assistantship is also available in the Jewish Student Center.

Jewish fraternities and sororities are on campus, as well as more than 100 Jewish faculty and staff who play an active role in advising and mentoring Jewish students. Jewish students are excused from classes on all major holidays as declared by the Provost. Nearly all Jewish students on campus are either Conservative or Reform. Members of the local Jewish community are actively involved with Lehigh's Jewish students and often invite them to Shabbat dinners and holiday celebrations.

Jewish students are very active campus leaders in a variety of activities from NCAA Division I athletics to the student newspaper. A number of successful "Jewish Program" fund drives have been executed with support from the institution.

MILLERSVILLE UNIVERSITY

Enrollment 6,000 (UG 5,500; GR 500)
Jewish 50

Hillel
c/o Potter House
Millersville University
Millersville, PA 17551
(717) 872-3555

Professor Jack R. Fischel, Advisor

Jewish Studies

1 course.

Kosher Food

Frozen dinners on request in dining hall.

ON CAMPUS

Each year, Hillel at Millersville co-sponsors a major conference on the Holocaust that brings important speakers to campus. The local Jewish community is very supportive of Jewish students and provides home hospitality for Shabbat and holidays. Jewish interests are supported at Millersville through a good relationship with the campus ministry.

MONTGOMERY COUNTY COMMUNITY COLLEGE

Enrollment 8,700
Jewish 170

c/o Multi-Campus Hillel Center
2014 North Broad Street
Philadelphia, PA 19121
(215) 641-6326 (Albert Rauer)
(215) 898-8265
Fax: (215) 763-9686
E-mail: hillel@vm.temple.edu

Marla Meyers, Director
Hila Reichman, Associate Director
Ken Krivitzky, Program Director
Professor Albert Rauer, Faculty Advisor

 Kosher Food
Vegetarian options available in dining hall.

Students at MCCC, a totally commuter college, participate in city-wide projects and events sponsored by the Multi-Campus Hillel Center, Hillel of Philadelphia. See listing for Temple University. Served by Multi-Campus Hillel Center.

MORAVIAN COLLEGE

Enrollment 1,300
Jewish 30

Hillel
c/o Dr. Stacey Zaremba
Department of Psychology
Moravian College
Bethlehem, PA 18018
(610) 861-1563
(610) 861-1391
Fax: (610) 861-1577
E-mail: mesbz01@moravian.edu

Dr. Stacey Zaremba, Advisor
Dr. George Diamond, LVAIC Hillel Liaison

 Jewish Studies
The Lehigh Valley Association of Independent Colleges, which includes Moravian, offers a B.A. in Jewish Studies through the Berman Center for Jewish Studies centered at Lehigh University.

 Study in Israel
Semester or year at Hebrew, Tel Aviv, or Ben-Gurion University.

Kosher Food
Vegetarian dining alternatives; dormitory cooking facilities.

 Housing
Jewish Residence: Lehigh Hillel.

ON CAMPUS

With a small but dynamic membership, the Moravian College Hillel, revitalized and reorganized, is in the process of establishing independent status although it will continue its association with Lehigh University and the Hillels of other Lehigh Valley colleges for mutual benefit. The number of Jewish students at Moravian College is small, but the college is warm, welcoming, and most ecumenical, as is the atmosphere of the Bethlehem community at large. The Berman Center for Jewish Studies, which won the Hillel 1991 William Haber Agency Award for Outstanding Service to the Jewish Campus Community, is centered at Lehigh University. However, the Berman Center's professors frequently offer Jewish content courses on the Moravian campus. Moravian students can take these courses and others on the Lehigh campus, and can major or minor in Jewish studies. In addition, the Berman Center has a crowded calendar of lectures, performances, and conferences in which Moravian students can participate.

MUHLENBERG COLLEGE

Enrollment 1,950
Jewish 480

Muhlenberg College Hillel
2400 Chew Street
Allentown, PA 18104
(610) 821-3244
Fax: (610) 821-3234
E-mail: hillel@muhlenberg.edu

Patti Mittleman, Director
Professor Holmes Miller, Advisor

 Jewish Studies
Minor in Jewish Studies.

 Study in Israel
Cooperative arrangements exist with Hebrew University and Tel Aviv University. Transfer credits are accepted from other institutions in Israel.

 Kosher Food
Students may prepare meals for themselves in the Hillel kitchen. Hillel has a Shabbat dinner program as well as a Sunday Bagel Brunch program and holiday meals. The College Food Service provides frozen kosher meals on request at no additional cost and a vegetarian dining alternative. Some dormitories have dining facilities.

ON CAMPUS

Muhlenberg College is very supportive of campus Jewish life, and provides a Hillel House—the center of Jewish activities, with a kosher kitchen and a growing library. Yom Kippur is an official college holiday, and Jewish students are excused from classes on all other major holidays, by order of the Dean. Muhlenberg Hillel has received the President's Award, presented annually to the student organization that has made the most significant contribution to the Muhlenberg community: "Their Passover seder has become a campus-wide celebration of community; their bagel brunches and Shabbat dinners provide the kind of informal gatherings that make the college experience such a wonderfully rich time," according to college president Arthur R. Taylor.

Programming includes a full range of social, educational, social action, and religious activities. Hillel representatives serve on campus boards such as the college Hunger Task Force, and Jewish students hold offices on the student council. The College is located in the center of Allentown's Jewish community, and there is much support from and interaction with the local community. Muhlenberg's advisors work in good relationship with the college chaplaincy and the administration.

The Institute for Jewish-Christian Understanding, located on the campus, is a college-funded center offering educational programs on the campus and in the community.

Study in Israel
Diverse study programs available in academic and non-academic settings in Israel.

Kosher Food
Hillel offers weekly Shabbat dinners. Kosher food available at local food stores. Vegetarian options also available. Hillel sponsors Passover seders and dinners. Frozen meals for Passover are available in the dining halls.

ON CAMPUS

The Penn State Hillel Foundation has been home away from home for tens of thousands of Jewish students since it was established in 1935, when only 300 Jewish students were on campus. Penn State Hillel is the foundation of Jewish life at the University, providing, and encouraging students to develop, those social and cultural activities of greatest interest to them.

Hillel operates out of Eisenhower Chapel, the Center for Ethics and Religious Affairs, which is centrally located on campus. Penn State Hillel's active program includes Sunday brunches, films, concerts, speakers, classes in contemporary Jewish Issues, the Jewish Freshman Council, the Jewish Greek Community, the Jewish Athletic League, Penn State Group (GAP), ice skating, bowling, barbecues, Shabbat dinners, and numerous other opportunities for socializing and enjoying being Jewish.

PENNSYLVANIA STATE UNIVERSITY

Enrollment 37,000
Jewish 3,700

Penn State Hillel Foundation
110 Eisenhower Chapel
University Park, PA 16802
(814) 863-3816
Fax: (814) 863-6170
E-mail: err4@psu.edu
Web: www.psu.edu

Tuvia Abramson, Executive Director
Elana Rivel, Program Director
Susan Rose, Development Director
Jeremy Adelman, Jewish Campus Service Corps Fellow

Jewish Studies
44 courses annually; minor. Chair in Jewish Studies. Specializations are available in Hebrew language and literature; Ancient Israelite religion, culture, history, and archaeology; modern Zionism; and anti-Semitism. 9 full-time Jewish Studies faculty; 15 interdisciplinary. 103 Weaver Building, University Park, PA 16802; (814) 863-8939.

PENNSYLVANIA STATE UNIVERSITY—ABINGTON

Enrollment 3,200
Jewish 500

Penn State Abington Hillel
Lares Student Union
Abington, PA 19001
(215) 881-7510
(215) 769-1174
E-mail: jzd1@psu.edu
marlaj@vm.temple.edu

Marla Meyers, Director, Multi-Campus Hillel Center
Hila Reichman, Associate Director, Multi-Campus Hillel Center
Ken Krivitzky, Program Director
Professor Judy Dorfman, Faculty Advisor
Rachel Salis, Jewish Campus Service Corps Fellow

Kosher Food
Vegetarian dining alternatives available in dining hall.

ON CAMPUS

Jewish students at PSA enjoy activities on campus and in the surrounding neighborhoods. Hillel is one of the more active groups on campus. Popular activities include monthly Lunch 'n' Learns, social dinners, the annual Israeli Culture Day, and holiday celebrations. Students also participate in citywide events sponsored by the Multi-Campus Hillel Center.

See listing for Temple University.

PENNSYLVANIA STATE UNIVERSITY—BEHREND COLLEGE

Enrollment 2,377
Jewish Few

Hillel at Behrend, Penn State
Brith Sholom Congregation
3207 State Street
Erie, PA 16508
(814) 454-2431

Rabbi Leonard Lifshen, Advisor

Behrend is served part-time by the rabbi from the local congregation.

PHILADELPHIA COLLEGE OF TEXTILES AND SCIENCE

Enrollment 2,000
Jewish 150

Philadelphia University Student Center
Schoolhouse Lane & Henry Avenue
Philadelphia, PA 19144-5497
(215) 951-2856
(215) 898-8265
E-mail: mandlen@philacol.edu

Marla Meyers, Director
Hila Reichman, Associate Director
Ken Krivitzky, Program Director

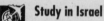 **Study in Israel**
Credits are accepted for study at Israeli institutions.

 Kosher Food
Available upon request.

ON CAMPUS
Occasional activities for Jewish students are held on campus, and students may participate in city-wide activities sponsored by the Hillel Multi-Campus Center, Hillel of Philadelphia. In addition, the College provides a rabbinic intern on campus as part of the Spiritual Development Department.

See listing for Temple University.

SUSQUEHANNA UNIVERSITY

Enrollment 1,600
Jewish 16

Hillel Student Organization at Susquehanna University
c/o Dr. Laurence Roth
Department of English
Susquehanna University
Selinsgrove, PA 17870-1001
(570) 372-4202
Fax: (570) 372-2774
E-mail: roth@susqu.edu

Dr. Laurence Roth, Co-Advisor
Dr. Gabriel Finder, Co-Advisor
David Silverman, Rabbi

Jewish Studies
The university offers a minor in Jewish studies comprising 14 courses across several disciplines. The purpose of the Jewish Studies minor is to enable and enrich student knowledge of Jewish spirituality, literature, history, and cultural diversity. The interdisciplinary curriculum provides a range of courses that facilitate student explorations of Judaism and Jewish experience, and thus fosters among students an understanding of Jewish Studies as the analysis of a diverse religious civilization. The minor is open to those students in a wide variety of academic majors interested in broadening their perspectives about spirituality and ethnicity.

Study in Israel
Students have arranged for semester-long study at Hebrew University.

Kosher Food
The College Food Service provides a daily vegetarian dining alternative and kosher meals during High Holy Days.

ON CAMPUS
The university respects all major religious holidays; absences are excused at these times. The university circulates a calendar and notice requesting faculty to respect Jewish holidays when composing class and examination schedules. An active Genocide-Holocaust Studies Committee sponsors several programs and guest speakers each semester.

SWARTHMORE COLLEGE

Enrollment 1,500
    Jewish 300

> Ruach
> Swarthmore College
> 500 College Avenue
> Swarthmore, PA 19081
> (610) 328-8615
> (215) 898-8265
> Fax: (610) 328-8673
> E-mail: mpiknat1@swarthmore.edu
>
> **Rabbi Marsha Pik-Nathan**, Director
> **Rebecca Grabiner**, Program Associate

Jewish Studies
A few courses. 1 full-time Jewish Studies professor. Students may also take classes at Bryn Mawr, Haverford, and the University of Pennsylvania.

Study in Israel
Students can receive credit for study in Israel through a variety of programs.

Kosher Food
A vegetarian kosher kitchen is located in one of the residence halls. Kosher Shabbat dinners weekly, and holiday meals. Vegetarian foods are always available in the dining center.

ON CAMPUS
Hillel offers a wide variety of religious, cultural, and social activities to choose from. Among the numerous programs sponsored by Hillel are weekly Friday night Shabbat services and kosher Shabbat dinners, and observances for all the Jewish holidays. Hillel also sponsors cultural and social events, such as semi-annual bagel brunches, study breaks, speakers, and performances. Recent speakers and performers have included Syd Leiberman, a storyteller; a Jewish *a cappella* group; and Marjorie Agosin, poet and human rights activist. Other events include visits to Philadelphia, discussions with other religious groups, and delivering Purim packages to a retirement home. Zionist Connection, an active Zionist group, holds weekly informal discussions on Israeli politics and history, and sponsors speakers, films, and cultural events. Students also participate in citywide programming coordinated by Hillel of Greater Pennsylvania, the Hillel Regional Center.

Swarthmore is served by the Center for Suburban Campuses, Hillel of Greater Philadelphia, based at Haverford and Bryn Mawr Colleges.

TEMPLE UNIVERSITY—MAIN AND AMBLER

Enrollment 33,000 (UG 21,000; GR 12,000)
    Jewish 1,300 (UG 800; GR 500)

> Temple Hillel
> 2014 North Broad Street
> Philadelphia, PA 19121
> (215) 769-1174
> (215) 898-8265
> Fax: (215) 763-9686
> E-mail: hillel@vm.temple.edu
>
> **Marla Meyers**, Director
> **Hila Reichman**, Associate Director
> **Ken Krivitzky**, Program Director
> **Rachel Salis**, Jewish Campus Service Corps Fellow

Jewish Studies
34 courses; B.A., M.A., Ph.D./Joint Program: Gratz College. The Stanley Merves Award in Jewish Studies, established by the Gilroy and Lilian Roberts Foundation, will be made to a current or incoming student who plans to major in Jewish Studies. Dr. Norbert Samuelson; Director, Jewish Studies Program; (215) 204-1748.

Study in Israel
Junior year abroad/summer semester: Tel Aviv Law School.

Kosher Food
Kosher food locally available.

ON CAMPUS
Temple's comprehensive program is designed to serve the needs and interests of its commuter population. Highlights of Temple Hillel's programming include monthly home-cooked Shabbat dinners, an annual Israel fair, an active Greek Jewish Council, and many opportunities to socialize. Students also participate in a wide range of citywide activities, both on campus and in Philadelphia neighborhoods.

Temple Hillel is home to the Multi-Campus Hillel Center, a regional program of Hillel of Greater Philadelphia, which serves students at numerous colleges and universities throughout the Philadelphia area. The special citywide program actively involves Jewish students in social and other events, and meets in homes or in other easily accessible locations throughout Philadelphia.

UNIVERSITY OF PENNSYLVANIA

Enrollment 18,000 (UG 10,000; GR 8,000)
Jewish 6,000

Hillel at the University of Pennsylvania
Jewish Campus Activities Center
202 South 36th Street
Philadelphia, PA 19104
(215) 898-7391
(215) 898-5443
Fax: (215) 898-8259
E-mail: hillel@dolphin.upenn.edu
Web: dolphin.upenn.edu/~hillel/

Jeremy Brochin, Director
Geoff Menkowitz, Project Coordinator JRP
Elizabeth Minkin, Program Associate
Rabbi Howard Alpert, Executive Director, Hillel of
    Greater Philadelphia
Emily Cook, Senior Jewish Campus Service Corps Fellow

Jewish Studies

30–35 courses annually; 50 in catalog; B.A., M.A.,
Ph.D. 2 Chairs in Jewish Studies. 3 different major/mi-
nors in Jewish Studies available: Department of Asian
and Middle Eastern Studies, concentrating upon language, literature, and culture; Religious Studies, focusing on comparative religious aspects; and an interdisciplinary major in Jewish Studies combining history, literature, and religion. A separate major in Modern
Middle Eastern Studies is also available, as are graduate
programs in many disciplines. Special strengths are in
Bible and Biblical Interpretation, Jewish Intellectual
History, and Modern Jewish History. The Program sponsors a Faculty Seminar, lectures, and undergraduate and
graduate student organizations.

The University of Pennsylvania also houses the Robert and Molly Freedman Jewish Music Archive of more
than 3,000 songbooks, reference works, and sound recordings related to Yiddish music, which is supported
by a database of more than 25,000 entries. Because of
the quality of the database, the collection is used exten-
sively for research by scholars, performers, and com-
posers. Dr. Jeffrey Tigay, Director, Jewish Studies
Program, 647 Williams Hall; (215) 898-6654;
jsp-info@ccat.sas.upenn.edu.

Study in Israel

Students may participate in year/summer credit
programs throughout Israel on University and independent programs. Penn Hillel serves as a resource for hundreds of Israel tours, programs, internships, and volun-
teer/job opportunities.

Kosher Food

7 days a week, 2 meals daily. The University runs
the kosher dining program. More than 300 students go
to Hillel's Shabbat dinner each week, and more than
200 eat lunch and dinner daily at kosher dining. The
University also provides vegetarian dining alternatives
in all dining facilities, and some dorms have cooking
facilities. For information about kosher dining, call
(215) 898-7013.

ON CAMPUS

The University of Pennsylvania's large Hillel facility is
centrally located on campus, and is the meeting place
for a large, active Jewish community. Hillel provides a
warm environment where Jewish students can explore
their Jewish identity, celebrate Jewish life, and build
community. In addition, Penn Hillel has opened a Jewish outreach office—the Jewish Activities Center—in
the Quad, the predominantly first-year student residence. This new center involves first-year students, students in the Greek system, and students from Reform
backgrounds in Jewish campus life.

Hillel's programs represent a wide range of Jewish
cultural, political, religious, intellectual, and social interests. Penn Hillel hosts more than 25 active student
groups, including social action, Jewish theatre, UJA,
Israel, Israeli dance, women, Holocaust education, and
a variety of other social, cultural, political, and religious
groups. Hillel is also very involved in programs throughout campus, often in cooperation with other groups.

The Jewish Grad group at Penn consists of students
from all of Penn's graduate programs and offers a variety of programs and activities for Jewish graduate
students.

*"The Hillel at Penn is committed not only to
providing opportunities for everyone, but even
more importantly, to students creating their
own opportunities. Through innovative programs, Penn's Hillel has succeeded in creating
an atmosphere that welcomes Jews of all backgrounds."*

Merav Kushner, '02

*"When I came to Penn, I found that the Reform
Jewish community (RJC) was very welcoming. I
quickly became very involved in the community by attending services and many of the social programs. By the end of my freshman year,
I felt comfortable calling the people of RJC a
community that functioned like a family
I could trust and lean on for support and
friendship."*

Stephanie Foster, '01

*"Jewish life at Penn has been a major part of
my undergraduate experience, and I have
made some of my closest friends at Hillel. There
are always so many different activities going
on and myriad ways for students to get involved and find their own niche. I have experienced 'Jewish life' not only by going to services
and participating in Hillel-sponsored activities,*

but also by spending time with Jewish friends I've made in classes or from living on their halls. Whatever you're looking for Jewishly, Penn has it, and if it doesn't, people make it happen."

Andrea Brustein, '00

UNIVERSITY OF PITTSBURGH

Enrollment 28,000 (UG 17,000; GR 11,000)
Jewish 2,550

Hillel Jewish University Center of Pittsburgh
4551 Forbes Avenue, 2nd Floor
Pittsburgh, PA 15213-3510
(412) 621-8875
Fax: (412) 621-8861
E-mail: hillel@sgi.net
Web: www.pitt.edu

Daniel Wiseman, Director
Amy Stein, Program Director
Mike Levinstein, Jewish Campus Service Corps
Senior Fellow

Jewish Studies

14–18 courses offered each year; 35 courses in catalog. 500 student registrations per year. Courses are offered in Hebrew language, Jewish history, Jewish thought, rabbinics, modern Israel, and contemporary Jewish problems. Jewish Studies is organized as an interdisciplinary program. A minor is available, requiring an independent study course with a significant paper. Courses are taught by 4 faculty, 2 regular part-time faculty, and 4 faculty, from other departments. There is an excellent Judaic collection in the University library, as well as a beautiful, museum-quality Israel Heritage Classroom. 6–10 public lectures annually. Dr. Jerome Rosenberg, Director, Faculty of Arts and Sciences, Jewish Studies Program, 2409 Cathedral of Learning, Pittsburgh, PA 15260; (412) 624-3007.

Study in Israel

Students can receive credit for study in Israel through a variety of programs.

Kosher Food

The University of Pittsburgh Food Services offers 2 kosher lunch options and 2 dinner options 7 days a week. The Hillel Foundation of Pittsburgh offers Shabbat dinners, holiday meals, and vegetarian dining alternatives. Many residence halls have cooking facilities.

ON CAMPUS

Hillel at the University of Pittsburgh offers a wide range of social, cultural, social action, Zionist, educational, and religious activities, with a strong emphasis on student involvement and student leadership development.

The campus is located close to the geographic center of Pittsburgh's Jewish community, which has a Jewish Community Center, kosher restaurants, stores, and synagogues. The Pittsburgh community is very supportive of campus Jewish life and offers home hospitality and part-time and full-time employment opportunities.

The Hillel Foundation of Pittsburgh is the center for programming and service to Carnegie-Mellon University, the University of Pittsburgh, Point Park College, Chatham College, and Duquesne University.

URSINUS COLLEGE

Enrollment 1,100
Jewish 50

Hillel at Ursinus
Ursinus College
Collegeville, PA 19426
(610) 489-4111
Fax: (610) 489-0627
E-mail: fnovack@acad.ursinus.edu

Marla Meyers, Director
Hila Reichman, Associate Director
Ken Krivitzky, Program Director
Professor Frances Novack, Advisor
Paul Stern, Advisor

Jewish Studies

Occasional courses, including a course on the Holocaust in the History Department.

Study in Israel

Junior year abroad and summer study programs for credit are available.

Kosher Food

Dormitory cooking facilities. Vegetarian dining alternatives in the College dining room. Food service will get kosher-for-Passover food on request.

ON CAMPUS

Activities for Jewish students at Ursinus vary according to the interest and enthusiasm of the students, but there are always holiday celebrations, a seder, an annual Holocaust commemoration, and other social and cultural programs either on campus or through participation in Philadelphia-area and national Hillel campus programs. In recent years, students have participated in programs on Israel in Washington, D.C., in the Hillel Leadership Conference, and in Hillel programs in Israel. The Hillel advisor has been honored by Hillel of Greater Philadelphia with the Netsky award for "distinguished contribution to Jewish student life."

Served by Multi-Campus Hillel Center. See listing for Temple University.

VILLANOVA UNIVERSITY

Enrollment 8,000
Jewish 65

Hillel at Villanova University
Lancaster Avenue
Villanova, PA 19085
(610) 519-7792
(215) 898-8265
Fax: (610) 446-2625

Rabbi Marsha Pik-Nathan, Advisor

Support for Jewish student activities at Villanova is provided by the Center for Suburban Campuses, Hillel of Greater Philadelphia.

WASHINGTON AND JEFFERSON COLLEGE

Enrollment 1,150
Jewish 50

Hillel Society
c/o Professor Michael Orstein
Washington and Jefferson College
Washington, PA 15301
(724) 223-6061

Professor Michael Orstein, Advisor

 Kosher Food
Vegetarian dining alternatives.

ON CAMPUS
The Jewish student population is small at Washington and Jefferson College, but the administration and local Jewish community are both very supportive of activities and holidays. Hillel sponsors an annual convocation with a Jewish/Israeli theme for the college and the community and monthly bagel brunches. There is also a Passover seder on campus. The community provides home hospitality for Shabbat and holidays.

WEST CHESTER UNIVERSITY

Enrollment 9,500 (UG 7,500; GR 2,000)
Jewish 1,000

Hillel/Jewish Student Union
Sykes Union Building
West Chester University
West Chester, PA 19383
(610) 436-2225
E-mail: rbarth@wcupa.edu

Professor Roger Barth, Advisor

 Jewish Studies
3 courses; minor in Holocaust Studies.

 Study in Israel
Junior year abroad at Tel Aviv University.

 Kosher Food
Vegetarian dining alternatives and dormitory cooking facilities. Kosher food is locally available.

ON CAMPUS
West Chester has an active Hillel group, with its own office, which plans on-campus events and also participates in regional activities through close affiliation with the Hillel Commuter Service, Hillel of Greater Philadelphia. Activities have included bagel brunches, seders, Hanukkah parties, and strong Israel programming.

See listing for Temple University.

WIDENER UNIVERSITY

Enrollment 3,800 (UG 2,300; GR 1,500)
Jewish 65

Hillel Club
1 University Place
Widener University
Chester, PA 19013
(610) 499-1146
(215) 898-8265
Fax: (610) 499-4059
E-mail: mersky@widener.edu
Web: www.widener.edu

Professor Ron Mersky, Advisor

 Jewish Studies
1 course, occasionally.

 Study in Israel
Can be arranged through Hillel.

 Kosher Food
Dormitory cooking facilities.

ON CAMPUS
Widener is located a short distance from Philadelphia, which enables students to hold some activities jointly with other schools and attend events at other campuses.

Support for Jewish student activities at Widener is provided by the Center for Suburban Campuses, Hillel of Greater Philadelphia.

YORK COLLEGE

Enrollment 3,300
Jewish 200

Hillel at York College
Country Club Road
York, PA 17405-7199
(717) 815-1426
(717) 846-7788
Fax: (717) 849-1619

Professor Irene H. Trachtenberg, Advisor

Kosher Food
Hillel offers kosher food on holidays; occasional meals; vegetarian dining alternatives. Kosher food is locally available.

ON CAMPUS
The Jewish community is very supportive of student initiatives.

RHODE ISLAND

BROWN UNIVERSITY

Enrollment 7,300 (UG 5,700; GR 1,600)
Jewish 1,600

Brown-RISD Hillel Foundation
80 Brown Street
Providence, RI 02906
(401) 863-2805
Fax: (401) 863-1591
E-mail: hillel@brown.edu
Web: www.brown.edu/students/jewish_student_union/

Rabbi Alan C. Flam, Executive Director
Cynthia G. Weinger, Program Director

Jewish Studies
26 courses annually; B.A., Ph.D. 7 full-time Jewish Studies faculty, including 1 endowed chair. The Judaic Studies Program is interdisciplinary; most of the faculty have joint appointments with other departments. The Program is particularly strong in Hebrew language instruction; Judaism in antiquity (Tanakh, second Temple period, and rabbinic texts); and Judaism in modern times (history, literature, sociology). The Program annually sponsors numerous lectures, movies, symposia, etc. Brown University, Program in Judaic Studies, Box 1826, Providence, RI 02912. Director: Professor Shaye J.D. Cohen; Undergraduate Advisor: Professor Lynn Davidman; (401) 863-3900; Fax: (401) 863-3938; annette_boulay@brown.edu.; Web: www.brown.edu/Departments/Judaic_Studies.

Study in Israel
Study abroad.

Kosher Food
Brown has a University-sponsored kosher meal plan; holiday meals including Passover lunches and dinners at Hillel; vegetarian options are always available.

Housing
Hebrew language and culture house.

ON CAMPUS
Brown Hillel's central location on Brown University's campus is symbolic of the centrality of Jewish life at Brown. Hillel offers students the space and opportunity to take part in a rich and varied range of social, cultural, educational, and religious activities. Students plan, participate, and benefit from the diverse scope of opportunities ranging from public service projects to a Jewish women's group, informal classes to Israeli dancing, outdoor hiking trips to a Jewish *a cappella* group, Shabbat programming to Israel activism. Jewish students are also well integrated into campus life and involved in many organizations and programs at Brown University. Brown Hillel created the first campus-based Jewish Community Relations Council in the country. The CRC builds relationships between other campus organizations and with the Jewish students who may be involved with those organizations. Hillel fosters and supports a pluralistic environment both in terms of religious expression and degree of Jewish involvement.

Brown Hillel is also close to the center of Providence's Jewish community, with its 4 synagogues, a Jewish Community Center, and Bureau of Jewish Education. Students go off campus to teach in the local religious schools, read Torah, and advise youth groups, or to meet the mentor with whom they were matched through a career mentoring program. As a strong and vibrant foundation, Brown-RISD Hillel has been recognized nationally not only for its dynamic student leaders and creativity in programming, but also for its community service/social justice initiatives. Brown-RISD Hillel has been named 1 of the 4 lead campuses in the Tzedek Hillel project, a national initiative to integrate service and justice into all aspects of Jewish life.

"Before Brown, I had never been in a school in which there were more than five other Jewish students. Here, I am a part of a large, vibrant community of Jewish students whose interests run the gamut of academic disciplines and activities. Within this community, I have found challenges and friends that have helped me to grow, making my college experience very memorable and enjoyable."

David Pressman, sophomore

"Going to a school that had a strong Jewish community was a priority in my college search, and I have found everything that I was looking for and more at Brown. With amazingly diverse programming, opportunities for leadership right from the beginning, a large, active Jewish population and a supportive university environment, there are so many different ways to express your connection to Judaism. Brown is a place full of passion and Jewish life on campus is very much reflective of that feeling."

Marissa Kifshen, junior

BRYANT COLLEGE

Enrollment 4,000
Jewish 300

Jewish Students Organization
Bryant College
1150 Douglas Pike
Smithfield, RI 02917
(401) 232-6266
(401) 232-6045

Professor Lawrence Silverman, Campus Chaplain
Professor Alan Olinsky, Advisor
Melissa Chernofsky, Jewish Campus Service Corps Fellow

 Study in Israel
Study abroad program; Israel possibilities.

 Kosher Food
Vegetarian options available. Kosher food available for holidays at Brown University.

ON CAMPUS
Bryant College Hillel is part of the Rhode Island Hillel Council. Joint programs are held with other schools in the area, including statewide retreats. The local community and the College administration are supportive of Jewish campus life at Bryant College.

JOHNSON AND WALES UNIVERSITY

Enrollment 9,000
Jewish 900

Hillel
Johnson and Wales University
8 Abbot Park Place
Providence, RI 02903
(401) 598-1837
Fax: (401) 598-2490
E-mail: mneckes@jwu.edu

Professor Mark Neckes, Advisor
Ronni Neckes, Advisor
Rabbi Lefkowitz, Chaplain

 Kosher Food
Available at nearby Brown University Hillel. Passover seders; kosher-for-Passover food is served all week in one of the cafeterias.

ON CAMPUS
Johnson and Wales Hillel is part of the Rhode Island Hillel Council. Hillel participates in joint programs with other area schools and statewide retreats.

RHODE ISLAND SCHOOL OF DESIGN

Enrollment 1,900
Jewish 150

Brown-RISD Hillel Foundation
80 Brown Street
Providence, RI 02906
(401) 863-2805
Fax: (401) 863-1591
E-mail: hillel@brown.edu
Web: www.brown.edu/students/jewish_student_union/

Rabbi Alan C. Flam, Executive Director
Cynthia G. Weinger, Program Director

 Kosher Food
Brown University sponsors the kosher meal plan. Lunch and dinner are served daily.

ON CAMPUS
RISD has a joint program with Hillel at Brown University. Activities include Jewish hiking trips, student art shows, Israeli dancing, community service projects, and a Jewish *a cappella* group. Hillel also sponsors a number of Jewish student groups, such as Kol Ishah, a women's issues group; *Mahberet*, a journal for progressive Jewish expression; and the Jewish Student Union, Hillel's student coordinating body.

The Jewish Cultural Arts Society (JCAS) supports student pieces in both the performing and visual arts, and seeks to stimulate students' thinking about Jewish identity, community, and values. Past activities have included a Jewish Film Festival, menorah and mezuzah-making workshops, and several guest artists who performed on campus, showcased their art work, and spoke to JCAS students.

In addition, Hillel provides other services such as a kosher meal plan, an informal Jewish education program, a Judaica library, and extensive files on study opportunities in Israel. Meeting room, study lounges, gallery space, and a piano are available for student use. Hillel also serves as a liaison for work and study opportunities within the larger Jewish community in Rhode Island and beyond.

See listing for Brown University.

ROGER WILLIAMS UNIVERSITY

Enrollment 2,000
Jewish 250

Hillel
Roger Williams University
1 Old Ferry Road
Bristol, RI 02809
(401) 254-3386

Michael Cunningham, Interim Advisor

 Jewish Studies
Jewish History.

 Study in Israel
Occasional programs in Israel.

 Kosher Food
Weekly lunches; holiday meals.

ON CAMPUS

Roger Williams' Jewish student group is part of the Rhode Island Hillel Council, which is based at Brown University. Students participate in joint programs with students at other area schools, and have on campus gatherings such as holiday baking. They have made a trip to the U.S. Holocaust Memorial Museum in Washington, D.C.

UNIVERSITY OF RHODE ISLAND

Enrollment 13,400 (UG 10,300; GR 3,100)
Jewish 1,700 (UG 1,500; GR 200)

B'nai B'rith Hillel Foundation
34 Lower College Road
Kingston, RI 02881
(401) 874-2740
(401) 874-2274
Fax: (401) 874-2136
E-mail: glbermel@uri.edu
Web: www.uri.edu/student_life/chaps/hillel.html

Guy L. Bermel, Director
Amy Sapherstein, Program Director
Sharon Grainer, Jewish Campus Service Corps Fellow

 Jewish Studies
8 courses; 4 Hebrew courses. Jewish Studies minor.

 Study in Israel
Study Abroad at Hebrew, Tel Aviv, and Ben-Gurion Universities.

 Kosher Food
Kosher co-op at Hillel; all meals available; vegetarian dining alternatives; Passover meal plan.

ON CAMPUS

URI is located in a very beautiful rural setting. Hillel is a growing presence on campus with a wide range of social and educational programs. The University of Rhode Island is a very supportive environment for these and other campus-wide Jewish activities. URI also has a very strong fraternity/sorority system. Within the last five years, the Jewish population at URI has grown from 8 to 18 percent because of the large influx of out-of-state students.

SOUTH CAROLINA

CLEMSON UNIVERSITY

Enrollment 16,000
Jewish 120

B'nai B'rith Hillel Student Organization
c/o Undergraduate Admissions
106 Sikes Hall
Clemson, SC 29634-5124
(864) 656-7729
E-mail: pcohen@clemson.edu

Dr. Peter Cohen, Advisor

Jewish Studies
2 courses.

 Study in Israel
Study abroad coordinated through Hebrew University.

 Kosher Food
Locally available (limited).

ON CAMPUS

Clemson University is a land grant institution situated in the foothills of South Carolina's Blue Ridge Mountains. The University is situated about 30 miles from Greenville, South Carolina, and about 2 hours' drive from Atlanta. Jewish students participate in all facets of Clemson University life, from being Clemson Ambassadors and members of sports teams to participating in the Calhoun College Honors Program. There are no "Jewish" fraternities or sororities, but Jewish students are members and officers of many Greek organizations.

Hillel at Clemson holds monthly social events, such as bagel brunches, pizza parties, and TV program evenings, and Jewish discussion groups are held every other Sunday evening. Hillel participates in interfaith activities with other religious denominations, and co-sponsors the annual Holocaust Awareness Month activities.

The Jewish communities of Clemson and Greenville are very supportive of campus Jewish life. Hillel enjoys an excellent working relationship with the campus ministry. Jewish religious objects such as Hanukkah candles, yahrzeit candles, and Jewish calendars are available from the Faculty Advisor.

COLLEGE OF CHARLESTON

Enrollment 8,800 (UG 7,100; GR 1,700)
Jewish 250

Jewish Student Union
c/o Department of History
College of Charleston
Charleston, SC 29424
(843) 953-8030
E-mail: bodekr@cofc.edu

Professor Martin Perlmutter, Advisor
Professor Richard Bodek, Advisor

 Jewish Studies
18-credit minor with core requirements in history and Jewish Studies. Wide selection of electives in religion, political science, American literature, Hebrew language, sociology, and interdisciplinary honors.

 Study in Israel
Junior year abroad programs as well as summer study in Israel.

 Kosher Food
Kosher butcher and bakery in town; frozen kosher meat at local supermarkets.

 Housing
Contact local rabbis.

ON CAMPUS

The Jewish Student Union is a registered student organization that sponsors regular events, including a Break Fast, building of a campus sukkah, and regular social events such as films, pizza, and beach get-togethers.

The College is the academic home of the South Carolina Jewish Historical Society and the Jewish Heritage Project, which is actively collecting South Carolina Jewish archives. Evening mini-courses, lectures, and brown bag lunches supplement the Jewish Studies courses offered in the curriculum. Home hospitality is available for Shabbat and the holidays from the Charleston Jewish community.

THE CITADEL—MILITARY COLLEGE OF SOUTH CAROLINA

Enrollment 3,800 (UG 2,000; GR 1,800)
Jewish 30 (UG 20; GR 10)

Hillel
182 Rutledge Avenue
Charleston, SC 29403
(843) 577-6599

Rabbi David J. Radinsky, Advisor
Rabbi Edward Friedman, Advisor

 Kosher Food
By special arrangement only.

ON CAMPUS

The Citadel is a military school, now coed on both undergraduate (cadets) and graduate levels. All undergraduates are required to live in the barracks (dormitories) and eat in the mess hall. Therefore, it is very difficult to maintain a Jewish lifestyle at this school. Yet, every Monday, Jewish students meet for a discussion group and occasionally for holiday home-stays. Students are welcomed into the local Jewish community.

UNIVERSITY OF SOUTH CAROLINA

Enrollment 28,000 (UG 20,000; GR 8,000)
Jewish 400 (UG 300; GR 100)

> Hillel at the University of South Carolina
> 1136 Washington Street, Suite 502
> Columbia, SC 29201
> (803) 799-9132
> E-mail: hillelc@univscvm.cso.sc.edu
>
> **Bernard L. Friedman**, Advisor

 Jewish Studies
12 courses in Departments of Religious Studies and Foreign Languages.

Kosher Food
Vegetarian dining alternatives; kosher food locally available.

ON CAMPUS

Hillel at the University of South Carolina meets in the Student Union building. The University is supportive of Jewish activities, and Hillel enjoys a good relationship on the campus and locally. Activities include social gatherings, active social action, Soviet Jewry and Israel programs, and celebration of all holidays. The Columbia Jewish community is very supportive of Jewish students at USC, and provides home hospitality for Shabbat and holidays.

TENNESSEE

RHODES COLLEGE

Enrollment 1,400
Jewish 20

> Jewish Student Union
> 3581 Midland
> University of Memphis
> Memphis, TN 38111
> (901) 452-2453
> Fax: (901) 767-9339
> E-mail: jsunion@cc.memphis.edu
> Web: www.people.memphis.edu/~jsunion
>
> **Scott Ostrow**, Director

Kosher Food
Available through JSU programs.

ON CAMPUS

Monthly events and holiday celebrations.

See listing for University of Memphis.

SOUTHERN COLLEGE OF OPTOMETRY

Enrollment 600
Jewish 10

> Jewish Student Union
> 3581 Midland
> University of Memphis
> Memphis, TN 38111
> (901) 452-2453
> Fax: (901) 767-9339
> E-mail: jsunion@cc.memphis.edu/~jsunion
>
> **Scott Ostrow**, Director
> **Professor Joel Spiegler**, Advisor

See listing for University of Memphis.

UNIVERSITY OF MEMPHIS

Enrollment 21,500
Jewish 250

> Jewish Student Union
> 3581 Midland
> Memphis, TN 38111
> (901) 452-2453
> Fax: (901) 767-9339
> E-mail: jsunion@cc.memphis.edu
> Web: www.people.memphis.edu/~jsunion
>
> **Scott Ostrow**, Director

Jewish Studies
Courses in Bornblum Judaic Studies Program/ Chair of Excellence rotating appointment. Bachelor of Liberal Studies degree offered; an Independent Studies degree in Jewish Studies.

 Study in Israel
New agreement with Tel Aviv University.

Kosher Food
Kosher kitchen in JSU facility. Lunches and Shabbat dinners throughout the year, and a full-service kosher-for-Passover cafe.

ON CAMPUS

The Jewish Student Union provides a dynamic center of Jewish life for all college and university students in the Mid-South. In addition, through the JSU, students often connect to the full range of services offered in the Memphis Jewish community.

The JSU sponsors a variety of social, community service, cultural, and religious events that reflect the interest of the students. Activities include monthly Shabbat dinners, holiday celebrations, on-campus lunches, speakers, and community-based events. The JSU also sponsors an active Graduate Student Network, which brings together students from all of the Memphis area graduate programs, and includes special affinity groups for Jewish law students and Jewish medical students. Professional mentoring and social opportunities are the cornerstones of the Network.

The JSU offers a newly renovated facility adjacent to the University of Memphis campus, which features a pool table, a TV/VCR, a fireplace, computers, a kosher kitchen, and a Jewish periodical library.

The Jewish Student Union is a program of the Memphis Jewish Federation.

UNIVERSITY OF TENNESSEE—CHATTANOOGA

Enrollment 8,200 (UG 6,800; GR 1,400)
Jewish 60

Jewish Student Organization
c/o Professor Irven M. Resnick
Department of Philosophy and Religion
232 Holt Hall, UTC
Chattanooga, TN 37403-2598
(423) 755-4446
Fax: (423) 744-4279
E-mail: iresnick@cecasun.utc.edu

Professor Irven M. Resnick, Advisor

Jewish Studies

Although no degree program in Judaic Studies exists at UTC, UTC does have an endowed chair in Judaic Studies within the Department of Philosophy and Religion. The Chairholder normally offers 2-4 courses each year, sponsors an annual series of public lectures, and brings various programs to the local Jewish community. Contact Professor Irven M. Resnick, Dept. of Philosophy and Religion, 232 Holt Hall, UTC, 615 McCallie Avenue, Chattanooga, TN 37403-2598.

Study in Israel

The Judaic Studies Chairholder coordinates a UTC in Haifa program, enabling students to work on a kibbutz and study at the University of Haifa. Designated scholarships are available for Jewish students, both to attend UTC and to support study in Israel.

Kosher Food

At Congregation Beth Sholom on holidays; occasional meals; kosher food brought from Atlanta.

ON CAMPUS

The Jewish Student Organization meets monthly primarily for social purposes. The Chattanooga Jewish community is very supportive of Jewish students at the university, and provides home hospitality for Shabbat and holidays.

UNIVERSITY OF TENNESSEE—KNOXVILLE

Enrollment 25,900
Jewish 300

Jewish Student Center
University of Tennessee
2100 Terrace Avenue
Knoxville, TN 37916
(865) 546-5226
Fax: (423) 694-4861 (at Federation)
E-mail: furtado48@hotmail.com; mfurtado@utk.edu
Web: www.jewishknoxville.org

Professor Moema Furtado, Director
Dr. Jeffrey Beeker, Advisor
Dr. Gilya Schmidt, Advisor

Jewish Studies

10 courses; major and minor. Interdisciplinary course of study: Hebrew and Germanic languages; Biblical and Modern Hebrew available through Religious Studies. Courses in philosophy and art also included. Todays Scholar of Religion; conferences. Contact Dr. Gilya Schmidt, Endowed Chair in Judaic Studies.

Study in Israel

The university accepts credits for study at Israeli universities.

Kosher Food

The Jewish Student Center provides kosher-style or vegetarian food for activities. Kosher foods are locally available, and there is a kosher restaurant close to campus. The University can offer kosher Passover food.

Housing

The JSC has housing for both Jewish men and women.

ON CAMPUS

The Jewish Student Center at Knoxville is a student-run organization that engages in cultural, social, religious and educational programs for the Jewish students, University staff and faculty. The Jewish Student Center is well located on campus, and a strong effort is made to provide a warm, friendly, comfortable place to meet new people, make friends, and deepen existing ties. JSC students participate in social action projects such as food drives and aiding in campus awareness by displaying annually a Simon Wiesenthal Holocaust exhibit for the school and Knoxville community. There is an all-Jewish fraternity, AEPi; membership in AEPi includes membership at the JSC. The JSC actively invites new students through strong recruitment efforts, a new student mixer, and a Graduate Students group.

UNIVERSITY OF TENNESSEE—MEMPHIS: MEDICAL, NURSING SCHOOL, AND ALLIED HEALTH

Enrollment 1,900
Jewish 50

Jewish Student Union
3581 Midland
University of Memphis
Memphis, TN 38111
(901) 452-2453
Fax: (901) 452-9339
E-mail: jsunion@cc.memphis.edu

Scott Ostrow, Director

ON CAMPUS

On-campus programming includes a very successful medical students mentoring program and a monthly kosher pizza lunch.

See listing for University of Memphis.

VANDERBILT UNIVERSITY

Enrollment 6,000+
Jewish 350 (UG 200; GR 150)

Vanderbilt Hillel: The Center for Jewish Life on Campus
2417 West End Avenue
Nashville, TN 37240
(615) 343-1953
(615) 343-6299
Fax: (615) 343-8355
E-mail: hillel@vanderbilt.edu
Web: www.vanderbilt.edu/hillel/

Shaiva Baer, Director

Jewish Studies

10 courses; minor; Hebrew. Vanderbilt is home to the largest Judaica library in the Southeast, begun in 1945. The University has recently acquired the Nahum Glatzer collection, including a large quantity of original material from Franz Rosenzweig.

Study in Israel

Semester at Hebrew University.

Kosher Food

Students may use the kosher kitchenette in the Hillel office for lunch.

ON CAMPUS

Vanderbilt Hillel prides itself in offering creative holiday programs and cultural venues. Our Shabbat, Sukkot, and Passover program draws a significant number of students and faculty.

AUSTIN COLLEGE

Enrollment 1,200
Jewish 25

Haverim Austin College
PO Box 1177, Suite 6J
Sherman, TX 75091-1177
(903) 892-4196

Janet Heeter, Advisor

BAYLOR COLLEGE OF MEDICINE— TEXAS MEDICAL CENTER

Enrollment 1,144
Jewish 100

Hillel Foundation of Greater Houston
Baylor College of Medicine
A.D. Bruce Religion Center
University of Houston
Houston, TX 77204-3621
(713) 743-5397
Fax: (713) 743-5995
E-mail: hillel@houstonhillel.org
afrankfort@houstonhillel.org

Anna Frankfort, Program Director
Julie Gutman, Program Associate
Dr. Amir Halevy, Faculty Advisor
Illan Gauss, Jewish Campus Service Corps Fellow

Kosher Food

Hillel offers monthly kosher Shabbat dinners and kosher meals for various holidays and special events. Hillel also serves kosher lunches on campus once a month.

ON CAMPUS

Students interested in Jewish life find abundant ways to participate in social, cultural, religious, social action, and academic events. Some of the activities offered include Shabbat dinners and services, which are offered twice monthly, Sunday brunches at faculty members' homes, and Happy Hours. Lunchtime programs are held monthly featuring faculty and community members discussing topics relating to Judaism and medicine. Holiday celebrations include High Holiday services and a break-the-fast held at Rice University, Simchat Torah observance with Chabad, and a Pesach seder "Match Up."

The Hillel Foundation of Greater Houston serves as the center of programming for Hillels at Baylor College of Medicine at the Texas Medical Center, the University of Texas Medical School, the South Texas College of Law, the University of Houston Law School, the University of Houston, and Rice University.

See listing for University of Houston.

RICE UNIVERSITY

Enrollment 4,051 (UG 2,645; GR 1,406)
Jewish 400 (UG 300; GR 100)

Hillel Foundation of Greater Houston
1700 Bissonnet
Houston, TX 77005
(713) 526-4918
Fax: (713) 526-4966
E-mail: hillel@houstonhillel.org

Anna Frankfort, Program Director
Julie Gutman, Program Associate
Dr. Paul Lockey, Faculty Advisor
Illana Gauss, Jewish Campus Service Corps Fellow

Jewish Studies
12 Jewish studies courses, including Hebrew.

Study in Israel
Junior year abroad; summer courses at many universities.

Kosher Food
Hillel offers a kosher Shabbat dinner once a month, as well as kosher meals for various holidays and special events. Kosher lunches and snacks are ocassionally served on campus.

See listing for University of Houston.

SOUTH TEXAS COLLEGE OF LAW

Enrollment 1,259
Jewish 100

Hillel Foundation of Greater Houston
1700 Bissonnet
Houston, TX 77005
(713) 743-5397
Fax: (713) 743-5995
E-mail: houstonhillel@hotmail.com

Rabbi David Moss, Executive Director
Anna Frankfort, Program Director
Julie Gutman, Program Associate
Illana Gauss, Jewish Campus Service Corps Fellow

Kosher Food

Hillel offers a kosher Shabbat dinner once a month, as well as kosher meals for various holidays and

special events. Kosher lunch is ocassionally served on campus.

ON CAMPUS
The Hillel Foundation of Greater Houston provides innovative social, cultural, religious, community service, and educational programs and opportunities for Jewish students in Houston. Some of the events include a Back to School Barbecue, Coffeehouse Night, Shabbat dinners, which are held once a month, Israel Night, Dinner & Jewish Learning, and a Judicial Reception for the law students. We co-sponsor events with guest speakers with organizations such as Young Judea, the Israeli Consulate, AIPAC, Holocaust Museum Houston, ADL, JNF, and Lights in Action. Lunchtime programs are offered for the students at the University of Houston, the Medical Center, and the law schools. Holiday celebrations include High Holiday service and Break Fast, a Hanukkah event, a dinner for Purim, a Passover seder "Match Up" program, an annual Yom Hashoah observance, and an event for Yom Ha'atzmaut. In conjunction with UJA, Hillel sponsors community service projects. At Hillel, a Jewish Resource Center is available to all students, and the University of Houston has a chapter of AEPi. Hillel subsidizes students so that they may participate in the UJA Students Mission to Israel program, and offers assistance to students to attend Jewish conferences and programs in Israel. The city of Houston has many synagogues and Jewish organizations, including the Jewish Community Center, which offers programs for Jewish singles.

The Hillel Foundation of Greater Houston serves as the center of programming for Rice University, Baylor College of Medicine, the University of Texas Medical School, South Texas College of Law affiliated with Texas A&M University, the University of Houston, the University of Houston Law Center, and other Houston-area universities with smaller Jewish populations.

SOUTHERN METHODIST UNIVERSITY

Enrollment 9,000 (UG 5,000; GR 4,000)
Jewish 290 (UG 140; GR 150)

Jewish Students Association/Hillel
Box 282, Campus Ministries
Dallas, TX 75275
(214) 768-4508
Fax: (214) 768-4514

Geralda Miller, Advisor

Jewish Studies
10 courses in the Religious Studies Department. The Bridwell Library at SMU houses an extensive Judaica collection.

Kosher Food
Locally available.

ON CAMPUS

The Jewish Students Association/Hillel at SMU provides a Jewish community for students on campus. Students may participate in a wide variety of social, religious, educational, and political activities. JSA/Hillel takes advantage of the many resources for Jewish life within the Dallas Jewish community, and a host family program is offered to students who are not from Dallas. A mentoring program, which matches SMU students with Jewish professionals in their field of interest, has been very successful. The Jewish Faculty and Staff Association is involved in student programming, and students are invited into the homes of faculty and staff for holiday celebrations. There is also an active Jewish Law Students' Association at SMU.

TEXAS A&M UNIVERSITY

Enrollment 43,000
Jewish 1,200

 Texas A&M Hillel Foundation
800 George Bush Drive
College Station, TX 77840
(409) 696-7313
E-mail: hillel@startel.net
Web: www.startel.net/hillel

Rabbi Peter Tarlow, Director

 Jewish Studies
4 courses.

 Study in Israel
Texas A&M accepts credit for study at Israeli universities.

 Kosher Food
Holidays and occasional meals at Hillel. Hillel has a kosher dairy kitchen that students use.

ON CAMPUS

Hillel at Texas A&M provides a wide range of social and cultural activities for Jewish students, including an annual Jewish book festival, an active Oppressed Jewry program, a Big Brother/Big Sister program, a tutoring program for undergraduates who wish to have a bar or bat mitzvah or learn Hebrew, an Israel Day celebration, and other activities according to student interest. Hillel enjoys a good working relationship with the campus ministry.

TEXAS TECH UNIVERSITY

Enrollment 23,000
Jewish 150

Hillel at Texas Tech University,
Department of English
Box 43092
Lubbock, TX 79409-3092
(806) 742-2524
(806) 742-3275

Professor James Foster, Advisor

ON CAMPUS

The local Jewish community is very supportive of Jewish campus life, and provides home hospitality for students for Shabbat and holidays. Texas Tech's campus population is divided rather equally between residential and commuter students.

UNIVERSITY OF HOUSTON/ LAW CENTER AT THE UNIVERSITY OF HOUSTON

Enrollment 35,000 (UG 25,000; GR 10,000)
Jewish 1,000 (UG 750; GR 250)

 Hillel Foundation of Greater Houston
A.D. Bruce Religion Center
University of Houston
Houston, TX 77004
(713) 743-5397
Fax: (713) 526-4966
E-mail: hillel@houstonhillel.org

Rabbi David Moss, Executive Director
Anna Frankfort, Program Director
Julie Gutman, Program Associate
Ilana Gauss, Jewish Campus Service Corps Fellow

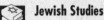 **Jewish Studies**
Approximately 2 courses per semester. Hebrew is offered at Rice University, 15 minutes away.

 Study in Israel
Junior year abroad; summer courses at many universities.

Kosher Food
Hillel offers a kosher Shabbat dinner once a month, as well as kosher meals for various holidays and special events. Kosher lunch is occasionally served on campus.

ON CAMPUS

The Hillel Foundation of Greater Houston provides innovative social, cultural, religious, community service, and educational programs and opportunities for Jewish students throughout the Houston area. These events include a Back to School Barbecue, Coffeehouse Night, Shabbat dinners, which are held once a month, Israel Night, Dinner & Jewish Learning, and a Judicial Reception for the law students. Hillel also co-sponsors events and guest speakers with organizations such as Young Judea, the Israeli Consulate, AIPAC, Holocaust Museum Houston, ADL, JNF, and Lights in Action.

Lunchtime programs are offered for the students at the University of Houston, the Medical Center, and the law schools. Holiday celebrations include High Holy Day service and Break Fast, a Hanukkah event, a dinner for Purim, a Passover seder "Match Up" program, an annual Yom Hashoah observance, and an event for Yom Ha'atzmaut. In conjunction with UJA, Hillel sponsors community service projects. At Hillel, a Jewish Resource Center is available to all students, and the University of Houston has a chapter of AEPi. Hillel subsidizes students so that they may participate in the UJA Students Mission to Israel program, and offers assistance to students to attend Jewish conferences and programs in Israel.

The city of Houston has many synagogues and Jewish organizations, including the Jewish Community Center, which offers programs for Jewish singles.

The Hillel Foundation of Greater Houston serves as the center of programming for students at Rice University, Baylor College of Medicine, the University of Texas Medical School, South Texas College of Law affiliated with Texas A&M University, the University of Houston, and the University of Houston Law Center, as well as at other Houston-area universities with smaller Jewish populations.

UNIVERSITY OF NORTH TEXAS

Enrollment 25,000
Jewish 250

> Jewish Student Association
> c/o Dr. Richard Ruderman
> Department of Political Science
> UNT—PO Box 1621
> Denton, TX 76203
> (817) 565-4944
>
> **Dr. Richard Ruderman**, JSA Advisor

UNIVERSITY OF TEXAS
MEDICAL SCHOOL/HEALTH SCIENCE CENTER

Enrollment 3,100
Jewish 300

> Hillel Foundation of Greater Houston
> 1700 Bissonett
> University of Houston
> Houston, TX 77005
> (713) 743-5397
> Fax: (713) 743-5995
>
> **Rabbi David Moss**, Executive Director
> **Anna Frankfort**, Program Director
> **Julie Gutman**, Program Associate
> **Dr. Nachum Dafny**, Advisor
> **Illana Gauss**, Jewish Campus Service Corps Fellow

Kosher Food
Hillel offers monthly kosher Shabbat dinners and kosher meals for various holidays and social events. Hillel also serves kosher lunches on campus once a month.

See listing for University of Houston.

UNIVERSITY OF TEXAS—AUSTIN

Enrollment 48,000
Jewish 4,000

> Hillel Foundation at the University of Texas
> 2105 San Antonio
> Austin, TX 78705
> (512) 476-0125
> Fax: (512) 476-0128
> Web: www.utexas-edu/students/hillel
>
> **Rabbi David Kessel**, Executive Director
> **Margo Sack**, Associate Director
> **Deena Waite**, Development Associate
> **Aaron Lippman**, Jewish Campus Service Corps Fellow

Jewish Studies
30 courses; B.A., M.A., Ph.D. in Hebrew Studies; and an undergraduate concentration in Jewish Studies. In addition to Hebrew, Yiddish, and Jewish Studies classes, UT's Middle East Studies Center and Department of Middle Eastern Languages and Cultures sponsors programs of Jewish interest.

The Perry Castaneda Library contains a sizable collection of Judaica in Hebrew, Yiddish, and other modern languages. Also available on campus are rare holdings at the Harry Ransom Center for the Humanities, such as early texts, periodicals, and the papers of Isaac Bashevis Singer. An extensive collection of videos and audio recordings is distributed among UT's many specialized libraries. Each year UT hosts a lecture or series of lectures organized by the Gale Chair of Jewish Studies that are open to the entire Austin community.

Study in Israel

Junior year abroad; summer archaeological programs in Israel; exchange program with Haifa University; and Mediterranean Crossroads, an interdisciplinary program with a summer field course in Israel and Turkey.

Kosher Food

Weekly Shabbat dinners, and other holiday and occasional meals; kosher-for-Passover meal plan. Vegetarian dining alternatives; dormitory cooking facilities.

ON CAMPUS

The University of Texas—Austin has emerged as a campus with a varied and inviting Jewish life. The Jewish population is a significant portion of the broader university. Jewish students are active in all areas of campus life, including student government, the student union, journalism, performing arts, and other programs. Hillel is run through a set of 12 student-run committees, which program for specific interests. In addition, several independent Jewish organizations work with Hillel, such as the newspaper, *The Jewish Texan*, an Israeli-American group, a Rosh Chodesh women's group, an AIPAC-Hamagshimim group known as Texans For Israel, and Latin American Jewish Students. Other Jewish organizations on campus include Plan II Jews, Jewish Law Students, Jewish Business Students, Israeli Students Organization, and Latin American Jewish Students. Students are also free to work with Hillel on independent initiatives.

Hillel is one of the most active organizations on campus. Among the more than 200 events available through Hillel annually are weekly Shabbat dinners, large parties for Purim and Hanukkah, a large celebration for Simchat Torah, intramural sports, weekly Shabbat services for the 3 major movements, a Jewish women's group, a campuswide UJA campaign, Israeli dancing, student-directed plays, social action activities, diversity programming, speakers and informal classes on a variety of topics, a film series, and others according to student interest.

Several Jewish sororities and fraternities (AEPhi, AEPi, PiLamdaPhi, SAM, and SDT) are present at UT, with many of their members involved in Hillel and the Greek-Jewish Council. Graduate student programming was recently combined with a young professional group with great success. The graduate and young professional group has had momentum to sponsor a host of activities, with active participation from the graduate community.

Hillel is located just 1 block from campus, and the student center is complete with a computer center, big screen television, pool table, lounge, and library. Students are free to come in almost any time of the day and most nights.

UNIVERSITY OF TEXAS, DALLAS

Enrollment 900
Jewish 150

Hillel
Box 830688, SU 21
Richardson, TX 75083-0688
(972) 231-0471
(972) 596-0832
Fax: (972) 231-0471
E-mail: Hillel@utdallas.edu
Web: www.utdallas.edu/orgs/hillel/

Professor Ronald Yasbin, Faculty Advisor

ON CAMPUS

UTD is a young school that is just developing an active campus life, and Hillel is a new group just getting started. Hillel sponsors occasional activities according to students' interests.

UNIVERSITY OF TEXAS—EL PASO

Enrollment 13,000
Jewish 50

Hillel
c/o Jewish Federation of El Paso
405 Wallenberg Drive
El Paso, TX 79912
(915) 584-4437
Fax: (915) 584-0243
E-mail: jfed1@huntleigh.net

Larry Harris, Executive Director, Jewish Federation

ON CAMPUS

A new Hillel group is being established at El Paso.

UNIVERSITY OF TEXAS—SAN ANTONIO

Enrollment 19,000
Jewish 1,000 (including other San Antonio colleges)

Hillel at University of Texas—San Antonio
R. Horowitz
Division of Education
San Antonio, TX 78249-0654
(210) 691-5418
Fax: (210) 458-5848
E-mail: horowitz@lonestar.utsa.edu

Dr. Rosalind Horowitz, Advisor

Jewish Studies

Hebrew is offered in the Division of Foreign Languages, and there are also courses in American Jewish Literature. The University of Texas—Austin, an hour and 15 minutes away, has a Jewish Studies program and extensive Judaic library holdings.

Study in Israel

Through the University of Texas—Austin.

Kosher Food

The University makes no provisions for kosher food, but Hillel at UTSA provides kosher food at all functions. Kosher food is available locally.

ON CAMPUS

The campus is located 150 miles from the border of Mexico. UTSA is the fastest-growing university/college in Texas. Hillel at UTSA was formed to meet the social, educational, and religious needs of this South Texas academic community. It includes students and faculty from the University of Texas—San Antonio, and also from Trinity University, St. Mary's University, Our Lady of the Lake, Incarnate Word, and San Antonio College, as well as from abroad. Jewish faculty come from across the world and participate in programs.

Because the school is rather isolated from large Jewish communities, opportunities to get together, such as kosher Shabbat dinners at the director's home, are valued and held as often as possible.

Student government, activities, lectures, and the school newspaper, *The Paesano*, allow students the opportunity to assume leadership roles. There is an annual UTSA Israel Fair so that students may learn of programs available to them. Special resources at the university include a campus Judaic collection in the John Peace Library. Local synagogues also offer opportunities for Jewish study.

Hillel sponsors films, lectures, and musical performances throughout the year.

UTAH

UNIVERSITY OF UTAH

Enrollment 25,000
Jewish 300

Hillel at University of Utah
332 S. 1400 East Front
University of Utah
Salt Lake City, UT 84112
(801) 585-5201
E-mail: hillel@lists.utah.edu
Web: www.utah.edu/hillel

Professor Dan Greenwood, Advisor

 Jewish Studies

10 courses; B.A., M.A., Ph.D. through the Middle East Center. Degree programs in Jewish studies combine area studies available through the Middle East Center with courses in Hebrew.

 Study in Israel

Junior year abroad.

Kosher Food

Vegetarian dining alternatives; kosher food locally available.

ON CAMPUS

Hillel at the University of Utah is the center of campus Jewish life for students at all the area schools, including Brigham Young University (with several Israeli students), Utah State University, Weber State University, and Salt Lake Community College. Many of the Jewish students are from out of state, especially California and New York. Activities vary with the interest of the students. There are monthly meetings and social activities such as bagel get-togethers and attendance at sports events. The university is supportive of the Hillel program, as is Salt Lake City's Jewish community, which offers home hospitality. A full listing of all events for the last two years is available on the Web site.

VERMONT

MIDDLEBURY COLLEGE

Enrollment 2,000
Jewish 150

Hillel
Middlebury College
Middlebury, VT 05753
(802) 443-5000
(802) 443-5151 (Schine)
(802) 443-5141 (Margolis)
Fax: (802) 443-2084
E-mail: schine@middlebury.edu
Web: www.middlebury.edu/~hillel/

Professor Robert Schine, Advisor
Professor Gary Margolis, Advisor

Jewish Studies

9 courses; minor. Focus on Jewish studies possible within existing majors such as Religion or History. Strong curricular offerings in Jewish thought, modern Jewish history, and Biblical Hebrew enroll from 30 to 50 students each semester. In 1994, the College received initial funding for the Silberman Chair in Jewish Studies, to be established within 5 years. The College also has an annual Quint Lecture in Jewish Studies and

other endowments supporting special cultural and academic programs of Jewish interest. Dr. Schine is Professor of Jewish Studies.

 Study in Israel

Several students study in Israel each year.

Kosher Food

Middlebury College now has a fully functional kosher kitchen. Dining halls always have vegetarian menu, but no kosher kitchen. Students cook regular Friday evening supper in the Jewish Center.

ON CAMPUS

The establishment of the Middlebury College Jewish Center in the fall of 1993 has given Jewish life a true focal point on campus. It is the locale of a rich and varied program of lectures, discussions, brunches, weekly Hillel lunch meetings, and regular Sabbath evening dinners. The college administration is supportive of Jewish life on campus, as is the local Chavurah. Students from the college teach in the local Hebrew School. Students are also frequently hosted for dinners in faculty homes and are included in many Chavurah events. All these factors combine to make Middlebury an increasingly congenial environment for students from Reform, Conservative, and occasionally, Orthodox backgrounds. Recent graduates have gone on to rabbinical school, internships in Israel, and graduate school in Judaic studies.

UNIVERSITY OF VERMONT

Enrollment 12,000
    Jewish 800 (UG 700; GR 100)

Hillel at UVM Center for Jewish Life
University of Vermont
Allen House Center for Cultural Pluralism
Burlington, VT 05405-0010
(802) 656-1153
Fax: (802) 656-3348
E-mail: hillel@zoo.uvm.edu

Liz Theisen, Director

 Jewish Studies

Hebrew in the Department of Religion.

 Study in Israel

Junior year abroad at Tel Aviv and Hebrew Universities.

 Kosher Food

Hillel is currently in the process of establishing kosher dining options on campus.

ON CAMPUS

Students are in charge of all program planning at Vermont Hillel/Jewish Student Union, and work cooperatively with the Jewish Action Coalition, Chabad, and many other campus organizations. The result is a wide variety of social, cultural, and educational activities responsive to students' interests. These include trips such as the Montreal Weekend, the Dartmouth Ski Shabbaton, a Fall Foliage Hike, and a trip to the U.S. Holocaust Memorial Museum in Washington, DC Students also gather for weekly Shabbat dinners, Jewish holiday celebrations, Paperbag Torah study, speakers, and many other events.

Hillel is a co-sponsor of the University of Vermont's Winterfest, National Women's Week, and Building Our Community, and Hillel members are guest speakers in Race and Culture Courses. The director represents Hillel in various settings, such as a panelist for the Center for Cultural Pluralism and a workshop leader in intergroup meetings. Hillel also serves as a resource center for students to gather information about travel and study in Israel, scholarships, and campus events.

VIRGINIA

COLLEGE OF WILLIAM AND MARY

Enrollment 5,300
    Jewish 370

College of William and Mary Hillel
Tucker Hall
English Department
Williamsburg, VA 27187
(804) 229-8795
(804) 221-3910
Fax: (804) 221-1844
E-mail: rjscho@facstaff.wm.edu
Web: www.wm.edu/SO/balfour-hillel

Professor Robert Scholnick, Advisor
Rabbi Sylvia Scholnick, Advisor

Jewish Studies

8 courses. The College of William and Mary offers a concentration in Judaic Studies within the Department of Religion. Biblical Hebrew is offered as well as courses in the major periods of Jewish history. For information about the Judaic Studies program, contact Professor M.L. Raphael, Dept. of Religion, College of William and Mary, Williamsburg, VA 23185; (757) 221-2172; mlraph@facstaff.wm.edu.

Study in Israel

While there is no college-sponsored program, William and Mary offers 1 scholarship to support summer study in Israel.

Kosher Food

By special arrangement with the University. Vegetarian dining alternatives; dormitory cooking facilities.

ON CAMPUS

William and Mary has an active and varied program of activities for Jewish students, with special events annually. Both Temple Beth El and the Religion Department sponsor an extensive program of visiting speakers and musical groups. Social events sponsored by Hillel include bagel brunches, evening gatherings, and outings to nearby beaches and parks.

GEORGE MASON UNIVERSITY

Enrollment 24,000
Jewish 1,500 (UG 1,000; GR 500)

 George Mason University Hillel
SUB 1, Room 207, MSN 2C7
4400 University Drive
Fairfax, VA 22030-4444
(703) 993-3321
Fax: (703) 993-3332
E-mail: hillel@gmu.edu
Web: www.mason.gmu.edu/~hillel

Scott Bailey, Director

 Jewish Studies

Courses of Jewish content and interest are offered in various departments.

Study in Israel

The Study Abroad Office refers students directly to the programs and universities in Israel. Credit is generally accepted.

ON CAMPUS

George Mason University is located 15 miles west of Washington, DC, and is predominantly a commuter campus, having an on-campus dorm community of about 3,000 students.

George Mason hosts a growing, active Jewish campus community, and Hillel offers a full range of cultural, social, educational, political, and religious activities. These include bi-monthly Shabbat dinners, holiday celebrations, Lunch 'n' Learn discussion series, and an annual Holocaust Remembrance Day program. Students also have the opportunity to participate in the many regional programs and attend activities at the other area Hillels. GMU Hillel has a close relationship with local synagogues and the JCC of Northern Virginia, which offer holiday home hospitality to students for Shabbat and the holidays.

George Mason is served by Hillel of Greater Washington DC.

JAMES MADISON UNIVERSITY

Enrollment 15,000
Jewish 400

Hillel of JMU
Box 8058, James Madison University
Harrisonburg, VA 22807
(540) 568-6365
(540) 568-6145
Fax: (540) 568-2800
E-mail: club-bbhillel@jmu.edu

Dr. Don Chodrow, Advisor
Dr. Michael Goldberger, Faculty Advisor

 Jewish Studies

8 courses.

 Study in Israel

Semester in Tel Aviv or Ben-Gurion University. There is also a 7-week summer program for college credit at an archaeological dig at Tel Miqne-Ekron.

 Kosher Food

Kosher meals unavailable. The JMU Dining Services offers "Passover Friendly" menus during that time.

ON CAMPUS

Student leaders run Hillel at JMU. Approximately 50–100 students participate in Hillel activities. Student leaders plan and conduct an extensive program of religious and social activities. In the fall, the Jewish faculty provide home hospitality during the High Holidays, and students are invited to join their host families for High Holiday services at the local synagogue. Hillel also sponsors a wide range of social, cultural, and religious events every month. Such events may include: joint social events with the University of Virginia and or Virginia Tech, a field trip to the U.S. Holocaust Memorial Museum in Washington, DC, and a popular seder service for other ministries on campus.

"This isn't as easy a place to be a Jew as at other schools. It's an effort, but it is friendly. I haven't encountered anti-Semitism or problems, but most people are Christian. Hillel is the one place for Jews—it's a more social than religious organization. The community is small but willing to help. Holocaust Remembrance Day is our big day of the year, but I am looking to draw attention to other times of the year to show that not only negative things happen!"

Suzanne Hecht, junior

MARY WASHINGTON COLLEGE

Enrollment 3,100
Jewish 250

215 George Washington Hall
1301 College Avenue
Fredericksburg, VA 22401-5358
(540) 654-1063
Fax: (703) 899-4123
E-mail: cdiamant@mwc.edu
Web: www.mwc.edu/ccc/campmin/hillel.html

Constance Diamant, Advisor

 Jewish Studies
Special-topics courses available.

 Kosher Food
Vegetarian dining alternatives.

ON CAMPUS

Hillel is an organization for students interested in Jewish culture with chapters on college campuses throughout the nation. At MWC's Hillel, student leaders plan and run a variety of activities under the supervision of the faculty advisor. These activities generally include Shabbat gatherings, attendance at social functions at nearby Hillel chapters, educational programming, and holiday observances.

MWC Hillel serves as the students' liaison to the Fredericksburg Jewish community. Temple Beth Sholom, a reform congregation, welcomes the participation of MWC students. Students generally attend High Holiday and Shabbat services and enjoy all non-voting privileges accorded to Temple members. Activities include choir, weekly adult Hebrew class, Torah study, and adult introduction to Judaism classes.

MWC Hillel provides a nurturing environment that allows students to strengthen their Jewish identities. The local Jewish community is very active and supportive.

NORTHERN VIRGINIA COMMUNITY COLLEGE

Enrollment 34,500
Jewish 150

Hillel
SUB 1, Room 207, MSN 2C7
4400 University Drive
Fairfax, VA 22030-4444
(703) 993-3321
Fax: (703) 993-3332
E-mail: hillel@gmu.edu
Web: www.mason.gmu.edu/~hillel

Scott Bailey, Director

Northern Virginia Community College is served as an extension program of George Mason University Hillel. See listing for George Mason University.

OLD DOMINION UNIVERSITY

Enrollment 15,000
Jewish 200

Old Dominion University Hillel
c/o Jewish Community Center of Tidewater
7300 Newport Avenue
Norfolk, VA 23505
(757) 489-1371, ext. 106

Jodi Sachs, Jewish Federation Liason
Professor Karen Rostov, Advisor

 Jewish Studies
Several courses.

 Kosher Food
Vegetarian dining alternatives.

ON CAMPUS

On-campus programming is responsive to the interests and needs of students. Students also participate in national and regional Hillel events.

RADFORD UNIVERSITY

Enrollment 10,000
Jewish 300

Hillel
Box 6935
Radford, VA 24142
(540) 951-2628
E-mail: aweiss@ruacad.ac.runet.edu

Jeff Kurtz, Director
Professor Alexander Weiss, Advisor

ON CAMPUS

Program varies according to interests and activity of the students.

UNIVERSITY OF RICHMOND

Enrollment 4,700
Jewish 100 (UG 70; GR 30)

Richmond Jewish Students Association
5403 Monument Avenue
Jewish Community Center
Richmond, VA 23226
(804) 288-6091
E-mail: lbbjcc@aol.com

Lisa Brooke Looney, Director

 Jewish Studies
Religion major, minor.

 Study in Israel
The University accepts credits for study at Israeli universities.

 Kosher Food
Special arrangements can be made on request.

ON CAMPUS

RJSA is a program of the Jewish Community Center of Richmond and offers social, cultural, educational, and religious programs for students of University of Richmond as well as other Richmond-area campuses. The Weinstein/Rosenthal Chair in Judaic-Christian Studies sponsors lectures and programs throughout the year. The campus sponsors an annual interfaith Thanksgiving dinner and interfaith seder. The Richmond community will host students for the holidays.

RJLSA (Richmond Jewish Law Student Association) consists of about 30 students at the T.C. Williams School of Law at the University of Richmond. RJLSA is a program of the Jewish Community Center of Richmond and offers social, cultural, educational, and religious programs for the law students at UR. Programs include lunches, cookouts, guest speakers, an interfaith seder, and Thanksgiving dinner.

"In spite of the relatively small Jewish population at the University of Richmond, RJSA is an active group fully supported by the community. With monthly programs, the Jewish students have built up their own little Jewish community on campus."

Rebecca Kleinman, RJSA president, junior

UNIVERSITY OF VIRGINIA

Enrollment 18,000 (UG 12,000; GR 6,000)
Jewish 2,000

 University of Virginia Hillel
1824 University Circle
Charlottesville, VA 22903
(804) 295-4963
Fax: (804) 295-4909
E-mail: rabbijoe@bigfoot.com
Web: www.virginia.edu/~hillel/

Rabbi Joe Blair, Executive Director
TBA, Program Director
Donna Laskowski, Administrator
Laura Hinkes, Jewish Campus Service Corps Fellow

 Jewish Studies
More than 10 courses; a new undergraduate program in Judaic studies is currently being developed.

 Study in Israel
Semester and year abroad programs are available.

 Kosher Food
Hillel offers kosher meals on Friday nights and holidays. Full kosher-for-Passover meal service available at Hillel.

ON CAMPUS

The Hillel Jewish Center at the University of Virginia is the center of campus Jewish life and one of the oldest Hillels in the United States. The Hillel Center building, an architectural landmark built between 1913 and 1916, is a pleasant haven in Jefferson's academic village.

Social events, social justice activities, and coalition-building are all part of UVA Hillel's program. The Center's association of groups includes: Hillel Student Board, Greater Hillel Council, Jewish Law Students Association and Graduate/Medical Students Group, Task Force for Jewish Arts and Culture, Shalom Theatre Company, Israel Action Group, United Jewish Appeal, Kosher Cooking Cooperative, Jewish/African-American Relations, Charlottesville Institute for Jewish Studies, Conservative, Orthodox, Reform, and Progressive minyanim, Faculty Association, and Parents and Alumni Associations. Hillel works closely with the Judaic Studies program and plans activities that engage Jewish faculty members.

VIRGINIA COMMONWEALTH UNIVERSITY

Enrollment 16,400 (UG 9,800; GR 6,600)
Jewish 200

Richmond Jewish Students Association
5403 Monument Avenue
Jewish Community Center
Richmond, VA 23226
(804) 288-6091
E-mail: lbbjcc@aol.com

Lisa Brooke Looney, Director

 Jewish Studies
6 courses; minor.

 Study in Israel
Study Abroad in Israel.

 Kosher Food
Available on request.

ON CAMPUS

RJSA is a program of the Jewish Community Center of Richmond and offers social, cultural, educational, and religious programs for students at VCU. Such programs include home hospitality for the Jewish holidays, Passover programs, pizza parties, and speakers.

VIRGINIA POLYTECHNIC INSTITUTE AND STATE UNIVERSITY

Enrollment 24,000
Jewish 1000

Hillel at Virginia Tech
201 E. Roanoke Street
PO Box 708
Blacksburg, VA 24063
(540) 951-2060
E-mail: hillel@vt.edu
Web: www.vt.edu:10021/org/hillel/

Ellisha Greenhood, Hillel Advisor
Professor Brian Storrie, Faculty Advisor

 Jewish Studies
Minor in Judaic Studies.

 Study in Israel
Study abroad in Israel.

 Kosher Food
Vegetarian alternatives. Kosher food available in local stores.

ON CAMPUS

Activities for Jewish students at VPI are based in the Blacksburg Jewish Community Center. VPI has an active cultural and social program, including intramural sports, a spring retreat, and a graduate student group. The Department of Religion periodically hosts visiting faculty of special Jewish interest. Rabbi Margulis is in residence 2 weekends per month.

WASHINGTON AND LEE UNIVERSITY

Enrollment 1,900
Jewish 80

Hillel at Washington and Lee University
Department of Religion
Lexington, VA 24450
(540) 463-8788
Fax: (540) 463-8998
E-mail: marks.r@wlu.edu

Professor Richard Marks, Advisor

 Jewish Studies
5 courses; Judaic Studies scholarship is available.

 Study in Israel
Credit is accepted for study at Israeli universities.

ON CAMPUS

Jewish enrollment at Washington and Lee is increasing. Hillel organizes monthly Shabbat dinners at professors' homes, a student seder, High Holy Day services and carpools to local synagogues, and Sukkot, Hanukkah, and Purim activities. Annual Judaic Studies lectures and Jewish film series. The Jewish communities of Lexington, Staunton, and Roanoke actively support Hillel at Washington and Lee.

"Jewish student life at Washington and Lee varies according to the initiative of the student. We have a very small Jewish student population, so Jewish students must be self-motivated. Our Hillel is very well-funded, though, so we enjoy all sorts of luxuries, including dinners with speakers, use of university cars to get to services during the High Holy Days, kosher meals in the dining hall during Passover, and Shabbat dinners throughout the year. While it can be tough, with so few Jewish students, to get many people to come out to Jewish activities, the school is embarking on a plan to attract more Jewish students. The other students on campus are very open and accepting of Jews. For the most part, we just blend in like every other student."

Stephen Philipson, junior

UNIVERSITY OF PUGET SOUND

Enrollment 2,600
Jewish 50

Jewish Student Association
c/o Religious Life Office
University of Puget Sound
1500 N. Warner
Tacoma, WA 98416
(206) 564-7101
Fax: (206) 564-7103

Rabbi Richard Rosenthal, Advisor

 Jewish Studies
2 courses.

ON CAMPUS

The Jewish student group at Puget Sound meets periodically and offers annual campus seders for Passover.

UNIVERSITY OF WASHINGTON

Enrollment 29,500 (UG 20,500; GR 9,000)
Jewish 1,200

 University of Washington Hillel Foundation
4745—17th Avenue NE
Seattle, WA 98105
(206) 527-1997
Fax: (206) 527-1999
E-mail: hilleluw@halcyon.com
Web: www.halcyon.com/hilleluw/index.html

Rabbi Daniel E. Bridge, Director
Renee Cohen, Program Director
Stephanie Hader, Jewish Campus Service Corps Fellow

 Jewish Studies
40 courses; B.A. in Jewish Studies; M.A. in Middle Eastern or Near Eastern Languages and Civilization. The Jewish Studies Program has some 20 faculty, and offers the Stroum Lecture series and bi-weekly colloquium meetings. The Hazel D. Cole Fellowship in Jewish Studies may be used for either doctoral or postdoctoral research in Jewish history, religious studies, Hebrew literature, or contemporary Jewish Studies. Jewish Studies Program, Box 353650, University of Washington, Seattle, WA 98195-3650; (206) 543-6811; Fax: (206) 685-0668; eulenbrg@u.washington.edu.

 Study in Israel
Credit exchange agreement with Hebrew University. Opportunity to meet with shaliach and/or Hillel staff to explore additional options.

 Kosher Food
Hillel offers Friday evening meals, a Passover seder, and lunches. Hillel has a kosher kitchen and students are invited to enjoy leftovers from the many programs and/or make lunch with the staff. Kosher foods are also available at local grocery stores in the University district.

ON CAMPUS

Hillel offers a wide variety of social, educational, cultural, and religious programs tailored to popular student interest. (Please contact Hillel to request a current calendar of events.) Students are encouraged to be as active as they like: to come to just one event or serve on a Project Team of their choice, helping to plan and implement programming.

There are no longer any Jewish Greek houses on campus, although the Greek system is fairly large. Members of the fraternities and sororities, as well as dorm residents, have found Hillel to be a great place to meet other Jewish students. Hillel, through its Israel Cultural Group and the local AIPAC chapter, is coalition-building with other campus groups to encourage positive feelings toward Israel on campus. Hillel can be a place to study, meet friends, or check in with the rabbi and staff. There is limited exercise equipment, Asteroids, a pool table, and a newly updated Judaica library including 20 national magazines and newspapers. Come in to enjoy a free latte—this is Seattle, you know!

WASHINGTON STATE UNIVERSITY

Enrollment 17,000
Jewish 250–500

Jewish Student Organization
Compton Union Building
Washington State University
Pullman, WA 99164-6340
(509) 335-8327
(509) 332-7903
Fax: (509) 335-0880
E-mail: kahn@wsu.edu

Professor Michael L. Kahn, Advisor
Professor David Stiller, Advisor

 Jewish Studies
Informal with the adult group.

 Study in Israel
On a case-by-case basis.

Kosher Food
Vegetarian dining alternatives.

ON CAMPUS
Students get together for friendship and social activities, such as ski trips, movies, and Shabbat dinners. Activities at Washington State are generally held with students from the University of Idaho, 8 miles away, and the adult group, the Jewish Community of the Palouse.

WESTERN WASHINGTON UNIVERSITY

Enrollment 10,300 (UG 9,300; GR 1,000)
Jewish 200

Hillel at Western Washington University
V.U. 202 #A1
Bellingham, WA 98225
(360) 650-7356
(360) 733-3400
Fax: (360) 650-6507
E-mail: hillel@henson.cc.wwu.edu
Web: www.wwu.edu/~hillel

Rabbi Yossi Liebowitz, Rabbinical Advisor

Jewish Studies
History of the Jews, Holocaust Studies, and Religious Studies.

Study in Israel
Information is available.

Kosher Food
Available in the community.

ON CAMPUS
Western's Hillel is the center of Jewish campus life for all students. Hillel provides a variety of social, cultural, and religious activities such as: "Rapp'n with the Rabbi," weekly coffeehouse, Shabbat dinner and services, Israeli dancing, sports activities, an annual Passover seder, and much more. Hillel is located in the Shalom Center, directly across the street from the center of campus, and is open daily for relaxing and studying.

MARSHALL UNIVERSITY

Enrollment 12,000
Jewish 35

Jewish Student Group
PO Box 2311
Huntington, WV 25724
(304) 696-2960

Professor William Paynter, Advisor

ON CAMPUS
Small Jewish student group with focus on Israel programming.

WEST VIRGINIA UNIVERSITY

Enrollment 25,000
Jewish 700 (UG 625; GR 75)

Hillel at West Virginia University
1420 University Avenue
Morgantown, WV 26505
(304) 296-2660
E-mail: aegm29d@prodigy.com
Web: www.wvu.edu/~hillel/

Richard Gutmann, Director
Professor James Friedberg, Faculty Advisor
Amy Feinberg, Advisor
Linda Hausman, Advisor

Jewish Studies
The University offers several classes addressing Judaism, and the library has significant Judaica holdings.

Study in Israel
Students may study abroad in Israel. Credits are generally accepted.

Kosher Food
Kosher food is provided at each Shabbat dinner and at all holidays and some special programs. A vegetarian store is located next door to Hillel. Several restaurants offer vegetarian fare, as does the University at its residence dining halls. Kosher food is available in several local grocery stores.

ON CAMPUS
Morgantown and the campus community comprise a friendly, homogenous community devoid of anti-Semitic and Israel-Arab conflicts. Hillel sponsors a wonderfully acclaimed Yom HaShoah program during

Holocaust Remembrance Week and offers numerous popular social, educational, religious, and cultural programs designed to provide Jewish students the opportunity to interact with each other. Hillel sponsors a film series, discussion groups, guest speakers, and other events.

Students may be as active as they desire: They may actively plan and run events or they may merely attend. Although the Greek system is large, there are no longer any Jewish fraternities or sororities on campus. Hillel is a great place to meet other Jewish students. Hillel is conveniently located near campus, much of student housing, and public/university transportation.

Contact Hillel at the above address or telephone number for more information or if you desire a calendar of events.

WISCONSIN

BELOIT COLLEGE

Enrollment 1,100
Jewish 80-100

> Am Yisrael
> Beloit College Box 24
> Beloit, WI 53511
> (608) 363-2262
> (608) 363-2071
> Fax: (608) 363-2052
> E-mail: mikeyg@beloit.edu
>
> **Professor Michael Goldweber**, Advisor

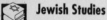 **Jewish Studies**

6 courses; B.A./Joint Program: University of Wisconsin—Madison.

 Study in Israel

Study Abroad at Tel Aviv and Hebrew Universities. The University offers a semester in Israel and Egypt for science students on problems of water sharing.

 Kosher Food

Holidays; occasional meals.

ON CAMPUS

Am Yisrael welcomes all who are interested in discovering and practicing Judaism on any level. Popular activities include a Yom Kippur Feast and Fast, a Hanukkah dinner, and a seder.

MARQUETTE UNIVERSITY

Enrollment 12,000
Jewish 120

> JSU-Hillel
> c/o Hillel Foundation of Milwaukee
> 3035 North Stowell Avenue
> Milwaukee, WI 53211
> (414) 961-2010
> Fax: (414) 961-7791
> E-mail: hillel@execpc.com
>
> **Andrea Hoffman**, Director

 Kosher Food

Marquette Kosher Lunch (MKL)—once a month.

ON CAMPUS

The Jewish Student Union at Marquette meets once a week for Schmooze with the Jews, and participates actively and regularly on campus. Marquette students participate in citywide programming based at UWM. JSU has an office in the Marquette University Ministry, Alumni Memorial Union, POB 1881. Students regularly participate in city-wide activities.

Marquette University is served by Hillel at the University of Wisconsin—Milwaukee.

UNIVERSITY OF WISCONSIN—MADISON

Enrollment 40,200 (UG 26,200; GR 14,000)
Jewish 4,500 (UG 3,000; GR 1,500)

> Hillel Foundation
> 611 Langdon Street
> Madison, WI 53703
> (608) 256-8361
> Fax: (608) 256-2451
> E-mail: stein@chorus.net
>
> **Greg Steinberger**, Director
> **TBA**, Program Director
> **Andrea Lerner**, Campus Rabbi
> **Julie Seltzer**, Jewish Campus Service Corps Fellow

Jewish Studies

43 courses; minor in Jewish Studies. The Center for Jewish Studies is an interdisciplinary program that includes 7 full-time faculty members and 12 part-time faculty who together teach approximately 2,000 students annually. The Center for Jewish Studies builds on the strength of the Department of Hebrew and Semitic Studies by drawing together faculty from across campus who offer courses crosslisted with such disciplines as English, French, German, Slavic studies, philosophy, anthropology, law, history, and music. The Department of Hebrew and Semitic Studies offers 65 courses, a B.A., an M.A., and a Ph.D., and administers an overseas pro-

gram at the Hebrew University in Jerusalem. Center for Jewish Studies, 308 Ingraham, 1155 Observatory Drive, Madison, WI 53706; (608) 265-4763.

Study in Israel
Most students attend Hebrew University Year Abroad; a few attend Tel Aviv and Haifa University programs.

Kosher Food
Weekly Shabbat dinners at Hillel, including vegetarian alternative; vegetarian alternatives in dining hall. Wednesday take-out available.

Housing
Ofek Shalom, Jewish cooperative, has room for 15-20 students.

ON CAMPUS
Madison Hillel is the center of Jewish campus activities for both undergraduates and graduates. Hillel serves as the foundation for 15 student groups that offer a variety of programs including social action projects, Israel programs, and social events. Hillel was instrumental in establishing the student advocacy group the Jewish Coalition, and the Jewish Task Force, a committee made up of faculty, students, university workers, and people from the community that works to protect the rights of Jewish students. Madison Hillel also created and maintains the nationally recognized Celebrate Difference Campaign, which has promoted positive intergroup relations at Wisconsin and on other campuses throughout the country.

Hillel is among the most active student organizations on campus, and is involved with many university-based groups, with Hillel students serving on several campus committees. Hillel works closely with other university groups to plan programs and to organize funding applications. There are 3 predominately Jewish fraternities and 2 predominately Jewish sororities on campus.

"Being Jewish at Wisconsin is a wonderful experience. The Jewish population is large and strong, and Hillel is particularly active. I immediately felt welcome and I had a ball, getting involved in whatever I could."

Sandra Krider, recent graduate

UNIVERSITY OF WISCONSIN—MILWAUKEE

Enrollment 25,000 (UG 11,100; GR 13,900)
Jewish 800

Hillel Foundation—Milwaukee
3035 North Stowell Avenue
Milwaukee, WI 53211
(414) 961-2010
(414) 961-1240
Fax: (414) 961-7791
E-mail: hillel@execpc.com
Web: www.execpc.com/~hillel

Andrea Hoffman, Director
Diane Boland, Program Director
Carmit Harari, Jewish Campus Service Corps Fellow

Jewish Studies
M.A. through Masters in Arts and Foreign Languages and Literature; Ph.D. through Comparative Literature program. Hebrew/Jewish Studies at UWM consist of 3 entities: Hebrew and Judaic Studies Program, Certificate Program in Jewish Studies, and a forthcoming Center for Jewish Studies. The Hebrew and Judaic Studies program offers modern and Biblical Hebrew in all levels, modern Hebrew literature, Holocaust literature, Hebrew drama, Hebrew Children's literature, Israeli film, The Bible as literature, Introduction to the Bible/Mishna/Talmud, Jewish Civilization in all historical periods, Women in the Bible, and The Dead Sea Scrolls. In addition, more than 85 courses relating to Jewish Studies are offered through the departments of history, philosophy, anthropology, sociology, political science, music, art history, film, visual arts, architecture, Holocaust Studies, philosophy of religion, and drama and theater. Professor Yair Mazor, University of Wisconsin—Milwaukee, Curtin Hall, PO Box 413, Milwaukee, WI 53201; (414) 229-5984/4433.

Study in Israel
At Hebrew University and Ber Zeit through the Political Science Department.

Kosher Food
Hillel offers Shabbat dinners every other week.

ON CAMPUS
Hillel at Milwaukee offers the full range of social, cultural, educational, and religious programming designed to serve its primarily commuter campus population. Activities include community leadership opportunities, a strong social action component, a mentor program, as well as a special trip, "Imagine Israel," for students who have never been to Israel. Milwaukee Hillel has a strong student leadership core. Milwaukee Hillel offers a special program for students from the former Soviet Union, which includes English-as-a-second-language courses for Russian immigrants. Professors often hold brown-bag breakfast meetings at Hillel.

UNIVERSITY OF WYOMING

Enrollment 11,000
Jewish 10

Jewish Students Organization
Campus Activities Center
University of Wyoming
Laramie, WY 82071
(307) 742-5161
(307) 766-3396
Fax: (307) 766-6771
E-mail: augies@uwyo.edu

Dr. Frederic D. Homer, Faculty Advisor

ON CAMPUS

The Jewish community of Laramie is quite small (about 100 people), but warm and welcoming to the few Jewish students on campus. The community holds a Passover seder, and Hannukah and Purim parties, and there are other gatherings as well. The Jewish Students Organization is funded by student fees, and the student government has been quite accommodating to JSO programs. However, according to a bill passed by the Student Senate, no religious activities (by any organization) may be held on campus. The University of Wyoming is very concerned about promoting diversity. Although there is no policy concerning students taking time off for Jewish holidays, students have not experienced problems in this area.

CANADA

ALBERTA

UNIVERSITY OF ALBERTA

Enrollment 30,000
Jewish 250

Hillel Jewish Students Association
Jewish Community Center
7200 156th Street
Edmonton, ALB T5R 2Z3
(403) 487-0585
Fax: (403) 481-1854
E-mail: ejfed@net.com.ca

Alissia Horwitz, Director

 Jewish Studies
3 courses in Hebrew; others in the Religious Studies Department.

 Study in Israel
One year abroad and summer programs.

Kosher Food
One kosher restaurant in Edmonton at the Jewish Community Centre.

ON CAMPUS

The University of Alberta has an increasingly active Jewish student community/Hillel with a full range of social, cultural, educational, and Israel programming. The student group meets regularly each month. Home-stays in the community are possible during the holidays.

The director at the University of Alberta also coordinates the program for Jewish students at Grant Macewan College, Alberta College, and Nait College.

UNIVERSITY OF CALGARY

Enrollment 20,000 (UG 16,000; GR 4,000)
Jewish 400 (UG 275; GR 125)

Jewish Students' Association of Calgary
c/o Calgary Jewish Center
1607 90th Avenue, SW
Calgary, ALB T2V 4V7
(403) 253-8600
Fax: (403) 253-7915

Stephen Shapiro, Director

BRITISH COLUMBIA

UNIVERSITY OF BRITISH COLUMBIA

Enrollment 30,000
Jewish 1,000

 Vancouver Hillel Foundation
Box 43 SUB
University of British Columbia
Vancouver, BC V6T 1Z1
(604) 224-4748
Fax: (604) 224-2512
E-mail: hillel@unixg.ubc.ca

Gabriel Meranda, Director
TBA, Program Director
TBA, Jewish Campus Service Corps Fellow

Jewish Studies
3 courses.

 Study in Israel
Credit available for study at Hebrew University and Tel-Aviv University.

 Kosher Food
Hillel offers a weekly hot vegetarian lunch, occasional dinner parties, and Oneg Shabbats. Kosher food is also locally available.

ON CAMPUS

A very popular feature of University of British Columbia's Hillel program are the Tuesday hot lunches. Hillel also offers a wide range of social, educational, and cultural programming for students and also for the numerous Israeli faculty on sabbatical in Vancouver. The University is very supportive of Jewish activities, and Hillel has an excellent relationship with the campus ministry.

Hillel, the Jewish center on campus at the University of British Columbia, also serves Simon Fraser University and Vancouver city colleges, with a very active Outreach program.

MANITOBA

UNIVERSITY OF MANITOBA

Enrollment 22,347 (UG 19,305; GR 3,042)
Jewish 549 (UG 500; GR 49)

Jewish Students' Association
370 Hargrave Street
Winnipeg, MB R3B 2K1
(204) 474-9325
Fax: (204) 956-0609
E-mail: herstein@cc.umanitoba.ca

Adam Herstein, Director

 Kosher Food
All JSA-sponsored programs are kosher.

ON CAMPUS

JSA at Manitoba holds an interfaith seder, and twice yearly Shabbat dinners, and has general social and political programming. Programs are planned jointly with the University of Winnipeg and other area schools.

UNIVERSITY OF WINNIPEG

Enrollment 5,000
Jewish 100

Jewish Students' Association
370 Hargrave Street
Lockhart Hall
Winnipeg, MB R3B 2K1
(204) 474-9325
Fax: (204) 956-0609
E-mail: herstein@cc.umanitoba.ca

Adam Herstein, Director

 Jewish Studies
3 courses.

Winnipeg's programs are held jointly with the University of Manitoba and other area schools.

NOVA SCOTIA

DALHOUSIE UNIVERSITY

Chaplaincy at Dalhousie University
c/o Rabbi Shlomo Grafstein
6136 University Avenue
Halifax, NS B3H 4J2
(902) 494-2287
Fax: (902) 494-6848

Rabbi Shlomo Z. Elazer Grafstein, Jewish Chaplain

ONTARIO

CARLETON UNIVERSITY

Enrollment 18,000
Jewish 400

Jewish Students Union—Hillel
559 King Edward, Room 102
Ottawa, ONT K1N 6N5
(613) 562-5800 ext. 3095
Fax: (613) 789-4593
E-mail: jsuottawa@cyberus.ca

Stacia Benovitch, Director
Ron Singer, Chair
Mitchell Bellman, Advisor

Jewish Studies
9 courses.

Kosher Food
Vegetarian dining alternatives.

ON CAMPUS

A wide variety of Jewish programming is offered throughout the academic year. The local community offers home hospitality and welcomes students to religious services.

MCMASTER UNIVERSITY

Enrollment 15,000
Jewish 300

McMaster Jewish Student Association
McMaster University
Commons Room B103
Hamilton, ONT L8S 4K1
(905) 522-7215
Fax: (905) 639-3769

Sheila Freedman, Advisor

Jewish Studies
2 courses; Joint Program: Maimonides.

Kosher Food
McMaster Hillel offers 1 lunch and holiday and occasional meals; vegetarian dining alternatives; dormitory cooking facilities. Kosher food is available locally.

ON CAMPUS

The community members and the Lubavitcher rabbi offer home hospitality for Shabbat and holidays, Passover, and Hanukkah lunches.

QUEEN'S UNIVERSITY

Enrollment 15,000
Jewish 500

Hillel House
124 Center Street
Kingston, ONT K7L 4E6
(613) 542-1120
Fax: (519) 545-6300

Jewish Studies
Queen's has a fairly new Jewish studies department in which one can take a variety of courses ranging from general surveys of Judaism through the ages to courses on Jewish mysticism, introductory Hebrew courses, and courses in Talmudic study. Currently one can minor in Jewish studies, and the program is expected to expand in the next few years to offer the option of a major.

Kosher Food
Kosher food can be ordered throughout the year from the Beth Israel synagogue. In addition, families open their homes to students for Pesach seders, and the Queen's cafeteria orders kosher-for-Passover food for students at Pesach.

ON CAMPUS

Queen's Hillel has a beautiful, spacious house located 5 minutes from campus. The house is used for many Hillel activities including Shabbat dinners, bagel brunches, and other get-togethers. Queen's Hillel generally holds at least 2 activities per month: dinners, parties, learning sessions, sporting events, etc.

In addition, students are often invited to Adult Education seminars, learning sessions, holiday celebrations, and dinners. The Jewish community in Kingston is very welcoming to the students and often invites students to Shabbat dinners and other celebrations in their homes.

UNIVERSITY OF OTTAWA

Enrollment 22,000
Jewish 350

Jewish Students Union—Hillel
559 King Edward, Room 102
Ottawa, ONT K1N 6N5
(613) 562-5800 ext. 3095
Fax: (613) 789-4593
E-mail: jsuottawa@cyberus.ca

Stacia Benovitch, Director
Ron Singer, Chair
Mitchell Bellman, Advisor

Jewish Studies
2 courses.

Kosher Food
Vegetarian dining alternatives.

ON CAMPUS

A wide variety of Jewish programming is offered throughout the academic year. The local community offers home hospitality and welcomes students to religious services.

UNIVERSITY OF TORONTO

Enrollment 37,000 (UG 25,000; GR 17,000)
Jewish 3,000 (UG 2,000; GR 1,000)

Jewish Students Union
15 King's College Circle
Toronto, ONT M5S 1A1
(416) 978-0421
(416) 978-0422
Fax: (416) 971-3085
E-mail: lance_davis@campuslife.utoronto.ca
Web: www.campuslife.utoronto.ca/groups/jsu/

Lance Davis, Programme Director

 Jewish Studies
60 courses; B.A., M.A., Ph.D.

 Kosher Food
Diablo's campus café is located next to the JSU.
Serves kosher muffins, bagels, pastries, etc.

ON CAMPUS

The Jewish Students' Union House serves as a drop-in center on campus for a broad range of social, cultural, political action, social action, religious, and educational programs. Programs are offered on campus as well as throughout Greater Toronto. JSU is the umbrella for fifteen active committees, including Israel Affairs, Holocaust Education, United Jewish Appeal, and Environmental Action. The Jewish Students' Union offers students a gateway to explore and experience any facet of Judaism in a pluralistic and accepting environment. The JSU also organizes citywide programs with the other Jewish student groups in Toronto.

"Our university is huge and it's easy to get lost. The campus is very spaced out, so the JSU moved to a more central location. Jewish campus activities are pretty strong, especially some of the intergroup programs. There was a joint soup kitchen with a church, and many Hillel members volunteered."

Fran Rothenberg, senior

"In the coming year, I would like to see more people come out to enjoy social events, learning, the Sabbath or any other activity which makes a person Jewish. Professors could become much more active to help students learn what it means to be Jewish."

Jonathan Friedman, senior

UT is part of Jewish Campus Services of Greater Toronto, which also serves Jewish students at York University, Ryerson University, and Seneca College. Executive Director, Rabbi Zac Kaye; Coordinator of Citywide Engagement Programs, Barbara Friedman; Program Coordinator for Ryerson and Seneca,

Stephanie Wener; 3101 Bathurst St., Suite 401, North York, ON M6A 2A6; (416) 785-1465; Fax: (416) 785-8271; zkaye@yorku.ca.

UNIVERSITY OF WATERLOO

Enrollment 26,121 (UG 24,049; GR 2,072)
Jewish 300

WJSA—Hillel
Campus Center Room 235
Waterloo, ONT N2L 3G1
(519) 885-1211
(519) 743-8422
E-mail: jewish@calum.csclu.uwaterloo.ca

Laurent Mydlarski, Advisor
Eric Golombek, Advisor
Michael Heitner, Advisor
Shi Sherabin, Advisor

UNIVERSITY OF WESTERN ONTARIO

Enrollment 25,000 (UG 23,000; GR 2,000)
Jewish 3,000 (UG 2,600; GR 400)

Jewish Students' Union
University Community Centre, Room 312
University of Western Ontario
536 Huron Street
London, ONT N6A 3K7
(519) 679-2111, ext. 2634
Fax: (519) 673-1161
E-mail: jsu@julian.uwo.ca
Web: www.usc.uwo.ca/clubs/jsu

Professor David Keypour, Advisor

 Jewish Studies
4 courses available at Huron College.

 Kosher Food
Arrangements can be made with Food Services for kosher food in dormitories throughout the year and at High Holiday time. Shabbat meals are organized by Hillel and by Chabad. Kosher food is locally available.

ON CAMPUS

The Jewish Students' Union provides a pluralistic and welcoming environment on campus. The JSU is composed of 15 active chairs that make up the Union executive. They divide their concern for all phases of Jewish student life and include a group for graduate students as well as undergraduates. Jewish students at Western Ontario work in collaboration with students on other campuses, and participate in regional and national activities. The university now has a very extensive Holocaust Literature Research Institute in the middle of campus. There are 2 predominantly Jewish fraternities on campus. The local community provides home hospitality for Shabbat and holidays.

UNIVERSITY OF WINDSOR

Jewish 225

Hillel
c/o Windsor Jewish Community Center
1641 Ouellette Avenue
Windsor, ONT N8X 1K9
(519) 973-1772
Fax: (519) 973-1774

Rabbi Garson Herzfeld, Advisor
Vivian Herzenberg, Advisor

 ### Jewish Studies
4 courses.

 ### Kosher Food
WJCC; frozen, on request.

ON CAMPUS

Holiday celebrations, Erev Shabbat dinners, lectures, discussions, and social events for students are held either on campus or at the WJCC throughout the academic year. Events at Wayne State University and University of Michigan Hillels are open and easily accessible to University of Windsor students. CJF Canada provides some subsidies for Jewish students to network with other Canadian Jewish students at regional and national gatherings. The local Jewish community provides home hospitality for Shabbat and holidays.

YORK UNIVERSITY

Enrollment 42,000
Jewish 4,000

Jewish Student Federation of York University
Room 442, Student Centre
4700 Keele Street
Willowdale, ONT M3J 1P3
(416) 736-5178
(416) 736-5179
Fax: (416) 736-5102
E-mail: pgropper@yorku.ca
Web: www.yucc.yorku.ca/~jsf

Pearl Gropper, Director
Rabbi Michael Skobac, Director of Jewish Educational
  Programming

 ### Jewish Studies
Centre for Jewish Studies offers a B.A. in Religious Studies (Jewish Studies Stream), a combined B.A.-B.Ed. program in Jewish Teacher Education (2 degrees, certification in both Jewish and general studies), and a certificate program in Hebrew and Jewish Studies.

 ### Study in Israel
Exchange program with Hebrew University; York scholarships are available for study in Israel.

Kosher Food
Kosher deli on campus.

ON CAMPUS

Although York is largely a commuter school, the dormitories, a kosher restaurant, and a range of Jewish activities make York a very "Jewish friendly" environment. From its lounge and office, the Jewish Student Federation runs a full program, including well-attended dances, an active student newspaper, and a variety of social and community action programs. The University cancels classes for Rosh Hashanah, Yom Kippur, and the first days of Passover.

The University is located about a half-hour drive from Toronto's major Jewish population center, with a JCC, synagogues, sports facilities, and other resources. Toronto's Jewish community is large (about 150,000) and supportive of Jewish campus activities, and provides home hospitality for holidays.

"There is a relaxed and comfortable place for a Jewish students at York. We are a commuter campus which makes it harder to become involved here. Our campus is very liberal. This year, we are working on more intergroup relations."

Teri Rothenberg, senior

York Hillel is part of Jewish Campus Services of Greater Toronto, which also serves Jewish students at the University of Toronto, Ryerson University, and Seneca College. Executive Director, Rabbi Zac Kaye; Coordinator of Citywide Engagement Programs, Barbara Friedman; Program Coordinator for Ryerson and Seneca, Stephanie Wener; 3101 Bathurst St., Suite 401, North York, ON M6A 2A6; (416) 785-1465; Fax: (416) 785-8271; zkaye@yorku.ca.

QUEBEC

CEGEP ST. LAURENT

Jewish 80

Centre Hillel
5325 Gatineau Avenue
Montreal, QUE H3T 1X1
(514) 738-2655
(514) 845-9171
Fax: (514) 738-1684

Avi Krispine, Program Director

CEGEP St. Laurent is served by the Hillel Foundation of Montreal, 3460 Stanley Street, Montreal, Quebec H3A 1R8, Canada. See listing for Université de Montréal.

CONCORDIA UNIVERSITY—SIR GEORGE AND LOYOLA CAMPUSES

Enrollment 20,000
Jewish 700

Concordia Hillel
2020 McKay Street P-205
Montreal, QUE H3G 2J1
(514) 848-7487
Fax: (514) 842-6405

Steve Spodek, Director, Hillel of Montreal
Joelle Elbaz, Program Director

 Jewish Studies

39 courses; interdisciplinary. B.A., M.A. in Judaic Studies; Ph.D. in Religion with JS concentration. Judaic Studies is an integrated program within the Department of Religion. Courses range from Jewish History, Jewish Thought, and Jewish Law to issues of contemporary concern such as Religion and State, Identity Construction, and gender topics. A Chair is being established in Quebec and Canadian Jewish History. Conferences, colloquia, and activities are offered annually. Michael Oppenheim, Chair, Judaic Studies, Department of Religion, 1455 de Maisonneuve West, Montreal, QUE H3M 1G8; (514) 848-2065; nojo@vax2.concordia.ca; Web: artsci-ccwin.concordia.ca/religion/reli.html.

 Kosher Food

Sandwiches and pastries in cafeteria; meals available at McGill Hillel.

Housing

At kosher student residence at McGill University.

ON CAMPUS

Concordia is an urban school with few dormitory facilities. Many student activities are in conjunction with McGill Hillel, which is within walking distance.

Concordia is served by the B'nai B'rith Hillel Foundations of Montreal, 3460 Stanley Street, Montreal, QUE H3A 1R8.

DAWSON (CEGEP) COLLEGE

Enrollment 8,000
Jewish 800

Dawson Hillel, 2C.3
Dawson College
3040 Sherbrooke Street West
Montreal, QUE H3Z 1A4
(514) 931-8731 ext. 1107
(514) 845-9171
Fax: (514) 842-6405
E-mail: steve@vir.com

Steven Spodek, Director, Hillel of Montreal
Sharon Tansky, Program Director

 Jewish Studies
12 courses.

 Study in Israel
Credit courses in Israel.

 Kosher Food
Served at McGill Hillel.

 Housing
At kosher student residence at McGill Hillel.

Dawson CEGEP is served by the B'nai B'rith Hillel Foundation of Montreal, 3460 Stanley Street, Montreal QUE H3A 1R8. See listing for McGill University.

JOHN ABBOTT COLLEGE

Enrollment 5,000
Jewish 150

Hillel
c/o SUJAC
21275 Lakeshore Road
St. Anne de Bellevue, QUE H9X 3L9
(514) 845-9171

Joelle Elbaz, Program Director
Steven Spodek, Director, Hillel of Montreal

John Abbot College is served as an extension program of McGill Hillel. See listing for McGill University.

MARIANOPOLIS (CEGEP) COLLEGE

Enrollment 1,650
Jewish 400

Hillel Extension
3460 Stanley Street
Montreal, QUE H3A 1R8
(514) 931-8792 ext. 294
(514) 845-9171
Fax: (514) 842-6405
E-mail: steve@vir.com
Web: www.vir.com/shalom/zionet.html

Steven Spodek, Director, Hillel of Montreal
Sharon Tansky, Program Director

 Kosher Food
Served by McGill University Hillel.

 Housing
Available at McGill Hillel House.

Marianopolis CEGEP is served by the B'nai B'rith Hillel Foundation of Montreal at McGill.

MCGILL UNIVERSITY

Enrollment 18,000
Jewish 3,500

Hillel Foundation
3460 Stanley Street
Montreal, QUE H3A 1R8
(514) 845-9171
Fax: (514) 842-6405
E-mail: steve@vir.com
Web: www.vir.com/shalom/zionet.html

Luni Bendayan, Director
Jodi Goroff, Jewish Campus Service Corps Fellow

Jewish Studies
50 courses; B.A., M.A., Ph.D., Jewish Teacher Training Program.

Study in Israel
McGill has strong junior year abroad programs in cooperation with all major Israeli universities.

Kosher Food
Hillel's kosher cafeteria offers daily lunch and dinner. Hillel holds a bi-weekly Shabbat dinner. Vegetarian dining alternatives.

 Housing
Kosher student residence in the Stanley Building.

ON CAMPUS

McGill Hillel is housed in a beautiful old Victorian mansion close to campus. It is the center of programming for Jewish students throughout the campus and throughout the metropolitan area, including a full range of cultural, social, and religious events such as Israel advocacy and MIPAC; an annual Human Rights lecture series; a Jewish Women's Circle; and fundraising for the local Jewish community and for Israel.

"McGill has a strong Jewish community both on campus and as part of the Montreal community. It is a very comfortable place and a good place for Jewish students. Jewish events with political, educational or religious themes are 'hot' on campus. The administration and academics are very supportive of campus Jewish life."

Amy Shore, junior

McGill Hillel is the center of services for Jewish students at Concordia, the Montreal CEGEPs, the Université de Montréal, and the Université du Quebec à Montréal. McGill Hillel is a service of the B'nai B'rith Hillel Foundation of Montreal.

UNIVERSITÉ DE MONTRÉAL

Jewish 500

Centre Hillel
5325 Gatineau Avenue
Montreal, QUE H3T 1X2
(514) 738-2655
(514) 845-9171
Fax: (514) 738-1684

Joseph Muyal, Director
Avi Krispine, Program Director

 Kosher Food
Kosher cafeteria 11 a.m.–8 p.m. (closed Shabbat).

ON CAMPUS

Centre Hillel provides strong summer and winter social programming for students at the Université de Montréal, the Université du Quebec à Montréal, and CEGEPs at the house near campus, as well as French-language speakers and other events for the entire Jewish and non-Jewish university community. Centre Hillel serves a large Sephardic Jewish campus population at these commuter schools.

Université de Montréal is served by the B'nai B'rith Hillel Foundation of Montreal, 3460 Stanley Street, Montreal, QUE, H3A 1R8.

UNIVERSITÉ DU QUEBEC À MONTRÉAL

Jewish 50

Centre Hillel
5325 Gatineau Avenue
Montreal, QUE H3T 1X1
(514) 738-2655
(514) 845-9171
Fax: (514) 738-1684

Joseph Muyal, Director
Avi Krispine, Program Director

See listing for Université de Montréal.

VANIER (CEGEP) COLLEGE

Enrollment 5,000
Jewish 500

Hillel Vanier
820 St. Croix Boulevard
Montreal, QUE H4L 3X9
(514) 845-9171
Fax: (514) 842-6405
Web: www.vir.com/shalom/zionet.html

Avi Krispine, Program Director

 Kosher Food
Available in the cafeteria.

Vanier College is served by the B'nai B'rith Hillel Foundation of Montreal, 3460 Stanley Street, QUE H3A 1R8.

SASKATCHEWAN

UNIVERSITY OF SASKATCHEWAN

Enrollment 19,000
Jewish 80

Jewish Students' Association of Saskatoon
715 McKinnon Avenue South
Saskatoon, Saskatchewan S7H 2G2
(306) 343-7023
Fax: (306) 343-1244
E-mail: tmr@jon.cjf.org

Sarah Floyd, Director

 Jewish Studies
Religious Studies program at the University includes courses relating to Judaism.

ISRAEL

BAR ILAN UNIVERSITY

Enrollment 21,000

Bar Ilan University
91 Fifth Avenue, Suite 200
New York, NY 10003
(212) 337-1286
Fax: (212) 337-1274
E-mail: tobiu@village.ios.com
Web: www.roxcorp.com/barilan

Robert Katz, Director of Academic Affairs

ON CAMPUS

Situated in Ramat Gan, Bar Ilan is Israel's third-largest university. Students are invited to participate in all regular as well as these special programs: the Junior Year (or Semester) of Jewish Heritage; the first-year "Tochnit Achat"; and the 1-year MBA in English. All programs blend academic excellence and a strong focus on Jewish heritage exploration. Bar Ilan is fully accredited by the New York State Board of Regents.

BEN-GURION UNIVERSITY OF THE NEGEV

Enrollment 11,000
Jewish 9,500 (Overseas Student Program, 65)

Overseas Student Program
Ben-Gurion University of the Negev
PO Box 653
Beer-Sheva, 84105
(972) (7) 461-144
Fax: (972) (7) 3-472-948
E-mail: osp@bgumail.bgu.ac.il

Professor Mark Gelber, Director, Overseas Student Program

 Jewish Studies
Complete program in history, literature, and Bible for English-speaking students.

 Kosher Food
Available on campus.

 Housing
Students in the Overseas Programs share BGU dorm apartments with Israeli roommates.

ON CAMPUS

Ben-Gurion University's Overseas Student Program provides a unique and challenging semester or year abroad for undergraduate and graduate students. Located in Beer-Sheva, BGU offers the opportunity to live with Israelis in student dorms, learn Hebrew, and be truly immersed in Israeli culture and society. Students can participate in community-based or academic internships in a wide range of fields, or conduct their own independent research with BGU faculty members. Courses are taught in English in several areas such as Environmental Studies, Archaeology, Anthropology, History, Judaic Studies, and Political Science. The academic side of the program is supplemented by exciting touring trips throughout Israel, extracurricular activities, a kibbutz stay, and an archaeological dig. Need-based scholarships and Hillel Leadership Scholarships are available.

North American Office: Ben-Gurion University of the Negev, Overseas Student Program, 342 Madison Avenue, Suite 1224, New York, NY 10173; (212) 687-7721; Fax: (212) 370-0805; BGUOSP@haven.ios.com. Caroline Fox, Associate Director; Samanta Feiner, Admissions Officer.

HAIFA UNIVERSITY

Enrollment 12,500 (UG 10,500; GR 2,000)
Jewish 10,000

> Haifa University Hillel Foundation
> Haifa University
> Haifa, 34481
> (972) (04) 8240-762
> (972) (04) 8240-684
> Fax: (972) (04) 8260-334
>
> **Rabbi Bernard Och**, Director

Kosher Food

All University cafeterias are kosher and there are dormitory cooking facilities.

ON CAMPUS

Hillel is the center for cultural and social activities for students at Haifa University. Numerous activities deal with the many social and ideological problems facing Israeli society. Hillel also provides a program for the integration of Russian and Ethiopian students in Haifa. Haifa's accredited overseas program includes a kibbutz-university semester and an option for internships.

North American Office: Fran Yacoubov, Director, Friends of Haifa University, 1110 Finch Avenue West, Suite #510, Downsview, ONT M3J 2T2; (800) 388-2134, Fax: (416) 665-4468.

HEBREW UNION COLLEGE— JEWISH INSTITUTE OF RELIGION

13 King David Street
Jerusalem 94101
(972) (02) 6203-333
Fax: (972) (02) 6225-1478

Dr. Michael Klein, Dean

ON CAMPUS

The five-acre Jerusalem campus is the center for the Israel Progressive Movement; Jewish liberal study and the study of the American Jewish experience for Israelis; and North American Reform Movement youth programs in Israel. HUC-JIR educates Israeli students for rabbinic ordination to serve the Israel Progressive Movement and provides first-year training for rabbinical, cantorial, educational, and specialized Jewish communal service students from the American campuses; teacher training programs for Israeli educators and professional communal leadership training programs for Russian immigrants; postgraduate studies in Bible, archaeology, and the history of ancient Israel; archaeological excavations; ulpan courses for new immigrants; and cultural programs for the Jerusalem community.

See listing for HUC-JIR's other campuses in the section "Rabbinical Schools and Specialized Educational programs."

HEBREW UNIVERSITY

Enrollment 23,000 (UG 16,000; GR 7,000)
Jewish 18,000

> Beit Hillel
> Hebrew University
> Mt. Scopus Campus
> Jerusalem, 91905
> (972) (02) 5882-483
> (972) (02) 5817-714
> Fax: (972) (02) 5811-140
> E-mail: msjoseph@pluto.mscc.huji.ac.il;
> mseast@pluto.mscc.huji.ac.il
>
> **Rabbi Yossie Goldman**, Director
> **Esther Abramowitz**, Assistant Director
> **Eli Bareket**, Program Director, Hebrew Language Program
> **Cindy Friedman**, Jewish Campus Service Corps Fellow

Jewish Studies

Rothberg School for Overseas Students: Freshman Year Program, One Year Program (including Pre-Med Specialization), Graduate Year Program, and summer courses in English. Emphasis is on Jewish, Israel, and Middle East studies, with courses also in business, science, environmental studies, and other fields. Opportunities are available for internships, independent study, and, on the graduate level, research tutorials. Many options for Hebrew language study, plus courses in Biblical Hebrew, Yiddish, and Arabic. Summer offerings have included: workshop for journalists, Jerusalem video workshop, archaeological digs, and marine science in the gulf of Eilat. All programs are complemented by extracurricular activities, seminars, and trips. Contact the North American Office (below).

Hillel, in conjunction with UJA and Hebrew University, offers 2 academically accredited courses about North America and World Jewry, entitled Sociology of American Jewry, and The History of the Jews in the Former Soviet Union from 1917 to the Present.

Kosher Food

The university offers several kosher cafeterias, vegetarian dining alternatives, and dormitory cooking facilities.

ON CAMPUS

Hillel offers a range of programs designed to welcome the visiting student and integrate him or her into college life and Israeli society. The Hillel Theater Workshop produces a play every semester, bringing together students from a variety of backgrounds. The Hillel Orchestra performs 3 concerts annually involving students, faculty, and new immigrants. Hillel's Hiking Club for Israeli and overseas students offers weekend trips and extended visits to all parts of Israel. Hillel also sponsors weekly lectures on current issues in Hebrew and in English. Hillel sponsors an Arab-Jewish Project and an award-winning Students for Social Action Project, and offers special mini-courses such as aerobics and yoga. Jewish learning opportunities are available for both Israeli and overseas students. Special programs for overseas students include home hospitality, volunteer internships, trips, movie nights, and holiday programming. Counseling is also available at Hillel.

Students who have been accepted to the One Year Program at Hebrew University can apply for Hillel Leadership Scholarships through their local Hillels.

The Hillel Foundation at Hebrew University serves as the center for supervision and training for the new Hillels in the former Soviet Union. Rabbi Yossie Goldman, Hillel International Vice President and Director of Israel and the Former Soviet Union, and Rabbi David Ebstein, Special Assistant for Projects in the Former Soviet Union, supervise these programs.

North American Office: Judith Silverman, Director, Hebrew University of Jerusalem, Office of Academic Affairs, 11 East 69th Street, New York, NY 10021; (800) 404-8622; (212) 472-2288; Fax: (212) 517-4548; 74542.340@compuserve.com; Web: www2.huji.ac.il.www_sfos/top.html.

TECHNION — ISRAEL INSTITUTE OF TECHNOLOGY

Enrollment 11,000 (UG 9,000; GR 2,000)
Jewish 10,000

> Haifa University Hillel Foundation
> Haifa University
> Haifa 34481
> (972) (04) 8240-762
> (972) (04) 8240-684
> Fax: (972) (04) 8260-334
>
> **Rabbi Bernard Och**, Director

Kosher Food

All University cafeterias are kosher and there are dormitory cooking facilities.

ON CAMPUS

Hillel is the center for cultural and social activities for students at Technion. Numerous activities deal with the many social and ideological problems facing Israeli society. Hillel also provides a program to integrate Russian and Ethiopian students in Haifa. At Technion, there are undergraduate year or semester programs offered in English in Industrial Engineering and Management. Graduate programs are also available.

Registration and Admissions Center: Technion City, Haifa, 32000 Israel; Brouria Tamir, Director, Undergraduate Studies, (972) 4 293-306; Fax: (972) 4 221-581; Rodika Levy, Director, Graduate Studies, (972) 4 292-573; Fax: (972) 4 221-600.

North American Development Office: 810 7th Avenue, 24th Floor, New York, NY 10019; (212) 262-6200.

TEL AVIV UNIVERSITY

Enrollment 26,000
Overseas Student Program 500 students annually

> The Ellin H. Mitchell Hillel Program
> Tel Aviv University
> Student Dormitory, Building G5
> Ramat Aviv, 69978
> (972) (03) 640-7961
> Fax: (972) (03) 640-9582
>
> **Shmuel Bowman**, Director

Jewish Studies

North American students can apply to the Lowy School for Overseas Students for a year, semester, or summer programs. Intensive Hebrew language instruction (Ulpan) is offered prior to the start of each semester, at a range of proficiencies. Middle Eastern Studies: M.A. Conducted under the auspices of the Moshe Dayan

Center for Middle Eastern and African Studies, in cooperation with the Lowy School for Overseas Students. Designed for English-speaking students, it is 2 years in length. Sackler School of Medicine—New York/American Program: 4-year M.D. program for Americans and Canadians. Taught in English, the curriculum is equivalent to that of U.S. medical schools. New York State accredited.

University-sponsored touring is a mandatory part of the Lowy School for Overseas Students, and 3 or 4 weekend seminars on political and social issues are held outside the campus in varied settings throughout the country.

Kosher Food
The university is home to 15 cafeterias (meat and vegetarian) and coffee shops (all kosher), including the Apropos cafe and a Chinese restaurant, all offering reduced prices for students. Every 2 dorm suites features a small kitchen and a dining area for in-house preparation.

ON CAMPUS
Utilizing halls, gardens, and an outdoor amphitheater, in addition to its centrally located office and lounge, Hillel is an integral part of campus life. Hillel works closely with the Office for Student Programming to create opportunities for students to gain a broad Israel experience and to interact with Israelis. Through volunteer internships, home hospitality, lectures, and special programs for the holidays, students encounter Israeli society, current issues, and Jewish life in Israel. Hillel offers leadership seminars and coordinates field placement work in conjunction with selected courses. The Hillel Theater Troupe, open to all students, produces 1 play a year.

Classes are scheduled for a 4-day week to permit time for travel. All of Tel Aviv University's extensive sports facilities are open to overseas students, including 3 pools (1 Olympic-sized), tennis courts, track, soccer, and fitness rooms. The OSP social activities include events throughout the week, hiking, movies, and special lectures. A 1-day trip to Jerusalem and 2 3-day trips to the Galilee/Golan Heights and Negev Desert are arranged by the OSP counselors. Tel Aviv University is a half-hour bus ride from downtown Tel Aviv, the Carmel market (shuk), the ancient port city of Jaffa, and the beaches of the Mediterranean Sea.

North American Office: Moshe Margolin, Director, Friends of Tel Aviv University, Office of Academic Affairs, 360 Lexington Avenue, 3rd Floor, New York, NY 10017; (212) 557-5820; Fax: (212) 687-4085.

WEITZMANN INSTITUTE OF SCIENCE

The Feinberg Graduate School of the Weizmann Institute of Science
Rehovot, 76100
(212) 779-2500
Fax: (972) (8) 9344114
E-mail: nfinfo@weizmann.weizmann.ac.il
Web: www.weizman.ac.il/feinberg

Batya Kfir, Assistant to the Dean
Diane Sarnoff, Coordinator of Special Projects

ON CAMPUS
The Feinberg Graduate School, located on the campus of the Weizmann Institute in Rehovot, accepts applications from students holding undergraduate degrees in the Natural and Exact Sciences who wish to pursue M.Sc. or Ph.D. degrees. Courses include Mathematics and Computer Science, Physics, Life Sciences, Chemistry, Geosciences, and Science Teaching. Financial aid is also available to all students.

M.Sc. studies begin in October and last up to 2 years. Courses are held in English. Registration for Ph.D. studies is open throughout the year to students holding a M.Sc. or M.D. degree. The Feinberg Graduate School is accredited by the New York State Board of Regents.

North American Office: American Committee for the Weizmann Institute of Science, 51 Madison Avenue, Suite 117, New York, NY 10010; (212) 779-2500; Fax: (212) 779-3209.

ADDITIONAL OPPORTUNITIES FOR STUDY IN ISRAEL

Information about other programs in Israel is available through the University Students Department of the World Zionist Organization, 110 East 59th Street, Third Floor, New York, NY 10022; (800) 27-ISRAEL.

OTHER PARTS OF THE WORLD

ARGENTINA

BUENOS AIRES

Jewish 15,000

B'nai B'rith Hillel
Juncal 2573
Buenos Aires, 1425
(54) (1) 824-4625
(54) (1) 826-6802
Fax: (54) (1) 824-3821

Jorge Burkman, District Director
Julio Schuchner, Chair, Hillel Department

ON CAMPUS

Hillel in Buenos Aires offers a comprehensive social and cultural program for all Jewish students in the metropolitan area. Students, who commute to college throughout the area, meet at the Hillel House.

AUSTRALIA

MONASH UNIVERSITY

Enrollment 18,000 (UG 12,000; GR 6,000)
Jewish 1,100

Hillel Foundation of Victoria
306 Hawthorn Road
Caulfield South
Victoria, 3162
(61) (03) 9272 5621
(61) (03) 9272 5624
Fax: (61) (03) 9272 5540
Web: www-mugc.cc.monash.edu.au/~rebhersh/hillel/
index.html

TBA, Director
Dani Gostin, Programming Staff
Cheryl Blankfield, Programming Staff

Jewish Studies
Chair of Jewish Civilization, Holocaust, and Jewish History units.

Kosher Food
Kosher sandwiches; vegetarian dining alternatives.

ON CAMPUS

Monash University is a 15-minute car ride from major Jewish centers. Students are very active on campus and in the community.

UNIVERSITY OF MELBOURNE

Enrollment 16,000 (UG 12,000; GR 4,000)
Jewish 400

Hillel Foundation of Victoria
306 Hawthorn Road
Caulfield South
Victoria, 3162
(61) (03) 9272 5621
(61) (03) 9272 5624
Fax: (61) (03) 9272 5540

TBA, Director
Dani Gostin, Programming Staff
Cheryl Blankfield, Programming Staff

Jewish Studies
3 courses; Hebrew, Jewish History.

Kosher Food
Kosher sandwiches; vegetarian dining alternatives.

ON CAMPUS

University of Melbourne students are active on campus and in the community.

UNIVERSITY OF NEW SOUTH WALES

Enrollment 25,000
Jewish 800

Hillel Foundation of New South Wales
Shalom College
Sydney
New South Wales, 2052
(61) (2) 9663-1366
Fax: (61) (2) 9313-7145
E-mail: hilleloz@magna.com.au

Dr. Hilton Immerman, Executive Director
Elena Rosin, Director, Community Affairs
Jeremy Hayman, Director, Student Affairs

Jewish Studies

Holocaust Studies, Jewish history, Arab-Israeli relations, Talmudic Law, and other Jewish Studies courses.

Kosher Food

Shalom College offers full board, 7 days a week, including vegetarian dining alternatives.

Housing

Jewish Residence: Shalom College, run by Hillel.

ON CAMPUS

U.S. Study Abroad Students: Hillel's Jewish residential college, Shalom College, is available to foreign students. Located on campus in Sydney at Australia's largest university, Shalom College is an ideal way of meeting and making friends with Australian students. Hillel also welcomes overseas students and faculty for kosher meals at Shalom College. The local Jewish community is very friendly and helpful.

The Hillel Foundation of New South Wales also serves Jewish university students throughout the Sydney area, at the following schools: University of Sydney, University of Newcastle, Macquarie University, University of New England, University of Technology, University of Western Sydney, and other tertiary technical institutions.

UNIVERSITY OF SYDNEY

Enrollment 19,000
Jewish 300

B'nai B'rith Hillel Foundation
Shalom College
New South Wales, 2033
(61) (2) 9663-1366
Fax: (61) (2) 9313-7145
E-mail: hilleloz@magna.com.au

Dr. Hilton Immerman, Executive Director
Elena Rosin, Director, Community Affairs
Jeremy Hayman, Director, Student Affairs

Jewish Studies

Hebrew, Biblical Studies, Jewish Civilization, Thought and Culture.

Kosher Food

Available at University of New South Wales, 20 minutes away.

Housing

Mandelbaum House.

See listing for University of New South Wales.

VIENNA

Jewish Community of Vienna
Seitenstettengasse 4
Vienna, 1010
(43) (1) 531 04 0
Fax: (43) (1) 533 15 77

Chaim Eisenberg, Chief Rabbi
Dr. Avshalom Hodik, Director

Jewish Studies

Offered at the Universities of Vienna and Graz.

Kosher Food

Available at local restaurant, Arche Noah, Seitestettengasse 2, 1010 Vienna (43 1 533 13 74). There are also 2 kosher shops (Hollandstrasse 10 and Ferdinandstrasse 2).

ON CAMPUS

Nearby in Vienna is the Simon Wiesenthal Documentation Center. People interested in visiting the Center should call first. It is located at Salztorgasse 6, 1010 Vienna (43 1 533 91 31). There is also the Jewish Museum of the City of Vienna, located at Dorotheergasse 11, 1010 Vienna (43 1 535 0431). The Union of Jewish Students is active in Vienna and headquartered at Wahringer Strasse 24, 1090 Vienna.

BELGIUM

BRUSSELS

European Union of Jewish Students
89, Chaussee de Vieurgat
1050 Brussels

Gideon Simon, Chair

BULGARIA

SOFIA

UJSYB
50 Stamsolijski Boulevard
Sofia, 1003
(35) (92) 717-544
(35) (92) 583-005

Solomon Bally, Advisor

CHILE

SANTIAGO

Jewish 1,000

B'nai B'rith International—Hillel
Avda Ricardo Lyon 1933
Santiago, Chile
(56) (2) 223-66-80
Fax: (56) (2) 225-20-39

Ram Tapia Adler, District Director

ON CAMPUS

Jewish students from throughout the Santiago area meet weekly on B'nai B'rith premises for social and cultural events. This program is sponsored and coordinated by B'nai B'rith District 27–Chile.

THE CZECH REPUBLIC

PRAGUE

Bejt Praha/The Open Prague Jewish Community
PO Box 195
Praha 1, Czech Republic
(42 2) 24 81 41 62
Fax: (42 2) 24 81 41 64

TBA, Director
Peter Gyori, Program Director
Renata Kabiljo, Assistant Program Director

Kosher Food
Kosher food is served daily at lunchtime and on Shabbat at the Czech Jewish Community Town Hall in the Old Jewish Town, Maislova 18, Prague 1. There is also a shop nearby with kosher food.

ON CAMPUS

All Jewish holidays are celebrated, and an Israeli folk dancing group meets each Thursday from 6:30 to 8:30 p.m. at Hastalska 20. Both advanced and beginners are welcome.

FRANCE

PARIS

UEJF—Union des Etudiants Juifs de France
27 ter Avenue de Lowendal
75015 Paris
(47) 34 62 00
Fax: (47) 34 48 65
E-mail: UEJF@poly.polytechnique.fr

Jewish Studies
Jewish studies are offered through the Sorbonne.

Kosher Food
Kosher food is widely available in Paris.

ON CAMPUS

UEJF is represented at most of the universities in Paris, and has unions as well in Bordeaux, Dijon, Grenoble, Lyon, Marseille, Metz, Montpellier, Nancy, Nice, Strasbourg, and Toulouse. UEJF has a membership of 15,000 students throughout France, and is a member of the World Union of Jewish Students and the European Union of Jewish Students.

NICE

Jewish 1–2,000

Centre Hillel de le Riviera
c/o prof. Albert Marouani
Board Chair and Advisor
(33) 93 97 70 33
Fax: (33) 93 97 71 01

ON CAMPUS

This new Hillel program is sponsored in cooperation with the EUJF and sponsors educational, cultural, and social activities. The programs are held at the B'nai B'rith Center and at the various campuses of the University of Nice.

GERMANY

BERLIN

Hillel-Jewish Student Union
Fasanenstrasse 79
Berlin, 80
(49) (30) 881-3538

Jewish Studies

The Free University of Berlin offers courses in Jewish Studies, and there are some courses also at other universities.

ON CAMPUS

There are groups of Jewish students in various universities who are loosely confederated through the Union of Jewish Students of Germany. The best contact for students is through the offices of the Jewish community. This office can also advise on availability of kosher food in many of the Western communities.

FRANKFURT

Zentralwohlfahrtsstelle der Juden
in Deustchland
Hebelstrasse 6
D 60318 Frankfurt/Main
(69) (49) 69.944371-0
Fax: (69) (49) 69.494817

Benjamin Bloch, Director

Kosher Food

Kosher restaurant: Savignystr. 66, phone: (069) 75 23 41.

The Zentralwohlfahrtsstelle der Juden in Deutschland is the welfare board of the Jewish communities in Germany, which serves as the social and educational center.

HEIDELBERG

Enrollment 153
Jewish 153

Hochschule fur Judische Studien
Friedrichstrasse 9
Heidelberg 69117
(62) (21) 2-25-76
Fax: (62) (21) 16-76-96

Professor Dr. Michael Graetz, Rector

Jewish Studies

M.A., Ph.D. 6 full professors; 6 assistant professors. Major areas of study at the College include Bible and Jewish Biblical Exegesis; Talmud, Codices and Rabbinic Literature; Hebrew Language and Literature; Yiddish, History of the Jewish People; and Jewish Philosophy and Thought. Subsidiary areas of study include Jewish Art and Contemporary Judaism.

Kosher Food

Kosher food is available for students and faculty members in the kosher Mensa during lecture period (October-February/April-July).

ON CAMPUS

With compulsory and simultaneous study in the University of Heidleberg (Ruprech-Karls-Universitat), students can elect to specialize in Jewish Studies (Hauptfach) with a minor in the University, or vice versa. The college has a library of about 40,000 volumes and has built up a unique collection of slides of Jewish art. Publications include a scholarly journal, *Trumah*, which is published annually, as well as occasional collections of symposia papers. Although the College is open to both Jewish and non-Jewish students, it also prepares Jewish students for communal service. The language of instruction is German.

GREAT BRITAIN

CAMBRIDGE

University of Cambridge Jewish Society
Cambridge Jewish Student Center
3 Thompson's Lane
Cambridge, England CB5 8AQ
(44) (01223) 354783
Web: www.cam.ac.uk/cambuniv/societies/cujs

Simon Colton, Contact

Kosher Food

Currently, there is no kosher student accommodation, but in self-catering colleges it may be possible to kosher the kitchen. Kosher food is locally available.

ON CAMPUS

The Jewish atmosphere in Cambridge is lively due to the large number of Jewish students. The Jewish Society offers a wide range of activities. The local community invites students home for Shabbat lunches and social events.

EDINBURGH

B'nai B'rith Hillel
20 Bartongate Terrace
Edinburgh, Scotland, EH4 8BA
(44) (131) 339 8201
Web: www.ed.ac.uk/~jsoc

Myrna Kaplan, Advisor

 Kosher Food

Kosher kitchen at Hillel facility. Kosher food and restaurants in neighboring community.

Housing

Hillel house has housing for 4 students.

ON CAMPUS

Hillel House in Edinburgh is a brand-new facility located less than 1 mile from both the city center and most of the campus facilities at the University of Edinburgh. The community is very supportive, hospitable, and welcoming to students during the holidays.

LEEDS

Jewish 230

Leeds Hillel Foundation
c/o Professor Roger D. Pollard
Department of Electrical Engineering
The University of Leeds
Leeds LS2 9JT
(44) (0113) 233-2080
E-mail: roger@elec-eng.leeds.ac.uk
Web: www.elec-eng.leeds.ac.uk/een6rdp/hillel.html

Professor Roger D. Pollard, Advisor

ON CAMPUS

Leeds Hillel, based at the Hillel House, 2 Springfield Mount, Leeds 2, is a 2-minute walk to most departments of Leeds University, and a 10-minute walk to a full range of shops in the city center. Hillel has its own synagogue services; Orthodox and Reform synagogues are in town. Hillel is strictly kosher, and kosher food is locally available. Local Jewish families will house students.

LONDON

Hillel Foundation
1/2 Endsleigh Street
London, WC1H 0DS
(44) (0171) 388-0801
Fax: (44) (0171) 916-3973
E-mail: hillel@ort.org

Gerry Lucas, Executive Director
Shirley Goldwater, Administrative Director, UJS
Rabbi Jonathan Dove, Student Chaplain

Jewish Studies

Regular shiurim are held for students in the London area. There are lunchtime discussion groups and the one-to-one Learning Exchange. For further details, apply to Rabbi Jonathan Dove.

Study in Israel

Apply to Shirley Goldwater in the UJS Office: (0171) 387-4644 or (0171) 380-0111.

Kosher Food

Kosher restaurant (low prices for students with identification) open during summer.

Housing

At residential Hillel houses. Application details available from Rachel Lewis.

ON CAMPUS

Hillel House in London, which houses the Union of Jewish Students, is the center of and clearinghouse for information about activities for Jewish students throughout the city and throughout Great Britain. In London, Hillel House sponsors a broad range of programs, including a citywide Jewish students arts festival, retreats, speakers, Israel Cultural Evening and activism, a leadership training seminar, and the Jewish student newspaper Aleph. A fully licensed bar and snack area is available for student use during the evening, complete with cable TV and pool table. A twice-monthly publication, *Renewal*, is distributed throughout the UK.

Hillel sponsors Jewish residence houses in Aberdeen, Birmingham, Bournemouth, Brighton, Bristol, Cardiff, Edinburgh, Glasgow, Hull, Leeds, Leicester, Liverpool, London, Manchester, Newcastle, Nottingham, Reading, Southampton Surrey, and Warwick. For complete details of UK campus facilities for Jewish students, write to the above address for the guide *The AJ6 Guide to College Life.*

LONDON

The Sternberg Centre for Judaism
Youth and Students Division, Reform Synagogues
of Great Britain
80 East End Road
London, N32SY
England
(44) (0181) 349 4731
Fax: (44) (0181) 343 4972
E-mail: students.rsgb@ort.org

Nick Lambert, Student Coordinator
Rabbi Warren Elf, RSGB Northern Region Chaplain
Deborah Myers-Weinsten, ULPS London Region Chaplain

ON CAMPUS

The Division provides for the religious and cultural needs of Reform and Progressive students on campuses throughout the United Kingdom. It provides a range of activities, including a summer tour of Israel, and works closely with the Union of Jewish Students and their affiliated Jewish societies. Two part-time chaplains are based in Manchester and Cambridge.

OXFORD

University of Oxford Jewish Society
Jewish Centre
21 Richmond Road
Oxford
England
(44) (01865) 270 000

Jewish Studies

The Oxford Institute for Yiddish Studies offers a full-time teaching diploma course in Yiddish literature during the year, suitable for graduates with a reasonable standard of Yiddish, as well as summer courses. Maris Wright, Director of Projects, Oxford Institute for Yiddish Studies, 4 Cornmarket, Golden Cross Court, Oxford, OX1 3EX, England; (44) (01865) 798 989; Fax: (44) (01865) 798 987; mwright@oxf-inst.demon.co.uk.

Kosher Food

Kosher food is possible in your own apartment, especially during upperclass years. Some kosher food is available locally.

ON CAMPUS

Oxford has a positive Jewish atmosphere, which varies according to college. The local Jewish community is small but hospitable to students. The Jewish Society is one of the largest in the country, and offers social events, weekly Friday night Shabbatons, and a well-attended Seudah on Shabbat afternoon.

See listing under Short-Term and Summer Programs.

HUNGARY

BUDAPEST

Union of Jewish Students
c/o JDC Suip Utca 12
1075 Budapest, Hungary
(36) (1) 122.0411
Fax: (36) (1) 122.2037

ON CAMPUS

Jewish studies offered through Lorand Eotvos University in Budapest. Kosher food available at 2 kosher restaurants in Budapest.

JAPAN

KOBE

The Jewish Community of Kansai
No. 12/12 Kitano-cho
4-Chome, Chuo-ku
Kobe
(81) (78) 221-7236
(81) (78) 222-3950
Fax: (81) (78) 221-6188

Bruce M. Benson, Advisor

ON CAMPUS

Some 30 Jewish families live in Kobe, which has had a Jewish population for more than a century, and was a transit point for Jewish refugees during World War II. The very interesting Jewish cemetery testifies to this history. Jewish students are welcome to services at the grand synagogue Ohel Shelomoh.

TOKYO

Jewish Community of Japan
Hiroo 3-8-8, Shibuya-ku
Tokyo, 150
(81) (03) 3400-2559
Fax: (81) (03) 3400-1827

Carnie Rose, Director

Jewish Studies
Modern Hebrew is taught as a selective course at Tokyo University of Foreign Studies and Osaka University of Foreign Studies.

Kosher Food
Kosher meat kitchen at the Jewish Community Center. JCC assists members in importing kosher meat and Passover products; meal service for take-out. Kosher products available in some areas. Shabbat dinner on Friday evenings and Kiddush on Shabbat mornings.

ON CAMPUS
The Jewish Community of Japan welcomes Jewish students to events such as Tuesday evening Israeli dancing, socials, Wednesday evening Adult Education, and other activities. Arrangements can be made for home hospitality so that Jewish students studying at universities outside of Tokyo can attend Passover seder. The Center has a swimming pool and a 1,000-volume circulation library. Discount membership for students. Take the subway to Shibuya, Bus #03 to the stop Tokyo Jo-Gakkanmae, 1-minute walk to JCC.

THE NETHERLANDS

AMSTERDAM

Hillel-IJAR
Union of Jewish Students of the Netherlands
de Lairessestrast
1071 HV Amsterdam

DELFT

Hillelhouse
Koornmarkt 9
2611 EA
Delft
E-mail: d.zwaaf@lr.tudelft.nl

Akiva Tor, Advisor

NEW ZEALAND

UNIVERSITY OF AUCKLAND
Jewish 130

Hillel-N.Z. Union of Jewish Students
16 Harper Place
Birkenhead
Auckland 10, New Zealand
(64) (09) 4184 134

Ari Phillips, Advisor
Roniel Lavi, Advisor

ON CAMPUS
Australian Union of Jewish Students (AUJS) is on campus.

SLOVAKIA

BRATISLAVA

Slovak Union of Jewish Students
c/o Union of Jewish Religious Communities in Slovakia
Kozla 21/11 SK
Bratislava, 81447
(421) (7) 5312167
(421) (7) 5318714 (SUJY: ph/fax)
Fax: (421) (7) 5311106
E-mail: feroalex@decef.elf.stuba.sk

Fero Alexander, Executive Chairman
Martin Urbanik, Chairman

ON CAMPUS
Spring and autumn seminars, as well as a summer camp connected with an activity, such as cleaning an abandoned Jewish cemetery.

RAND AFRIKAANS UNIVERSITY (AFRIKAANS SPEAKING)

Enrollment 15,000
Jewish 110

> South African Union of Jewish Students
> Building No. 1
> Anerley Office Park
> 7 Anerley Road
> Parktown, 2193
> (27) (11) 486-1981
> Fax: (27) (11) 486-0204
>
> **Charles Ancer**, President

 Jewish Studies
Hebrew studies.

ON CAMPUS

Apolitical campus. SAUJS organizes shiurim and social functions.

UNIVERSITY OF CAPE TOWN (UCT)

Enrollment 14,672
Jewish 600

> Kaplan Centre
> U.C.T.
> Private Bag
> Rondebosch, 7700
> (27) (21) 650 3062
> Fax: (27) (21) 650 3726
>
> **Dr. Milton Shain**, Director

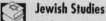 **Jewish Studies**
Hebrew, Jewish civilization, Jewish history. Holocaust studies are offered every 2 years.

 Kosher Food
Kosher canteen and catering facilities. No kosher food provided at the residences.

ON CAMPUS

The University is on the outskirts of the city center. The Kaplan Centre is situated on campus and provides an environment for Jewish learning and social interaction. It consists of a Jewish Studies library and Chaplaincy book and tape library, and organizes regular shiurim during lunch.

UNIVERSITY OF PRETORIA

Enrollment 25,000
Jewish 80

> South Africa Union of Jewish Students
> Building No. 1
> Anerley Office Park
> 7 Anerley Road
> Parktown, 2193
> (27) (11) 486-1981
> Fax: (27) (11) 486-0204
>
> **Charles Ancer**, President

 Jewish Studies
Ancient Hebrew Department.

ON CAMPUS

The University is on the outskirts of the city center. Every Jewish student is a member of SAUJS, which organizes social functions as well as lectures for the general student body.

UNIVERSITY OF THE WITWATERSRAND

Enrollment 17,716
Jewish 1,000

> South African Union of Jewish Students
> Anerley Office Park, Building 1
> 7 Anerley Road
> Parktown, 2193
> (27) (11) 486-1981
> Fax: (27) (11) 486-0204
>
> **Charles Ancer**, President

 Jewish Studies
Jewish Studies and Hebrew Department.

ON CAMPUS

Jewish students at the University of the Witwatersrand are active on campus through the South African Union of Jewish Students (SAUJS), which organizes regular shiurim and weekends away. The university is situated near the city center and offers a vibrant student life.

FORMER SOVIET UNION

KHARKOV

Jewish Population 50,000

> The Kharkov Hillel Center
> c/o Ina Belyakovich
> Kharkov Jewish Day School
> Kharkov, Ukraine
> Former Soviet Union
> (380) 572 43 1981
> Fax: (380) 572 43 1981
>
> **Ina Belyakovich**, Director

ON CAMPUS

The Kharkov Hillel Center serves Jewish students throughout the Kharkov area. It offers a range of programs designed to introduce students to various Jewish and Israeli topics. Activities include student theater, Jewish holiday celebrations, Hebrew study, Jewish learning, Israeli dancing and music, a monthly newspaper, Jewish history, and an outreach program to elderly in the Kharkov community assisting them with shopping and other needs.

See listing for Moscow.

KISHINEV

Jewish Population 40,000

> Kishinev Hillel
> c/o Anna Gurshenzon
> 24 Dacia Boulevard, Apt. 78
> Kishinev, Moldova
> Former Soviet Union
> (373) 2-341446
> Fax: (373) 2-438400
> E-mail: office@joint.moldova.su
>
> **Anna Gurshenzon**, Chairperson

ON CAMPUS

The Kishinev Hillel serves young adult Jews throughout the Kishinev area. It offers programs designed to introduce young Jews to Judaism and to Israel, and to provide a forum for them to meet each other and to interact with the Kishinev Jewish community. Current programs include weekly Kabbalat Shabbat, intellectual games, student-led tours of Jewish Kishinev, and a theater group.

See listing for Moscow.

KIEV

Jewish Population 80,000

> Kiev Hillel
> Dimitrova St. 6, Apt. 25
> Kiev, Ukraine
> Former Soviet Union
> (38) 044 220 6436
> Fax: (38) 044 220 6436
> E-mail: aharon@jcu.kiev.ua
>
> **Osik Akselrud**, Director

ON CAMPUS

The Kiev Hillel Center serves Jewish students attending the International Solomon University and others living throughout the metropolitan area. Activities include a theater workshop producing original works based on Jewish themes; a well-known and respected Jewish dance and choral group; a monthly newspaper; Jewish learning; weekly Kabbalat Shabbat celebrations throughout the Kiev Jewish community; and outreach to the elderly by delivering food packages and providing other services.

> *"Our university is the first Jewish university in Ukraine. And as far as it is Jewish, our students feel themselves comfortable and relaxing. They are interested in participating in Hillel activity because for them it's a great opportunity to spend their leisure among friends with a Jewish background. Our university administration helps us in many ways both financially and spiritually. Among our academic program there are such subjects as Hebrew and Jewish history, which help in crystallizing Jewish identity."*
>
> **Darina Privalko, recent graduate**

See listing for Moscow.

LVOV

> Lvov Hillel
> c/o Kiev Hillel
> Dimitrova St. 6, Apt. 25
> Kiev, Ukraine
> Former Soviet Union
> (38) 0322 22 74 90
>
> **Irina Gelston**, Coordinator

ON CAMPUS

The Lvov Hillel serves Jewish students and young people throughout Lvov. It offers programming enabling them to become better acquainted with Judaism and Israel through cultural, religious, social, and educational programming.

See listing for Moscow.

MINSK

Jewish Population 90,000

The Minsk Hillel Center
Mogilovskaya St. 16, Apt. 143
Minsk, Belarus
Former Soviet Union
(375) (172) 245-208
Fax: (375) (172) 102 569 (c/o Minsk JDC office)

Genya Zelotnik, Director

ON CAMPUS

The Minsk Hillel Student Center serves Jewish students attending Minsk State University and in the surrounding area. In an atmosphere where young Jews can meet and create a community, the Minsk Hillel offers a variety of programs designed to introduce students to various Jewish and Israeli topics. Activities include Friday night Shabbat celebrations, intellectual quiz shows, Jewish debating club, program on Judaism, Torah, Jewish culture, and Israeli dancing.

See listing for Moscow.

MOSCOW

Moscow Hillel
2 Bobrov Street Apt. 50
Moscow, Russia
Former Soviet Union
(7) (095) 923-7459
Fax: (7) (095) 331-3953
E-mail: hillel@glas.ape.org

Jenya Michaelova, Director

ON CAMPUS

The Moscow Hillel Center serves Jewish students who live throughout the metropolitan area. It offers a range of programs designed to introduce students to various Jewish and Israeli topics. Activities include a monthly newspaper; an art cafe featuring original poetry, stories and performances; weekly Kabbalat Shabbat programs; monthly Havdalah programming; Jewish learning opportunities; song, dance, and theater groups; and outreach to Moscow's Jewish elderly.

Hillel in the former Soviet Union (FSU) is under the supervision of Hillel's divisional headquaters in Jerusalem. The Hillel Foundation at Hebrew University serves as the center for the development of new student groups and for the supervision and training of the new Hillels in the FSU. Rabbi Yossie Goldman, Hillel International Assistant Vice President and Director for Israel and the FSU, assisted by Rabbi David Ebstein in Jerusalem, supervises all FSU programming. In addition to local Hillel programming, regional leadership seminars

held throughout the year are run by a combined staff from Israel and the FSU. Contact Rabbi Yossie Goldman for further information: 011-972-2-5817714; Fax: 011-972-2-5811140; msjoseph@olive.mscc.huji.ac.il.

ST. PETERSBURG

Jewish Population 100,000

St. Petersburg Hillel Center
56 Zimbalina Street, Apt. 71
St. Petersburg, Russia
(7) (812) 275-5441
Fax: (7) (812) 560-2314
E-mail: hillel@infopro.spb.su

Misha Levin, Director

ON CAMPUS

The St. Petersburg Hillel Center serves Jewish students who live throughout the metropolitan area. It offers a range of programs designed to introduce students to various Jewish and Israeli topics. Activities include puppet theater; theater workshop featuring original experiential and avant-garde works based on biblical texts; monthly newspaper; Arts Studio showcasing original works; a dance group; Jewish learning opportunities; and Shabbat and holiday celebrations.

See listing for Moscow.

URALS

Urals Regional Hillel
8 Mamina-Sibiryka St., Apt. 92
Ekaterinburg, Russia
Former Soviet Union
(7) 3432 296211
Fax: (7) 3422 592930
E-mail: uraljdc@online.ru

Yan Yankovsky, Student Coordinator

ON CAMPUS

The founding of Hillel in the Urals is taking place on a regional basis, with the center in Ekaterinburg. Hillel has two components in the Urals: local programming in communities with Jewish students and young people, and twice-yearly regional activities, which will be held in different cities on a rotating basis.

Hillel throughout the Urals region seeks to foster an atmosphere where young Jews may meet and create a community. Programming is offered in a wide variety of areas in order to introduce students to various Jewish and Israeli topics.

See listing for Moscow.

URUGUAY

MONTEVIDEO

B'nai B'rith International—Hillel
Canelones 1216
Montevideo
(598) (02) 910 522
Fax: (598) (02) 921 303

Dr. Eduardo Kohn, District Director

ON CAMPUS

B'nai B'rith District 28 organizes activities for Jewish students throughout the Montevideo metropolitan area.

VENEZUELA

CARACAS

Hogar B'nai B'rith
Apdo. 68927 Altamira 1062-A-9a
Transv. entre 7a Avenida y
Luis Roche
Caracas
(58) (02) 2621346
Fax: (58) (02) 5736657

Claudio B. Avruj, Advisor

ON CAMPUS

Outreach program serves youth in Colombia, Venezuela, Panama, Costa Rica, Guatemala, Mexico, and Netherland Antilles/Curacao.

PART FIVE | *Resources*

Short-Term and Summer Programs

Additional information about some of the institutions and organizations sponsoring the following programs may be found in the listings of National Agencies and Institutions.

UNITED STATES

American Jewish Joint Distribution Committee, Inc.: Jewish Service Corps

This annual program places volunteers in various Jewish communities throughout the world for a year of service. Volunteers are placed in countries such as Bulgaria, Poland, Morocco, and Yugoslavia where they serve as teachers, youth organizers, and social workers. Applications are accepted on an ongoing basis; most placements begin in the late summer/early fall. Yael Mueller, 711 Third Avenue, New York, NY 10017; (212) 885-0841; Fax: (212) 370-5467; E-mail: yael-m@jdcny.org.

American Jewish Joint Distribution Committee, Inc.: Ralph I. Goldman Fellowship in International Jewish Communal Service

This is a one-year work-study fellowship with the AJJDC. Preference is given to candidates in the early stages of their careers in the practice and/or study of communal service showing a strong interest in international Jewish communal affairs and international social welfare. A master's degree is preferred. Interested candidates should send a letter of advocacy to: Ralph I. Goldman Fellowship, AJJDC, 711 Third Avenue, New York, NY 10017, on or before November 1.

Brandeis Collegiate Institute

BCI, a program of The Brandeis-Bardin Institute, is a leadership institute for young Jewish men and women (aged eighteen to twenty-six). BCI welcomes all, regardless of affiliation or depth of Judaic knowledge and experience. During two one-month summer sessions, participants from around the world explore their Jewish identity and heritage through the study of Jewish thought and text, as well as through hands-on experiences in Jewish art, music, drama, and dance. BCI is located on a 3,100-acre campus in southern California. Scholarships are available through the Institute and local communities. BCI, 1101 Peppertree Lane, Brandeis, CA 93064; (805) 582-4450; Fax: (805) 526-1398; E-mail: bbibci4u@aol.com. Dr. Alvin Mars, Director; Gary Rothstein, Program Administrator.

Drisha Institute for Jewish Education: Summer Institute (women)

Drisha provides women with the opportunity to engage in traditional Jewish text study in an environment that encourages seriousness of purpose, free

inquiry, and respect for classical texts. Drisha offers a wide variety of study options for women of all backgrounds and levels. Full-time learning programs, twenty-five part-time classes every semester, full time Summer Institutes, a co-ed Winter Week of Learning, co-ed community lectures, and the Drisha Tape Project offer multilevel opportunities for college and graduate students, teachers, and others. Yesodot (Foundations) courses enable students to focus on strengthening their text skills. Drisha Institute for Jewish Education, 131 West 86th Street, New York, NY 10024; (212) 595-0307; Fax: (212) 595-0679; E-mail: inquiry@drisha.org. Nina Bruder, Executive Director; Leslie Lautin, Communications Coordinator. For full-time programs, see listing under "Rabbinical Schools and Specialized Educational Programs."

Elat Chayyim: A Center for Healing and Renewal

Intensive courses in Jewish spirituality, including prayer, meditation, text study, arts, song, dance, and interfaith dialogues. Some internships are available. Elat Chayyim, 99 Mill Hook Road, Accord, NY 12404; (800) 398-2630; Fax: (914) 626-2037; E-mail: elatchayyi@aol.com. Rabbi Jeff Roth, Director. See listing for ALEPH, in the section "National Agencies and Institutions with Resources and Programs for Jewish College Students."

Hebrew College: Kerem Summer Institute

The Kerem Summer Institute is a trans-denominational one-month intensive immersion program focusing on Jewish learning, living, and self-discovery. Students get a historical overview of Judaism, study the major classical texts, improve their Hebrew skills, discuss important contemporary issues, and earn six academic credits. The faculty includes outstanding scholars from Boston-area universities as well as celebrated Jewish community leaders. Each participant receives a substantial fellowship. Additional funding is available for those with financial need. 120 Colborne Road, Boston, MA 02135; (800) 40-KEREM; Fax: (617) 734-9769; E-mail: haroesty@lynx.neu.edu.

Jewish Theological Seminary

Recently ranked by the National Research Council as the only program of Judaic studies among the top ten ranked religion programs, the Graduate School of JTS offers the most comprehensive program of advanced Jewish studies in the United States. The library of JTS houses the most complete collection of Judaica in the Western Hemisphere, and students benefit from the Graduate School's renowned faculty, the largest in the country devoted solely to the advanced study of Judaica, as well as consortia with other prestigious universities. Financial aid based on need and/or merit is available to matriculated students in the form of scholarships, grants, loans, and employment opportunities. The Graduate School offers degrees of Master of Arts, Doctor of Hebrew Literature, and Doctor of Philosophy in ancient Judaism, Bible and ancient Semitic languages, interdepartmental studies, Jewish art and material culture, Jewish history, Jewish literature, Jewish philosophy, Jewish women's studies, liturgy, medieval Jewish studies, Midrash, modern Jewish studies, and Talmud and Rabbinics, as well as a dual degree program with Columbia University's School of Social Work. The Graduate School of JTS, 3080 Broadway, New York, NY 10027; (212) 678-8022; Fax: (212) 678-8947; E-mail: gradschool@itsa.edu. Michael Goldberg, Graduate Admissions Coordinator.

National Havurah Summer Institute

For young adults with potential for Jewish leadership, this week-long study will give students a look at the various pathways to Jewish living. National Havurah Committee: (215) 248-9760; Fax: (215) 247-9703.

Schusterman Hillel International Student Leaders Assembly

Located at Camp Moshava in the Pocono Mountains, the Schusterman Hillel International Student Leaders Assembly brings together student leaders from the United States, Canada, and the former Soviet Union. This conference offers leadership training, a marketplace of programs and ideas, text study, and networking opportunities for student leaders from large and small campuses. Participants must be nominated by Hillel Directors or on-campus advisors. Late August. Contact your Hillel representative on campus, or contact Laura Siegel at the Hillel International Center, 1640 Rhode Island Avenue, NW, Washington, DC 20036; (202) 857-6559; Fax: (202) 857-6693; E-mail: lsiegel@hillel.org.

Skidmore College & The American Jewish Committee: Seminars in Judaic Study

Three one-week, noncredit seminars to deepen understanding of Jews and Judaism, held at Skidmore College, Saratoga Springs, NY 12866; (518) 584-5000, ext. 2264; Fax: (518) 584-7963.

YIVO Institute for Jewish Research: Uriel Weinreich Program

An intensive Yiddish language program with an emphasis on Yiddish culture. Coursework is offered at all levels. 555 West 57th Street, New York, NY 10019; (212) 246-6080; Fax: (212) 292-1892.

ISRAEL AND OVERSEAS

ARCHAEOLOGICAL PROGRAMS

Archaeological Excavations in Israel: www.israel.org/archdigs.html

Both volunteer and college credit digs are available at various sites. Contact the Biblical Archaeology Review, 4710 41st Street, NW, Washington, D.C. 20016; (202) 364-3300; or check the list of volunteer opportunities on the Web site of the Israel Ministry of Foreign Affairs: www.israel.org/archdigs.html.

Hebrew University: Hazor Excavations (in memory of Yigal Yadin)

Participate in the excavation of Tel-Hazor, the largest biblical site in Israel, located in the upper Galilee. Amnon Ben-Tor, Institute of Archaeology, Hebrew University, Jerusalem 91905, Israel; (972) 2-882403; Fax: (972) 2-825548.

Israel Archaeological Society: Summer Expeditions

Digs in Israel, Jordan, and possibly Egypt. Explore these three countries and Syria. Accommodations in comfortable hotels. June 19 to July 31. Participants can join for one to six weeks. College credit is available. Israel Archaeological Society, 467 Levering Avenue, Los Angeles, CA 90024-6259; (800) 477-2358; Fax: (310) 476-6259. Arthur D. Greenberg, Director.

Harvard University: Ashkelon Excavations—The Leon Levy Expedition

This program takes place at an urban site with habitation from 3500 B.C.E. to 1150 C.E. on the Mediterranean Coast. Eight academic credits can be received through Harvard University Summer School for an additional fee. Ashkelon Excavations, Harvard Semitic Museum, 6 Divinity Avenue, Cambridge, MA 02138; (617) 495-9385; Fax: (617) 496-8904.

Tel Aviv University: Archaeological Excavation at Ancient Jaffa

The current project explores the governmental stronghold of the Rameseside Period. Remains belonging to the Iron Age and Persian Period are investigated while digging down to the Late Bronze Age strata. This program carries six credits from Tel Aviv University. The Institute of Archaeology, Tel Aviv University, Ramat Aviv, 69978; (972) 3-6409578; Fax: (972) 3-5497842.

EDUCATIONAL PROGRAMS: YEARLONG, SEMESTER, AND SUMMER STUDY

Many of the following study programs also offer touring or volunteer opportunities. In addition, numerous colleges and universities have arranged for their own study programs in Israel. Discuss your interests with the Study Abroad office on campus, or with the Judaic Studies program or Hillel staff. If you select a program independent of your university and wish to receive course credit for your work, check with the relevant department before enrolling to be certain the credits offered will be recognized.

The Embassy of Israel offers a publication, "Higher Education in Israel," which may be obtained by contacting (202) 364-5500; E-mail: ask@israelemb.org; Web: www.israelemb.org.

Beit Midrash/A Liberal Yeshiva

The Beit Midrash/A Liberal Yeshiva is an egalitarian community of prayer and study. Year program, September to June; part-time and one-term study is also possible. Classical Jewish texts are taught by lecture, discussion, and hevruta (study partner). Issues of contemporary relevance, including Jewish values, spirituality, and ethics, are key subjects. Students are guided as they fill in gaps in their knowledge of, and experience with, Judaism, prayer, and Israel. They explore all positions and points of view while remaining free to draw their own conclusions. This is a joint project of the World Union for Progressive Judaism and Hebrew Union College-JIR, in cooperation with the Reconstructionist Rabbinical College and the Leo Baeck College, London. 838 Fifth Avenue, New York, NY 10021 (212) 650-4090; Fax: (212) 650-4099; E-mail: landisbd@ix.netcom.com. Betsy Miller Landis, Director of Development and Recruitment.

Ben-Gurion University of the Negev—Overseas Student Program

Semester and one-year programs for overseas students: Ulpan, touring, kibbutz stay, archaeological dig. Live with Israelis. 342 Madison Avenue, Suite 1924, New York, NY 10173; (212) 687-7721; Fax: (212) 370-0805; E-mail: BGUOSP@haven.ios.com; Web: www.bgu.ac.il/osp.

See listing for Ben-Gurion University in the Israel section of this guide.

Bezalel Academy of Arts and Design: Summer Study

Bezalel, Israel's national academy of arts, design, and architecture, offers two summer courses for international students. Jerusalem Through the Ages is a history course consisting of classroom lectures and discussions, combined with site exploration of the city and surrounding hills. Introduction to Fine Arts offers both beginning and experienced students the opportunity to work independently in both studio and outdoor settings. Morning and afternoon classes, at least five days a week. Housing is at Eyal Hotel; college credit is offered. The program is co-sponsored by the CRB Foundation of Montreal and Jerusalem and the Joint Authority for Jewish Zionist Education. Friends of Bezalel, 654 Madison Avenue, Suite 409, New York, NY 10021; (212) 935-1900; Fax: (212) 935-2210.

Dorot Fellowship in Israel

The Dorot Fellowship is a one-year immersion in Israel for college graduates in their 20s and 30s. No prior experience in Israel is expected, and individuals maintaining all levels of Jewish religious observance, from secular to Orthodox, are welcomed and accommodated. The Fellowship has five main components: summertime ulpan study; part-time study of Hebrew texts or Jewish studies, which takes place at an approved co-ed institution of your choice (ap-

proved institutions currently include the Pardes Institute for Jewish Studies, the Shalom Hartman Institute, Elul, Yakar, the Conservative Yeshiva, the Liberal Yeshiva, and any Israeli university); a part-time voluntary internship; a series of monthly seminars and trips within Israel that examine contemporary Israeli and Jewish life; and living with Israelis. The Fellowship year begins in July, with an ulpan. It is anticipated that Fellows will gain proficiency in Hebrew during the course of the year. The Fellowship's aim is to enhance the skills and personal development of future Jewish lay leaders and Fellows are expected to be involved in their communities and in the network of Fellowship alumni when they return to North America. The Fellowship provides a generous living stipend and tuition at the Fellows' academic institutions. Each year there are approximately fifteen Fellows. Dorot Foundation, 439 Benefit Street, Providence, RI 02906; (401) 351-8866; Fax: (401) 351-4975; E-mail: info@dorot.org; Web: www.dorot.org/fellowship. Daniel Stein, Assistant Director.

Hebrew University

Hebrew University offers many different programs for undergraduate and graduate students. archaeology, modern Hebrew, and marine biology and international relations (Marine Science in the Gulf of Eilat). Two graduate programs include America and the Holy Land and the Graduate Summer Institute with a concentration on Christian-Jewish dialogue in early modern Europe and comparative perspectives. Office of Academic Affairs, Hebrew University, Mt. Scopus Campus, Jerusalem 91905, Israel; (212) 472-2288, (800) 404-8622; Fax: (212) 517-4548.

See listing for Hebrew University in the Israel section of this guide.

Isralight Institute

The Isralight Institute offers three- and six-week programs throughout the year that include classes, seminars, and touring. Isralight is independent and non-political. Curriculum includes philosophy, written and oral tradition, Jewish ethics, mysticism, and gender issues. Scholarships and college credit are available. IsraLight Institute, 25 Misgav Ladach Street, Old City, Jerusalem 97500; (972) 2-6274-890; Fax: (972) 2-6273-875; E-mail: Islight@netvision.net.il. In the U.S.: PO Box 640563, Miami, FL 33164-0563; (800) 694-4949; E-mail: sharelite@aol.com. Leah Benchimol, North American Representative.

The Jerusalem Fellowships

The Jerusalem Fellowships at the Aish HaTorah College of Jewish Studies are intense three-week (winter) or four-week (summer) field study programs in Israel for college students and young professionals aged nineteen to twenty-nine. These programs are designed for those who want to learn about their Jewish heritage, see the beauty of the land, learn more about Israeli society and politics, and meet with top Israeli officials. We offer three different programs: The Jerusalem Fellowships Internship for Leaders for freshmen, sophomores, and juniors in college; The Jerusalem Fellowships Summer/ Winter Break Program for undergraduates, grads and young professionals; and The Jerusalem Fellowships MBA Leadership Mission (two weeks). Scholarships are available for all three programs. 2124 Broadway, MPB 224, New York, NY 10023; (800) FELLOWS (335-5697); Fax: (914) 425-8255; E-mail: jf@aish.edu; Web: www.jerusalemfellowships.org. Chaim Dubin, Director.

Jewish Learning Exchange Summer Break Program: Ohr Somayach

Yeshiva study and touring program for students and young professional men. 38 East 29th Street, 8th Floor, New York, NY 10016; (212) 213-3100, (800) 431-2272; Fax: (212) 213-8717.

Kayitz Bar-Ilan

Six-week session. English-language courses in biology, English literature, economics, marketing, Bible, Arab-Israel conflict, and Jewish history. Bar-Ilan University, Academic Affairs Department, 91 Fifth Avenue, Suite 200, New York, NY 10003; (212) 337-1286; Fax: (212) 337-1274.

See listing for Bar-Ilan University in the Israel section of this guide.

Machon Meir (men)

Studies in Bible, Talmud, Jewish philosophy, mysticism, and Hebrew Ulpan (four levels). Tours throughout Israel integrate Torah with the experience of modern Israel; (718) 373-8390.

Mayanot Institute of Jewish Studies

Mayanot is an accredited institute of Jewish studies dedicated to providing opportunities to study the classic texts of Jewish civilization in an open environment. The progressive curriculum is designed to examine the breadth and depth of Jewish texts, thus giving the student a diverse perspective on Jewish thought, experience, and culture. The program also features organized tours, field trips, and specialized seminars. Mayanot's academic year is divided into fall and spring semesters. 15 Mesilat Yesharim Street,

Jerusalem 94584 (972) 2-624-9167; Fax: (972) 2-624-9168; E-mail: mayanot@netvision.net.il; Web: www.mayanot.edu. Shlomo Gestetner, Executive Director. In the U.S. and Canada: American Friends of Mayanot, 14 Farwell Street, West Haven, CT 06516; (888) MAYANOT (629-2668).

Oxford Institute for Yiddish Studies

Annual residential summer courses in Yiddish language and literature at Oxford, in England. Students can design their own course from twenty-six modules; a minimum of three modules must be taken. The Institute also offers a one-year Yiddish diploma course for graduates. Oxford Institute for Yiddish Studies, 4 Cornmarket, Golden Cross Court, Oxford, OX1 3EX, England; (44) 01865-798989; Fax: (44) 01865-798987; E-mail: mwright@oxf-inst.demon.co.uk. Maris Wright, Director of Projects.

See listing for Oxford University in this guide.

Pardes Institute of Jewish Studies

Pardes, located in Jerusalem and unaffiliated with any denominational or political group, provides full-year, semester, and summer coeducational programs. Students from all streams of Jewish life are taught classical Jewish texts with no expectation that they adhere to a particular level of observance. Areas of study include Bible, Jewish law, Midrash, Talmud, and philosophy. Seminars are offered on topics such as Gender Roles in Judaism and Modern Zionist Thought. Year-program students participate in tours throughout Israel and a weekly community project of their choice. Pardes faculty are available to lecture on college campuses in North America. Pardes Institute of Jewish Studies, PO Box 8575, Jerusalem, Israel; (972) 2-673-5210; Fax: (972) 2-673-5160; E-mail: pardesinst@netmedia.net.il. In the U.S.: American Pardes Foundation, 165 East 56th Street, New York, NY; (212) 230-1316; Fax: (212) 230-1265. Paula Steisel, National Program Director.

Project Interchange: An Institute of The American Jewish Committee

Project Interchange is the only national organization dedicated solely to providing educational seminars in Israel for America's political, ethnic, civic, and religious leaders. Since 1982, more than 2,500 distinguished Americans have participated in our educational programs in Israel. Project Interchange continues to update seminar alumni on issues facing Israel through timely briefing papers, alumni conferences, and local speakers. Project Interchange offers internship opportunities throughout the year. 1156 15th Street, NW, Suite 1201, Washington, D.C. 20005; (202) 833-0025; Fax: (202) 331-7702; E-mail: pi@ajc.org; Web: www.ajc.org/wwa/pi. Lisa B. Eisen, Executive Director.

The Shalem Center

The Shalem Center was founded in 1994 as a research and educational institution focusing on Jewish social thought and Israeli public policy. Combining theoretical inquiry with the study of practical policy, the Center seeks to offer the Jewish nation a coherent alternative to an increasingly post-Zionist Israel. Though a rigorous program of research, publishing, and seminars, the Center produces innovative analyses and proposals for the improvement of Jewish national public life. At the same time, the Center seeks to develop future intellectual and political leaders to build a better Israel.

Shalem Graduate Fellowships support the work of a select group of students pursuing a full-time program of research and study in diverse areas of Jewish national life at the Shalem Center in Jerusalem. Graduate Fellows research theoretical and practical problems facing Israel and the Jewish people and develop innovative approaches to solving them. The Shalem study program is an interdisciplinary examination of the works, ideas, and facts that form the foundations of public life. Graduate Fellows participate in weekly seminars, occasional symposiums, and workshops on topics of interest. 1140 Connecticut Avenue, NW, Suite 801, Washington, D.C. 20036; (202) 887-1277; Fax: (202) 887-1277; Web: www.shalem.org.il. Yoram Hazony, President; Kenneth Weinstein, Director, Washington Office.

Technion—Israel Institute of Technology

Semester and one-year programs are available for both undergraduate and graduate students in engineering, mathematics, and the sciences. American Friends of Technion Society, 810 Seventh Avenue, 24th Floor, New York, NY 10019; (212) 262-6200; Fax: (212) 262-6155.

Tel Aviv University: Lowy School for Overseas Students Summer Session

Located in the heart of Israel and world-renowned for academic excellence, Tel Aviv University (TAU) is the country's largest, most comprehensive, and most dynamic university with more than 26,000 students. TAU is a vibrant center of learning that reflects Israel, her region, and her people. Through its Lowy School for Overseas Students, TAU offers a matchless academic and personal experience to share with students from all over the world. All Lowy School programs are taught in English. It offers a wide range of excellent courses in major disciplines taught by members of TAU's superb faculty. 360 Lexington Avenue, New York, NY 10017; (800) 665-9828; Fax: (212) 687-4085; E-mail: tauoaa@aol.com; Web: www.telavivuniv.org. Hal Klopper, Director.

See listing for Tel Aviv University in the Israel section of this guide.

Temple University Law School/Tel Aviv University School of Law

ABA-approved international and comparative law joint program operated by Temple and Tel Aviv University Law Schools. This six-week summer session has been operating for twenty years. Courses such as Legal Aspects of the Middle East Peace Process, Comparative Religious Law, and Comparative Constitutional Law are taught in English by Israeli and U.S. law professors, many of whom have been involved in peace negotiations. Field trips, guest speakers, and special events are featured. Temple University School of Law, International Programs—Room 710, 1719 N. Broad Street, Philadelphia, PA 19122; (215) 204-8982; Fax: (215) 204-1185; E-mail: intl-law@vm.temple.edu.

Tulane Law School/Cardozo Law School/Hebrew University Law School

ABA-approved international and comparative law program at Hebrew University. Two-week summer sessions, with three classes offered each session. English-language courses include Comparative U.S. and Israeli Business Law, The Law of International Trade, Civil Liberties in Israel and the U.S., and Discrimination Law in the U.S. and Israel. (504) 865-5980; Fax: (504) 862-8846; E-mail: jfriedman@law.tulane.edu. Prof. Joel Friedman, University School of Law.

Ulpan Akiva Netanya: International Hebrew Study Center

The Center offers intensive Hebrew and Arabic courses on all levels, as well as tours and special Shabbat activities. Ulpan Akiva Netanya, PO Box 6086, 42160 Netanya, Israel; (972) 9-8352312 (Sundays to Thursdays 9 a.m. to 2 P.M.); Fax: (972) 9-8652919; E-mail: ulpanakv@netvision.net.il; Web: www.ulpan-akiva.org.il.

University of Haifa

The University offers college students an opportunity to spend a semester, one year, or a summer in Israel on internationally accredited programs. The overseas program offers undergraduate courses in Hebrew and Arabic, such as Middle East, religious studies and Israel, archaeology, history, comparative literature, communications, fine arts, environmental studies and maritime studies, psychology honors program, accredited internships, Kibbutz University Program, International Summer Hebrew Ulpan, and Summer Travel and Study Seminar. You must have completed at least one semester of college to be eligible. Department of Overseas Studies, 220 Fifth Avenue, Suite 1301, New York, NY 10001; (888) 562-8813; Fax: (212) 685-7883; E-mail: university~of~haifa@worldnet.att.net; Web: www.haifa.ac.il. Stacey Sanders, North American Director.

The Weizmann Institute of Science: The Karen Kupcinet International Science School Summer Work Program

The Weizmann Institute accepts a small number of overseas junior- and senior-year college students in the exact and natural sciences for a ten- to twelve-week summer program. Candidates must give evidence of a serious interest in and aptitude for research. Modest stipends cover food, lodging, and incidental expenses but not travel. Application deadline early January. American Committee for the Weizmann Institute of Science, 51 Madison Avenue, Suite 117, New York, NY 10010; (212) 779-2500; Fax: (212) 779-3209.

Yeshiva Study

Yeshiva Study provides many opportunities for both men and women. Torah Education Department, 110 East 59th Street, New York, NY 10022; (212) 339-6080; Fax: (212) 318-6177.

VOLUNTEER, EXPERIENTIAL, AND TOURING PROGRAMS

While most of the following programs offer learning components, their primary focus is on experiencing Israel through hands-on involvement or through travel.

American Jewish World Service: Jewish Volunteer Corps

AJWS is a not-for-profit organization that provides nonsectarian humanitarian support, technical assistance, skilled volunteers, and emergency relief to people in need—regardless of race, ethnicity, or religion—in Africa, Asia, Latin America, the Middle East, Russia, and the Ukraine. Founded in 1985, AJWS has supported projects in more than fifty countries. AJWS is a Jewish response to international need. AJWS empowers American Jews to act upon the Jewish ideals of tzedakah and tikkun olam. Through AJWS' International Jewish College Corps Program, college students and recent graduates have the opportunity to travel to Zimbabwe and Honduras where they will engage in a service project with an AJWS partner organization. Upon completion of their time in the developing world, students travel to Israel where they learn about Israel's role as a leader in international development. Throughout the following year, students gather for seminars, retreats, service projects, and meetings with activists, rabbis, and educators. 989 Avenue of the Americas, 10th Floor, New York, NY 10018; (212) 736-2597; Fax: (212) 736-3463; E-mail: sfingeroth@jws.org; Web: www.ajws.org. Ruth Messinger, President; Stephanie Fingeroth, Assistant to the President.

America-Israel Friendship League: Exchange of Young Journalists

The Exchange of Young Journalists program arranges a four-week visit to Israel for students in undergraduate/graduate studies in communications, media, and journalism. AIFL, 134 East 39th Street, New York, NY 10016; (212) 213-8630; Fax: (212) 683-3475. Stanley A. Urman, Senior Executive Vice President.

AMITIM: The Israel-Diaspora Service Project

AMITIM is a hands-on movement for global change in which a select group of North Americans and Israelis, aged twenty-one to twenty-seven, dedicate eight to ten months of service to underdeveloped Jewish communities in the former Soviet Union. AMITIM offers Jewish communities a framework in which they may reconnect with their heritage, reclaim their past, and determine their position in the world of today and tomorrow. Rebuild and strengthen the communities and yourself—physically, emotionally, spiritually—and return with valuable skills and international experience that will enhance any resume or graduate school application. AMTIM seeks college graduates with significant leadership skills who are independent, innovative, flexible and comfortable working as part of a team. Placements begin in late summer/early fall. 1440 Spring Street, NW, Atlanta, GA 30309; (404) 874-7043; E-mail: jaziman@atljf.org; Web: www.aljf.org. Jessica Aziman, Director.

Israel Aliyah Program Center (IAPC): Stagerim

Two- to six-month internship employment in all fields with any Hebrew level. Apply three months in advance. (212) 339-6060; Fax: (212) 832-2597.

Kibbutz Program Center

The Kibbutz Program Center helps young adults select the kibbutz program that best fits their needs. The Center offers three main programs. Kibbutz Volunteers is a two-month commitment to volunteer on a kibbutz, in exchange for room and board. Starting dates throughout the year. Kibbutz Ulpan is a five-month program for individuals agred eighteen to twenty-eight. Intensive Hebrew study while living and working on a kibbutz. Starting dates throughout the year. Project Oren Kibbutz Programs are five months of combining kibbutz life and work and Hebrew study with one of four educational programs, all of which offer tours and Israel exploration. Program options are Israel Through Drama, Creative Arts, Environmental Studies, and Jerusalem Studies & Archaeology. The Center has numerous other summer program options. Kibbutz Program Center, 633 Third Avenue, New York, NY 10017; (212) 318-6132; (800) 247-7852; Fax: (212) 318-6134; E-mail: kibbutzdsk@aol.com. Merav Segal, Milka Eliav, Alisha Goodman.

Livnot U'Lehibanot

Livnot U'Lehibanot (To Build and to Be Built) is a community-oriented, three-month or three-week work, study, community service, and hiking program with locations in both ancient Tzfat and historic Jerusalem. By literally "digging into their roots," young Jewish adults aged twenty-one to thirty with little or no Jewish background are introduced to the foundations of Jewish tradition in an open and questioning atmosphere. Livnot offers a course of study in Jewish history, philosophy, ethics, holidays, and current events. Participants also work in construction and community service projects to aid Israel's needy and go on weekly hikes throughout the country. Programs run throughout the year. Livnot

U'Lehibanot, 110 East 59th Street, 3rd Floor, New York, NY 10022; (888) LIVNOT-0; (212) 752-2390; Fax: (212) 832-2597; E-mail: sammyrose@aol.com. Stacy "Sam" Rosen, North American Coordinator.

Masada Israel Summer Programs

Masada Maccabi Israel Summer Programs is an independent, Zionist, educational, non-profit organization dedicated to offering Jewish youth the opportunity to explore Israel through cultural, social, outdoor, and educational activities. Spend a week in each region of Israel hiking through the desert, bike riding in the north, spending nights under the stars, and many more adventurous activities. Some programs are Adventure Israel (four weeks), Scuba Program (five weeks), Adventure Extreme (five weeks), Teen Age Tour (three weeks), Masada Student Program (four weeks), Masada Student Sinai Adventure (five weeks), and Young Professionals Israel Experience (two weeks). 4 East 34th Street, New York, NY 10016; (800) 732-1266 (outside New York), (212) 481-1500 (in New York); Fax: (212) 481-1513; E-mail: masadamac@aol.com; Web: www.masadamac.com. Yaffa Shoshan, Central Shlicha; Avi Maidenberg, National Program Director.

New Israel Fund/Shatil Volunteer and Internship Placement Service (in Israel)

Shatil, New Israel Fund's Capacity-Building Center for Social Change Organizations, coordinates a volunteer placement service that matches qualified individuals with grassroots organizations that work to advance democracy and social justice in Israel. Programs include safeguarding civil and human rights, promoting Jewish-Arab co-existence, advancing the status of women, fostering tolerance and religious pluralism, bridging social and economic gaps, increasing government accountability, and assisting citizen efforts to protect the environment. Shatil volunteers work side by side with Israeli activists. Internships usually span three months to a full year, from four to forty hours per week;

some summer internships may be available. Stipends for qualified candidates who speak Hebrew or Arabic and will volunteer for at least twenty-one hours per week for a minimum of six months. PO Box 53395, Jerusalem 91533, Israel; Fax: (972) 2-735149; E-mail: volunteer@shatil.nif.org.il. Brenda Needle, Coordinator, Volunteer Program. In the U.S.: 1625 K Street, NW, Suite 500, Washington, D.C. 20006; (202) 223-3333; Fax: (202) 659-2789; E-mail: info@nif.org. Roger Bennett, Coordinator of Leadership Development Programs.

Project Otzma

Otzma is a volunteer fellowship in Israel that provides its participants with the opportunity to live and work with Israelis on immigrant absorption centers, regions of urban renewal, kibbutzim, and youth aliyah villages. Otzma also includes an intensive educational program, hiking throughout the country, and the unique experience of an Israeli adoptive family. Upon return to North America, OTZMA graduates apply their skills and knowledge to serve their local Jewish communities. United Jewish Communities, 111 Eight Avenue, Suite 11E, New York, NY 10011; (212) 284-6721, (877) GO-OTZMA; Fax: (212) 284-6844; E-mail: otzma@ujcna.org; Web: www.projectotzma.org.

Project Otzma/Council of Jewish Federations

Project Otzma is a ten-month volunteer leadership development fellowship designed to offer young Jewish adults aged twenty to twenty-four (college graduates preferred) the opportunity to live and volunteer in Israel in a variety of settings. Participants work on kibbutzim and in youth village boarding schools and immigrant absorption centers, and volunteer in regions of urban renewal paired with their local communities in North America. Project Otzma's important educational component gives participants a better understanding of Israeli society. It includes an intensive three-month Hebrew language course, seminars on topical issues, and hiking trips. Each participant is paired with an adoptive family whose house and members serve as a "home away from home" for the duration of the program. Project Otzma, Council of Jewish Federations, 730 Broadway, New York, NY 10003; (212) 598-3532; Fax: (212) 529-5842; E-mail: sherry_moss@cjfny.org. Sherry Moss, CJF Otzma Coordinator.

Project Oren Kibbutz Programs

Project Oren Kibbutz Programs offers an experience unlike any other in Israel. Students live on kibbutz, work three days a week in one of the kibbutz branches, and study Hebrew three days a week on kibbutz for either a summer or a semester. By working with kibbutzniks and studying Hebrew with fellow Ulpanists, students have the opportunity to see Israel from the inside while creating their own community. Students also participate in a rich program of stimulating lectures and trips that discuss various Jewish issues, such as Zionism, Israel-Diaspora relations, history, the peace process, and more. Lastly, Project Oren also offers three educational tracks for the semester programs from which the participants choose one particular topic to study: creative arts; Israel through drama; or Jerusalem studies and archaeology. These topics are studied twice a week through lectures, trips, and workshops. 633 3rd Avenue, 21st Floor, New York, NY 10017; (800) 247-7852, (212) 318-6136; Fax: (212) 318-6134; E-mail: projoren@aol.com; Web: www.kibbutz.org.il/oren. Alisha Goodman, North American Director.

Sephardic Education Center— Tour Israel

Young adults aged eighteen to twenty-six can tour Israel and on the way stay in four- and five-star hotel accommodations. Sephardic Education Center, (800) 484-9987 ext. 7365; Fax: (213) 653-9985.

Sherut La'am—Youth and Hechalutz/ World Zionist Organization

Sherut La'am is a one-year program for recent college graduates up to age twenty-five. Working as volunteers, participants become integral members of the communities in which they live and work. The first four months are devoted to intensive Hebrew study (Ulpan) on Kibbutz Ramat Yochnan (half day study/half day work). Participants are then placed in volunteer positions, most often in development towns throughout Israel. A six-month program is available to those who already know Hebrew. Sherut La-am, 110 East 59th Street, New York, NY 10022; (212) 339-6916/6933, (800) 27-ISRAEL; Fax: (212) 755-4781. Miriam Stern, Director.

Shoreshim College Program

Bicultural program for American and Israeli students exploring Jewish and Israeli culture. Participants have the option to go to Poland as part of the program. College credit and scholarship are available. 323 N. Clark Street, #768, Chicago, IL 60657; (708) 982-9347, (708) 328-0706, Fax: (708) 328-7504.

Society for the Protection of Nature in Israel (SPNI): Israel Nature Trails

More than a dozen different tours from Tel Aviv or Jerusalem ranging from one to twelve days. All tours are in English with experienced guides. SPNI-Israel Nature Trails, 3 Hashfela Street, Tel Aviv, 66183; (972) 3-6388677. In the U.S.: 89 Fifth Avenue, Suite 800, New York, NY 10003; (800) 323-0035, (212) 645-8732; Fax: (212) 645-8749.

Tagar Israel Experience

Tagar offers two programs. Tagar Israel Experience includes three weeks volunteering on an army base and two weeks touring. We Are One has previous Israel program participants perform community service. Tagar Student Movement, (212) 650-1231, (800) 846-2382; Fax: (212) 658-1413.

Theater in Israel

The Israel Theatre Program offers American students the opportunity to understand the social, political, and ideological dilemmas of Israeli society as reflected in its theatre. Participants meet Israeli artists, educators, producers, and therapists, and visit Israeli sites. Courses are sponsored by Seminar Hakibbutzim, the State Teachers College of Israel in Tel Aviv, and the

Theatre Program of Kansas State University. Nine undergraduate or graduate credits may be transferrable. Six weeks during the summer. 129 Nichols, Manhattan, KS 66506-2304; (913) 532-6875; Fax: (913) 532-7004; E-mail: fedder@ksu.edu. Dr. Norman J. Fedder, Theatre Program, Kansas State University.

UAHC College Academy in Israel

A thirty-six-day adventure in Israel combining twenty-four days of touring with a twelve-day kibbutz stay or archaeological dig. UAHC, NFTY in Israel: (914) 987-6300.

UJA Student Winter Missions

Winter missions to Israel to observe how UJA contributions help Israel. UJA University Programs, 99 Park Avenue, Suite 300, New York, NY 10016; (212) 880-1437; Fax: (212) 867-1074.

University Student Division of the Hagshama Department, World Zionist Organization: Study and Touring

USD/Hagshama/WZO serves as a resource for all Israel programs as well as programs of its own. These include short-term tours, academic study, kibbutz, art, internships/volunteer, Ulpan, teaching English, and other opportunities. USD/Hagshama also has a leadership training program that involves seminars in the U.S. and a trip to Israel. USD/Hagshama's goal is to bring Israel to college campuses and college campuses to Israel. USD/Hagshama fosters Zionist ideals and trains students for Israel activism on campus. (800) 27-ISRAEL; Fax: (212) 318-6193; E-mail: info@usd.org.

Volunteers for Israel

Volunteers for Israel participants get an insider's view of Israel by spending three weeks on army bases or in hospitals performing community service. On specific dates, archaeological digs, trips to botanical gardens, and two-week tours are also available. College credit is available. Low program fees include round-trip airfare, airport taxes, room and kosher board, day tour, and lectures. Volunteers for Israel, 330 West

42nd Street, Suite 1618, New York, NY 10036; (212) 643-4848; Fax: (212) 643-4855; E-mail: vol4israel@aol.com. Edie Silberstein, Executive Director; Marna Chester, National Student Coordinator.

WUJS Institute at Arad

The WUJS Institute in Arad, Israel, offers Jewish college graduates (aged twenty-one to thirty-five) seven months of Hebrew language instruction, Jewish/Israeli studies courses, travel, and community volunteer experiences with five months or more of career development and job placement in all professions throughout Israel. 24 Yoshiyahu Street, Arad 89022, Israel; E-mail: wujsarad@netvision.net.il; Web: www.wujs-arad.org. In the U.S.: WUJS Institute, PO Box 6177, East Brunswick, NJ 08816; Toll free: (888) WUJS-INS; Phone/Fax: (732) 238-2998; E-mail: wujsusa@cwixmail.com, wujs@aol.com. Ami Blaszkowsky, Director.

Yad Vashem: Institute for Educators

Teaching the Shoah and Antisemitism is a program open twice a year to graduates and post-graduates. It provides the appropriate academic and pedagogic tools to enable educators to teach, confront, and discuss the main issues concerning the causes and effects of the Shoah. Yad Vashem International School for Holocaust Studies, PO Box 3477, Jerusalem 91304, Israel; Fax: (972) 2-6433511; E-mail: edu@yad-vashem.org.il.

Yavnh Olami—Summer Internship Program

In this program that includes regular shiurim and tiyyulim, religious Zionist students gain actual experience in their chosen field. 110 East 59th Street, 4th Floor, New York, NY 10022; (212) 339-6942.

National Agencies and Institutions

Hillel works in close cooperation with many other agencies and institutions with excellent programs for college students. Many of these organizations, and the resources they offer to Jewish college students, are listed on the following pages. Because of the complexity and vitality of the Jewish organizational world, it is possible that a program of national interest has been inadvertently omitted. Note: Organizations that provide short-term or summer programs for college students are listed in the preceding section.

Information about most of these programs is available through Hillel, or you may contact the agency or institution through the campus liaison at the national headquarters.

Abraham Fund

477 Madison Avenue
New York, NY 10022
(212) 303-9421, (800) 301-FUND
Fax: (212) 935-1834
E-mail: abrahamfun@aol.com
Web: www.coexistence.org

Founded in 1989, the Abraham Fund is a not-for-profit fundraising and educational organization dedicated to promoting Jewish-Arab co-existence in Israel. As a financial and educational resource for grassroots programs that enhance mutual understanding and tolerance, The Abraham Fund provides grants to numerous organizations and institutions in Israel in such areas as culture, education, health, and social services, among others. In the United States, the Abraham Fund's educational and cultural programs provide information that enhances understanding about the necessary cooperation between Israel's Jewish majority and Arab minority.

ALEPH: Alliance for Jewish Renewal

7318 Germantown Avenue
Philadelphia, PA 19119
(215) 247-9700
Fax: (215) 247-9703

Rabbi Daniel Siegel,
Executive Director

Founded by Rabbi Zalman Schachter-Shalomi, ALEPH is a transdenominational organization dedicated to the advancement of vital, engaged, and spiritually meaningful Judaism. ALEPH sponsors conference, seminars, and retreats; publishes a quarterly journal, *New Menorah*;

and is home to a variety of programs, including The Shalom Center, the Network of Jewish Renewal Communities, The Jewish Renewal Life Center, The Spiritual Eldering Institute, Elat Chayyim, a summer and holiday retreat center, and a Professional Development Program leading to private smicha (rabbinic ordination).

Alpha Epsilon Phi Sorority

111 Prospect Street, 2nd Floor
Stamford, CT 06901
(203) 358-8744
Fax: (203) 357-7975
E-mail: aephinatl@aol.com

Bonnie Rubenstein Wunsch, Executive Director

Alpha Epsilon Pi Fraternity

8815 Wesleyan Road
Indianapolis, IN 46268-1171
(317) 876-1913
Fax: (317) 876-1057
E-mail: sid@aepi.org
Web: www.aepi.org

Sidney Dunn, Executive Vice President

Alpha Epsilon Pi national fraternity was founded "to provide opportunities for the Jewish college man seeking camaraderie as well as personal growth in a Jewish social and cultural organization." Since its inception in 1913 at New York University, more than 65,000 men have become members, and approximately 1,500 more men are initiated annually. The fraternity "encourages the Jewish student to remain dedicated to Judaism while preparing him to become one of tomorrow's leaders so that he may aid himself, his family, his community, and his people." AEPi works with Hillel and other Jewish organizations on political action, philanthropic, and social projects. Annual awards are given to members for service to the Jewish community.

America-Israel Friendship League

134 East 39th Street
New York, NY 10016
(212) 213-8630
Fax: (212) 683-3475
E-mail: aifl@nyworld.com
Web: www.aifl.org

Stanley A. Urman, Senior Executive Vice President

Neither a governmental nor a sectarian organization, the AIFL, founded in 1971, is a national membership organization that mobilizes broad support for people-to-people exchanges between Americans and Israelis of all ages, faiths, ethnic backgrounds, and political persuasions. Regional offices of the AIFL are located in Denver, Tucson, and San Francisco. The AIFL is dedicated to promoting and strengthening the mutually beneficial relationships between the people of the United States and Israel. It has developed a broad range of people-to-people programs, which include educa-

tional exchanges of youth and young adults, seminars and missions in Israel for key groups of present and future American leaders, and a variety of educational and cultural activities throughout the United States.

American Friends of Neve Shalom/ Wahat Al Salam: The Oasis of Peace

121 6th Avenue, Room 502
New York, NY 10013
(212) 226-9246
Fax: (212) 431-9783

Sharon Burde, Executive Director

Neve Shalom/Wahat Al Salam (NS/WAS) is a unique cooperative community where Jews and Palestinians of Israeli citizenship live together. The aim is to create a social, cultural, and political framework of equality and mutual respect in which citizens retain their own heritage and identity.

American Israel Public Affairs Committee

440 First Street, NW, Suite 600
Washington, D.C. 20001
(202) 639-5200
Fax: (202) 347-4918

Elissa Polan, National Leadership Coordinator

AIPAC is the only registered lobby that works with Congress and the administration to strengthen the U.S.-Israel relationship. AIPAC's Political Leadership Development Program educates and trains college students to become politically involved. Internships are offered in Washington, D.C., and nine regional offices, and interns get to lobby members of Congress. The Near East Report, a bi-weekly newsletter, the D.C. Political Job Bank, resource materials, and AIPAC on Campus are also available to members of the program.

American Jewish Committee

165 East 56th Street
New York, NY 10022-2746
(212) 751-4000
Fax: (212) 319-0975

Geri Rozanski, Director, Community Program Development

The American Jewish Committee seeks to prevent infraction of civil and religious rights of Jews in any part of the world; to advance the cause of human rights of all people; to interpret the position of Israel to the American public; and to help American Jews maintain and enrich their Jewish identity while achieving full integration in American life. The Committee sponsors research into current social issues affecting the American Jewish community.

American Jewish Congress

15 East 84th Street
New York, NY 10028
(212) 879-4500
Fax: (212) 472-2264

Phil Baum, Acting Director

The American Jewish Congress works to foster the creative cultural survival of the Jewish people; to help Israel develop in peace, freedom, and security; to eliminate all forms of racial and religious bigotry; and to advance civil rights, protect civil liberties, defend religious freedom, and safeguard the separation of church and state.

American Jewish Joint Distribution Committee, Inc.

711 Third Avenue
New York, NY 10017-4014
(212) 687-6200
Fax: (212) 370-5467

Linda Levi, Assistant Executive Vice President

JDC serves as the overseas arm of the American Jewish community, sponsoring programs of relief, rescue, and reconstruction in sixty countries, and fulfilling its commitment to the idea that all Jews are responsible for one another and that "to save one person is to save a world" (Mishna, Sanhedrin 4:5). JDC, in cooperation with Hillel and the Lynn and Charles Schusterman Family Foundation, is facilitating the creation of Hillels in the former Soviet Union. JDC also offers several volunteer opportunities abroad.

See listing under Short-Term and Summer Programs for Jewish University Students.

American Zionist Foundation

110 East 59th Street, 3rd Floor
New York, NY 10022
(212) 318-6100
Fax: (212) 935-3578

Amy Riesner, Program Associate

The American Zionist Foundation assists university students with Zionist and Israel programming by providing speakers, resources, and materials for Israel advocacy and education.

Anti-Defamation League

823 United Nations Plaza
New York, NY 10017
(212) 885-7813
(212) 490-2525
Fax: (212) 867-0779
E-mail: rossj@adl.org
Web: www.adl.org

Dr. Jeffrey A. Ross, Director, Department of Campus Affairs/
Higher Education

The Anti-Defamation League was founded in 1913 to combat anti-Semitism and all forms of bigotry. In doing so, it seeks to enhance and protect the interests of the Jewish community. The ADL sponsors conferences, a Crisis Management Team, missions to Israel, the Blacks and Jews in Conversation Program, and the Campus of Difference Program. The ADL's services are available to all members of the campus Jewish community.

Association for Jewish Studies

MB 0001
Brandeis University
PO Box 9110
Waltham, MA 02254-9110
(617) 736-2981
Fax: (617) 736-2982
E-mail: ajs@logos.cc.brandeis.edu

Robert M. Seltzer, President
Aaron L. Katchen, Executive Secretary

The AJS seeks to promote, maintain, and improve the teaching of Jewish studies in colleges and universities by sponsoring meetings and conferences, publishing a newsletter and other scholarly materials, aiding in the placement of teachers, coordinating research, and cooperating with scholarly organizations.

Association of Jewish Community Organization Personnel (AJCOP)

14619 Horseshoe Trace
Wellington, FL 33414
(561) 795-4853
Fax: (561) 798-0358
E-mail: marlene@ajcop.org
Web: www.ajcop.org

Louis B. Solomon, Executive Director

AJCOP is the professional association for the advancement of standards of community organization practice affiliated with the Jewish Communal Service Association. AJCOP welcomes all professionally trained or experienced individuals engaged in community organization work within and on behalf of the Jewish community. Individuals are employed by local, regional, national, and overseas Jewish community organizations, agencies, and institutions, as well as academicians engaged in the field. Jewish students preparing to enter the field and retired professionals are eligible for membership in AJCOP. We are dedicated to the development, enhancement, and strengthening of the professional practice of Jewish community service. We seek to improve standards, practices, scope, and public understanding of the professional practice of Jewish community organization. We recognize the importance of supporting these efforts toward creative Jewish survival. AJCOP exists to serve those who serve others.

AVODAH: The Jewish Service Corps

443 Park Avenue South, 11th Floor
New York, NY 10016
(212) 545-7759
Fax: (212) 686-1353
E-mail: info@avodah.net
Web: www.avodah.net

David Rosenn, Executive Director

AVODAH is a year-long full-time service corps program that combines front-line work on urban poverty issues in New York City with Jewish study and community building. AVODAH participants live together, creating a community of young people committed to integrating a vibrant Jewish life and a serious commitment to social change. Service placements include organizations addressing issues such as hunger, literacy, public health, and child welfare. AVODAH is not affiliated with any particular Jewish denomination or movement. Participants from all across the range of American Jewish life are encouraged to apply. Service corps members receive health insurance and a subsistence stipend. Applicants to AVODAH must be twenty-one or older.

B'nai B'rith International

1640 Rhode Island Avenue, NW
Washington, D.C. 20036
(202) 857-6600
Fax: (202) 857-1099
E-mail: bblb@cloudg.net

Jason Epstein, Assistant Director of Public Affairs

B'nai B'rith International, with affiliates in forty-seven countries, offers programs designed to ensure the preservation of Jewry and Judaism through education, community volunteer service, expansion of human rights, assistance to Israel, housing for the elderly, and advocating the rights of Jews wherever they live. There are new chapters in several of the countries of the former Soviet Union.

B'nai B'rith Lecture Bureau

823 United Nations Plaza, Room 400
New York, NY 10017
(212) 490-1170
Fax: (212) 687-3429
E-mail: bblb@cloudg.net

Ruth Wheat, Director

The B'nai B'rith Lecture Bureau, sponsored by the Commission on Continuing Jewish Education, is a major resource for speakers on subjects of Jewish interest in the United States and Canada. Its list of distinguished writers, performing artists, scholars, and teachers represents the full range of Jewish thought and opinion in the United States, Israel, and elsewhere.

Campus Outreach Opportunity League (COOL)

1531 P Street, NW
Lower Level
Washington, D.C. 20005
(202) 265-1200
Fax: (202) 265-3241
E-mail: outreach@cool2serve.org
Web: www.cool2serve.org

Sarah Pearlman, Director of Outreach

COOL is a national non-profit organization whose mission is to educate and empower college students to strengthen our nation through community service. We educate, mobilize, and connect students of all backgrounds to lead a movement that increases participation in our communities, promotes activism, and fosters the civic and social responsibility necessary to build a just society.

Chabad-Lubavitch World Center

770 Eastern Parkway
Brooklyn, NY 11213
(718) 774-4000
Fax: (718) 774-2718

Zalman Shmotkin, Director

Chabad-Lubavitch activities vary from campus to campus. Chabad Houses are located near campuses or in Jewish community neighborhoods. Chabad offers Torah classes, Shabbat/Holiday services and meals, Mitzvah observance campaigns, and other special programs geared to students. Chabad rabbis are available for student counseling and assistance with Jewish observance.

CLAL—The National Jewish Center for Learning and Leadership

440 Park Avenue South, 4th Floor
New York, NY 10016
(212) 779-3300
Fax: (212) 779-1009

Marla Egers, Director of Community Development

CLAL develops pluralistic learning experiences and programs to inform, motivate, and empower Jews in order to attract them to a more active involvement in Jewish life.

Coalition for the Advancement of Jewish Education (CAJE)

261 West 35th Street, #12A
New York, NY 10001
(212) 268-4210
Fax: (212) 268-4214
E-mail: cajeny@caje.org

Sylvia Abrams, Chairperson
Dr. Eliot G. Spack, Executive Director

CAJE brings together Jews from all ideologies who are involved in every facet of Jewish education and are committed to transmitting the Jewish heritage. The organization sponsors the annual Conference on Alternatives in Jewish Education, maintains a Web site with downloadable curricular materials, publishes a wide variety of publications, organizes shared-interest networks, and offers small grants for special projects.

Coalition on the Environment and Jewish Life (COEJL)

443 Park Avenue South, 11th Floor
New York, NY 10016-7322
(212) 684-6950 ext. 210
Fax: (212) 686-1353
E-mail: coejl@aol.com
Web: www.coejl.org

Mark Jacobs, Director

COEJL promotes environmental education, scholarship, advocacy, and action in the American Jewish community through publications, public education campaigns, conferences, Jewish environmental leadership development, and a Legislative Advocacy Network. COEJL's mission is to integrate Jewishly informed environmental education and action into the fabric of American Jewish life. Resource materials, speakers, and technical assistance are available to campus groups. A collaboration of Jewish institutions from a broad spectrum of Jewish religious and communal life, COEJL is the Jewish member of the National Religious Partnership for the Environment. Internships are available.

College Democrats of America

430 South Capitol Street, SE
Washington, D.C. 20003
(202) 479-5189
Fax: (202) 488-5075
E-mail: cda@collegedems.org
Web: www.collegedems.org/cda

Lisa Kohnke, National Field Director

As the student arm of the Democratic Party, College Democrats of America is a national organization working to expand and coordinate student involvement in the political process. We stand on the front lines in the battle to protect student aid and the ongoing fight for affordable health care, access to education, a cleaner environment, and equal opportunity for all Americans. CDA continuously registers students to vote and aggressively fights to reverse the constituency's low voter turnout in order to restore young America as a viable political force for the 2000 campaign. CDA hosts a National Convention in Washington, D.C., every summer to engage America's Democratic student activists. The convention includes intensive campaign and grassroots training, keynote addresses, meetings with elected officials, a rally on Capitol Hill, national CDA officer elections, social events, and a community service project.

Committee for Accuracy in Middle East Reporting in America (CAMERA)

PO Box 428
Boston, MA 02456
(617) 789-3672
Fax: (617) 787-7853
Web: www.camera.org

Andrea Levin, Director
Josh Chadajo, Campus Programs

CAMERA is a non-profit media-watch organization dedicated to promoting balanced and accurate coverage of Israel and the Middle East. CAMERA responds directly to students' requests for information, allowing them to respond knowledgeably to anti-Israel activities on campus. CAMERA On Campus educates students about key issues by featuring articles on current events and the history of the region, and also recommends resources for further research. CAMERA On Campus is available to students, Hillels, and other campus organizations free of charge. For a subscription, provide CAMERA with the name, address, school, and year of graduation. Organizations should indicate the desired number of copies per issue.

Council of Jewish Federations

730 Broadway
New York, NY 10003
(212) 475-5000 ext. 583
(800) 899-4480 Tone: 395-225
Fax: (212) 529-5842
E-mail: lance_jacobs@cjf.org

Lance Jacobs, Consultant, Personnel Services

CJF is the Continental Association of almost 200 North American Jewish Federations. CJF develops programs, provides consultation and the exchange of successful experiences, supports fundraising, and engages in planning and action on common community needs. CJF administers the Federation Executive Recruitment and Education Program (FEREP), which provides graduate school scholarships to exceptional individuals wishing to pursue a career track in the Jewish Federation field.

FEREP

United Jewish Communities
111 Eighth Avenue, Suite 11E
New York, NY 10011
(212) 284-6710
Fax: (212) 284-6843
E-mail: susan_sherr@cjfny.org
Web: www.generationj.com

Susan Sherr, Consultant, Personnel Services

FEREP is a scholarship program that offers various levels of tuition grants toward specific graduate programs leading to careers in the Jewish federation field. The unique curricula coordinate graduate study with field work internships in Jewish federations. FEREP awardees commit to working in a Jewish federation in North America for two to three years upon completion of graduate school. FEREP offers a limited number of full tuition grants (capped at $20,000 per year for each year of graduate study) and partial tuition grants ($7,500 per year for each year of graduate study). In addition, FEREP awardees receive priority referral to appropriate entry-level positions in federations upon graduation as well as ongoing career counseling and professional development opportunities.

Hadassah: The Women's Zionist Organization of America, Inc.

50 West 58th Street
New York, NY 10019
(212) 303-8156
(212) 303-4597
Fax: (212) 303-4525

Susan Mark, Hadassah National Outreach Chair
Larry Hoffman, National Assistant Director, Young Judaea

Hadassah is one of the foremost women's groups in the United States and the largest women's Zionist organization in the world. Founded in New York in 1912 by Henrietta Szold to provide modern health care for those in Palestine, Hadassah is now comprised of more than 300,000 women dedicated to healing, education, and volunteerism. Young Judaea, Hadassah's Zionist youth movement, offers clubs and summer camps in the United States and work-study programs in Israel. Hadassah also sponsors five of Hillel's Jewish Campus Service Corps Fellows.

Hamagshimim

50 West 58th Street
New York, NY 10019
(212) 303-4582
(877) GO-HAMAG
Fax: (212) 303-4572
E-mail: hamagshimim@hadassah.org

Lisa Samick, Director
Steve Klein, Shaliach

Hamagshimim is a pluralistic, non-partisan Zionist movement on campuses nationwide. Our goal is to build Zionist and Jewish identity by emphasizing the centrality of Israel in Jewish life. Hamagshimim sponsors several events both in the U.S. and in Israel: National Convention, the Get Back to Israel Retreats, *Mesamnei Shvilim* (leadership enrichment seminar in

Israel), Sharsheret (a junior year abroad add-on program), and Destination Israel. *Ad Kahn*, our bi-monthly newsletter, is available free of charge to all students, Hillels, and other campus organizations. Additionally, Hamagshimim offers several services to assist students and recent graduates in getting to Israel. *B'derech* (on the way) is a free individualized counseling service to assist you in choosing the best program. *Reshet* (network) is a free service designed to aid your search for job and internship opportunities while you are still in the States.

International Association of Jewish Vocational Services (IAJVS)

1845 Walnut Street, Suite 640
Philadelphia, PA 19103
(215) 854-0233
Fax: (215) 854-0212
Web: www.iajvs.org

Genie Cohen, Executive Director

IAJVS is a not-for-profit trade association of social service agencies located across the United States and in Canada and Israel. College-age individuals can find career counseling, connections to internships, and scholarship assistance at member agencies. Additional services include career management workshops, skills training, and rehabilitation programs. These are available to people across the social spectrum, including dislocated workers, people changing careers, welfare recipients, refugees, persons with disabilities, and the elderly. IAJVS provides its member agencies with technical, informational, fundraising, and communications support. IAJVS organizes an annual meeting for member agency executives, staff, and lay leaders. To locate the nearest IAJVS agency, visit the IAJVS Web site or contact the IAJVS office.

Israel Aliyah Program Center

110 East 59th Street, 3rd Floor
New York, NY 10022
(212) 339-6060
Fax: (212) 832-2597

IAPC reaches out to students interested in exploring Israel or making aliyah. IAPC sponsors aliyah support groups on campuses and furnishes them and other Jewish organizations with literature, materials, and speakers. IAPC offers summer employment internships and tour opportunities in Israel.

CONSULATES OF THE STATE OF ISRAEL

Atlanta

1100 Spring Street, Suite 440
Atlanta, GA 30309-2823
(404) 875-7851
Fax: (404) 874-5364

Boston

1020 Statler Office Building
20 Park Plaza
Boston, MA 02116
(617) 542-0041
Fax: (617) 338-4995

Chicago

111 E. Wacker Drive, Suite 1308
Chicago, IL 60601
(312) 565-3300
Fax: (312) 565-3871

Houston

24 Greenway Plaza, Suite 1500
Houston, TX 77046
(713) 627-3780
Fax: (713) 627-0149

Los Angeles

6380 Wilshire Boulevard, Suite 1700
Los Angeles, CA 90048
(323) 852-5500
Fax: (323) 852-5555

Miami

100 N. Biscayne Boulevard, #1800
Miami, FL 33132
(305) 358-8111
Fax: (305) 371-5034

Montreal

1155 Boul, Rene Levesque Quest
Montreal, Quebec H3B 4S6
Canada
(514) 940-8500
Fax: (514) 940-8555

New York

800 Second Avenue
New York, NY 10017
(212) 499-5439
Fax: (212) 499-5435

Ottawa

50 O'Connor Street, Suite 1005
Ottawa, Ontario KIP GL2
Canada
(613) 567-6450
Fax: (613) 237-8865

Philadelphia

230 South 15th Street, 8th floor
Philadelphia, PA 19102
(215) 546-5556
Fax: (215) 545-3986

San Francisco

456 Montgomery St., Suite 2100
San Francisco, CA 94104
(415) 398-8885
Fax: (415) 398-8589

Toronto

180 Bloor Street West, Suite 700
Toronto, Ontario M5S 2VG
Canada
(416) 640-8500
Fax: (416) 640-8555

Israel: Embassy of Israel

3514 International Drive, NW
Washington, D.C. 20008
(202) 364-5500
Fax: (202) 364-5423
Web: www.israelemb.org

Avi Granot, Minister for Public and Interreligious Affairs
Yair Kalush, Chief of Public Affairs (364-5546)
Mitchell Gersten, Academic Liaison (364-5676)

The Embassy of Israel and Israel's Consular offices throughout North America are resources for material dealing with Israeli politics, culture, geography, economy, and current social issues. Israeli academic and political guest lecturers are also available for various seminars, symposia, or classroom lectures throughout the academic year.

Israel: State of Israel Office of Academic Affairs in the USA (IOAA)

Consulate General of Israel
800 Second Avenue
New York, NY 10017
(212) 499-5430
Fax: (212) 499-5435
E-mail: ioaa@idt.net

Orly Gil, Consul for Academic Affairs in the USA
Mara Baylis, Director of Student Affairs

IOAA is the official liaison of Israel to the university community in the USA. The goal of the IOAA is to foster cooperation with university faculty and students by making Israel-related information, programs, and activities available to college campuses around the country. The office works together with faculty, departments, student associations, and other organizations interested in Israel.

The Jewish Chautauqua Society

838 Fifth Avenue
New York, NY 10021
(800) 765-6200
(212) 570-0707
Fax: (212) 570-0960

Doug Barden, Executive Director
Dora Lee, Program Director

JCS works to promote interfaith understanding by sponsoring accredited college courses and one-day lectures on Judaic topics, producing educational videotapes on interfaith topics, and convening interfaith institutes. JCS is sponsored by the National Federation of Temple Brotherhoods.

Jewish Community Centers Association of North America

15 East 26th Street, 10th floor
New York, NY 10010-1579
(212) 532-4949
Fax: (212) 481-4174

Steven Rod, Director of Professional Development

The Jewish Community Centers Association is the central leadership and service organization for the North American Jewish Community Center/YM-YWHA movement. Its 275 JCCs, YM-YWHAs, and summer camps in the United States and Canada have a constituency of more than one million Jews. JCC Association is also the United States Government–accredited agency for serving the Jewish needs of U.S. Jewish military personnel and their families and hospitalized veterans through the services of the JWB Jewish Chaplains Council. Local JCCs provide employment opportunities for college students as group leaders, camp staff, and clerical workers. JCCs organize programs for singles during school vacations.

Jewish Council for Public Affairs (JCPA)

1640 Rhode Island Avenue, NW
Washington, D.C. 20036
(202) 293-1649
Fax: (202) 293-2154
Web: www.jewishpublicaffairs.org

Reva Price, Washington Representative

The national policy-making and coordinating body for the Jewish community relations field, JCPA and its 13 national and 122 local member Jewish community relations agencies address a wide range of domestic and international public affairs issues. JCPA and local groups consult and work with campus groups on a range of community relations and public policy issues, strategies, and advocacy and provide information, material, speakers, and other resources. Hillel's annual public policy forum, the Spitzer Forum, is held in conjunction with the annual JCPA Plenum.

Jewish Education Service of North America, Inc. (JESNA)

111 8th Avenue
New York, NY 10011-5201
(212) 284-6950
Fax: (212) 284-6951
E-mail: info@jesna.org

Paul A. Flexner, Director, Human Resources Development

JESNA was created in 1981 as the Jewish Federation system's educational coordinating, planning, and development agency. JESNA is widely recognized for its leadership in the areas of research and program evaluation, professional recruitment and development, media and technology, organizational change, and effective program design and dissemination. JESNA operates the Lainer Interns for Jewish Education program at the Hebrew University and Tel Aviv University. In North America, JESNA encourages university students to pursue careers in Jewish education and Jewish communal service.

Jewish Fund for Justice

260 Fifth Avenue, Suite 701
New York, NY 10001-6408
(212) 213-2113
Fax: (212) 213-2233
E-mail: justice@aol.com

Janet Leuchter, Jewish Outreach Coordinator

The Jewish Fund for Justice is a national philanthropy organization that, in partnership with Hillel, provides grants and technical assistance to grassroots groups fighting poverty in their own communities. JFJ offers grants to on- or off-campus anti-poverty projects with Jewish student involvement, including those undertaken in coalition with other campus groups. JFJ also offers program materials for Chanukah, Purim, and Pesach that link these holidays with contemporary social justice issues.

Jewish Heritage Program (JHP)

4032 Spruce Street
Philadelphia, PA 19104
(212) 222-9618
Fax: (215) 222-9635
E-mail: jheritage@aol.com
Web: www.jhp.org

Rabbi Menachem Schmidt, Executive Director
Rabbi Ephraim Levin, Associate Director

JHP is a unique campus outreach organization that began on the University of Pennsylvania campus five years ago. The goal of JHP is to help students provide peer-to-peer-based Jewish identity programming geared toward unaffiliated students. The programs are designed to inspire students to celebrate their heritage and instill a sense of identity and pride in their religion. JHP offers leadership training and mentoring opportunities with Jewish professionals from a variety of fields. Other activities include Shabbat dinners, historical programs, and holiday celebrations. The program also offers a number of retreats and trips, including an annual Israel excursion.

Jewish Life Network: A Judy and Michael Steinhardt Foundation

6 East 39th Street, 10th Floor
New York, NY 10016
(212) 279-2288
Fax: (212) 279-1155
E-mail: info@jewishlife.org
Web: www.jewishlife.org

Jonathan J. Greenberg, Executive Director

The Jewish Life Network, a Judy and Michael Steinhardt foundation, seeks to revitalize Jewish identity through educational, religious, and cultural initiatives designed to reach out to all Jews with an emphasis on those who are on the margins of Jewish life. In designing its programs, JLN favors imaginative breakthroughs, new strategies, and articulating Judaism in contemporary terms. This means supporting new programs and underwriting new institutions that could meaningfully change the community capacity for reaching groups who are not strongly connected to Jewish life. The basic pillars of Jewish identity formation should consist of day school education, Jewish camping, youth groups and college movements, experiences in Israel, intensive adult learning, and service. JLN supports and creates projects that will help to build this infrastructure.

Jewish Literacy Foundation

17 Warren Road, Suite 18
Pikesville, MD 21208
(410) 602-1020
Fax: (410) 602-4033
E-mail: ysegal@aol.com

Rabbi Yigal Segal, Executive Director

The Jewish Literacy Foundation is a non-profit organization established to promote the development and distribution of written educational materials which provide essential Jewish knowledge for the 75 percent of American Jewish households that currently have no synagogue affiliation and little or no personal contact with a rabbi or Jewish educator of any kind.

Jewish National Fund—College Activists Program

42 E. 69th Street
New York, NY 10021
(212) 879-9305 ext. 330
Fax: (212) 879-3980

Stephanie R. Stein, College Activists Department

The JNF College Activists Department (JNF On Campus) is the student arm of the Jewish National Fund. We are dedicated to ensuring that the campus community develops a growing understanding of "eco-zionism" and the Jewish connection to the natural world. Our programs offer college students the opportunity to foster their love for Ha'aretz, the land of Israel, become active campus leaders, and help improve the ecology of our planet. Programs include "Plant Your Roots in Israel" Tree Drives, Campus Hill Project, Annual Eco-Zionism Conference, Israel Experience Adventure Mission, Eco-Shabbat Evenings, Student Leadership Conferences, BGU Fellowship, Bi-Coastal Hanukkah Gatherings and Tu Bi'Shevat & Jewish Environmental Programs.

Jewish Renewal Life Center

6445 Greene Street, Room B202
Philadelphia, PA 19119
(215) 843-4345
Fax: (215) 247-9703

Rabbi Julie Greenberg, Director

Among the Center's activities is a year of immersion in Jewish living and learning with emphasis on development of skills in spiritual leadership and community building.

Jewish Student Press Service and New Voices Magazine

27 W. 20th Street, Suite 901
New York, NY 10011
(212) 675-1168
Fax: (212) 929-3459
E-mail: nvoices@idt.net
Web: www.jsps.com

Sam Apple, Director/Editor

The Jewish Student Press Service gives Jewish students an independent media to voice their ideas, opinions, and concerns. It provides resources and assistance to local campus Jewish publications, works to help today's Jewish students develop into tomorrow's topnotch journalists, and publishes the national Jewish student newspaper, *New Voices*. Contributors welcome.

Jewish Women International

1828 L Street, NW, Suite 250
Washington, D.C. 20036
(202) 857-1370
Fax: (202) 857-1380

Neil Sutton, Program Manager

Jewish Women International, formerly B'nai B'rith Women, strengthens the effectiveness of women in improving the quality of life for themselves, their families, and society; fosters the emotional well-being of children and youth; and perpetuates Jewish life and values. Goals include educating and advocating on issues of domestic violence in the Jewish community and building bridges through educational programs for youth.

Jewish Women's Archive

68 Harvard Street
Brookline, MA 02445
(617) 232-2258
Fax: (617) 975-0109
E-mail: jwarchive@rcn.org
Web: www.jwa.org

Gail Twersky Reimer, Director

Combining both the latest technology and the oldest oral traditions, the Jewish Women's Archive is working to bring a buried history back to life. JWA's award-winning Web site has laid the foundation for our comprehensive, state-of-the-art Virtual Archive. This pioneering resource will make it possible for anyone anywhere to instantly locate sources documenting the history of Jewish women in North America. Our *Women of Valor* posters, educational materials, and Web exhibits, created in collaboration with Ma'yan: The Jewish Women's Project in New York, bring the lives and accomplishments of noteworthy Jewish women out of obscurity and into the mainstream. Resource materials, speakers, and programs are available to campus groups. Student internships at JWA are available year-round.

Jews for Racial and Economic Justice

140 West 22nd Street, Suite 302
New York, NY 10011
(212) 647-8966
Fax: (212) 647-7124
E-mail: jfrej@igc.org
Web: www.jfrej.org

Andy Settner, Executive Director
Cindy Greenberg, Associate Director

Since our founding in 1990, the mission of JFREJ has been to connect Jewish struggles against anti-Semitism and for pluralism with broader social justice struggles. JFREJ strengthens a progressive Jewish voice in debates over NYC's future and activates the Jewish community as partner in the struggle for justice. JFREJ offers two community education anti-bias workshops ("Understanding & Fighting Racism as Jews" and "Anti-Semitism and Jewish Identity"); organizes public educational forums on pressing social justice issues; is involved in multiracial, interfaith, and cross-class coalition work; conducts outreach and provides support to Jewish students of all ages; hosts a weekly radio show (*Beyond the Pale: The Progressive Jewish Radio Hour*); has contacts at local universities and colleges; and has an extensive speakers bureau of scholars, activists, artists, and theologians who are experts on topics such as law, economics, feminism, and American culture.

KESHER—Reform Students on Campus

633 Third Avenue
New York, NY 10017-6778
(212) 650-4070
Fax: (212) 650-4199
E-mail: kesher@uahc.org

Rabbi Jonathan Klein, Director

KESHER is the Reform movement's college outreach program, engaging students through campus chavurot and events, and supplementing these experiences with an annual College Convention, e-mail networks, and summer/winter trips to Israel. To assist in funding Reform campus events, KESHER, in conjunction with the North American Federation of Temple Brotherhoods, offers grants to students and Hillel professionals. In addition, KESHER offers year-long academic programs in Israel and colloquia through the Hebrew Union College—Jewish Institute of Religion.

KIRUV College Outreach Program

500 W. 185th Street
New York, NY 10033
(212) 960-5263
Fax: (212) 960-5228

Barry Bender, Executive Director

KIRUV, sponsored by the Rabbinical Assembly of America and Yeshiva University, provides Jewish identity programming to campuses throughout North America. KIRUV's student volunteers provide on-campus peer teaching, exploratory programs, and experiential workshops utilizing more than fifty different program topics and seven different program formats.

KOACH—The Center for Conservative Judaism on Campus

601 Skokie Boulevard, Suite 402
Northbrook, IL 60062
(847) 714-9130
Fax: (847) 714-9133
E-mail: moline@uscj.org
Web: www.uscj.org/koach

Richard Moline, Director
Robyn Fryar, Jewish Campus Service Corps Fellow

KOACH provides support to Conservative students on campus. KOACH's Creative Grants Program funds religious services and cultural, educational, and social programs. KOACH produces a student newsletter with wide distribution; holds local, regional, and North American conferences; and has a wide array of programs and services, both in North America and in Israel. The KOACH E-mail network provides students with a forum to discuss issues of Jewish concern on campus. KOACH also serves as a clearinghouse for speakers and materials published by the Conservative movement and as a resource for questions on Conservative Judaism.

Lights in Action

220 5th Avenue, 13th Floor
New York, NY 10001
(212) 685-7886
Fax: (212) 685-7909
E-mail: liahq@lia.org
Web: www.lia.org

Sara Horwitz, Tali Rosenblatt, Shari Goldberg, Co-Directors

Lights in Action, a student-run group in operation for about six years, strives through creativity and a direct approach to bring Judaism to the 70,000 unaffiliated Jewish college students nationwide. Projects include mass mailings (reaching more than 200 campuses), leadership training seminars, a national student Shabbat, and a summer Institute in Israel. Supported by both philanthropists and institutions, LIA's purpose is to vest students with the tools to lead their peers and empower others to embrace Judaism.

MAZON: A Jewish Response to Hunger

12401 Wilshire Boulevard, Suite 303
Los Angeles, CA 90025-1015
(310) 442-0020
Fax: (310) 442-0030
E-mail: mazonmail@aol.com
Web: www.mazon.org

Susan Cramer, Executive Director

MAZON is a vehicle through which American Jews can respond to the tragedy of hunger in the United States and abroad. Its dual purpose is to help those who are hungry today and to alleviate the poverty that causes hunger. MAZON offers grants to non-profit organizations that provide assistance to hungry people or that seek effective, long-term solutions to the problems of hunger; it also assists students in finding volunteer opportunities with soup kitchens, pantries, and anti-hunger coalitions in their area. MAZON encourages students to organize campuswide appeals during Pesach and Yom Kippur to benefit MAZON, and to contribute 3 percent of the cost of simchas, Shabbat dinners, and other food-based gatherings to benefit the hungry.

Menora: The Authority for the Repatriation of Diaspora Synagogues to Israel

25 West 45th Street
Suite 1405
New York, NY 10036
(212) 840-1166
Fax: (212) 840-1514
E-mail: perryd6301@aol.com

Perry Davis, Contact

10 Keren Kayemet LeIsrael Street
PO Box 71197
Jerusalem 91711
Israel
(972) 2-241724
Fax: (972) 2-252025

Moshe Moskovic, Contact

Menora was founded to rescue (and restore, when possible) Jewish artifacts such as Torahs, books, etc., from Diaspora communities that no longer have active Jewish communities.

MERCAZ USA, The Zionist Organization of the Conservative Movement

155 Fifth Avenue
New York, NY 10010
(212) 533-7800 ext. 2016
Fax: (212) 533-2601
E-mail: mercaz@compuserve.com
Web: www.mercazusa.org

Rabbi Robert R. Golub, Executive Director

MERCAZ USA is the Zionist organization, representing all arms of the Conservative Movement within the World Zionist Organization and the Jewish Agency for Israel. As the voice of the Conservative Movement within the international forums of the Jewish people, MERCAZ works to increase the impact and influence of Conservative Judaism on Israeli society and acts as a force for supporting religious pluralism and securing equality of funding and opportunities for Masorti rabbis and institutions. At the same time, in the Diaspora, MERCAZ promotes Zionist education and activities and the study of the Hebrew language, and provides stipends and scholarships for short- and long-term visits to Israel. MERCAZ is a grassroots organization supported by individual and family memberships. A special student membership rate is available.

National Center for Jewish Film

Brandeis University, Lown Building #102 MS053
Waltham, MA 02254
(781) 899-7044
Fax: (781) 736-2070
E-mail: ncjf@logos.cc.brandeis.edu
Web: www.JewishFilm.org

Sharon Rivo, Executive Director

The National Center for Jewish Film is an award-winning non-profit film archive and distributor dedicated to preserving and sharing Jewish heritage. The Center's unique collection of more than 12,000 reels of film includes features, documentaries, shorts, newsreels, and home movies. The Center also distributes its own newly restored versions of rare Yiddish feature films. NCJF services hundreds of venues worldwide, including theaters, film festivals, educators, filmmakers, researchers, universities, senior groups, synagogues, and museums.

National Coalition for the Homeless

1012 14th Street, NW, #600
Washington, DC 20005-3406
(202) 737-6444 ext. 311
Fax: (202) 737-6445
E-mail: nch@ari.net
Web: www.nch.ari.net

Michael Stoops, Director, Field Organizing Projects

Founded in 1982, the NCH is the nation's oldest and largest national homelessness advocacy group. Our mission is to create the systemic and attitudinal changes necessary to prevent and end homelessness, while concurrently working to increase the capacity of local supportive housing and service providers to better meet the urgent needs of those families and individuals now homeless in their communities. We focus on four content areas: housing that is affordable to those with the lowest incomes; accessible/comprehensive health care and other needed support services; livable incomes that make it possible to afford basic necessities; and the civil rights of those who are without homes. We work in partnership with those who are or have been homeless, local homeless/housing programs, faith-based groups, students, and other individuals committed to preventing and ending homelessness for the children, men, and women who suffer it or are at risk of doing so. Faces of Homelessness Speakers Bureau and National Hunger & Homelessness Awareness Week (always the first full week before Thanksgiving) are two campus-oriented programs that NCH sponsors nationwide. Our Speakers Bureau features a panel of local homeless/formerly homeless people and an advocate, along with a multimedia slide show/video presentation on homelessness. Contact us about booking a "Faces" panel on your campus or Hillel Center. We also have an organizing manual for National Hunger & Homelessness Awareness Week.

National Conference on Soviet Jewry

1640 Rhode Island Avenue, NW, Suite 501
Washington, D.C. 20036-3278
(202) 898-2500
Fax: (202) 898-0822
E-mail: ncsj@erols.com
Web: www.ncsj.org

823 UN Plaza
New York, NY 10017

Mark B. Levin, Executive Director

The NCSJ, a voluntary, non-profit agency created in 1971, is the mandated central coordinating agency of the organized Jewish community for policy and activities on behalf of the estimated two to three million Jews in the former Soviet Union. The mission of the NCSJ is to safeguard the individual and communal political rights of Jews living in the former Soviet Union and to secure their religious and political freedom. NCSJ seeks to assure the right of Jews to emigrate from

the former Soviet Union without impediment, and monitors and combats anti-Semitism in the successor states.

National Council of Young Israel

3 West 16th Street
New York, NY 10011
(212) 929-1525

Rabbi Pesach Lerner, National Executive Director

The National Council of Young Israel maintains a program of spiritual, cultural, social, and communal activity aimed at the advancement and perpetuation of traditional, Torah-true Judaism. The Council also seeks to instill in American youth an understanding and appreciation of the ethical and spiritual values of Judaism by its sponsorship of kosher kitchens, fraternity houses, and Israel programs.

National Foundation for Jewish Culture (NFJC)

330 Seventh Avenue, 21st Floor
New York, NY 10001
(212) 629-0500 ext. 204
Fax: (212) 629-0508

Daniel Schifrin, Director of Communications

The NFJC is dedicated to strengthening Jewish life by fostering an American Jewish cultural identity. Working with artists, scholars, cultural institutions, and community agencies, the NFJC provides programs, services, grants, and awards in every region of the country. The NFJC's best-known programs are the Doctoral Dissertation Fellowships in Jewish Studies, which have helped hundreds of students earn Ph.D.s in Jewish studies, and the Fund for Jewish Documentary Filmmaking, the largest such fund of its kind. The NFJC also coordinates the Council of Jewish Theatres, the Council of American Jewish Museums, and the Council of Archives and Research Libraries in Jewish Studies, as well as the National Institute for Cultural Presenters.

National Havurah Committee

National Administrative Office
7318 Germantown Avenue
Philadelphia, PA 19119-1720
(215) 248-9760
Fax: (215) 247-9703
E-mail: 73073.601@compuserve.com

Quentin Davis, Office Manager

One of the National Havurah Committee's (NHC) primary functions has been to organize and sponsor Summer Institutes, which are weeklong gatherings for study, prayer, and idea and resource exchange among havurah members. NHC also organizes regional retreats in New England, the Mid-Atlantic region, and the Chesapeake Region; publishes a newsletter, *Havurah*, which is devoted to ritual, tradition, and culture from a havurah perspective; and maintains a directory of havurot throughout the country and a Teacher's Bureau to send havurah teachers to communities with few Jewish resources.

National Jewish Democratic Council (NJDC)

PO Box 75308
Washington, D.C. 20013
(202) 216-9060
Fax: (202) 216-9061
E-mail: njdconline@aol.com

Ira N. Forman, Executive Director

NJDC is the national voice for Jewish Democrats. Through its grassroots political network operating from coast to coast, NJDC plays a multidimensional role in the democratic process. As an organization advocating the separation of church and state, strong U.S.-Israel relations, and reproductive freedom, NJDC educates candidates for public office, distributes voter guides to Jewish voters, and advocates for our issues on Capitol Hill and in state capitals. NJDC offers unpaid internships year-round to qualified undergraduates.

National Jewish Law Students Association (NJLSA)

233 Bay State Road
Boston, MA 02215
(617) 624-6781
Fax: (617) 353-7214
E-mail: njlsa@aol.com
Web: seamless.com/njlsa

Daniel D. Sudit, President

The NJSLA has as its mission to foster Jewish identity in legal professionals and students and to promote their active involvement in the Jewish community. It is a resource and communication network for Jewish law students and student groups, a member organization of the Student Initiatives Committee of Hillel, and an advisory organization to the American Bar Association /Law Student Division Board of Governors. The NJLSA holds an annual national conference and regional caucuses, and produces several publications.

National Jewish Outreach Program

485 5th Avenue, #701
New York, NY 10017
(800) 44 HEBRE(W)
(212) 986-7450
Fax: (212) 986-7476
E-mail: info@njop.org
Web: www.njop.org

Rabbi Yitzchak Rosenbaum, Program Director

NJOP is an independent, nondenominational organization dedicated to providing Jewish adults with accessible basic Jewish programming, including the Hebrew Reading Crash Course, Crash Course in Basic Judaism, Turn Friday Night into Shabbat, and The Beginners Service. NJOP also sponsors Shabbat Across America and Read Hebrew America. Programs are free (except Shabbat program) and available on and off campus at hundreds of locations throughout North America.

National Student Campaign Against Hunger and Homelessness

11965 Venice Boulevard, #408
Los Angeles, CA 90066
(800) 664-8647 ext. 323
Fax: (310) 391-0053
E-mail: nscah@aol.com
Web: www.pirg.org/nscahh

Julie Miles, Executive Director

The NSCAHH works to effectively engage college and high school students in the fight against hunger and homelessness through education, service, and action. Recognizing that students are the next generation of leaders and advocates, NSCAHH sponsors several national programs to raise money, awareness, and action; trains students through our conference and campus site visits; and serves as a clearinghouse of information and contacts. Started by the student PIRGs and U.S.A. for Africa in 1985, NSCAHH is the largest student network fighting hunger and homelessness with more than 600 active campuses. Through our programs, thousands of students educate their peers about the severity of the problems of hunger; provide volunteer power and raise food, clothing, and money for community programs; and advocate for fundamental changes. In addition, our annual conference brings students together to learn more about the problems and receive training to become more effective as student leaders and activists. Our staff is currently made up of a director and two field organizers. Our primary programs include our advocacy program, SPLASH (Students Pushing Legislative Action to Stop Hunger and Homelessness), along with our conference, National Hunger and Homelessness Awareness Week, the Student Food Salvage Program, and the Hunger Cleanup.

National Wildlife Federation

Campus Ecology
8925 Leesburg Pike
Vienna, VA 22184
Fax: (703) 790-4468
E-mail: campus@nwf.org
Web: www.nwf.org/campus

Campus Ecology works with administrators, faculty, staff, and students in transforming colleges and universities into learning and teaching models of environmental sustainability by assisting with the design and implementation of practical conservation projects, providing training and incentives, and helping to document and share lessons learned nationally and beyond.

Od Yosef Chai

1556 58th Street
Brooklyn, NY 11219
(718) 633-5299
Fax: (718) 633-9439

Jacob Krasny

Od Yosef Chai is a Tzedakah and Chesed organization whose purpose is to provide support for our needy fellow Jews in Israel. Support is provided to the poor of Israel throughout the year through various programs. In conjunction with our fundraising projects, extensive educational materials are distributed to inculcate in Jewish students across North America an appreciation and understanding of the mitzvoth of Tzedakah and Chesed.

Outreach Judaism

71D Edison Court
Monsey, NY 10952
(800) 315-JEWS
Fax: (914) 356-1915
E-mail: tovia@j51.com

Rabbi Tovia Singer, National Director of Outreach Judaism

Outreach Judaism (formerly Jews for Judaism) is a national organization that responds directly to the issues raised by missionaries and cults by exploring Judaism in contradistinction to Christianity. The organization's goal is to generate a lasting connection between Jewish families and Judaism through building immediate awareness of the current Hebrew-Christian movement worldwide. As a result, Outreach Judaism offers lectures on college campuses and in Jewish communities with multilevel informational resources, campus outreach, counseling, discussion groups, and networking with other Jewish organizations that deal with the dangers of the Messianic movement and cults.

Oxfam America

26 West Street
Boston, MA 02111
(800) 597-3278
(617) 728-2596
E-mail: fast@oxfamamerica.org
Web: www.oxfamamerica.org

Liz Carty, National Outreach Coordinator

Oxfam America fights global hunger and poverty by working in partnership with grassroots organizations promoting sustainable development in Africa, Asia, and the Americas, including the United States. In order to foster an environment supportive of long-term development, Oxfam America also advocates for policy change and supports colleges, schools, religious organizations and community groups in their efforts to fight hunger and poverty through our Fast for a World Harvest campaign. Oxfam provides free materials and technical assistance to groups organizing events to educate, advocate, and raise funds for Oxfam's anti-poverty work.

Progressive Zionist Caucus

27 West 20th Street, #901
New York, NY 10011
(212) 675-1168
E-mail: jonospin@aol.com

Jonathan Glick, National Director

The Progressive Zionist Caucus is a movement of Zionist activities on college campuses around the world concerned with the questions currently facing the Zionist movement and the Jewish people. Through proactive education, PZC works to restore vision, dreams, and energy to the Zionist movement, believing that striving for peace, social justice, religious pluralism, and economic democracy is essential for the realization of positive and responsible Zionism.

Project Gesher

126 High Street
Boston, MA 02110
(617) 457-8789
Fax: (617) 988-6262
E-mail: info@gesher.net
Web: www.gesher.net

Rachel Alexander, Director

Project Gesher brings young adults into the Jewish community by providing personal connections and access to information and resources.

Religious Action Center of Reform Judaism (RAC)

2027 Massachusetts Avenue, NW
Washington, D.C. 20036
(202) 387-2800
Fax: (202) 667-9070
E-mail: rac@uach.org
Web: rj.org/rac

Mark Pelavin, Associate Director

The RAC is the Washington office of the Reform Jewish movement and serves as its advocate in the nation's capital for issues of social justice and religious liberty. Full-time college and postcollege interns monitor legislation of concern to the American Jewish community and provide social action programming to Jewish congregations across the country. The RAC is a joint instrumentality of the Union of American Hebrew Congregations and the Central Conference of American Rabbis.

Republican Jewish Coalition

415 Second Street, NE
Washington, DC 20002
(202) 547-7701
Fax: (202) 544-2434
E-mail: rjc@rjchq.org
Web: www.rjchq.org

Matthew Brooks, Executive Director

The RJC (formerly the National Jewish Coalition) is the national organization of Jewish Republicans. Its mandate is to represent the views of our members to Republican decision-makers at all levels of government and to articulate Republican ideas in the Jewish community. The RJC lobbies on a number of important issues, including education, defense, Israel, taxes, and the budget. The RJC has chapters around the country and a network of Jewish Republican activists in key states, in addition to its strong presence in Washington, D.C. The RJC has an internship program for college students, with applications accepted for the fall and spring semesters (part-time) and the summer (full-time). A stipend is available for students not receiving academic credit for the internship.

The Shalom Center

7318 Germantown Avenue
Philadelphia, PA 19119
(215) 247-9700
Fax: (215) 247-9703
E-mail: alephajr@aol.com, malkhut@aol.com

Rabbi Arthur Waskow, Director

The Shalom Center (a division of ALEPH: Alliance for Jewish Renewal) draws on Jewish tradition and history to address the basic spiritual, political, and economic issues beneath environmental destruction, disemployment, overwork, and the destruction of community. The Shalom Center sponsors training institutes for Jewishly rooted social activists and community organizers.

Simon Wiesenthal Center

9760 West Pico Boulevard
Los Angeles, CA 90035
(310) 553-9036 ext. 311
Fax: (310) 277-5558

Francine Lis, Assistant Director, Museum Education

The Simon Wiesenthal Center is an international human rights organization dedicated to preserving the memory of the Holocaust and to fostering tolerance and understanding through community involvement, educational outreach, and social action. The Center and its Museum of Tolerance confront bigotry, racism, anti-Semitism, terrorism, and genocide. The research department and library are open to the public; group tours are available. The Center provides speakers upon request.

SPNI—Israel Nature Trails

89 Fifth Avenue, Suite 800
New York, NY 10003
(800) 323-0035
(212) 645-8732
Fax: (212) 645-8749

Stephanie P. Glickman, Manager, North and Central America

The Society for the Protection of Nature in Israel (SPNI) is an education and conservation organization focusing on Israel's natural and historical heritage. The SPNI's nature tour programs offer educational excursions and ecology hikes in Israel.

See listing under Short-Term and Summer Programs for Jewish University Students.

TAGAR Zionist Student Activist Movement

218 E. 79th Street
New York, NY 10021
(212) 650-1231
Fax: (212) 650-1413

Ofer Laufman, Central Shaliach

TAGAR, the student division of the Betar Zionist Youth Movement, organizes campus groups across America to teach Zionism, Jewish pride, and love of Israel. TAGAR sponsors summer and winter programs in Israel.

See listing under Short-Term and Summer Programs for Jewish University Students.

Teach for America

315 West 36th Street
New York, NY 10018
(800) 832-1230 ext. 225
Fax: (212) 279-2081
Web: www.teachforamerica.org

Dan Park, Director of National Program Support

Teach for America is the national corps of outstanding and diverse recent college graduates of all academic majors who commit two years to teach in under-resourced urban and rural public schools. We bring together individuals from a wide range of racial, ethnic, and cultural backgrounds who will be lifelong leaders in the pursuit of educational excellence for all children. At any given time, more than 1,000 corps members in thirteen regions around the country are reaching 100,000 students. For more information call us at the above number, check out our Web site, or visit your career service office.

United Jewish Appeal—University Programs

99 Park Avenue, Suite 300
New York, NY 10016-1599
(212) 880-1435
Fax: (212) 867-1074
E-mail: sharyn_lubin_levi@cuja.com

Sharyn Lubin Levitt, Director

UJA's University Programs strengthen the American Jewish student relationship with UJA, Israel, and world Jewry through education, leadership development, Israel experiences, and campus campaigns. UJA prepares college students to assume responsibility for maintaining and strengthening these relationships by providing enrichment opportunities on campus, in Israel, and in the broader Jewish community. Annual programs include the National Leadership Training Conference, Freedom Week, university-based campaigns, missions to Israel, and regional cluster conferences. Programs in Israel include a UJA/UIO/Hillel leadership course at Hebrew University, a Thanksgiving dinner, and an end-of-the-year leadership conference.

United States Holocaust Memorial Museum

Volunteer and Intern Services
100 Raoul Wallenberg Place, SW
Washington, D.C. 20024
(202) 479-9738
Fax: (202) 488-6568
Web: www.ushmm.org

Jill Wexler Greenstein, Manager of Volunteer and Intern Services

The Volunteer and Intern Services Branch of the United States Holocaust Memorial Museum represents more than 350 volunteers and interns who work in the Media Relations, Survivor Affairs, Legal, International Programs, Photo Archives, Collections, Exhibitions, Academic Publications, Records Management, Archives, Education, Oral History, Technical Services, Historian, Library, Learning Center, Survivor Registry, Volunteer Services, and Visitor Services divisions of the Museum. The volunteers and interns serve to further the Museum's mission to memorialize and educate about the Holocaust. The Museum has two million visitors from all over the world each year.

University Programs Department

United Jewish Communities
111 Eighth Avenue, Suite 11E
New York, NY 10011
(212) 284-6547
Fax: (212) 285-6838
E-mail: mirm_kreigel@uja.com
Web: www.generationj.com

As United Jewish Communities' educational and fundraising arm on college campuses nationwide, University Programs (UP) serves to foster a sense of collective social responsibility among Jewish college students on campus and beyond. Through educational programming, community service projects, leadership development training, Israel experiences, and campus campaigns, UP serves to strengthen the relationship between North American Jewish college students and their Jewish communities at home, in Israel, and around the world.

University Student Division of the Hagshama Department, World Zionist Organization

633 3rd Avenue, 21st Floor
New York, NY 10017
(800) 27-ISRAEL
(212) 339-6941
Fax: (212) 318-6193
E-mail: info@usd.org

Naftali Raz, Israeli Shaliach
Melissa Barron, National Director

A non-partisan, multi-ideological network of student Zionist activists, USD/Hagshama trains students in organizational and leadership skills in order to promote Israel awareness and Zionism on college campuses effectively. USD/Hagshama regional directors are located in Boston, Chicago, Miami, New York, and Oakland.

The Washington Institute for Jewish Leadership and Values

6101 Montrose Road, Suite 200
Rockville, MD 20852
(301) 770-5070
Fax: (301) 770-6365
E-mail: wijlv@aol.com
Web: www.wijlv.org

Jerry Kiewe, Assistant Director

The Washington Institute for Jewish Leadership and Values is a non-profit educational foundation advancing tikkun olam, activism, and civic engagement by American Jews, grounded in Torah and Jewish values. We conduct seminars in Washington, D.C., which examine Jewish perspectives on contemporary political issues; conduct workshops that encourage activism and community service; and offer several one-year Fellowships which provide a rich variety of experiences. The Washington Institute is a non-partisan, transdenominational agency.

The Wexner Foundation—Graduate Fellowship Program

158 W. Main Street
PO Box 668
New Albany, OH 43054
(614) 939-6060
Fax: (614) 939-6066

Larry Moses, President

The Wexner Graduate Fellowship Program offers annual fellowships for full-time graduate study in the fields of Jewish education, Jewish communal service, the Rabbinate, the Cantorate, and Jewish studies. The program provides complete tuition, a generous stipend, and unique learning experiences to outstanding candidates who demonstrate leadership potential, a commitment to the Jewish community, and academic excellence.

World Congress of Gay, Lesbian, and Bisexual Jewish Organizations

PO Box 23379
Washington, DC 20026-3379
(202) 452-7424
E-mail: info@wcgljo.org
Web: www.wcgljo.org/wcgljo

Lee Walter, Vice President

The World Congress of Gay, Lesbian, and Bisexual Jewish Organizations, established in 1980, consists of sixty-five member organizations throughout the world: from Argentina to Australia, from Los Angeles to Paris, from Mexico City to Israel. We act to combat homophobia in the Jewish community and anti-Semitism wherever it exists. We hold world conferences every two years, with the next one scheduled for July 2000 in New Jersey. In off years, we hold regional conferences.

World Union of Jewish Students

PO Box 7914
Rechavia
Jerusalem, 91077
Israel
(972) 2-561-0133
Fax: (972) 2-561-0741
E-mail: wujs@netvision.net.il

Benjamin Rutland, Chairperson

WUJS seeks to unite the national independent student unions from all countries and to help in the exchange of ideas and information between its members. It seeks to promote Israel and Zionism, address women's issues, encourage Jewish learning and culture, and secure and defend the rights, status, and interests of Jews and Jewish communities worldwide.

Ziv Tzedakah Fund

384 Wyoming Avenue
Millburn, NJ 07041
(973) 763-9396
Fax: (973) 275-0346
E-mail: naomike@aol.com
Web: www.ziv.org

The Ziv Tzedakah Fund is a non-profit, tax-exempt organization dedicated to the collection and distribution of funds to various little-known Tzedakah projects. It is devoted to providing money and support for individuals and programs that offer direct, significant, and effective services with a minimum of overhead and bureaucracy. Ziv is also involved in bringing the educational message of Tzedakah to communities and Jewish schools throughout the United States, Canada, and Israel.

SORORITIES AND FRATERNITIES

At a number of campuses, certain formerly all-Jewish fraternities and sororities maintain a predominantly Jewish membership. This does not necessarily mean that there will be Jewish programming or social events. The national offices below will provide more detailed information. It is important to also contact and visit the chapter on the campus you are considering.

Alpha Epsilon Phi Sorority

111 Prospect Street, 2nd Floor
Stamford, CT 06901
(203) 358-8744
Fax: (203) 357-7975
E-mail: aephinatl@aol.com

Bonnie Rubenstein Wunsch, Executive Director

Alpha Epsilon Pi Fraternity

8815 Wesleyan Road
Indianapolis, IN 46268-1171
(317) 876-1913
Fax: (317) 876-1057
E-mail: sid@aepi.org
Web: www.aepi.org

Sidney Dunn, Executive Vice President

Sigma Alpha Mu Fraternity

651 North Range Line Road
Carmel, IN 46032
(317) 846-0600
Fax: (317) 846-9462
E-mail: samhq@msn.com

Aaron Girson, Executive Director

Sigma Delta Tau Sorority

111 Congressional Boulevard., Suite 110
Carmel, IN 46032
(317) 846-7747
(317) 575-5578 ext. 587
Fax: (317) 575-5562
E-mail: nationaloffice@sigmadeltatau.com
Web: www.sigmadeltatau.com

Ann Braly, Executive Director

Tau Epsilon Phi Fraternity

617 White Horse Pike
Haddon Heights, NJ 08035
(609) 573-9575
Fax: (609) 573-9441

Beau Davidson, Director of Chapter Services

Zeta Beta Tau Fraternity

3905 Vincennes Road, Suite 101
Indianapolis, IN 46268
(317) 334-1898
Fax: (317) 334-1899
E-mail: zbt@zbtnational.org
Web: www.zbt.org

Jonathan I. Yulish, Executive Director
Michael D. Cimini, Director of Expansion

Specialized Educational Opportunities

For educational opportunities in Israel, see the Israel section of this guide. Additional information may be found in the section Short-Term or Summer Opportunities for Jewish University Students, or by calling the University Students Department of the World Zionist Organization at (800) 27-ISRAEL.

DEGREE PROGRAMS IN JEWISH COMMUNAL SERVICE

Baltimore Hebrew University

5800 Park Heights Avenue
Baltimore, MD 21215
(410) 578-6900
Fax: (410) 578-6940
E-mail: bhu@bhu.edu

Dr. Robert O. Freedman, President
Dr. Barry M. Gittlen, Dean, Peggy Meyerhoff Pearlstone School of Graduate Studies
Dr. George Berlin, Dean, Bernard Manekin School of Undergraduate Studies

M.A. and Ph.D. programs in Jewish Studies; M.A. program in Jewish Education (with plentiful networking opportunities available for Jewish educators); Baltimore Institute for Jewish Communal Service; Ulpan Modern Hebrew Department; Joseph Meyerhoff Library; Elderhostel; Center for Jewish Communal Dialogue (CJCD); Matmid Program (through the Leonard and Helen R. Stulman School of Continuing Education); and frequent academic conferences, lectures, and special courses offered by distinguished visiting professors and community leaders.

Baltimore Institute for Jewish Communal Service

5800 Park Heights Avenue
Baltimore, MD 21215
(410) 578-6932
Fax: (410) 578-1803
E-mail: lsalkov@bijcs.edu

Karen S. Bernstein and **Cindy Goldstein**, Co-Directors

Two-year double Master's Program/Certificate in Jewish Communal Service; M.A. from Baltimore Hebrew University; M.S.W. from the University of Maryland School of Social Work; M.A. in Policy Sciences from the University of Maryland, Baltimore County; and M.A. in Jewish Education from Baltimore Hebrew University. This innovative program also features internships in Baltimore's large and thriving Jewish community, as well as monthly seminars, a mentor program, and an overseas mission.

Bar Ilan University, Program of Jewish Heritage

235 Park Avenue South, 3rd Floor
New York, NY 10003
(888) BIU-YEAR, (212) 673-4991
Fax: (212) 673-4856
E-mail: tobiu@idt.net
Web: www.mindtravel.com/barilan

Deborah Neufeld, Director of Academic Affairs

The Program of Jewish Heritage is designed for students who wish to explore their Jewish identity in an academic setting. The program combines general and Judaic studies curricula taught by the members of the university's regular faculty. Ulpan, extracurricular activities, and trips are also available. The program is open to students who have completed at least one year of college. Credits are transferable to American colleges and universities.

Hebrew Union College—Jewish Institute of Religion

Irwin Daniels School of Jewish Communal Service
3077 University Avenue
Los Angeles, CA 90007-3796
(800) 899-0925
Fax: (213) 747-6128
E-mail: deisner@huc.edu
Web: www.huc.edu

Steven F. Windmueller, Director

The Irwin Daniels School of Jewish Communal Service offers several multidisciplined graduate programs including single master's, joint master's with the Rhea Hirsch School of Education and the Magnin School for Graduate Studies, and double master's with many different schools of the University of Southern California as well as double master's programs with the Schools of Social Work at Washington University in St. Louis and the University of Pittsburgh. The program includes study in Israel; pluralistic approach. Founded in 1968, this program was the first of its kind in the United States. The school has pioneered the development of dual master's programs, combining communal service and social work, public administration, gerontology, and communications management, and has recently added a dual program in business administration with USC's Marshall School of Business. A new program in informal Jewish education exists for those interested in careers as youth professionals and camp administration. Certificates as well as master's level degrees in synagogue administration are also offered.

Hornstein Program in Jewish Communal Service of Brandeis University

415 South Street
Waltham, MA 02254
(617) 736-2990
Fax: (617) 736-2070
E-mail: ngreene@binah.cc.brandeis.edu

Natalie Greene, Administrator

Two-year master's degree program in Jewish communal service and Jewish education; additional specializations in Jewish fundraising and Jewish advocacy. The Hornstein curriculum includes a required one-month seminar in Israel. Students may also take advantage of two dual degree programs: the three-year Hornstein

Program/Near Eastern and Judaic Studies program, and the two-year Hornstein Program/Heller School Master's in Human Service Management. Scholarship support is available for the two-year course of study.

Jewish Theological Seminary of America and Columbia University School of Social Work

3080 Broadway
New York, NY 10027
(212) 678-8022
Fax: (212) 678-8974
E-mail: socialwork@jtsa.edu

Michael Goldberg, Graduate Admissions Coordinator

Dual-degree program designed to prepare students for a career in Jewish communal service. Entails concurrent attendance at both schools and the awarding of an M.A. in Jewish studies from the Jewish Theological Seminary and an M.S. in social work from Columbia University. Students in the dual degree program may also apply for enrollment in the program, which leads to teacher certification for non-Jewish education majors.

The Mandel School of Applied Social Sciences

Case Western Reserve University
10900 Euclid Avenue
Cleveland, OH 44106-7164
(216) 368-8670
Web: www.msass.cwru.edu

Darlyne Bailey, Ph.D., Dean and Professor

The Mandel School of Applied Social Sciences (MSASS) is one of the nation's top graduate schools of social work. MSASS offers a master's degree in social work, a doctorate in social welfare, and joint degrees in social work and law; social work and business administration, social work and social welfare; and social work and nonprofit organizations.

Project StaR

School of Social Work
University of Michigan
Ann Arbor, MI 48109-1106
(734) 764-5392
Fax: (734) 763-3372
E-mail: ksholder@umich.edu
Web: www.ssw.umich.edu/star

Professor Armand Lauffer, Director
Katherine Funk Sholder, Administrator

Project StaR is a twenty-month graduate program in which students earn a Master of Social Work degree from the number one-rated School of Social Work in the country, plus a Certificate in Jewish Communal Service and Judaic Studies from the University's Frankel Center for Judaic Studies. StaR (Service, Training, and Research in Jewish Communal Development) prepares students for leadership careers in the Jewish community. Students can major in community organization, management, policy and evaluation, or interpersonal practice. They may also enroll in dual degree programs. Dozens of Judaic studies courses are available in history, social science, literature and the arts, Tanakh, and other sacred texts. Financial aid and fellowships are available. StaR has outstanding paid internships (locally, nationally, and overseas) and financial aid. StaR graduates have gone on to serve the Jewish community in Jewish federations, JCCs, Hillels, national Jewish social justice and environmental agencies, and Jewish education and congregational settings, and have continued their studies in rabbinic schools or at the doctoral level. The student-designed "StaRGate" section of Project StaR's Web site is a gateway for professionals, lay leaders, and students to the Jewish Internet. The website was recently nominated for the Computerworld Smithsonian Award as an innovative user of information technology, becoming part of the Smithsonian Institution's Permanent Research Collection. StaRGate provides access to hundreds of sites on Jewish communities, customs, religion, and history.

Wurzweiler School of Social Work

Yeshiva University
Belfer Hall, 9th Floor
2495 Amsterdam Avenue
New York, NY 10033-3299
(212) 960-0810
Fax: (212) 960-0055

Michele Sarracco, Director of Admissions

M.S.W. in Social Casework/Clinical, Social Group Work and Administration/Community Organization. Certificate in Jewish Communal Service and the D.S.W. Wurzweiler offers traditional two-year programs for full-time students and for those who are currently employed in approved social service positions (Concurrent and Plan for Employed Persons), as well as a special three-summer Block Program for students who must remain in their home communities. A student may earn a Certificate in Jewish Service concurrently with M.S.W. studies in all programs.

RABBINICAL SCHOOLS AND SPECIALIZED EDUCATIONAL PROGRAMS

Drisha Institute for Jewish Education

131 West 86th Street
New York, NY 10024
(212) 595-0307
Fax: (212) 595-0679
E-mail: inquiry@drisha.org

Nina Bruder, Executive Director
Lisa S. Taubenblat, Programs Assistant

Drisha provides women with the opportunity to engage in traditional Jewish text study in an environment that encourages seriousness of purpose, free inquiry, and respect for classical texts. Drisha offers a wide variety of study options for women of all backgrounds and levels. The Scholars Circle provides the opportunity for highly qualified students interested in careers in Jewish education and scholarship to immerse themselves for three years in full-time, intensive study of Talmud and Jewish law. Havuta (partner) study is a major part of the program. Students receive a certificate upon completion of the program and a living stipend to support their studies. The Talmud/Tanakh Program is an intensive, two-year program leading to a certificate in Talmud and Bible. Students participate in the same Talmud class as the Scholars Circle and pursue mentored independent study in a wide range of topics related to the Bible. Participants receive a living stipend to support their studies.

The Beit Midrash Program is an intermediate-level, one-year program of full-time biblical and rabbinic textual study. Living stipends are available for students pursuing careers in Jewish education.

Gratz College

> 7605 Old York Road
> Melrose Park, PA 19027
> (215) 635-7300 ext. 140
> (800) 475-4635 ext. 140
> Fax: (215) 635-7320
> E-mail: admissions@gratz.edu
> Web: www.gratzcollege.edu
>
> **Evelyn Klein**, Director of Admissions

Graduate programs in Jewish Communal Studies, Jewish Education, Jewish Studies, Jewish Music, Israel Studies, and Judaica Librarianship. Students are eligible to apply for the Council of Jewish Federations—FEREP and Wexner Graduate Fellowships, as well as for campus-based fellowships, scholarships, and work-study programs.

See listing in Pennsylvania section of this guide.

Hebrew College—Shoolman Graduate School of Jewish Education

> 43 Hawes Street
> Brookline, MA 02446
> (617) 278-4948
> Fax: (617) 264-9264
> E-mail: admissions@hebrewcollege.edu
> Web: www.hebrewcollege.edu
>
> **Ilana Kobrin**, Admissions and Recruitment Coordinator

At Hebrew College, we believe that Jewish educators need the capacity to integrate the fields of Jewish education, general education, and Jewish studies. Students here have the opportunity to study the content and structure of each of these fields while also specializing in their area of professional interest. The Shoolman Graduate School prepares its graduates for a career or advancement in the fields of day school teaching or supplementary school teaching, educational leadership and administration, early childhood education, family education and, nonformal education, including youth leadership, Jewish camping, and Israel program leadership.

See listing for Hebrew College in Massachusetts section of this guide.

Hebrew Theological College (Orthodox)

> 7135 N. Carpenter Road
> Skokie, IL 60077
> (847) 982-2500
> Fax: (847) 674-6381
> E-mail: htc@htcnet.edu
>
> **Rabbi Dr. Jerold Isenberg**, Chancellor

Hebrew Theological College, established in 1922, is the oldest rabbinical seminary and school of higher Jewish learning in the Midwest. Major programs include Rabbinical School, Bellows Kollel, Bressler School of Advanced Hebrew Studies, Blitstein Teachers Institute for Women, Kanter School of Liberal Arts and Sciences, Computer Training, Teacher Training, Silber Memorial Library, and Community Service Division.

Hebrew Union College—Jewish Institute of Religion (Reform)

> 3101 Clifton Avenue
> Cincinnati, OH 45220-2488
> (312) 221-1875
>
> **Rabbi Kenneth E. Ehrlich**, Dean

Hebrew Union College (NY)—Jewish Institute of Religion

> The Brookdale Center
> 1 West 4th Street
> New York, NY 10012-1186
> (212) 674-5300
>
> **Rabbi Zahara Davidowitz-Farkas**, Dean
>
> 3077 University Avenue
> Los Angeles, CA 90007-3796
> (213) 749-3424
>
> **Rabbi Lee Bycel**, Dean

Founded in 1875, Hebrew Union College—Jewish Institute of Religion is the nation's oldest institution of higher Jewish education and is the academic and professional leadership development center of Reform Judaism. HUC-JIR educates men and women for service to American and world Jewry as rabbis, cantors, educators, and communal workers, and offers graduate and postgraduate degree programs to scholars of all faiths. With campuses in New York, Cincinnati, Los Angeles, and Jerusalem, HUC-JIR's Skirball Cultural Center and Museums, Klau and Abramov Libraries, American Jewish Archives (10 million documents on Western Hemisphere Jewry and the Holocaust), and archaeological excavations in Israel provide extensive research opportunities for students in all programs and represent major centers of study, research, and publication.

See listing for HUC-JIR's Jerusalem campus in the Israel section of this guide.

Jewish Theological Seminary (Conservative)

3080 Broadway
New York, NY 10027
(212) 678-8817
Fax: (212) 678-8947
E-mail: stdickstein@jtsa.edu

Rabbi Stephanie Dickstein, Assistant Dean of the Rabbinical School

Founded in 1886, the Jewish Theological Seminary is the academic and spiritual center of the Conservative Movement in Judaism. Its New York City campus houses the Albert A. List College of Jewish Studies, the Graduate School, the William Davidson Graduate School of Jewish Education, the Rabbinical School, and the H.L. Miller Cantorial School and College of Jewish Music. Jerusalem is the site of The Morris and Nellie L. Kawaler Year in Israel Program and other extension programs of the Seminary. The Seminary has a student body of 600 and a faculty of some 100 full-time and part-time scholars.

Jewish Theological Seminary: The Davidson School

The William Davidson Graduate School of Jewish Education
3080 Broadway
New York, NY 10027
(212) 678-8030
Fax: (212) 749-9085
E-mail: edschool@jtsa.edu

Pauline Rotmil, Admissions Coordinator

The mission of the Davidson School is to help transform Jewish education in North America through teacher and leadership training. Through its master's program, the Davidson School prepares students to become educators in Jewish educational settings both formal (day schools and synagogue schools) and informal (youth groups, camps, Jewish community centers, and adult education programs). This program also prepares individuals to teach Judaica at the secondary level and beyond. The doctoral programs prepare students for work in administration, supervision, curriculum design, teaching education at the college or university level, and research and scholarship in Jewish education. Through a consortium with Teachers College, Columbia University, Davidson School students can design individualized programs to fit their special educational interests.

Ner Israel Rabbinical College (Orthodox)

400 Mt. Wilson Lane
Baltimore, MD 21208
(410) 484-7200
Fax: (410) 484-3060

Rabbi Beryl Weisbord, Director of Admissions

Ner Israel offers Semikhah (the traditional ordination) and bachelor's, master's, and doctoral degrees in Talmudic Law. A teaching certification is also available.

Ohr Somayach Tanenbaum Educational Center

244 Route 306
Monsey, NY 10952
(800) 647-7662
(914) 425-8862

Rabbi Naftali Reich, Director of Development
Jeff Maza, Director of Legacy

Ohr Somayach Tanenbaum Educational Center offers accredited courses geared to the introductory student. Ohr Somayach's main programs include Hebrew Language, Bible, and Jewish Philosophy and introductory Talmudics. Unaffiliated with any movement, Ohr Somayach also offers a variety of part-time programs under the aegis of its outreach division, Legacy, which is open to students from diverse Jewish backgrounds. A variety of Jewish learning aids are available for the off-campus student. A smicha program is being developed. Scholarship support is available. The newly opened Bodner Family Educational Facility offers modern amenities with housing provided on campus.

Rabbi Isaac Eichanan Theological Seminary (Orthodox)—REITS

Affiliate of Yeshiva University
2540 Amsterdam Avenue
New York, NY 10033-3299
(212) 960-5344
Fax: (212) 960-0061

Rabbi Zevulun Charlop, Dean

Offers a course of study leading to Semikhah (the traditional ordination), as well as a variety of Rabbinic and Talmudic programs leading to more advanced ordination. REITS also encompasses four distinct Kollelim—institutes for advanced studies in Talmud and codes, including its program in Israel, which meets on Yeshiva's Joseph and Caroline Gruss campus in Jerusalem. Integral to the REITS program are extensive rabbinic training and internship/apprenticeship programs. The Semikhah curriculum includes contemporary Jewish Halakhah and Halakhah L'Massaseh requisities, which view modern issues and needs through the authentic prism of Jewish law. Co-requisite programs include master's degrees at Yeshiva University's Bernard

Revel Graduate School in Bible, Jewish philosophy, Jewish history, and rabbinic literature; Azrieli Graduate School of Jewish Education and Administration; and Wurzweiler School of Social Work.

Reconstructionist Rabbinical College

1299 Church Road
Wyncote, PA 19095
(215) 576-0800
Fax: (215) 576-6143
Web: www.rrc.edu

Rabbi Daniel Aronson, Dean of Admissions

RRC offers a course of study leading to rabbinical ordination and an M.A. in Hebrew Letters. Students in the rabbinical program may choose specialized training, including course work and supervised field internships for congregational work, campus work, chaplaincy, geriatric chaplaincy, community organization work, or education. Substantial financial aid available in the form of fellowships and scholarships. The College also offers an M.A. in Jewish Studies program for those interested in combining academic and spiritual questions in their study of Torah; a Cantorial Investiture program, which is offered jointly with Gratz College; a Certificate in Jewish Women's Studies, offered jointly with Temple University; and a doctoral program leading to a D.H.L. (Doctorate in Hebrew Letters).

She'arim: College of Jewish Studies for Women

PO Box 35129
Jerusalem
Israel
(972) 2-651-4240
Fax: (972) 2-651-8370
E-mail: shearim@shearim.com
Web: www.shearim.com

Miriam Shaul, Administrator

She'arim's year-round academic program offers three levels of study: *Shi'ur Alef* (Beginners) is suited to students who have a positive identification with Judaism, and who are committed to the basics of Shabbat and Kashrut; *Shi'ur Bet* (Intermediate) is appropriate for students who are more advanced in Torah commitment and wish to develop their learning skills and broaden their philosophical knowledge; *Shi'ur Gimel* (Advanced) offers advanced students the opportunity to deepen their skills while being exposed to challenging, new levels of learning. Courses include Chumash with commentaries; Tanach with commentaries; Halacha on all levels; Jewish Thought including Mussar, Chassidut Rambam, Maharal, and others; and Interpersonal Relationships. She'arims Taste of Torah program is designed for those with a strong interest and curiosity about their Jewish heritage, but who do not necessarily have any knowledge or commitment. Courses cover fundamental concepts in Jewish law and philosophy, the holidays, and introduction to text study. Taste of Torah runs continuously in three-week cycles. Students may join at any stage in the cycle.

YIVO Institute for Jewish Research

Max Weinreich Center for Advanced Jewish Studies
555 West 57th Street, Suite 1100
New York, NY 10019
(212) 246-6080
Fax: (212) 292-1892

Dr. Allen Nadler, Director of Research and Dean
Portia Auguste-Smith, Dean's Assistant

YIVO is the major resource for study of East European and American Jewish culture, with more than 22 million items in 750 archival collections and a 330,000-volume multilingual library. Graduate studies are available at the Max Weinreich Center; several fellowships for postgraduate research are available. Six-week summer intensive language program is offered through the Uriel Weinreich Program in Yiddish Language, Literature, and Culture. The center does not offer certificates or degrees. Credits from courses are transferrable under a formal course exchange program with major universities in the New York area.

See listing in New York section of this guide.

Jewish Books on Campus

The following books have been recommended by students and Hillel staff throughout the country. Some are basic books; others reflect contemporary interests of Jewish college students.

THE TORAH

The Five Books of Moses: Genesis, Exodus, Leviticus, Numbers, Deuteronomy: A New Translation with Notes and Commentary. Everett Fox, trans. Schocken Books, 1995.

The JPS Torah Commentary (Five Volumes) by Nahum M. Sarna, Chaim Potok et. al. Jewish Publication Society, 1989.

The Tanakh: The Holy Scriptures. Jewish Publication Society, 1985.

BASIC JUDAISM

Back to the Sources by Barry Holtz. Summit Books, 1984.

Basic Judaism by Milton Steinberg. Harcourt Brace, 1987.

Contempoary Jewish Ethics by Menachem Kellner. Hebrew Publishing Company, 1972.

Ethics of the Fathers: Pirke Avot. Many editions.

Finding Our Way: Jewish Texts and the Life We Lead Today by Barry W. Holtz. Schocken Books, 1990.

How to Maintain a Traditional Jewish Household by Blu Greenberg. Jason Aronson, 1989.

The Jewish Holidays: A Guide and Commentary by Michael Strassfeld. Harper and Row, 1985.

Jewish Encyclopedia of Ethical and Moral Issues. Jason Aronson, 1996.

Jewish Literacy by Joseph Telushkin. Morrow, 1991.

Jewish Wisdom by Joseph Telushkin. Morrow, 1994.

On Wings of Awe: A Machzor for Rosh Hashanah and Yom Kippur by Rabbi Richard Levy, ed. and translator. Hillel and Ktav Publishing Company, 1985.

On Wings of Freedom: The Hillel Haggadah for the Nights of Passover by Rabbi Richard Levy. Hillel and Ktav Publishing Company, 1989.

Nine Questions People Ask About Judaism by Dennis Prager and Joseph Telushkin. Simon and Schuster, 1981.

The Schocken Guide to Jewish Books: Where to Start Reading About Jewish History, Literature, Culture, and Religion by Barry Holtz. Schocken Books, 1992.

This Is My God: The Jewish Way of Life by Herman Wouk. Souvenir Press, 1992.

To Be a Jew: A Guide to Jewish Observance in Contemporary Life by Hayim Halevy Donin. Basic Books, 1972.

What Do Jews Believe?: The Spiritual Foundations of Judaism by David Ariel. Schocken, 1995.

HISTORY

From Generation to Generation: How to Trace Your Jewish Genealogy and Personal History by Arthur Kurzwell. William Morrow Co., 1980.

A History of the Jews by Paul Johnson. Harper & Row, 1987.

The Jews of Islam by Bernard Lewis. Princeton University Press, 1984.

Life Is with People: The Culture of the Shtetl by Mark Zborowski and Elizabeth Herzog. Schocken, 1995

World of Our Fathers by Irving Howe. Schocken Books, 1989.

THE JEWISH EXPERIENCE

As a Driven Leaf by Milton Steinberg. Behrman House, 1939.

The Big Book of Jewish Humor by William Novak and Moshe Waldoks. Perennial Library, 1990.

The Book of Legends/Sefer Ha-aggadah, Hayim Nahman and Yeshosua Hana Ravitnitzky, eds., William G. Braude, trans. Schocken.

Chosen Tales: Stories Told by Jewish Storytellers by Peninnah Schram. Jason Aronson, 1995.

Conflicting Visions: Spiritual Possibilities of Modern Israel by David Hartman. Schocken, 1990.

Davita's Harp by Chaim Potok. Fawcett Press, 1986. (Other Chaim Potok books: *The Promise*. Ballantine Books, 1969; *The Chosen*. Ballantine Books, 1967.)

Down-to-Earth Judaism: Food, Money, Sex, and the Rest of Life by Arthur Waskow. William Morrow, 1995.

From Beirut to Jerusalem by Thomas Friedman. Anchor Books Doubleday, 1995.

Ellis Island to Ebbets Field: Sport and the American Jewish Experience by Peter Levine. Oxford University Press, 1992.

Exodus by Leon Uris. Bantam Books, 1987.

The First Jewish Catalog: A Do-It-Yourself Kit by Richard Siegel, Michael Strassfeld, Sharon Strassfield. Jewish Publication Society, 1973.

The Second Jewish Catalog: Sources and Resources by Sharon Strassfeld and Michael Strassfeld. Jewish Publication Society, 1976.

The Third Jewish Catalog: Creating Community by Sharon Strassfeld and Michael Strassfeld. Jewish Publication Society, 1980.

40 Things You Can Do to Save the Jewish People by Joel Lurie Gishaver. Jason Aronson, 1995.

The Gates of the Forest by Elie Wiesel. Schocken Books, 1966. (Also *Night*. Avon Books, 1972.)

Invisible Lines of Connection by Lawrence Kushner. Jewish Lights Publishing Co., 1997.

The Jew in the Lotus: A Poet's Rediscovery of Jewish Identity in Buddhist India by Rodger Kamenetz. Harper San Francisco, 1994.

The Jewish Holiday Kitchen by Joan Nathan. Schocken Books, 1988.

Jewish Meditation: A Practical Guide by Aryeh Kaplan. Schocken Books, 1995.

The Jewish Way: Living the Holidays by Irving Greenberg. Simon and Schuster, 1988.

Judaism and Vegetarianism by Richard H. Schwartz. Exposition Press, 1982.

Lifecycles by Debra Orenstein. Jewish Lights Publishing Company, 1994.

Tainted Greatness: Antisemitism and Cultural Heroes by Nancy A. Harrowitz. Temple University Press, 1994.

To Life!: A Celebration of Jewish Being and Thinking by Harold Kushner. Walker and Company, 1994.

The Passover Seder: An Anthropological Perspective on Jewish Culture by Ruth Fredman Cernea. University Press of America, 1995.

Seasons of Our Joy: A Modern Guide to the Jewish Holidays by Arthur Waskow. Beacon Press, 1990.

Twice Blessed: On Being Lesbian and Gay and Jewish by Christie Balka and Andy Rose. Beacon Press, 1989.

The World of Jewish Cooking by Claudia Roden. Knopf, 1997.

When Bad Things Happen to Good People by Harold Kushner. Schocken Books, 1981.

JEWISH FEMINISM

Deborah, Golda and Me: Being Female and Jewish in America by Letty Cottin Pogrebin. Crown, 1991.

Four Centuries of Jewish Women's Spirituality by Ellen M. Umansky and Diane Ashton. Beacon Press, 1992.

Miriam's Well: Rituals for Jewish Women Around the Year by Penina Adelman. Fresh Meadows, 1986.

On Being a Jewish Feminist: A Reader by Susannah Heschel. Schocken Books, 1983.

On Women and Judaism by Blu Greenberg. Schocken Books, 1983.

Standing Again at Sinai: Judaism from a Feminist Perspective by Judith Plaskow. Harper & Row, 1990.

CHOOSING JUDAISM

Choosing Judaism by Lydia Kukoff. Hippocrene Books, 1981.

Conversion to Judaism by Lawrence J. Epstein. Jason Aronson, 1994.

Your People, My People by Lena Romanoff. Jewish Publication Society, 1990.

Index

C

Jewish Holiday Calendar

Hillel
1640 Rhode Island Ave., NW
Washington, DC 20036

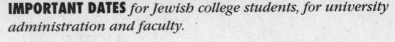

IMPORTANT DATES *for Jewish college students, for university administration and faculty.*

These dates should be noted well in advance to avoid conflicts between the academic and Jewish calendars.

Jewish holy days, religious festivals, and the weekly Sabbath begin at sunset on the day preceding the given date. On these days, Jews who follow traditional practices are not permitted to engage in day-to-day occupations and routine commitments. All Jews wishing to observe these days will need time for preparation or travel in advance of the actual observance.

YEAR / *Traditional Year*	1999-2000 / *5760*	2000-2001 / *5761*	2001-2002 / *5762*	2002-2003 / *5763*	2003-2004 / *5764*	2004-2005 / *5765*	2005-2006 / *5766*	2006-2007 / *5767*
SHABBAT — The Sabbath, every week from Friday evening to Saturday evening; one of the holiest days in the calendar.								
ROSH HASHANAH — The Jewish New Year; start of the Ten Days of Penitence (1)	Sat-Sun SEP 11-12	Sat-Sun SEP 30-OCT 1	Tue-Wed SEP 18-19	Sat-Sun SEP 7-8	Sat-Sun SEP 27-28	Thu-Fri SEP 16-17	Tues-Wed OCT 4-5	Sat-Sun SEP 23-24
YOM KIPPUR — Day of Atonement; a very solemn day of the year, devoted to fasting, prayer, and repentance.	Mon SEP 20	Mon OCT 9	Thu SEP 27	Mon SEP 16	Mon OCT 6	Sat SEP 25	Thurs OCT 13	Mon OCT 2
SUKKOT — First two days of Tabernacles; commemorating the dwelling of the Israelites in booths in the wilderness. (1)	Sat-Sun SEP 25-26	Sat-Sun OCT 14-15	Tue-Wed OCT 2-3	Sat-Sun SEP 21-22	Sat-Sun OCT 11-12	Thu-Fri SEP 30-OCT 1	Tues-Wed OCT 18-19	Sat-Sun OCT 7-8
SHEMINI ATZERET — Eighth Day of Assembly and **SIMCHAT TORAH** — Rejoicing of the Law. (1)	Sat-Sun OCT 2-3	Sat-Sun OCT 21-22	Tue-Wed SEP 9-10	Sat-Sun SEP 28-29	Sat-Sun OCT 18-19	Thu-Fri OCT 7-8	Tues-Wed OCT 25-26	Sat-Sun OCT 14-15
HANUKKAH — Feast of Lights; victory of the Maccabees and rededication of the Temple. (2)	Sat-Sun DEC 4-11	Fri-Fri DEC 22-29	Mon-Mon DEC 10-17	Sat-Sat NOV 30-DEC 7	Sat-Sun DEC 20-27	Wed-Wed DEC 9-15	Mon-Mon DEC 26-Jan2	Sat-Sun DEC 16-23
PURIM — Celebrates defeat of plot to destroy the Jews of Persia. (2)	Tue MAR 21	Fri MAR 9	Tue FEB 26	Tue MAR 18	Sun MAR 7	Fri MAR 25	Tues MAR 14	Sun MAR 4
PESACH — Passover; deliverance of the Jewish people from Egypt. The Seder service on the first two evenings recounts the story of the Exodus. (1) The last two days are also observed as full holy days. (1)	Thu-Fri APR 20-21 / Wed-Thu APR 26-27	Sun-Mon APR 8-9 / Sat-Sun APR 14-15	Thu-Fri MAR 28-2 / Wed-Thu APR 3-4	Thu-Fri APR 17-18 / Wed-Thu APR 23-24	Tue-Wed APR 6-7 / Tue-Wed APR 12-13	Sun-Mon APR 24-25 / Sat-Sun APR 30-MAY 1	Thurs-Fri APR 13-14 / Wed-Thu APR 19-20	Tue-Wed APR 3-4 / Mon-Tue APR 9-10
SHAVUOT — Feast of Weeks; marks the giving of the Law (Torah) at Mt. Sinai. (1)	Fri-Sat JUN 9-10	Mon-Tue MAY 28-29	Fri-Sat MAY 17-18	Fri-Sat JUN 6-7	Wed-Thu MAY 26-27	Mon-Tue JUN 13-14	Fri-Sat JUN 2-3	Wed-Thu MAY 23-24

NOTES:
(1) Reform Jews observe the first day only.
(2) These holidays do not require absence from routine commitments. Jewish law does not recognize gradations of importance among holy days. However, Jews who may not observe all holy days are, nevertheless, most likely to be at synagogue or home celebrations on Rosh Hashanah, Yom Kippur, and the first two evenings of Pesach.

NOTES

NOTES

Expert Advice

www.review.com

Talk About It

www.review.com

Pop Surveys

Paying for it

www.review.com

THE
PRINCETON
REVIEW

www.review.com

Getting in

Word du Jour

www.review.com

Find-O-Rama School & Career Search

www.review.com

Best Schools

Finding it

www.review.com

MORE EXPERT ADVICE

from

THE PRINCETON REVIEW

Find the right school • Get in • Get help paying for it

CRACKING THE SAT & PSAT
2000 EDITION
0-375-75403-2 • $18.00

CRACKING THE SAT & PSAT WITH
SAMPLE TESTS ON CD-ROM
2000 EDITION
0-375-75404-0 • $29.95

THE SCHOLARSHIP ADVISOR
2000 EDITION
0-375-75468-7 • $25.00

SAT MATH WORKOUT
0-679-75363-X • $15.00

SAT VERBAL WORKOUT
0-679-75362-1 • $16.00

CRACKING THE ACT WITH
SAMPLE TESTS ON CD-ROM
2000-2001 EDITION
0-375-75501-2 • $29.95

CRACKING THE ACT
2000-2001 EDITION
0-375-75500-4 • $18.00

CRASH COURSE FOR THE SAT
10 Easy Steps to Higher Score
0-375-75324-9 • $9.95

DOLLARS & SENSE FOR COLLEGE
STUDENTS
How Not to Run Out of Money by
Midterms
0-375-75206-4 • $10.95

PAYING FOR COLLEGE WITHOUT
GOING BROKE, 2000 EDITION
Insider Strategies to Maximize Financial
Aid and Minimize College Costs
0-375-75467-9 • $18.00

BEST 331 COLLEGES
2000 EDITION
The Buyer's Guide to College
0-375-75411-3 • $20.00

With Free
Apply!
Software

THE COMPLETE BOOK OF COLLEGES
2000 EDITION
0-375-75462-8 • $26.95

THE GUIDE TO PERFORMING ARTS
PROGRAMS
Profiles of Over 600 Colleges, High
Schools and Summer Programs
0-375-75095-9 • $24.95

POCKET GUIDE TO COLLEGES
2000 EDITION
0-375-75416-4 • $9.95

AFRICAN AMERICAN STUDENT'S GUIDE
TO COLLEGE
Making the Most of College: Getting In,
Staying In, and Graduating
0-679-77878-0 • $17.95

WE ALSO HAVE BOOKS TO HELP YOU SCORE HIGH ON

THE SAT II, AP, AND CLEP EXAMS:

CRACKING THE AP BIOLOGY EXAM 2000-2001 EDITION
0-375-75495-4 • $17.00

CRACKING THE AP CALCULUS EXAM AB & BC 2000-2001 EDITION
0-375-75499-7 • $18.00

CRACKING THE AP CHEMISTRY EXAM 2000-2001 EDITION
0-375-75497-0 • $17.00

CRACKING THE AP ECONOMICS EXAM (MACRO & MICRO) 2000-2001 EDITION
0-375-75507-1 • $17.00

CRACKING THE AP ENGLISH LITERATURE EXAM 2000-2001 EDITION
0-375-75493-8 • $17.00

CRACKING THE AP U.S. GOVERNMENT AND POLITICS EXAM 2000-2001 EDITION
0-375-75496-2 • $17.00

CRACKING THE AP U.S. HISTORY EXAM 2000-2001 EDITION
0-375-75494-6 • $17.00

CRACKING THE AP PHYSICS 2000-2001 EDITION
0-375-75492-X • $19.00

CRACKING THE AP PSYCHOLOGY 2000-2001 EDITION
0-375-75480-6 • $17.00

CRACKING THE AP EUROPEAN HISTORY 2000-2001 EDITION
0-375-75498-9 • $17.00

CRACKING THE AP SPANISH 2000-2001 EDITION
0-75401-4 • $17.00

CRACKING THE CLEP 4TH EDITION
0-375-76151-9 • $20.00

CRACKING THE SAT II: BIOLOGY SUBJECT TEST 1999-2000 EDITION
0-375-75297-8 • $17.00

CRACKING THE SAT II: CHEMISTRY SUBJECT TEST 1999-2000 EDITION
0-375-75298-6 • $17.00

CRACKING THE SAT II: ENGLISH SUBJECT TEST 1999-2000 EDITION
0-375-75295-1 • $17.00

CRACKING THE SAT II: FRENCH SUBJECT TEST 1999-2000 EDITION
0-375-75299-4 • $17.00

CRACKING THE SAT II: HISTORY SUBJECT TEST 1999-2000 EDITION
0-375-75300-1 • $17.00

CRACKING THE SAT II: MATH SUBJECT TEST 1999-2000 EDITION
0-375-75296-X • $17.00

CRACKING THE SAT II: PHYSICS SUBJECT TEST 1999-2000 EDITION
0-375-75302-8 • $17.00

CRACKING THE SAT II: SPANISH SUBJECT TEST 1999-2000 EDITION
0-375-75301-X • $17.00

THE PRINCETON REVIEW

Visit Your Local Bookstore or Order Direct by Calling 1-800-733-3000
www.randomhouse.com/princetonreview

FIND US...

International

Hong Kong
4/F Sun Hung Kai Centre
30 Harbour Road, Wan Chai,
Hong Kong
Tel: (011)85-2-517-3016

Japan
Fuji Building 40, 15-14
Sakuragaokacho, Shibuya Ku,
Tokyo 150, Japan
Tel: (011)81-3-3463-1343

Korea
Tae Young Bldg, 944-24,
Daechi- Dong, Kangnam-Ku
The Princeton Review- ANC
Seoul, Korea 135-280,
South Korea
Tel: (011)82-2-554-7763

Mexico City
PR Mex S De RL De Cv
Guanajuato 228 Col. Roma
06700 Mexico D.F., Mexico
Tel: 525-564-9468

Montreal
666 Sherbrooke St.
West, Suite 202
Montreal, QC H3A 1E7 Canada
Tel: 514-499-0870

Pakistan
1 Bawa Park - 90 Upper Mall
Lahore, Pakistan
Tel: (011)92-42-571-2315

Spain
Pza. Castilla, 3 - 5º A, 28046
Madrid, Spain
Tel: (011)341-323-4212

Taiwan
155 Chung Hsiao East Road
Section 4 - 4th Floor,
Taipei R.O.C., Taiwan
Tel: (011)886-2-751-1243

Thailand
Building One, 99 Wireless Road
Bangkok, Thailand 10330
Tel: 662-256-7080

Toronto
1240 Bay Street, Suite 300
Toronto M5R 2A7 Canada
Tel: 800-495-7737
Tel: 716-839-4391

Vancouver
4212 University Way NE,
Suite 204
Seattle, WA 98105
Tel: 206-548-1100

locations

REMOVED FROM THE COLLECTION
OF PRINCE WILLIAM PUBLIC
LIBRARY SYSTEM

National (U.S.)
We have over 60 offices around the U.S. and
run courses in over 400 sites. For courses and locations
within the U.S. call 1-800-2-Review and you will be
routed to the nearest office.